CAMBRIDGE
EDUCATIONAL SERVICES

AMERICA'S PREMIERE TESTING READINESS PROGRAM

The Practice Book
Turbo Training for the SAT® Test

Our Mission: Progress Through Partnership

Cambridge Educational Services partners with educators who share the significant mission of educational advancement for all students. By partnering together, we can best achieve our common goals: to build skills, raise test scores, enhance curriculum, and support instruction. A leading innovator in education for twenty years, Cambridge is the nation's premier provider of school-based test preparation and supplemental curriculum services.

Cambridge Publishing, Inc.
www.CambridgeEd.com

© 1994, 1995, 1996, 1997, 2000, 2003, 2004, 2005, 2010, 2012, 2015, 2016 by Cambridge Publishing, Inc.
All rights reserved. First edition 1994
Thirteenth edition 2016

Printed in the United States of America
19 18 17 16   1 2 3 4 5

ISBN-13: 978-1-58894-273-9

TABLE OF CONTENTS

How to Use This Book...v

WARM-UP QUIZZES   1

Reading Quizzes   3

Quiz I...3
Quiz II Brain Buster 8

Writing and Language Quizzes   17

Quiz I...17
Quiz II Brain Buster 25

Math: Multiple-Choice Quizzes   29

Quiz I—No Calculator 29
Quiz I—Calculator 31
Quiz II Brain Buster—No Calculator 34
Quiz II Brain Buster—Calculator 36

Math: Student-Produced Responses Quizzes   41

Quiz I—No Calculator 41
Quiz I—Calculator 43
Quiz II Brain Buster—No Calculator 46
Quiz II Brain Buster—Calculator 49

Essay Quiz   53

PRACTICE TESTS   55

Practice Test I   57

Section 1: Reading...59
Section 2: Writing and Language 75
Section 3: Math—No Calculator 87
Section 4: Math—Calculator 93
Section 5: Writing 106

Practice Test II   109

Section 1: Reading...111
Section 2: Writing and Language 126
Section 3: Math—No Calculator 140
Section 4: Math—Calculator 147
Section 5: Writing 158

Practice Test III 161

Section 1: Reading 163
Section 2: Writing and Language 179
Section 3: Math—No Calculator 193
Section 4: Math—Calculator 199
Section 5: Writing 211

APPENDIX A | ANSWERS AND EXPLANATIONS 213

Quizzes 215

Reading Quiz Explanations 215
Writing and Language Quiz Explanations 221
Math: Multiple-Choice Quiz Explanations 228
Math: Student-Produced Responses Quiz Explanations 236
Essay Quiz Explanations 239

Practice Tests 243

Practice Test I Explanations 243
Practice Test II Explanations 271
Practice Test III Explanations 299

Item Index 325

Error Correction and Suggestion Form 337

HOW TO USE THIS BOOK

Using This Practice Volume

This book is designed to help you practice to take the SAT test. It will help you:

- Practice your pacing on each test section.
- Measure your mastery of tested concepts.
- Improve your confidence for test day.

To use this book effectively, you should work through the warm-up quizzes first, pacing yourself as you go. After you finish each quiz, use the answer key to check your work and review the questions you got wrong. As you review, read the explanation provided in Appendix A and also look at the category path at the beginning of the explanation to see what type of item you missed.

Once you have finished the quizzes, work through each practice test. Try to complete the tests in one sitting, following the pacing guidelines, to build your testing endurance. After you finish a test, check your answers using the answer key and read the explanations to figure out why you missed the questions you did.

Cambridge's Victory Program

This book is most effectively used as part of Cambridge's *Victory* program. The categories used in the explanations and index of this volume match the categories in the *Victory* book, making it easy for you to review the concepts you miss in the quizzes and practice tests in this volume.

This book is designed to reinforce what your teacher covers in class in the *Victory* program. The program can be completed in six steps:

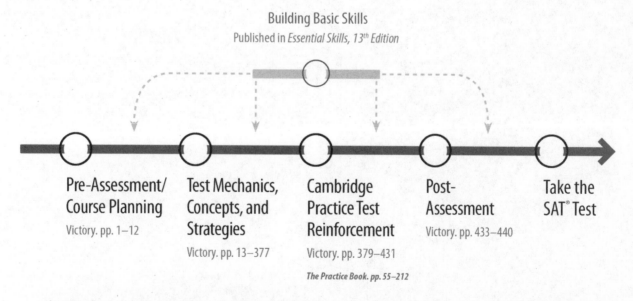

Building Basic Skills
Published in *Essential Skills, 13th Edition*

Pre-Assessment/   Test Mechanics,   Cambridge   Post-   Take the
Course Planning   Concepts, and   Practice Test   Assessment   SAT® Test
Victory. pp. 1–12   Strategies   Reinforcement   Victory. pp. 433–440

Victory. pp. 13–377   Victory. pp. 379–431

The Practice Book. pp. 55–212

- **Pre-Assessment/Course Planning.** A diagnostic pre-assessment and score reports help you identify your starting point and prepare for the course.

- **Building Basic Skills.** This review material, found in *Essential Skills, 13th Edition,* serves as a refresher on topics you may not have studied in a while.

- **Test Mechanics, Concepts, and Strategies.** Items resemble those on the real tests, which your instructor will use to teach tested concepts and applicable strategies.

- **Practice Test Reinforcement.** One full-length practice SAT test in the *Victory* book allows you to practice your skills in a testing format. Three additional full-length practice tests are available in this book.

- **Post-Assessment.** A diagnostic post-assessment helps you to see how far you've come, and recommended courses of action help you to continue your study after the course.

- **Take the SAT Test.** After you complete the course, you will take the test, using everything you will learn throughout this course to succeed on test day.

A Note for Teachers

You may choose to use this practice test book in three different ways:

- Administer the test in class, either in individual test sections or in an extended testing session. To make this exercise most effective, review the questions with your class when you complete the test.

- Assign the quizzes and tests as homework. This will be most effective if you collect the homework or have your students submit the progress reports available in the *Victory* teacher resource center.

- Use the practice material in this book as an "item bank," using the index at the back of this book to certify the different skills and concepts that are tested.

You know your students best. Make sure to guide them as they practice to ensure that they get the most out of their preparation time.

Warm-Up Quizzes

CAMBRIDGE
THE PRACTICE BOOK

READING QUIZZES

This section contains three Reading quizzes. Complete each quiz under timed conditions. Answers are on page 215.

Quiz I

(18 items; 15 minutes)

DIRECTIONS: Each passage or pair of passages is followed by a set of items. Choose the best answer to each question based on what is stated or implied in the passage or passages and in any accompanying graphics.

Passage I

Items #1–8 refer to the following two passages.

The following passages are excerpts from two different sources that discuss particular approaches to history.

Passage 1

As Carl Hempel demonstrates in his seminal essay "The Function of General Laws in History," a general law plays the same role in both history and
Line the natural sciences. According to Hempel's
5 deductive-nomological model, proper scientific explanation—whether for history or the natural sciences—includes three sorts of statements:

(A) A set of statements about conditions (that can be designated as C1, C2, and so on)
10 that are true at a particular place and time.

(B) A set of universal hypotheses connecting events of type C with events of type E.

(C) A statement asserting that E is logically deducible from the statements of A and B.

15 The "C" events are, of course, causes, while the "E" events are effects. Given a sufficiently precise description of background conditions by Set A and an adequately articulated set of empirical laws in Set B, a conclusion such as "A popular uprising
20 overthrew the government" can be logically deduced with as much certainty as that of a syllogism.*

The notion that a historian cannot study past events in the same way that a chemist studies
25 reactions or a physicist studies falling objects is due to a misunderstanding. Historical explanations intentionally omit from Set A statements about human nature that are well known to the sciences of psychology and sociology because they are too
30 numerous to mention. Further, many of the general laws used by historians do not seem susceptible to easy confirmation in the way that laboratory experiments are. It is difficult to find a sufficiently large number of revolutions to assess the validity of
35 the assertion that a drop of a certain magnitude in a population's standard of living will inevitably be followed by revolution.

Thus, we should more accurately speak not of scientific explanations of historical events but of
40 "sketches" of history. This terminology would call attention to the incompleteness and the imprecision in historical explanation, while at the same time reminding us that the form of explanation is the same as that of the natural sciences.

*A syllogism is a form of reasoning in which a conclusion is drawn from two statements:

Major Premise: All ruminants are quadrupeds.
Minor Premise: All cows are ruminants.
Conclusion: Therefore, all cows are quadrupeds.

Passage 2

45 The obvious distinction between history and the natural sciences is that history is concerned with human actions. The historian makes a distinction between what may be called the outside and the inside of an event. The outside of the event
50 is everything belonging to it that can be described in terms of bodies and their movements: the passage of Caesar across a river called the Rubicon on a certain date or the spilling of Caesar's blood on the senate-house floor on another. The inside of the
55 event can only be described in terms of thought:

Caesar's defiance of Republican law or the clash of constitutional policy between Caesar and Caesar's assassins. The historian is not investigating mere events (a mere event is one that has only an outside and no inside) but actions, and an action is the unity of the outside and inside of an event.

The task of the historian is thus distinguished from that of the natural scientist in two ways. On the one hand, the historian must undertake an additional investigation that is neither needed by nor available to the natural scientist. The historian must inquire after the "why" of an event, that is, the thought behind it. On the other hand, the task of the historian is somewhat simpler than that of the natural scientist because once that question has been answered there is no further question to be raised. There is no reason to look behind the thought associated with the event for a supervening general law.

Since the questions that the historian asks are different from those posed by the natural scientist, the historian will employ a different method. The historian penetrates to the inner aspect of the event by the technique of *Verstehen*.* To be sure, the historian will study whatever documents and other physical evidence are available, but these are important only insofar as they provide an access to the inside of the event.

A purely physical event can only be understood as a particular occurrence governed by a universal or general law, but the inside of an event is a thought—unique, and as such, not subject to a law-like explanation. Nor is this reason for disappointment. It is not the case that there are historical laws but the techniques just do not yet exist to find them. Rather, the laws just do not exist to be found. To expect to find causal explanation in history and to demand of history predictions about the course of future events is an illegitimate expectation conceived and fostered by the false analogy of history to the natural sciences and the incorrect assumption that the natural sciences are the paradigm for all human knowledge.

The positivist will object that this means that history is, in principle, less rigorous than natural science, but this objection ignores the point that there simply are no historical laws to be discovered. In fact, because a historical event has both an inside and an outside, it is the events of natural science that are, in a sense, deficient. As R. G. Collingwood wrote so boldly in the concluding section of *The Idea of History*, "Natural science . . . depends on historical thought for its existence." In history, there are no general scientific laws to be uncovered, and the search for them is the foolish pursuit of a will-o'-the-wisp that exists only in the fables of positivist literature.

Verstehen is the German word for "understanding."

1. As used in line 5, the word "nomological" most nearly means

   A) law-like.
   B) historical.
   C) accurate.
   D) logical.

2. In line 18, the phrase "adequately articulated" means

   A) verbally presented.
   B) only preliminary.
   C) confidently denoted.
   D) sufficiently detailed.

3. In the third paragraph of Passage A, the author suggests that a series of historical events could serve the same scientific function as

   A) eyewitness accounts.
   B) general laws.
   C) laboratory experiments.
   D) historical sketches.

4. According to the author of Passage A, it is difficult to formulate a general historical law about revolution because

   A) revolutions, by definition, involve the overthrow of an existing government.
   B) too few revolutions are available for study to yield valid conclusions.
   C) details about a revolution are generally only known to a few key participants.
   D) historical events ordinarily involve a large number of unidentified actors.

5. The attitude of the author of Passage A toward psychology and sociology is one of

   A) skepticism.
   B) indifference.
   C) confidence.
   D) outrage.

6. Passage A is primarily an argument against the position that

   A) revolutions are caused by factors that can be identified.
   B) history is not a science like physics or chemistry.
   C) science is an undertaking requiring the use of logic.
   D) history is more important than the physical sciences.

7. Passage B explains that the technique of *Verstehen* is used to enable the historian to study

   A) the outside of historical events.
   B) motives and intentions of historical actors.
   C) psychology and sociology.
   D) historical laws.

8. The author of Passage A and the author of Passage B would be most likely to agree with which of the following statements?

   A) Psychology and sociology use the same methodology as the natural sciences.
   B) Scientific historians should construct their explanations in the same way that the physicist does.
   C) The inability of historians to conduct laboratory testing shows that history is not a science.
   D) Events that have no element of thought are governed by law-like regularities.

Passage II

Items #9–18 refer to the following passage.

This passage reviews the basic physics of electromagnetic waves, specifically radar.

Whether used to control airplane traffic, detect speeding automobiles, or track a hurricane, radar is a very useful tool. Developed during World War II,
Line
5   this technology allows for remote sensing, that is, locating objects that are not seen directly. The word "radar" is a contraction of "radio detection and ranging." It works in much the same way as an echo. When you shout toward a cliff or a large building, part of the sound bounces back. In radar, waves of
10 electromagnetic radiation are sent out. When they strike an object, they bounce back and are picked up by a receiver. The returning signal indicates the direction of the object; the time it takes for the signal to return indicates the distance to the object.
15 Radar waves detect objects by their varying densities. They are not deflected by atmospheric layers and therefore always travel in a straight line—in all weather, both day and night.

Radar waves are electromagnetic waves, as are
20 light waves, electric waves, X-rays, cosmic rays, and radio waves. All electromagnetic waves travel at 300,000 kilometers per second—the speed of light. Waves differ from each other in the number of times they vibrate per second; this variable is
25 known as frequency and is usually expressed as cycles per second. Waves also differ in their size, or wavelength. The speed, frequency, and wavelength of a wave are related by the wave equation in which:

30      $$speed = frequency \cdot wavelength$$

This shows that the product of the frequency and wavelength of any given wave is always a constant—the speed of light. To find the wavelength of a wave, knowing the frequency, this formula is
35 used:

$$wavelength = \frac{speed}{frequency}$$

For example, if a radio station broadcasts waves at 600,000 cycles per second (cps), the wavelength would be calculated this way:

40 $$wavelength = \frac{300,000 \text{ km per sec}}{600,000 \text{ cps}} = 0.5 \text{ km} = 500 \text{ m}$$

If the frequency of the wave is doubled to 1,200,000 cycles per second, its wavelength would be cut in half to 250 meters. Since frequencies are so high, the unit "megahertz" is usually used;
45 $1 \text{ megahertz} = 1,000,000$ cycles per second.

Wavelengths within the electromagnetic spectrum vary greatly. Radar has wavelengths that measure from approximately one centimeter (0.01 meters) up to one meter. Each kind of wave has a
50 range of wavelengths. The table compares some sample wavelengths of several kinds of electromagnetic waves.

TYPE OF WAVE (METERS)	SAMPLE WAVELENGTH
cosmic rays	0.0000000000000001
X-rays	0.0000000001
ultraviolet rays	0.00000001
visible light	0.000001
infrared heat	0.0001
microwaves	0.001
radar	0.1
television	1.0
radio	100
long radio waves	10,000
electric power	1,000,000

9. Radio waves and radar waves have the same

   A) frequency.
   B) wavelength.
   C) cycles per second.
   D) speed.

10. A radar signal having a frequency of 3,000 megahertz would have a wavelength of

   A) 0.001 km.
   B) 0.01 km.
   C) 10 m.
   D) 0.1 m.

11. A radar set could not locate an airplane if it were flying

   A) faster than the speed of sound.
   B) above a heavy storm.
   C) above the atmosphere.
   D) below the horizon.

12. It is possible to find the distance to an object from a radar set because the

   A) wavelength of radar is known.
   B) frequency of radar is known.
   C) speed of radar is 300,000 kilometers per second.
   D) set operates at 10 megahertz.

13. The relationship between the frequency and wavelength of a wave is

   A) constant.
   B) directly proportional.
   C) exponential.
   D) inverse.

14. An antenna picks up a signal that has a wavelength of about one meter. It is likely to be

   A) in the visible spectrum.
   B) an ultraviolet ray.
   C) a television signal.
   D) an X-ray.

15. Radio waves will not penetrate the ionosphere, but microwaves will. Would you expect X-rays to penetrate the ionosphere?

   A) Yes, because they have a shorter wavelength than microwaves and radio waves.
   B) Yes, because they have a lower frequency than microwaves and radio waves.
   C) No, because they travel more slowly than microwaves.
   D) No, because they have fewer cycles per second than microwaves or radio waves.

16. Compared to cosmic rays, the frequency value of visible light waves is

   A) higher.
   B) lower.
   C) the same.
   D) Cannot be determined from the given information

17. Which of the following factors would be most important in order for radar to detect and track storms?

   A) Radar signals travel in straight lines.
   B) The densities of moist air masses are different from those of dry air masses.
   C) The atmosphere does not deflect radar signals.
   D) Radar signals travel much faster than storms.

18. Like a radar reflection, an echo can be used to determine the distance of an object. This must be because

   A) sound is a form of radar.
   B) sound travels at a relatively fixed rate.
   C) sound waves have different frequencies.
   D) sound waves are invisible.

Quiz II Brain Buster

(31 items; 25 minutes)

> **DIRECTIONS:** Each passage or pair of passages is followed by a set of items. Choose the best answer to each question based on what is stated or implied in the passage or passages and in any accompanying graphics.

Passage I

Items #1–11 refer to the following passage.

This passage discusses agricultural policy during Franklin D. Roosevelt's presidency.

President Roosevelt's administration suffered a devastating defeat when, on January 6, 1936, the Agricultural Adjustment Act (AAA) of 1933 was
Line declared unconstitutional. New Deal planners
5 quickly pushed through Congress the Soil Conservation and Domestic Allotment Act of 1935, one purpose of which was conservation. It also aimed to control surpluses by retiring land from production.

10 The law was intended as a stopgap measure until the administration could formulate a permanent farm program that would be constitutional and satisfy the nation's farmers. Roosevelt's landslide victory in 1936 obscured the
15 ambivalent nature of his support in the farm states. Despite extensive government propaganda, many farmers still refused to participate in the administration's voluntary production control programs because severe droughts had eliminated
20 the burdensome surpluses and low prices of 1933.

In February of 1937, Secretary of Agriculture Wallace convened a meeting of farm leaders to promote the concept of the ever-normal granary. This policy would encourage farmers to store crop
25 surpluses (rather than dump them on the market) until grain was needed in years of small harvests. The Commodity Credit Corporation would grant loans to be repaid when the grain was later sold for a reasonable profit. The conference chose the
30 Committee of Eighteen, which drafted a bill. However, the major farm organizations were divided. Since ten of the eighteen members were also members of the American Farm Bureau Federation, the measure was quickly labeled a Farm
35 Bureau bill, and there were protests from the small, but highly vocal, Farmer's Holiday Association. When debate on the bill began, Roosevelt himself was vague and elusive. He didn't move the proposed legislation into the "desirable" category until
40 midsummer. In addition, there were demands that the New Deal's deficit spending be curtailed. Opponents of the bill charged that the AAA was wasteful and primarily benefited corporations and large-scale farmers.

45 The Soil Conservation and Domestic Allotment Act failed to limit agricultural production as the administration had hoped. Farm prices and consumer demand were high, and many farmers, convinced that the drought had ended the need for
50 crop controls, refused to participate in the AAA's soil conservation program. Without direct crop controls, agricultural production skyrocketed in 1937. By late summer, there was panic in the farm belt as prices fell, triggering fears that they would
55 again be driven down to the disastrously low levels of 1933. Congressmen began to pressure Roosevelt to place a floor under farm prices by making loans through the Commodity Credit Corporation. However, Roosevelt made such loans contingent
60 upon the willingness of Congress to support the administration's plan for a new system of crop controls. Roosevelt's adroit political maneuver finally forced congressional representatives to agree to support a bill providing for crop controls
65 and the ever-normal granary. The following year Congress passed the Agricultural Adjustment Act of 1938.

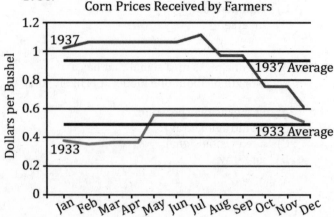

Corn Prices Received by Farmers

1. The primary purpose of the passage is to

    A) analyze the connection between weather
       conditions and agricultural prices.
    B) call attention to economic hardship
       suffered by farmers.
    C) pinpoint the weaknesses of Roosevelt's
       policies.
    D) describe events leading to the passage of
       the Agricultural Adjustment Act of 1938.

2. In context, "ambivalent" (line 15) means

    A) wavering.
    B) inadequate.
    C) insincere.
    D) involuntary.

3. According to the passage, all of the following
    were impediments to the passage of the
    Agricultural Adjustment Act of 1938 EXCEPT

    A) initial lack of clear Presidential support.
    B) prosperity enjoyed by the nation's farmers.
    C) opposition to the idea of a Farm Bureau bill.
    D) doubts about the constitutionality of the
       bill.

4. The author implies which of the following
    conclusions?

    A) Roosevelt's ability to gain passage of the
       Agricultural Adjustment Act of 1938 depended
       on the large harvests of 1937.
    B) Secretary of Agriculture Wallace alienated
       members of the American Farm Bureau
       Federation by proposing an ever-normal
       granary.
    C) The Agricultural Adjustment Act of 1933 was
       declared unconstitutional because it was
       written by the Farm Bureau.
    D) The Commodity Credit Corporation was
       created to offer farmers incentives for taking
       land out of production.

5. Which of the following excerpts from the text
    best supports the correct answer to the
    previous question?

    A) Lines 2–9 ("the Agricultural . . .
       production.")
    B) Lines 21–29 ("In February . . . profit.")
    C) Lines 29–36 ("the conference . . .
       Association.")
    D) Lines 51–62 ("Without . . . crop controls.")

6. It can be inferred from the passage that the
    Farmer's Holiday Association opposed the bill
    drafted by the Committee of Eighteen because

    A) the bill was not strongly supported by
       President Roosevelt.
    B) the Farmer's Holiday Association opposed
       the American Farm Bureau Federation.
    C) the Roosevelt administration had incurred
       excessive debt to finance its New Deal.
    D) its membership consisted primarily of
       large-scale farmers.

7. Which of the following excerpts from the text
    best supports the correct answer to the
    previous question?

    A) Lines 27–30 ("The Commodity . . . bill.")
    B) Lines 31–36 ("However . . . Association.")
    C) Lines 37–40 ("When debate . . .
       midsummer.")
    D) Lines 40–44 ("In addition . . . farmers.")

8. It can be inferred that loans granted by the
    Commodity Credit Corporation would
    encourage farmers to store surplus grain by

    A) providing farmers a financial incentive to
       take arable land out of production.
    B) implementing a comprehensive program of
       mandatory soil conservation practices.
    C) conditioning financial assistance on a
       promise to participate in the Agricultural
       Adjustment Administration's program.
    D) relieving farmers of the need to sell grain in
       order to obtain immediate cash.

9. Which of the following best describes the author's treatment of Roosevelt's farm policies?

    A) Scholarly but appreciative
    B) Objective but critical
    C) Analytical but abrasive
    D) Biased and condemnatory

10. In the context of the passage, "adroit" (line 61) means

    A) unsuccessful.
    B) skillful.
    C) inept.
    D) radical.

11. The data in the graph could best be used to support which of the following points made by the author?

    A) The Agricultural Adjustment Act of 1933 was a short-term solution. (line 9)
    B) Farmers were concerned about agricultural prices in late summer of 1937. (line 52)
    C) Roosevelt did not provide clear support for the Committee of Eighteen bill. (line 37)
    D) Farmers were reluctant to participate in voluntary production controls. (line 16)

Passage II

Items #12–21 refer to the following passage.

This passage discusses the political thought of James Burnham.

Most thinkers have distinguished three political entities: the individual, society, and state. It is normal to begin with the individual and then to consider society as the embodiment of his nature as a social being. Thus, the individual is considered to be both logically and historically prior to society. Furthermore, society is considered both logically and historically prior to the state. But in James Burnham's vision of the future state, the priority of the individual over the state is inverted. Burnham changed his mind on many points of detail between one book and the next, partly because he thought that what was happening in world politics at any given moment was decisive. But his general sense of the form political power would take didn't move far from the version of it he gave in *The Managerial Revolution*. In that book he predicted that the weaknesses of capitalism would eventually prove fatal. However, he thought the downfall of capitalism would not be the victory of the people followed by a Marxist paradise. Instead, capitalism would be replaced by an autocracy even more extreme than that in Stalin's Russia. Under this autocracy, the instruments of production would be controlled by the state. The state, in turn, would be controlled by a ruling elite of managers.

Burnham argued that managers would control the instruments of production in their own corporate favor. The economy of state ownership would provide the basis for domination and exploitation by a ruling class to an extreme never before known. The masses would be curbed or constantly diverted so that they would, as we say, go along with the managerial order. Also in Burnham's future state, history has come to an end. Existence has removed itself from historical process and become pure essence, its attributes those of official meaning. Perfection is defined as the state of being in complete accordance with the terms prescribed for it by the state, much as a proposition in logic or a theorem in mathematics might be faultless.

In *We*, Yevgeny Zamyatin envisaged a one-world state. Burnham allowed for three states. Three superstates would divide the world between them and would enter into shifting alliances with one another. In 1941, Burnham thought the three would be the United States, Europe, and Japan. The superpowers would wage war over territory. Burnham said, "These wars will be directed from each base for the conquest of the other bases. But it does not seem possible for any one of these to conquer the others. Even two of them in coalition could not win a lasting victory over the third."

By 1947, many of Burnham's predictions had already proved false, a result of his tendency to assume that present conditions would persist unchanged; but a more damning indictment of his vision is the hypocrisy concealed behind the attack on power. Burnham was infatuated with the image of totalitarianism; he was fascinated by the power he attacked. He despised the democracy he should have defended. Ultimately, Burnham voiced the secret desire of the English intelligentsia to destroy the old, egalitarian version of socialism and usher in a new hierarchical society in which the intellectual could at last get his hands on the whip.

12. The author's treatment of James Burnham's writing in the final paragraph can best be described as

   A) critical.
   B) neutral.
   C) speculative.
   D) detached.

13. According to the passage, Burnham's vision of the future state was methodologically flawed because it

   A) failed to consider the power inherent in controlling the means of production.
   B) uncritically projected existing conditions into the future.
   C) distinguished the individual, society, and state as distinct political entities.
   D) proposed that the downfall of capitalism would be a victory of the people over the elite.

14. Which of the following excerpts from the text provides the strongest support for the correct answer to the previous question?

    A) Lines 2–5 ("It is normal . . . being.")
    B) Lines 38–41 ("Perfection . . . faultless.")
    C) Lines 42–43 ("In *We* . . . states.")
    D) Lines 54–57 ("By 1947 . . . unchanged.")

15. The statement that Burnham inverted the logical priority of the individual over the state means that Burnham believed that

    A) people are seen as aspects of the state and not as individuals.
    B) history culminated in the existence of an all-powerful government.
    C) individuals can reach perfection only as social beings.
    D) the existence of individuals can be deduced from the existence of a state.

16. According to Burnham, in the completely autocratic state, history will have come to an end because

    A) the state will define the social forms to which individuals must conform.
    B) the means of production will be controlled by a managerial elite.
    C) no one superpower will be able to wage war successfully against any other superpower.
    D) individuals will be diverted from a study of past events by the state.

17. The author's primary concern is to

    A) present his own vision of the future.
    B) prove someone else's predictions were wrong.
    C) critique a political theory.
    D) criticize a literary style.

18. In context, the phrase "historically prior" (line 6) means

    A) occurring with.
    B) more important than.
    C) existing before.
    D) reliant upon.

19. In Burnham's view, the future as sketched in *The Managerial Revolution* could best be described as

    A) indeterminate.
    B) bleak.
    C) unstable.
    D) utopian.

20. Which of the following textual excerpts provides the strongest support for the correct answer to the previous question?

    A) Lines 10–17 ("Burnham . . . *Revolution*.")
    B) Lines 21–23 ("Instead . . . Russia.")
    C) Lines 43–46 ("Three . . . one another.")
    D) Lines 59–61 ("Burnham . . . attacked.")

21. In context, the phrase "get his hands on the whip" (line 66) means

    A) exercise power.
    B) avoid work.
    C) live peaceably.
    D) relinquish authority.

Passage III

Items #22–31 refer to the following passage.

This passage describes a meteorite that may have originated on Mars.

Meteorite ALH84001 is a member of a family of meteorites, half of which were found in Antarctica, that are believed to have originated on Mars. Oxygen isotopes, as distinctive as fingerprints, link these meteorites and clearly differentiate them from any Earth rock or other kind of meteorite. Another family member, ETA79001, was discovered to contain gas trapped by the impact that ejected it from Mars. Analysis of the trapped gas shows that it is identical to atmospheric gases analyzed by the spacecraft that landed on Mars in 1976.

The rock of ALH84001 was formed 4.5 billion years ago, but 3.6 billion years ago it was invaded by water containing mineral salts that precipitated out to form small carbonate globules with intricate chemical zoning. These carbonates are between 1 and 2 billion years old. Sixteen million years ago, an object from space, possibly a small asteroid, impacted Mars and blasted off rocks. One of these rocks traveled in space until it was captured by the earth's gravity and fell on Antarctica. Carbon-14 dating shows that this rock has been on Earth about 13,000 years.

The carbonate globules contain very small crystals of iron oxide (magnetite) and at least two kinds of iron sulfide (pyrrhotite and another mineral, possibly greigite). Small crystals of these minerals are commonly formed on Earth by bacteria, although inorganic processes can also form them. In addition, manganese is concentrated in the center of each carbonate globule, and most of the larger globules have rims of alternating iron-rich and magnesium-rich carbonates. The compositional variation of these carbonates is not what would be expected from high temperature equilibrium crystallization; in fact, it is more similar to the variation that occurs during low temperature crystallization. Furthermore, it is consistent with formation by non-equilibrium precipitation induced by microorganisms.

There are also unusually high concentrations of PAH-type hydrocarbons. These PAHs are unusually simple compared to most PAHs, including PAHs from the burning of coal, oil, or gasoline or the decay of vegetation. Other meteorites contain PAHs, but the pattern and abundances are different. Of course, PAHs can be formed by strictly inorganic reactions, and PAHs were produced in the early solar system and are preserved on some asteroids and comets. Meteorites from these objects fall to Earth and enable us to analyze the PAHs contained within the parent bodies. While some of these are similar to the PAHs in the Martian meteorite, all show some major differences. One reasonable interpretation of the PAHs is that they are decay products from bacteria.

Also present are unusual, very small forms that could be the remains of microorganisms. These spherical, ovoid, and elongated objects closely resemble the morphology of known bacteria, but many of them are smaller than any known bacteria on Earth. Furthermore, microfossil forms from very old Earth rocks are typically much larger than the forms that we see in the Mars meteorite. The microfossil-like forms may really be minerals and artifacts that superficially resemble small bacteria. Or, perhaps lower gravity and more restricted pore space in rocks promoted the development of smaller forms of microorganisms. Or, maybe such forms exist on Earth in the fossil record but have not yet been found. If the small objects are microfossils, are they from Mars or from Antarctica? So far, studies of the abundant microorganisms found in the rocks, soils, and lakes near the coast of Antarctica do not show PAHs or microorganisms that closely resemble those found in the Martian meteorite.

There is considerable evidence in the Martian meteorite that must be explained by other means if we are to definitely rule out evidence of past Martian life in this meteorite. So far, we have not seen a reasonable explanation by others that can explain all of the data.

PLANET	TEMPERATURE (CELSIUS)	ATMOSPHERIC PRESSURE (MILLIMETERS)	GRAVITY (METERS/SECOND^2)
Earth	20	760	9.87
Jupiter	−148	380	26.6
Mars	−50	4.56	3.72
Venus	470	6.99×10^4	8.87

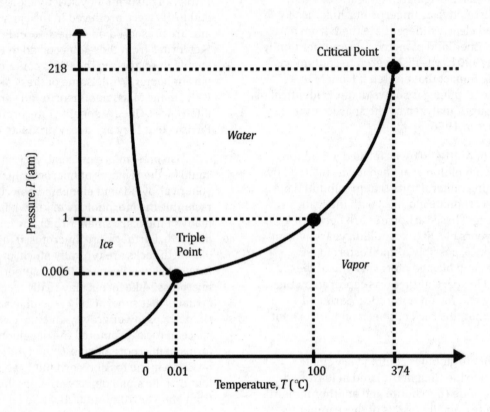

22. The main purpose of the passage is to

   A) argue that the available data support the conclusion that life once existed on Mars.
   B) examine various facts to determine what thesis about ALH84001 is most strongly supported.
   C) answer objections to the contention that Martian meteorites contain evidence of primitive life.
   D) pose challenges to scientists who hope to prove that ALH84001 proves that life exists on Mars.

23. According to the passage, what evidence most strongly establishes that meteorite ALH84001 originated on Mars?

   A) Comparison of trapped gases and the Martian atmosphere
   B) Presence of alternating iron and magnesium carbonates
   C) Evidence of shapes that resemble known bacteria
   D) Pattern of carbonate globules with unusual zoning

24. The passage mentions all of the following as tending to prove that ALH84001 may once have contained primitive life EXCEPT

A) distinctive oxygen isotopes trapped in gases.
B) extraordinarily high concentrations of unusual PAHs.
C) presence of iron oxide and iron sulfide crystals.
D) unusual zonings of carbonate globules.

25. According to the passage, the compositional variation of the carbonate deposits and the PAH–type hydrocarbons both

A) result from chemical processes more likely to occur on Mars than on Earth.
B) might be the product of an organic reaction or the product of an inorganic process.
C) tend to occur at relatively cooler temperatures than other similar reactions.
D) are evidence of chemical processes that occurred during the formation of the solar system.

26. The author mentions lower gravity and restricted pore space (lines 65–66) in order to explain why

A) bacteria on Mars might be smaller than bacteria found on Earth.
B) no microfossil record of bacteria has yet been found in Antarctica.
C) the spherical, ovoid, and elongated shapes in ALH84001 cannot be bacteria.
D) restricted pore space in Martian rocks would hinder bacterial growth.

27. As used in the passage, "morphology" (line 58) means

A) surface.
B) rot.
C) structure.
D) habitat.

28. With which of the following conclusions about the possibility of life on Mars would the author most likely agree?

A) The available evidence strongly suggests that conditions on Mars make it impossible for life to have developed there.
B) The scientific evidence is ambiguous and supports no conclusion about the possibility of life on Mars.
C) Scientific evidence cannot, in principle, ever demonstrate that life existed on Mars.
D) Scientific data derived from ALH84001 is consistent with the proposition that life once existed on Mars.

29. Which of the following textual excerpts provides the best support for the correct answer to the previous question?

A) Lines 6–11 ("Another . . . 1976.")
B) Lines 12–16 ("The rock . . . zoning.")
C) Lines 21–23 ("Carbon-14 dating . . . years.")
D) Lines 75–80 ("There is considerable . . . data.")

30. In context, "abundances" (line 45) means

A) excesses.
B) quantities.
C) disbursements.
D) limitations.

31. The figure given in the passage is a phase diagram for the compound H_2O showing the conditions under which H_2O will be ice, liquid, or a solid. Given the data provided for Selected Planets, is it reasonable to believe that Mars today has water to support the development of life?

A) Yes, because a pressure of below 5 millimeters and a temperature of –50°C permit unlimited quantities of H_2O to exist in liquid form.
B) Yes, because a pressure of less than 5 millimeters and a temperature of –50°C would produce minute quantities of water sufficient to support microbial life.
C) No, because a pressure of less than 5 millimeters and a temperature of –50°C means that H_2O would exist only as solid ice.
D) No, because a pressure of less than 5 millimeters and a temperature of –50°C would allow H_2O to exist only as vapor.

WRITING AND LANGUAGE QUIZZES

This section contains two Writing and Language quizzes. Complete each quiz under timed conditions. Answers are on page 221.

Quiz I

(34 items; 25 minutes)

> **DIRECTIONS:** Each passage is followed by a set of items. For each item, you will select the choice that improves the passage's expression of ideas or corrects errors in sentence structure, usage, or punctuation. A passage or a question may be accompanied by one or more graphics that you will consider as you make editing decisions.
>
> Some items will direct you to an underlined portion of a passage, and others will direct you to a location in a passage or ask you to think about the passage as a whole.
>
> For each item, choose the answer that most effectively improves the quality of writing in the passage or that makes the passage follow the conventions of standard written English. Choose the "NO CHANGE" option if you think the best choice is to leave the relevant portion of the passage as it is.

Passage I

The Con Game Is No Game

[1]

Most people have a certain crime **1** that one believes should be ranked as the worst of all crimes. For some, **2** its' murder; for others, it may be selling drugs to children. I believe, **3** moreover, that the worst of all crimes may be the confidence scheme.

[2]

The confidence scheme may seem an **4** odd choice for the worst crime since con games are usually **5** nonviolent. Although, it is a crime that ranks high in heartlessness. Con artists are the most

1. A) NO CHANGE
    B) that they believe
    C) which one believes
    D) that you believe

2. A) NO CHANGE
    B) they are
    C) it's
    D) its

3. A) NO CHANGE
    B) however
    C) further
    D) therefore

4. A) NO CHANGE
    B) obvious
    C) irrelevant
    D) apt

5. A) NO CHANGE
    B) nonviolent, though
    C) nonviolent, but
    D) nonviolent, and

devious, the most harmful, and the most disruptive members of society because **6** <u>they break</u> down **7** <u>honesty, and trust, the</u> most important bonds of the social order.

[3]

The con games themselves are **8** <u>simplistic almost infantile</u>. They work **9** <u>on account of a con artist can</u> win complete confidence, talk fast enough to keep the victim slightly confused, **10** <u>and dangling</u> enough temptation to suppress any suspicion or skepticism. Traditionally, the primary targets of these criminals **11** <u>will be</u> the elderly and **12** <u>women. (And they prefer to work in large crowds.)</u> In the past several years, however, as access to the web has become more widespread, the demographics have changed. **13**

6. A) NO CHANGE
    B) it breaks
    C) of its breaking
    D) of them breaking

7. A) NO CHANGE
    B) honesty, and trust the
    C) honesty and trust, the
    D) honesty and trust the

8. A) NO CHANGE
    B) simplistic; almost infantile
    C) simplistic, almost infantile
    D) simplistic, yet almost infantile

9. A) NO CHANGE
    B) on account of a con artist's ability to
    C) owing to a con artist's ability to
    D) because a con artist can

10. A) NO CHANGE
    B) and dangles
    C) and has dangled
    D) and dangle

11. A) NO CHANGE
    B) to be
    C) are
    D) is

12. A) NO CHANGE
    B) women, and the con artists prefer to work in large crowds.
    C) women, preferring, of course, to work in large crowds.
    D) women (who prefer to work in large crowds).

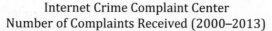

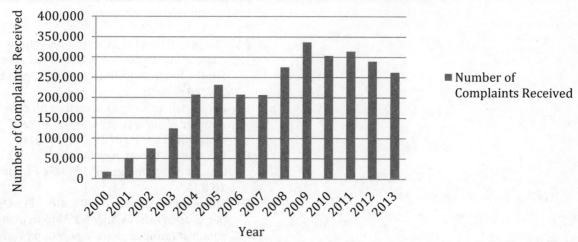

Internet Crime Complaint Center
Number of Complaints Received (2000–2013)

Internet Crime Complaints (2013)

AGE (IN YEARS)	NUMBER OF REPORTS BY MALES	TOTAL LOSS REPORTED BY MALES	NUMBER OF REPORTS BY FEMALES	TOTAL LOSS REPORTED BY FEMALES
Under 20	5,194	$103,298,649	3,602	$2,364,515
20–29	24,549	$42,144,452	23,483	$23,619,502
30–39	28,391	$71,022,425	26,389	$41,784,048
40–49	26,668	$89,559,205	29,170	$70,355,407
50–59	29,220	$93,705,383	26,239	$83,858,340
Over 60	23,074	$87,244,816	16,834	$72,884,870

13. The author wishes to include a sentence using data from the graphs to prove this point. Which of the following would best accomplish this purpose?

A) In 2013, for the age group 20 to 59, the number of complaints filed by males and the number filed by females have been similar, while the number filed by people age 60 and over has been less than other groups in that range.

B) In 2013, the total dollar value of the loss reported by males over 60 was greater than the total dollar value of the loss reported by females over 60.

C) The total number of complaints received by the Internet Crime Complaint Center in 2013 was 262,813, but ten years earlier, the number reported in 2004 was only 207,492.

D) The total number of complaints received by the Internet Crime Complaint Center declined from 336,655 in 2009 to 262,813 in 2013, though one year, 2011, did show an increase.

14. The writer wants to identify for the reader the age and gender of the group likely to suffer the greatest per person loss. Which of the following sentences best accomplishes that purpose?

   A) The group that filed the greatest number of complaints was males between the ages of 50 and 59; the individuals in this group filed a total of 29,220 reports.
   B) For females, the age group that filed the greatest number of complaints was the 40 to 49 group, which filed a total of 29,170 reports.
   C) For the age group over 60, more males filed complaints than females, 23,074 compared with 16,834.
   D) Males under the age of 20 suffered the greatest per person loss, as only 5,194 individuals, the smallest number of any age group of any gender, suffered a total loss of $103,298,649, the largest of any group.

15. The writer wants to conclude the essay by answering a possible objection that internet fraud will become less important in the future based on the data for years 2012 and 2013. Which of the following sentences would most effectively accomplish this goal?

   A) Between the years 2000 and 2005, the number of complaints filed with the Center increased, but the decline in that number in 2006 and 2007 strongly suggests that the importance of the internet is declining.
   B) From 2007 to 2009, the number of complaints filed with the Center increased to a high of 336,655 but declined thereafter to a total of 262,813 in 2013.
   C) In 2013, the total number of complaints filed with the Center was 262,813, which cumulatively resulted in hundreds of millions of dollars in losses.
   D) Between 2000 and 2011, the number of annual complaints filed with the Center declined twice, but then increased, so the pattern suggests that the declines reported in 2012 and 2013 are likely to be reversed.

Items #16–18 ask about the preceding passage as a whole.

16. Which of the following is most probably the author's opinion rather than a fact?

A) The most disruptive members of society are con artists.
B) The majority of con games are nonviolent.
C) The targets of con games are mostly the elderly and women.
D) The con artists succeed when they win the complete confidence of their targets.

17. What would be the most logical continuation of the essay?

A) A description of some confidence games
B) An account of the elderly as crime victims in society
C) An account of the author's experience with con artists
D) An explanation of crowd psychology

18. What would strengthen the author's contention that con games rank first in heartlessness?

A) Statistics to show the number of people who were taken in by the con artist
B) A discussion of the way the police handle the problem
C) An example that shows how the con artist breaks down honesty and trust
D) An example to illustrate that con games are nonviolent and simple

Passage II

Elizabeth I's Intellect Ruled Supreme

[1]

Elizabeth I had a sensuous and indulgent nature that she inherited from her mother, Anne Boleyn **19** (who was beheaded by Henry VIII). Splendor and pleasure **20** is the very air she breathed. She loved gaiety, laughter, and wit. Her vanity **21** remained even, to old age. The vanity of a coquette.

[2]

The statesmen **22** who she outwitted believed, almost to the end, that Elizabeth I was little more than a frivolous woman **23** who was very vain. However, the Elizabeth they saw was far from **24** being all of Elizabeth, the queen.

19. A) NO CHANGE
    B) (having been beheaded by Henry VIII)
    C) beheaded by Henry VIII
    D) OMIT the underlined portion.

20. A) NO CHANGE
    B) is,
    C) were
    D) were,

21. A) NO CHANGE
    B) remains, even to old age, the
    C) remains, even to old age the
    D) remained, even to old age, the

22. A) NO CHANGE
    B) that she outwitted
    C) whom she outwitted
    D) who she was outwitting

23. A) NO CHANGE
    B) and she was also very vain
    C) known for her great vanity
    D) OMIT the underlined portion.

24. A) NO CHANGE
    B) to be
    C) having been
    D) OMIT the underlined portion.

The willfulness of her father, Henry VIII, and the triviality of Anne played over the surface of a nature **25** so hard like steel—a purely intellectual temperament. Her vanity and caprice carried no weight **26** whatsoever in state affairs. The coquette of the presence chamber **27** had became the coolest and hardest of politicians at the council board.

[3]

It was this part that gave her marked **28** superiority over the statesmen of her time. No **29** more nobler a group of ministers ever gathered round the council board than those of Elizabeth, but she was the instrument of none. She listened and she weighed, but her policy, as a whole, was her own. It was the policy of good sense, **30** not genius, she endeavored to keep her throne, to keep England out of war, **31** and she wanted to restore civil and religious order.

25. A) NO CHANGE
    B) as hard as
    C) so hard as
    D) as hard like

26. A) NO CHANGE
    B) no matter what
    C) whatever, at all
    D) whatever, despite everything

27. A) NO CHANGE
    B) became
    C) used to become
    D) becomes

28. A) NO CHANGE
    B) superiority in regard to
    C) superiority about
    D) superior quality to

29. A) NO CHANGE
    B) nobler a group,
    C) nobler a group
    D) more nobler of a group,

30. A) NO CHANGE
    B) not genius she
    C) not genius. She
    D) —not genius, she

31. A) NO CHANGE
    B) wanting
    C) and wanting
    D) and

Items #32–34 ask about the preceding passage as a whole.

32. What might logically have preceded this essay?

A) Some biographical background on Elizabeth I
B) A discussion of the wives of Henry VIII
C) A discussion of the politics of Tudor England
D) A discussion of the policies of Elizabeth's ministers

33. This essay is most probably taken from a

A) scholarly work on Renaissance England.
B) biography of Elizabeth I.
C) diary kept by one of Elizabeth's ministers.
D) political science textbook.

34. Which of the following would most strengthen the essay?

A) Knowing who the ministers were and what their policies were
B) Examples of Elizabeth's dual nature
C) A discussion of Henry VIII's policies
D) A discussion of the role of the woman in Tudor England

Quiz II Brain Buster

(20 items; 10 minutes)

DIRECTIONS: In the sentences below, certain parts of the sentences have been underlined. The answer choices represent different ways of writing each underlined part; the original version is indicated by the "NO CHANGE" option. For each item, select the choice that best expresses the intended idea, is most acceptable in standard written English, or is most consistent with the overall tone and style of the sentence.

1. More than just a movie star, Audrey Hepburn was celebrated for her luminous beauty, for her acclaimed acting ability, <u>and everyone knew of her humanitarian work with organizations</u> such as UNICEF.

   A) NO CHANGE
   B) and everyone knew of her humanitarian organizations work
   C) and for her humanitarian work with organizations
   D) and her humanitarian work with organizations

2. Many geologists believe that the likelihood of a devastating earthquake of magnitude 8 or higher <u>is as great or greater in the eastern part of the United States than</u> in California.

   A) NO CHANGE
   B) may be at least as great or greater in the eastern part of the United States than
   C) is at least as great in the eastern part of the United States as
   D) can be at least so great in the eastern part of the United States as

3. The industry has seen a dramatic <u>increase in the churn of cell phone accounts caused by customer willingness to act on new promotional offers to switch</u> providers.

   A) NO CHANGE
   B) increase in the churn of cell phone accounts caused by willingness of customers to act on new promotional offers switching
   C) churn of cell phone accounts increase because of customer willingness to act on new promotional offers to switch
   D) increase in the churn of cell phone accounts because of customer willingness to act on new promotional offers to switch

4. <u>The Bichon Frisé is a breed of non-sporting dog, descending from the water spaniel and originating</u> in ancient times in the Mediterranean area.

   A) NO CHANGE
   B) The Bichon Frisé, which is a breed of non-sporting dog descending from the water spaniel, originated
   C) The Bichon Frisé, a breed of non-sporting dog descended from the water spaniel, originated
   D) The Bichon Frisé, a breed of non-sporting dog, descended from the water spaniel which originated

5. Although the defense found the only lead that was likely to defeat the contract, the declarer <u>ruffed in, sloughed her losing club on dummy's ace of diamonds,</u> after drawing trumps, was able to score six spade tricks to make the grand slam.

A) NO CHANGE
B) ruffed in, sloughed her losing club on dummy's ace of diamonds, and
C) ruffing in, sloughed her losing club on dummy's ace of diamonds
D) ruffed in, sloughing her losing club on dummy's ace of diamonds,

6. <u>Lincoln, discovering in young manhood the secret that the Yankee peddler has learned before him, knew</u> how to use a good story to generate good will.

A) NO CHANGE
B) Discovering in young manhood the secret that the Yankee peddler has learned before him, Lincoln knew
C) Lincoln, discovering the secret that the Yankee peddler had learned in young manhood before him, knew
D) In young manhood Lincoln discovered the secret that the Yankee peddler had learned before him:

7. The portfolio, which was apparently <u>left inadvertent on the bus, contained three completed watercolors, including several uncompleted sketches.</u>

A) NO CHANGE
B) left inadvertently on the bus, contained three completed watercolors, including several uncompleted sketches
C) inadvertently left on the bus containing three completed watercolors, including several uncompleted sketches
D) inadvertently left on the bus, contained three completed watercolors and several uncompleted sketches

8. Recent tests on a variety of herbal supplements designed to reduce cholesterol found that half did not contain the listed <u>ingredients, were so poorly manufactured that the active ingredients, when present,</u> could not be absorbed.

A) NO CHANGE
B) ingredients or were so poorly manufactured that the active ingredients, when present,
C) ingredients were so poorly manufactured that the present active ingredients,
D) ingredients, were so poorly manufactured, and that the active ingredients, when present,

9. Both Samuel Beckett and Joseph Conrad were brought up speaking one language <u>and they wrote in another language when they wrote novels.</u>

A) NO CHANGE
B) having written novels in another language altogether
C) but wrote their novels in another language
D) yet when they wrote novels, they wrote them in another language

10. <u>The relationship of smoking and lung cancer have been firmly established, yet people continue to ignore warnings, jeopardizing their health and that of others.</u>

A) NO CHANGE
B) The relationship of smoking to lung cancer has been firmly established, yet people continue to ignore the warnings, jeopardizing their health and that of others.
C) The relationship of smoking to lung cancer has been firmly established, yet people continually ignore the warnings that jeopardize their own health and that of others.
D) The relationship of smoking with lung cancer has been firmly established, with people continuing to ignore the warnings and jeopardizing their own health and others.

11. <u>Thrown onto the stage by adoring fans, the prima ballerina knelt gracefully and gathered up the bouquets of red roses.</u>

   A) NO CHANGE
   B) Thrown onto the stage by adoring fans, the prima ballerina had knelt gracefully before gathering up the bouquets of red roses.
   C) Thrown onto the stage by adoring fans, the bouquets of red roses were gathered up by the prima ballerina after she had knelt gracefully.
   D) The prima ballerina knelt gracefully and gathered up the bouquets of red roses that had been thrown onto the stage by adoring fans.

12. Although the Battle of Fort Ann is rarely mentioned in history texts, it <u>may have been the most significant engagement of the Revolutionary War because it led</u> ultimately to General Burgoyne's defeat at Saratoga.

   A) NO CHANGE
   B) could have been the most significant engagement of the Revolutionary War because it led
   C) could have been the most significant engagement of the Revolutionary War if it led
   D) might have been the more significant engagement of the Revolutionary War that led

13. The driving snow made the roadway slippery and reduced visibility to no more than a few feet, <u>and fortunately there were no</u> accidents despite the heavy volume of traffic.

   A) NO CHANGE
   B) but fortunately there were no
   C) while fortunately there were no
   D) so fortunately there were no

14. India's movie industry <u>may not be as well known as the United States, but it is much bigger because</u> film is the principal storytelling vehicle in a country where more than 40 percent of the population is illiterate and the cheapest ticket costs no more than a quarter.

   A) NO CHANGE
   B) may not be as well known as that of the United States, but it is much bigger because
   C) might not be as well known as that of the United States, but it is much bigger on account of
   D) could not be as well known as the United States, but they are much bigger because

15. <u>Although the American relay team did not qualify for the finals, the</u> anchor runner dropped the baton shortly after the hand-off.

   A) NO CHANGE
   B) When the American relay team did not qualify for the finals, the
   C) The American relay team did not qualify for the finals, and the
   D) The American relay team did not qualify for the finals because the

16. The <u>newly released worm is especially dangerous because</u> it directs infected computers to launch a distributed denial of service attack on the very web sites that offer instructions for combating the worm.

   A) NO CHANGE
   B) released new worm is especially dangerous because
   C) released new worm is dangerous especially because
   D) newly released worm is especially dangerous on account of

17. To protest their being underpaid in comparison to other city agencies, a strike was called by the sanitation workers.

A) NO CHANGE
B) To protest them being underpaid in comparison with other city agencies, the sanitation workers called a strike.
C) To protest their being comparatively underpaid with other city agencies, a strike was called by the sanitation workers.
D) To protest their being underpaid in comparison with workers of other city agencies, the sanitation workers called a strike.

18. Learning of the fall of Constantinople to the Turks in 1453, the failure of the Crusades became apparent to Christian Europe which had ignored earlier major defeats.

A) NO CHANGE
B) Christian Europe realized that the Crusades had failed, which had ignored earlier major defeats
C) Christian Europe, which had ignored earlier major defeats, realized that the Crusades had failed
D) Christian Europe, ignoring earlier major defeats, realized that the Crusades had failed

19. Insofar as poultry is a good bargain and often less than a dollar a pound, the per-person consumption of chicken and turkey has increased in the last ten years, while that of the more expensive meats such as beef and lamb has declined.

A) NO CHANGE
B) Because poultry is a good bargain and often less than a dollar a pound
C) For the reason that poultry is a good bargain at less than a dollar a pound
D) Because poultry is a good bargain at less than a dollar a pound

20. Because of the number of colleges and universities in and around the city, the population of Boston has more percentage of students than any other city in the United States of comparable size.

A) NO CHANGE
B) the population of Boston has more percentage of students than any
C) Boston's population has a greater percentage of students as any other
D) Boston has a higher percentage of students than any other

MATH: MULTIPLE-CHOICE QUIZZES

Take each quiz under the specified timing conditions. After each quiz, review the answers. Remember that the purpose of these quizzes is to practice pacing while implementing the various strategies you have learned.

Quiz I—No Calculator

(5 items; 8 minutes)

DIRECTIONS: Solve each item and choose the correct answer choice. Use any available space for scratchwork. The use of a calculator **is not permitted**. Answers are on page 228.

Notes:

(1) All expressions and equations represent real numbers unless otherwise indicated.

(2) Figures that accompany problems in this test are intended to provide information useful in solving the problems. They are drawn as accurately as possible EXCEPT when it is stated in a specific problem that the figure is not drawn to scale. All figures lie in a plane unless otherwise indicated.

(3) The domain of a given function f is the set of all real numbers x for which $f(x)$ is a real number unless otherwise indicated.

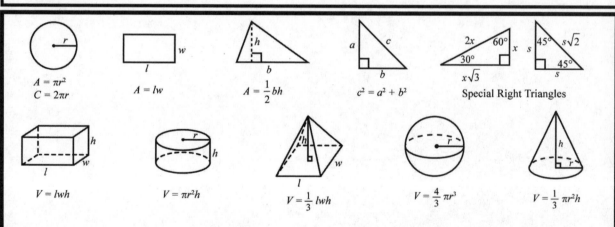

The number of degrees of arc in a circle is 360.

The sum of the measures in degrees of the angles of a triangle is 180.

The number of radians of arc in a circle is 2π.

1. If $f(3)=5$ and $f(7)=7$, what is the slope of the graph of $f(x)$ in the coordinate plane?

    A) -2
    B) $-\dfrac{1}{2}$
    C) 1
    D) $\dfrac{1}{2}$

2. The local modeling agency is looking for some new models for a specific job. The job requires that the model's height be within 2 inches of 70 inches. Which of the following absolute value inequalities describe this condition, where x is the model's height in inches?

    A) $|x+2| \le 70$
    B) $|x-2| < 70$
    C) $|x+70| < 2$
    D) $|x-70| < 2$

3. If $5^6 = \left(\sqrt{5}\right)^{-4x}$, what is 5^x?

    A) $\dfrac{1}{5^3}$
    B) $\dfrac{1}{5^2}$
    C) $\dfrac{1}{5}$
    D) 5

4. If $x^2 + 3x - 18 = 0$ and $2m = x$, which of the following could be a value of m?

    A) -3
    B) 1
    C) 3
    D) 6

5. A circle with center O has radii $\overline{OA}$ and $\overline{OB}$. The measure of angle AOB is $40°$ and the diameter of the circle is 36 centimeters. What is the length of $\overparen{AB}$ in centimeters?

    A) 2π
    B) 4π
    C) 8π
    D) 18π

Quiz I—Calculator

(10 items; 15 minutes)

DIRECTIONS: Solve each item and choose the correct answer choice. Use any available space for scratchwork. The use of a calculator **is permitted**. Answers are on page 228.

Notes:

(1) All expressions and equations represent real numbers unless otherwise indicated.

(2) Figures that accompany problems in this test are intended to provide information useful in solving the problems. They are drawn as accurately as possible EXCEPT when it is stated in a specific problem that the figure is not drawn to scale. All figures lie in a plane unless otherwise indicated.

(3) The domain of a given function f is the set of all real numbers x for which $f(x)$ is a real number unless otherwise indicated.

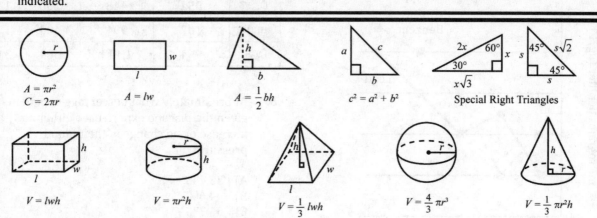

The number of degrees of arc in a circle is 360.
The sum of the measures in degrees of the angles of a triangle is 180.
The number of radians of arc in a circle is 2π.

1. If $\dfrac{x}{x+3} = \dfrac{3}{4}$, and $x \neq -3$, then what is the value of x?

   A) 3
   B) 4
   C) 5
   D) 9

2. Under certain conditions, a bicycle traveling k meters per second requires $\dfrac{k^2}{20} + k$ meters to stop. If $k = 10$, how many <u>meters</u> does the bicycle need to stop?

   A) 10
   B) 12
   C) 15
   D) 20

3. On the first day after being given an assignment, a student read $\frac{1}{2}$ the number of pages assigned, and on the second day, the student read 3 more pages. If the student still has 6 additional pages to read, how many pages were assigned?

A) 15
B) 18
C) 24
D) 30

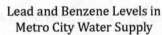

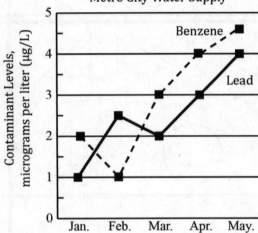

Lead and Benzene Levels in Metro City Water Supply

4. Once per month, Metro City tests the lead and benzene levels in the municipal wells. The graph above shows the measured lead and benzene levels for five months. What was the average monthly change in benzene levels from January to May?

A) 0.5 μg/L
B) 0.625 μg/L
C) 0.75 μg/L
D) 2.9 μg/L

5. The ratio of $a:b$ is $1:5$, the ratio of $b:c$ is $3:2$, and the ratio of $(2a+c):c$ can expressed as $8:w$. What is the value of w?

A) $\frac{1}{5}$

B) $\frac{1}{3}$

C) 3
D) 5

Questions 6 and 7 are based on the following information.

A pharmaceutical company conducted a study on the effectiveness of a new drug that is intended to decrease the blood pressure of patients.

The study included 3,000 randomly selected patients, each given either the new drug or the placebo. The table below summarizes the results from the study.

	DECREASE	NO CHANGE	INCREASE	TOTAL
Drug	852	448	200	1,500
Placebo	102	994	404	1,500
Total	954	1,442	604	3,000

6. Approximately what percentage of patients given the placebo experienced either an increase or no change in their blood pressure?

A) 33.7%
B) 44.6%
C) 66.3%
D) 93.2%

7. What is the probability that a patient either experienced a decrease in blood pressure or was given the drug?

A) $\frac{852}{3,000}$

B) $\frac{954}{3,000}$

C) $\frac{1,602}{3,000}$

D) $\frac{852}{1,500}$

8. Which of the following scatterplots shows a relationship that is appropriately modeled with the equation $y = ax^b$ where a is negative and b is positive?

A)

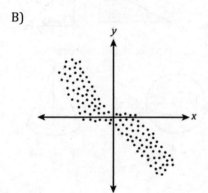

B)

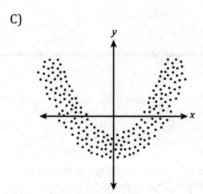

C)

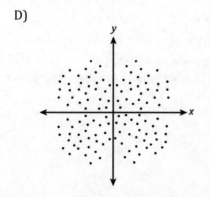

D)

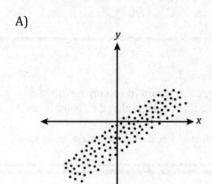

$$v = \sqrt{\frac{2(E - mgh)}{m}}$$

9. The formula above gives the velocity of an object in terms of its total mechanical energy E, mass m, and height h. The total mechanical energy E of an object is equal to the sum of the object's potential and kinetic energies. If an object's potential energy is mgh, which of the following is equivalent to the kinetic energy of the object?

    A) $2mv$
    B) $2mv^2$
    C) $\frac{1}{2}mv^2$
    D) $\frac{1}{2}v\sqrt{2m}$

10. Which of the following best describes the roots of $x^2 - 7x + 14 = 0$?

    A) real, unequal, and rational
    B) real, unequal, and irrational
    C) imaginary, unequal, and rational
    D) imaginary, unequal, and irrational

Quiz II Brain Buster—No Calculator

(5 items; 8 minutes)

DIRECTIONS: Solve each item and choose the correct answer choice. Use any available space for scratchwork. The use of a calculator **is not permitted**. Answers are on page 230.

Notes:

(1) All expressions and equations represent real numbers unless otherwise indicated.

(2) Figures that accompany problems in this test are intended to provide information useful in solving the problems. They are drawn as accurately as possible EXCEPT when it is stated in a specific problem that the figure is not drawn to scale. All figures lie in a plane unless otherwise indicated.

(3) The domain of a given function f is the set of all real numbers x for which $f(x)$ is a real number unless otherwise indicated.

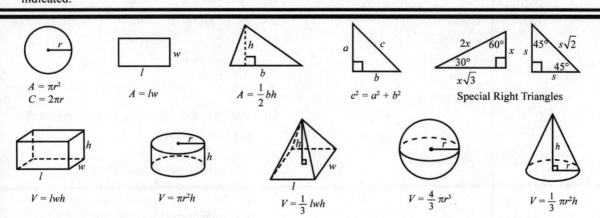

$$A = \pi r^2$$
$$C = 2\pi r$$

$$A = lw$$

$$A = \frac{1}{2}bh$$

$$c^2 = a^2 + b^2$$

Special Right Triangles

$$V = lwh$$

$$V = \pi r^2 h$$

$$V = \frac{1}{3}lwh$$

$$V = \frac{4}{3}\pi r^3$$

$$V = \frac{1}{3}\pi r^2 h$$

The number of degrees of arc in a circle is 360.

The sum of the measures in degrees of the angles of a triangle is 180.

The number of radians of arc in a circle is 2π.

$$m(t) = \frac{t}{10} + 10 , \; 0 \le t \le 48$$

1. The equation above models the change in mass, m, measured in grams, of a butterfly larva as a function of time, t, measured in hours. Which of the following must be true?

   I. The mass of the larva increases by 1% each hour when $0 \le t \le 48$.

  II. The mass of the larva at $t = 0$ is 10 grams.

 III. The average growth rate of the butterfly larva when $0 \le t \le 48$ is 0.1 grams per hour.

A) I only
B) I and II only
C) II and III only
D) I, II, and III

$$3y - 15 = 2x$$
$$-\frac{2}{3}x + y = 6$$

2. Which of the following is the solution to the system of equations above?

A) $(-3,3)$
B) $(0,5)$
C) There is no solution.
D) There is an infinite number of solutions.

3. If $-y+x>1$ and $3y+6x \leq -2$ form a system of inequalities, which of the following graphs shows the solution set for the system?

A)

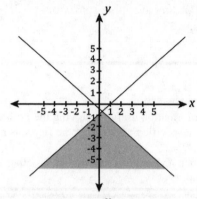

B)

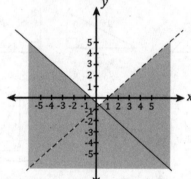

C)

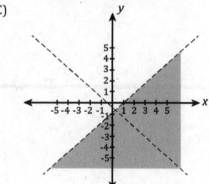

D)

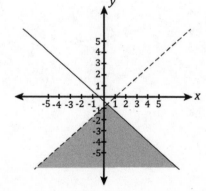

4. What are the solutions for x in the equation $x^2 + 4x = -6$? (Note: $i = \sqrt{-1}$)

A) $x = -1 \pm i\sqrt{2}$

B) $x = -2 \pm i\sqrt{2}$

C) $x = 1 \pm i\sqrt{2}$

D) $x = 2 \pm i\sqrt{2}$

$$\sqrt{x+m} - x = -1$$

5. If $m = 5$, what is the solution set to the equation above?

A) $\{-1, 4\}$

B) $\{-1\}$

C) $\{2\}$

D) $\{4\}$

Quiz II Brain Buster—Calculator

(10 items; 15 minutes)

DIRECTIONS: Solve each item and choose the correct answer choice. Use any available space for scratchwork. The use of a calculator **is permitted**. Answers are on page 231.

Notes:

(1) All expressions and equations represent real numbers unless otherwise indicated.

(2) Figures that accompany problems in this test are intended to provide information useful in solving the problems. They are drawn as accurately as possible EXCEPT when it is stated in a specific problem that the figure is not drawn to scale. All figures lie in a plane unless otherwise indicated.

(3) The domain of a given function f is the set of all real numbers x for which $f(x)$ is a real number unless otherwise indicated.

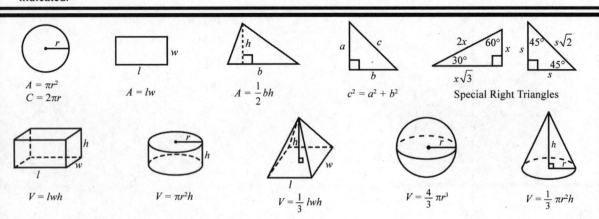

The number of degrees of arc in a circle is 360.

The sum of the measures in degrees of the angles of a triangle is 180.

The number of radians of arc in a circle is 2π.

1. The bill for a group at a restaurant listed a subtotal and 6 percent tax. The group left a $29.25 tip, paying $235.95 in all. What percentage of their bill's subtotal did the group tip?

   A) 10
   B) 15
   C) 17
   D) 20

2. A square that has vertices at points (3,4) and (1,4) has an area of 2. What is the length of the side of the square?

   A) $\sqrt{2}$
   B) 2
   C) 4
   D) Cannot be determined from the information given.

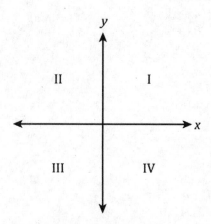

3. If the system of equations $y = x - 1$ and $y = -2x$ is graphed in the xy-plane above, which quadrant contains the solution to the system?

   A) Quadrant I
   B) Quadrant II
   C) Quadrant III
   D) Quadrant IV

4. In the xy-coordinate plane, if the line $y = 2x - 1$ is shifted down 2 units and shifted to the right 3 units, which of the following is the graph of the new line?

A)
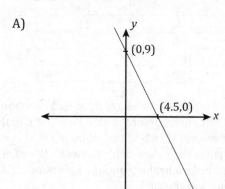

B)
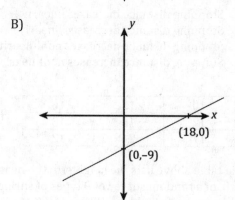

C)
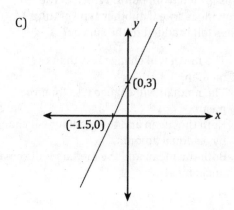

D)
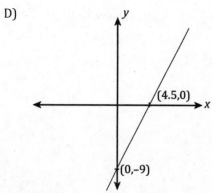

SPEED (KILOMETERS PER HOUR)	STOPPING DISTANCE (METERS)
40	10
60	21
80	36
100	50
120	78

5. The stopping distances of a car as a function of the car's speed before braking is shown in the table above. Which of the following best describes the relationship between the car's speed before braking and the stopping distance of the car?

A) Stopping distance increases linearly
B) Stopping distance decreases linearly
C) Stopping distance decreases nonlinearly
D) Stopping distance increases nonlinearly

10	13	16
12	16	18
17	21	12

6. The table above lists the heights, to the nearest inch, of a random survey of 9 types of spring tulips grown from bulbs. Which of the following is true if another type of tulip 14 inches tall is added to the survey?

A) The mean will change less than the median.
B) The median will change less than the mean.
C) Both the mean and the median will change by an equal amount.
D) Both the mean and the median will remain unchanged.

7. If $x + y = 5$, what is the value of $3^y \left(\sqrt[3]{9^{3x/2}} \right)$?

A) 5^3
B) 3^5
C) 3^9
D) 9^5

8. Assume an angle with radian measure θ exists such that $\cos\theta = -\dfrac{3}{5}$ and $\dfrac{\pi}{2} < \theta < \pi$. What is the value of $\sin\theta$?

A) $-\dfrac{5}{3}$

B) $-\dfrac{4}{5}$

C) $\dfrac{3}{5}$

D) $\dfrac{4}{5}$

9. A triangle has a height of $3x - 2$. If the area of the triangle is $12x^2 + x - 6$, which of the following is equivalent to the length of the base of the triangle?

A) $x - 6$
B) $4x - 3$
C) $4x + 3$
D) $8x + 6$

Number of Days Students Ate Fresh Vegetables

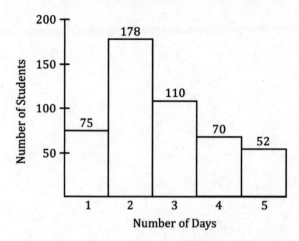

10. The histogram above summarizes a survey of 595 students at Prairie Middle School about the number of days in a five-day period that they ate fresh vegetables. The histogram is found to have an error: the number of students for the categories "2 days" and "3 days" have been switched. After the correction, which of the following statements is NOT necessarily true?

A) The corrected median is 3 days.
B) The corrected mode is 3 days.
C) The corrected mean is greater than the uncorrected mean.
D) The corrected mean is 2.2 days.

MATH: STUDENT-PRODUCED RESPONSES QUIZZES

This section contains two Math: Student-Produced Responses quizzes. Complete the quizzes in the specified time limit. Use any available space in the section for scratch work. Answers are on page 236.

Quiz I—No Calculator

(2 items; 4 minutes)

DIRECTIONS: Solve each item. Use any available space for scratchwork. The use of a calculator **is not permitted**.

Notes:

(1) All expressions and equations represent real numbers unless otherwise indicated.

(2) Figures that accompany problems in this test are intended to provide information useful in solving the problems. They are drawn as accurately as possible EXCEPT when it is stated in a specific problem that the figure is not drawn to scale. All figures lie in a plane unless otherwise indicated.

(3) The domain of a given function f is the set of all real numbers x for which $f(x)$ is a real number unless otherwise indicated.

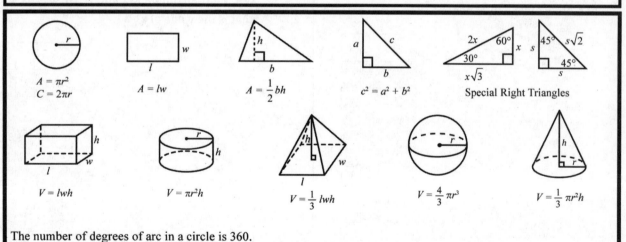

The number of degrees of arc in a circle is 360.

The sum of the measures in degrees of the angles of a triangle is 180.

The number of radians of arc in a circle is 2π.

Each item requires you to solve an item and mark your answer on a special answer grid. For each item, you should write your answer in the boxes at the top of each column and then fill in the ovals beneath each part of the answer you write. Here are some examples:

Answer: 7/2 and 3.5

NOTE: A mixed number such as $3\frac{1}{2}$ must be gridded as 7/2 or as 3.5. If gridded as "31/2," it will be read as "thirty-one halves."

Answer: 325

NOTE: Either position is correct.

Answer: 1/6, .166, or .167

NOTE: A decimal answer with more digits than the grid can accommodate must be truncated. A decimal such as $0.16\overline{6}$ must be gridded as .166 or .167. A less accurate value such as .16 or .17 will be scored as incorrect.

1. Ray is now 10 years older than Cindy. In 8 years, Ray will be twice as old as Cindy is then. How old is Cindy now?

2. Let the operation ✪ be defined by x ✪ $y = xy + y$ for all numbers x and y. If 2 ✪ $3 = z$ ✪ 1, what is the value of z?

Quiz I—Calculator

(3 items; 6 minutes)

DIRECTIONS: Solve each item. Use any available space for scratchwork. The use of a calculator **is permitted**.

Notes:

(1) All expressions and equations represent real numbers unless otherwise indicated.

(2) Figures that accompany problems in this test are intended to provide information useful in solving the problems. They are drawn as accurately as possible EXCEPT when it is stated in a specific problem that the figure is not drawn to scale. All figures lie in a plane unless otherwise indicated.

(3) The domain of a given function f is the set of all real numbers x for which $f(x)$ is a real number unless otherwise indicated.

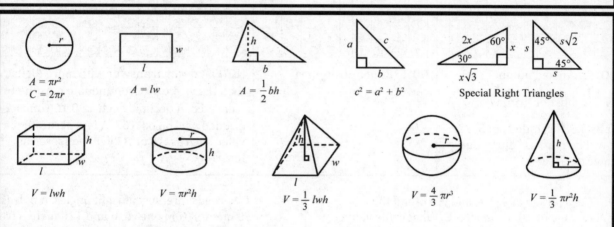

The number of degrees of arc in a circle is 360.

The sum of the measures in degrees of the angles of a triangle is 180.

The number of radians of arc in a circle is 2π.

Each item requires you to solve an item and mark your answer on a special answer grid. For each item, you should write your answer in the boxes at the top of each column and then fill in the ovals beneath each part of the answer you write. Here are some examples:

Answer: 7/2 and 3.5	Answer: 325	Answer: 1/6, .166, or .167

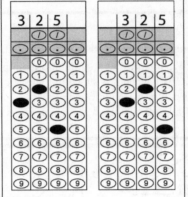

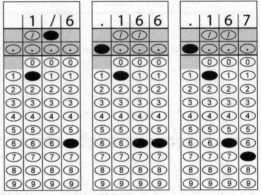

NOTE: A mixed number such as $3\frac{1}{2}$ must be gridded as 7/2 or as 3.5. If gridded as "31/2," it will be read as "thirty-one halves."

NOTE: Either position is correct.

NOTE: A decimal answer with more digits than the grid can accommodate must be truncated. A decimal such as $0.16\overline{6}$ must be gridded as .166 or .167. A less accurate value such as .16 or .17 will be scored as incorrect.

1. The average of 4, 5, x, and y is 6, and the average of x, z, 8, and 9 is 8. What is the value of $z - y$?

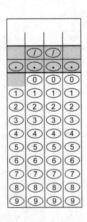

2. Two roads intersect at right angles. A pole is 50 meters from one road and 120 meters from the other road. How far (in meters) is the pole from the point where the roads intersect?

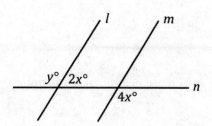

3. In the figure above, line *l* is parallel to line *m*. What is the value of *x*?

Quiz II Brain Buster—No Calculator

(2 items; 4 minutes)

DIRECTIONS: Solve each item. Use any available space for scratchwork. The use of a calculator **is not permitted**.

Notes:

(1) All expressions and equations represent real numbers unless otherwise indicated.

(2) Figures that accompany problems in this test are intended to provide information useful in solving the problems. They are drawn as accurately as possible EXCEPT when it is stated in a specific problem that the figure is not drawn to scale. All figures lie in a plane unless otherwise indicated.

(3) The domain of a given function f is the set of all real numbers x for which $f(x)$ is a real number unless otherwise indicated.

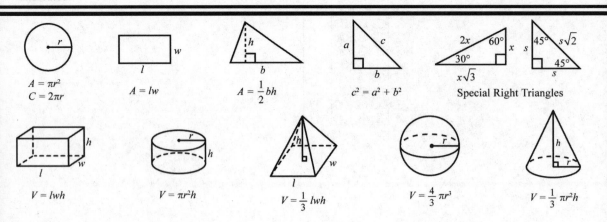

The number of degrees of arc in a circle is 360.

The sum of the measures in degrees of the angles of a triangle is 180.

The number of radians of arc in a circle is 2π.

Each item requires you to solve an item and mark your answer on a special answer grid. For each item, you should write your answer in the boxes at the top of each column and then fill in the ovals beneath each part of the answer you write. Here are some examples:

Answer: 7/2 and 3.5

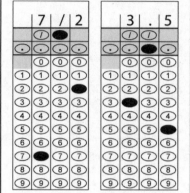

Answer: 325

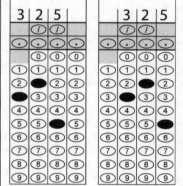

Answer: 1/6, .166, or .167

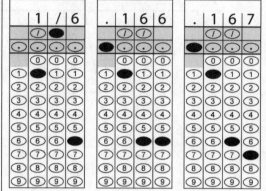

NOTE: A mixed number such as $3\frac{1}{2}$ must be gridded as 7/2 or as 3.5. If gridded as "31/2," it will be read as "thirty-one halves."

NOTE: Either position is correct.

NOTE: A decimal answer with more digits than the grid can accommodate must be truncated. A decimal such as $0.16\overline{6}$ must be gridded as .166 or .167. A less accurate value such as .16 or .17 will be scored as incorrect.

1.   If $2^{x+1} = 4^{x-1}$, what is the value of x?

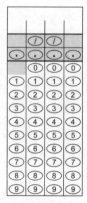

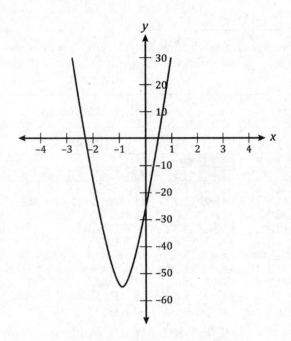

2. The function $f(x) = x^4 - 4x^3 + 10x^2 + 45x + k$ is graphed in the xy-plane above. If k is an integer, what could be the value of $|k|$?

Quiz II Brain Buster—Calculator

(3 items; 6 minutes)

DIRECTIONS: Solve each item. Use any available space for scratchwork. The use of a calculator **is permitted**.

Notes:

(1) All expressions and equations represent real numbers unless otherwise indicated.

(2) Figures that accompany problems in this test are intended to provide information useful in solving the problems. They are drawn as accurately as possible EXCEPT when it is stated in a specific problem that the figure is not drawn to scale. All figures lie in a plane unless otherwise indicated.

(3) The domain of a given function f is the set of all real numbers x for which $f(x)$ is a real number unless otherwise indicated.

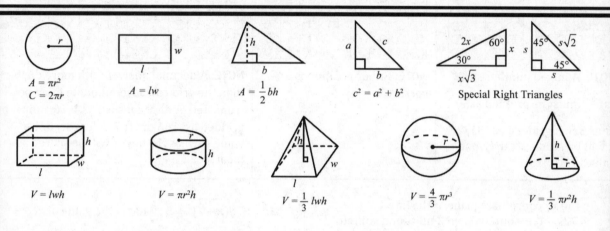

The number of degrees of arc in a circle is 360.

The sum of the measures in degrees of the angles of a triangle is 180.

The number of radians of arc in a circle is 2π.

Each item requires you to solve an item and mark your answer on a special answer grid. For each item, you should write your answer in the boxes at the top of each column and then fill in the ovals beneath each part of the answer you write. Here are some examples:

Answer: 7/2 and 3.5

NOTE: A mixed number such as $3\frac{1}{2}$ must be gridded as 7/2 or as 3.5. If gridded as "31/2," it will be read as "thirty-one halves."

Answer: 325

NOTE: Either position is correct.

Answer: 1/6, .166, or .167

NOTE: A decimal answer with more digits than the grid can accommodate must be truncated. A decimal such as $0.16\overline{6}$ must be gridded as .166 or .167. A less accurate value such as .16 or .17 will be scored as incorrect.

1. In the *xy*-coordinate plane, if the line $y = 2x - 1$ is shifted down 2 units and shifted to the left 6 units, what is the *y*-intercept of the new line?

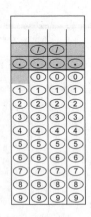

2. If $\sqrt[4]{(x+7)^2} = 5$, what is the value of *x*?

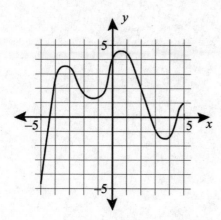

3.   The function $f(x)$ is graphed in the xy-plane above. If k is an integer such that the equation $f(x) = k$ has four real solutions, what is one possible value of k?

ESSAY QUIZ

This section contains a Writing quiz. Complete the quiz under timed conditions. Sample essay responses begin on page 239.

(1 Essay Prompt; 50 minutes)

DIRECTIONS: The Essay Test measures your ability to read and understand a passage and write an essay that analyzes the passage. In your essay, demonstrate that you have carefully read the passage, write a clear and logical analysis, and use language precisely.

You have 50 minutes to read the passage and write an essay in response to the provided prompt.

Read the passage below and think about how Michael Bloomberg uses
- evidence (facts, examples, etc.) to support claims.
- reasoning to develop the passage and to connect claims and evidence.
- rhetorical or persuasive elements, such as language choices or emotional appeals, to increase the impact of the ideas expressed.

Adapted from a May 13, 2012, graduation speech at the University of North Carolina at Chapel Hill by former New York City mayor Michael Bloomberg.

1 The smartphone is arguably the greatest invention the world has ever seen. And the reason is simple: it has democratized technology. Today, whether you're building an app, or writing a review on Yelp!, or checking in on Foursquare, you are making the computer, and everyone who uses it, smarter.

2 Since the dawn of time, we have been sharing knowledge with each other. But today, knowledge is being shared globally as quickly as it is being discovered individually. That revolution in computer-based communications, which started in government laboratories, and in Steve Jobs's garage, and in the little office I first rented 30 years ago, is now being led by the masses.

3 Whether you like it or not: the computer nerds have won. We're all computer nerds now.

4 The creation of the smartphone is the most visible symbol of the technological revolution we're experiencing. But it's happening all around us. In every industry, the speed of innovation is moving at a breathtaking pace. You can see it just down the road at Research Triangle Park. You can see it in Silicon Valley—and in Boston, Massachusetts, and Austin, Texas. All of those places are home to great universities where pioneering work is being done and good jobs are being created.

5 In New York City, we've joined forces with Cornell University, New York University, and Carnegie Mellon—as well as the Technion Institute of Technology in Israel, and universities in Canada, the UK, and India—to develop new, world-class applied science and engineering campuses. We know the future of the global economy is tied to the discoveries that are made by university-educated researchers and innovators. And if those discoveries happen in New York City, the companies that spin off from them will start in New York City.

6 I have no doubt that many of you here today will be part of those discoveries. Your work will reshape our understanding of the world—everything from the origins of the universe to the cure for cancer. For the non-

scientists here, you too will have an important role to play. You business and finance majors: you may be providing the capital for the discoveries to be brought to the market. Education and journalism majors: you may be writing or teaching about those discoveries. Nursing and pre-med students: you may be talking to patients about them. And you future lawyers—yes, lawyers always have to be involved in everything—you will be needed to protect patents, and of course, fight off other lawyers.

7 The technology revolution that is reshaping our understanding of the world, and the freedom that you enjoy to pursue your dreams, are complementary. They reinforce each other. The more we learn, the freer we will be. And the freer we are, the more we will learn.

8 *Lux Libertas.* Light and Liberty. That is the motto of your university. And that, I believe, will be the defining spirit of the twenty-first century. The more light we shed on the nature of the world, the more we advance knowledge in science and technology, the more liberty we will spread.

9 In fact, I would argue that the technological revolution that is now underway will not only be our most powerful weapon in the fight against poverty and disease, it will be our most powerful weapon in the fight against repression and intolerance. Because where there is light, liberty grows. And where there is liberty, light flows.

10 Now, it's up to all of you—in your own way—to take what you have learned here, and spread light and liberty wherever you go.

Write an essay explaining how Michael Bloomberg develops his argument that we are in the midst of a technological revolution that has the potential to greatly impact the world around us. In your essay, analyze how Bloomberg uses one or more of the elements listed above (or other elements) to make his argument more logical and persuasive. Be sure to focus on the most relevant aspects of the passage.

Your essay should not discuss whether you agree with Bloomberg's claims but rather discuss how Bloomberg develops his argument.

Practice Tests

CAMBRIDGE
THE PRACTICE BOOK

15SATB

Practice Test I

Outline

I. **Section 1:** Reading (pp. 59–74)

II. **Section 2:** Writing and Language (pp. 75–86)

III. **Section 3:** Math, No Calculator (pp. 87–92)

IV. **Section 4:** Math, Calculator (pp. 93–105)

V. **Section 5:** Essay (Optional) (pp. 106–107)

DIRECTIONS

Practice Test I includes five test sections: Reading, Writing and Language, Math, No Calculator, Math, Calculator, and the optional Essay. Calculator use is permitted on the Math, Calculator section only.

Cambridge offers several services for schools utilizing our practice tests. Ask your teacher whether your school has decided to send your answers to Cambridge for scoring or to score your answers at your school. If Cambridge is scoring your test, you will use a Scantron™ form provided by your teacher, or you will enter your answers online. If your school is scoring your test, you may use a Scantron™ form provided by your teacher, or you may write your answers on paper.

If you are entering your test answers on a Scantron™ form, please be sure to include the following information on the Scantron™:

Book and edition	*The Practice Book, 13th Edition*
Practice Test Form Code	**15SATB**

If you are only completing a single section of this practice test, make sure to also include the following information:

Subject	**Reading, Writing and Language,** or **Math**
Section Number	**Section 1**, **2**, **3** or **4**

The items in each test section are numbered and the multiple-choice answers are lettered. The Scantron™ form has numbered rows that correspond to the items on the test. Each row contains lettered ovals to match the answer choices for each item on the test. Each numbered row has a corresponding item on the test.

For each multiple-choice item, first decide on the best answer choice. Then, locate the row number that corresponds to the item. Next, find the oval in that row that matches the letter of the chosen answer. Then, use a soft lead pencil to fill in the oval. DO NOT use a ballpoint pen. For each student-produced response item on the math test sections, decide on the correct answer. Then, locate the SPR grid that corresponds to the item. Write your answer in the top of the grid and use a soft lead pencil to fill in each corresponding oval. DO NOT use a ballpoint pen.

Mark only one answer for each item. If you change your mind about an answer choice, thoroughly erase your first mark before marking your new answer.

Note that only responses marked on your Scantron™ form or written on your paper will be scored. Your score on each test will be based only on the number of items that are correctly answered during the time allowed for that test. You will not be penalized for guessing. Therefore, it is in your best interest to answer every item on the test, even if you must guess.

On the Essay, write your response to the prompt using the essay response sheets or loose-leaf paper provided by your teacher. (Note that the Writing Test is optional.)

You may work on each test only during the time allowed for that test. If you finish a test before time is called, use the time to review your answer choices or work on items about which you are uncertain. You may not return to a test on which time has already been called, and you may not preview another test. You must lay down your pencil immediately when time is called at the end of each test. You may not for any reason fill in or alter ovals for a test after time has expired for that test. Violation of these rules will result in immediate disqualification from the exam.

SECTION 1—READING

Time—65 minutes

52 items

> **DIRECTIONS:** Each passage or pair of passages is followed by a set of items. Choose the best answer to each question based on what is stated or implied in the passage or passages and in any accompanying graphics. Answers are on page 243.

Questions #1–10 are based on the following passage.

The following passage is an excerpt from "My Kinsman, Major Molineux" by Nathaniel Hawthorne.

It was near nine o'clock when a boat crossed with a single passenger, who had obtained conveyance at the late hour by promise of extra fare. He was a youth of eighteen years, country-
5 bred, and on his first visit to town. The youth drew from his pocket a little province bill of five shillings, which, in depreciation in that sort of currency, satisfied the ferryman's demand with the addition of a hexagonal piece of parchment,
10 valued at three pence. He headed into town with as light a step as if his day's journey had not already exceeded thirty miles and with as eager an eye as if he were entering London instead of the little metropolis of a New England colony.

15 Before Robin had proceeded far, it occurred to him that he knew not whither to direct his steps; so he paused and looked up and down the narrow street, scrutinizing the small and mean wooden buildings. "This low hovel cannot be my
20 kinsman's dwelling," thought he, "nor yonder old house; and truly I see none that might be worthy of him."

He resumed his walk and the houses became more respectable. He soon discerned a figure
25 moving on moderately in advance, and he hastened his steps to overtake it. Robin laid hold the man's coat, just where the light from the open door of a barber's shop fell.

"Good evening to you, honored sir," said he.
30 "I pray you tell me where is the dwelling of my kinsman, Major Molineux."

The citizen answered him with anger and annoyance. "I know not the man you speak of. Now, release my coat." Robin hastened away,
35 pursued by an ill-mannered roar of laughter from the barber's shop. At first surprised, he soon reflected, "This is some country representative, who has never seen the inside of my kinsman's door and lacks the breeding to answer a stranger
40 civilly."

He now became entangled in narrow streets. At length, on a corner, he beheld the swinging door of an inn. He was guided by voices to the public room and accosted by the innkeeper. "From
45 the country, Sir?" said the innkeeper, with a profound bow. "Beg to congratulate you on your arrival and trust you intend a long stay."

"The man sees a family likeness! The rogue has guessed that I am related to the Major!"
50 thought Robin. "My honest friend," he said, "my present business is merely to inquire my way to the dwelling of my kinsman, Major Molineux. I shall return another evening when my purse is full and enjoy your hospitality."

55 "Better trudge, boy," the innkeeper said, "better trudge!" Robin had begun to draw his hand toward the lighter end of his oak cudgel, but a strange hostility in every countenance induced him to relinquish his purpose of breaking the
60 courteous innkeeper's head.

"Is it not strange," thought Robin, "that a promise to return would provoke such rudeness?"

Suddenly, there appeared a watchman who carried a lantern. He turned to face Robin and
65 displayed a long staff, spiked at the end. "I say, friend! Will you guide me to the house of my kinsman, Major Molineux?"

Continue ➔

"Watch here an hour, and Major Molineux will pass by," said he gruffly.

70   After some time, Robin discerned a man at the foot of a nearby church building and addressed him in a loud and peevish cry, "Hallo, friend! Must I wait here all night for my kinsman, Major Molineux? I've been searching half the night
75 for Major Molineux; is there really such a person in these parts, or am I dreaming?"

"Major Molineux! The name is not altogether strange to me," said the gentleman. "The Major will very shortly pass through this very street. In
80 the meantime, as I'm curious to witness your meeting, I will sit down here upon the steps and bear you company."

Then Robin briefly related that his father was a clergyman and that he and Major Molineux
85 were brothers' children. The Major, having inherited riches and acquired civil and military rank, had visited his cousin, in great pomp, a year before; had manifested much interest in Robin; and, being childless himself, had thrown out hints
90 respecting the future of Robin. It was therefore determined that Robin should profit by his kinsman's generous intentions.

"Well, sir," continued Robin, "I thought it high time to begin the world. So I started for this
95 place, to pay the Major a visit."

While he spoke, a stream of boisterous people emptied into the street where they were standing. A single horseman thundered a command to halt. The shouts and laughter of the
100 people died away, and there remained only silence. Right before Robin's eyes was an open cart. There the torches blazed the brightest, and there, tarred and feathered, sat his kinsman Major Molineux!

1.   As it is used in line 18, the word "mean" means

   A) ill-mannered.
   B) destructive.
   C) unfinished.
   D) shabby.

2.   As it is used in line 25, the phrase "in advance" means

   A) higher.
   B) ahead.
   C) overdue.
   D) earlier.

3.   It can be inferred that no one would give Robin information about his kinsman because Major Molineux

   A) no longer lived in the town.
   B) had changed his name.
   C) had fallen into disgrace.
   D) did not wish to be found.

4.   Which of the following textual excerpts provides the strongest evidence for the correct answer to the previous question?

   A) Lines 34–36 ("Robin . . . barber's shop")
   B) Lines 57–60 ("a strange . . . head")
   C) Lines 64–65 ("He turned . . . end")
   D) Lines 102–104 ("There . . . Major Molineux")

5.   It can be inferred from the passage that the man Robin meets at the foot of the church building

   A) does not know Major Molineux but is anxious to meet him.
   B) knows that Major Molineux is Robin's relative.
   C) is aware that Major Molineux has been tarred and feathered.
   D) hopes that Robin will give him money for waiting with him.

6.   Which of the following statements by the man at the foot of the church building best supports the correct answer to the previous question?

   A) Lines 77–78 ("The name is not . . . me")
   B) Lines 78–79 ("The Major . . . street")
   C) Lines 79–81 ("In the meantime . . . meeting")
   D) Lines 81–82 ("I will sit . . . company")

Continue ▶

7. Which of the following best describes the development of the passage?

   A) Robin arrives in town expecting that his well-to-do relative will provide for him but learns that his relative is not the well-respected person he expected.
   B) Robin travels to town to find work but learns that the inhabitants are hostile toward strangers from the country.
   C) Major Molineux invites his cousin's son, Robin, to visit him in town, but when Robin arrives, the Major refuses to acknowledge him.
   D) Aware that Robin is coming to visit his relative Major Molineux, various townspeople play a practical joke on Robin.

8. The hostility among the people gathered at the public inn can best be explained by their

   A) mistrust of strangers from the country.
   B) animosity toward Robin's kinsman, Major Molineux.
   C) anticipation of a fight between Robin and the innkeeper.
   D) curiosity about the events that have brought Robin to town.

9. According to the passage, Robin enters the town with an attitude of

   A) resignation.
   B) fulfillment.
   C) anticipation.
   D) indifference.

10. Reflecting on his first encounter with townspeople (lines 36–40), Robin ironically

   A) ignores their advice on how to locate his kinsman, Major Molineux.
   B) concludes that their hostility is a universal trait of townspeople.
   C) suspects that the stranger is actually his kinsman, Major Molineux.
   D) attributes to the stranger characteristics that he could apply to himself.

Continue

Questions #11–20 are based on the following pair of passages.

The following two passages explain two different views on judicial review.

Passage 1

I think there's a misunderstanding of what the doctrine of judicial review means in practice. Obviously, members of Congress and the president and members of the executive branch
5 are obligated to obey the Constitution, and the doctrine of judicial review doesn't mean they do not.

If the majority of members of Congress find something to be desirable but unconstitutional,
10 they ought not to vote for it. If they vote for it and the president decides it's unconstitutional, he ought to veto it. And if two-thirds of Congress overrides the presidential veto, then the Supreme Court ought to throw it out. This is not a case of
15 one branch having supremacy over another; it is a case where you have got to pass everybody's notion of what is constitutional.

The alternative, if it is being suggested that the Supreme Court should lose its power to
20 declare acts unconstitutional, seems to me to be very unfortunate. While Congress has an obligation to take constitutionality into effect, the question is whether the Supreme Court should lose its power to say "no," and I would find that
25 disastrous.

I would add that there is no crisis of judicial activism, if that term is understood to mean judges letting personal beliefs on political or social issues dictate their decisions. Judicial activism is a
30 stick that politicians use with which to beat things that they don't like.

Various doctrines inherent in the notion of a judiciary restrict judicial activism. One of the most important is judicial restraint: a court should not
35 decide a matter prematurely, should not decide political questions, and should not decide a matter unless there is a genuine case involving controversy. Courts impose on themselves a strict requirement that there be real parties with real
40 interests at stake, that there be a real injury in fact, and that political questions are out of bounds.

Passage 2

Courts have an obligation to determine the constitutionality of federal statutes they are asked to apply, and not simply because they are
45 themselves required to obey the Constitution. As Marshall argued, judicial review is an essential element in the constitutional system of checks and balances—designed, as Hamilton said in *The Federalist*, to help keep the legislature within the
50 limits of its authority.

This does not mean that the courts have a monopoly on constitutional interpretation. Members of Congress, like all federal and state officers, are bound by their oaths to support the
55 Constitution. Whenever a bill is introduced, every member of Congress must inquire whether Congress has the power to enact it. Thus, Congress is continually engaged in interpreting the Constitution. So, of course, is the president. And
60 thus a great deal of constitutional law is made outside the courts, by the legislative and executive branches of government.

The vexing question is therefore not who has power to interpret the Constitution but whose
65 view prevails in case of conflict. What happens when different branches of government, each acting within its proper sphere of authority, disagree as to what the Constitution means?

There are times when other governmental
70 actors are plainly obliged to accept judicial decisions. Judicial power to decide a case implies authority to render a judgment that binds the parties. Thus, when President Roosevelt contemplated disobeying an anticipated judicial
75 decision requiring the government to pay bondholders in gold, he challenged the very essence of judicial power. Such a course could be defended, if at all, only as an exercise of the natural right of revolution; it was not consistent
80 with the Constitution.

It does not follow that other branches are bound in all cases by judicial interpretations of the Constitution. President Jackson vetoed a new charter for the Bank of the United States after the
85 Supreme Court had upheld congressional power to establish it. President Jefferson pardoned those convicted under the Sedition Act on constitutional grounds that had been rejected by the courts. Both Jackson and Jefferson were well within their

Continue ➡

90 rights. Neither of them did anything that interfered with the power of the courts to render binding judgments in particular cases. The pardon power is an express limitation on that principle, and it essentially allows the winning party to
95 waive a judgment in its favor. Nor was either Jefferson's or Jackson's action inconsistent with *Marbury*'s principle that the courts must have power to prevent other branches from exceeding their powers.

100   On the contrary, Jefferson and Jackson's actions provided an *additional* check that furnished even greater security for the rights of the states and the people. Indeed, what these two presidents did illustrates the core of our
105 constitutional separation of powers: no measure can be carried out to the detriment of the people or the states unless all three branches agree that it is constitutional.

11. It can be inferred that the author of Passage 1 believes that claims that judicial activism upsets the proper constitutional balance between the branches of government are

A) well-founded.
B) exaggerated.
C) misconstrued.
D) premature.

12. As it is used in line 52, the word "monopoly" means

A) a large business.
B) exclusive control.
C) unrestricted power.
D) unlimited authority.

13. It can be inferred that both authors agree that

A) only the courts have the power to consider the constitutionality of a law.
B) only the courts are required to consider the constitutionality of a law.
C) all three branches of government must assess the constitutionality of a law.
D) no branch of government is required to assess the constitutionality of a law.

14. Which of the following pairs of excerpts from the text best supports the correct answer to the previous question?

A) Lines 33–34 ("One . . . restraint") and lines 42–45 ("Courts . . . Constitution")
B) Lines 26–27 ("there is . . . activism") and lines 69–71 ("There . . . decisions")
C) Lines 21–25 ("While . . . disastrous") and lines 71–73 ("Judicial . . . parties")
D) Lines 15–17 ("it is . . . constitutional") and lines 105–108 ("no measure . . . constitutional")

15. It can be inferred that the author of Passage 2 believes that the Supreme Court's power to judge the constitutionality of a law is

A) the exclusive prerogative of the Court and not available to other branches of government.
B) more extensive than just the obligation of the justices to obey the Constitution.
C) always binding on the other branches of government when a court interprets the Constitution.
D) stated explicitly in the provisions of the Constitution itself.

16. Which of the following textual excerpts provides the strongest support for the correct answer to the previous question?

A) Lines 42–45 ("Courts . . . Constitution")
B) Lines 53–55 ("Members . . . Constitution")
C) Lines 60–62 ("a great . . . government")
D) Lines 81–83 ("It does . . . Constitution")

17. Which of the following, when substituted for the word "vexing" (line 63), would best preserve the intended meaning of the original sentence?

A) Painful
B) Difficult
C) Moot
D) Rhetorical

Continue

18. In the first paragraph of Passage 2, the author cites Marshall and Hamilton as authorities for the proposition that

A) judicial review of the constitutionality of legislation has a broader scope than just a required adherence to the Constitution.

B) courts should conduct a review of legislation pending before Congress to determine its constitutionality.

C) the authority of the legislature to pass laws is limited by the power of the courts.

D) checks and balances is a constitutional provision that increases the authority of the legislature.

19. The author of Passage 2 believes that Jefferson's pardon of those convicted under the Sedition Act was justified because

A) the courts had determined that the Sedition Act unfairly restricted free speech.

B) the executive branch, once it had won convictions, was free to give up its victory.

C) the executive is in a better position to judge the constitutionality of a law than the courts.

D) the pardon was necessary to prevent the legislature and the courts from exceeding their constitutional authority.

20. Which of the following best characterizes the exchange of views by the two authors?

A) Both authors agree that the doctrine of judicial review, while once important, has outlived its usefulness.

B) Both authors agree that the doctrine of judicial review remains an important element of Constitutional government.

C) The author of Passage 1 believes that the doctrine of judicial review should only rarely be invoked while the author of Passage 2 believes the Supreme Court should oversee all aspects of government.

D) The author of Passage 1 believes that all three branches of government have the power to review the acts of other branches while the author of Passage 2 believes that only the Supreme Court does.

Continue ➤

Questions #21–30 are based on the following passage.

The following passage describes how organisms respond to microwave radiation.

Behavior is one of two general responses available to endothermic (warm-blooded) species for the regulation of body temperature, the other being innate mechanisms of heat production and
5   heat loss. Human beings rely primarily on the first response to provide a hospitable thermal microclimate for themselves in which the transfer of heat between the body and the environment is accomplished with minimal involvement of innate
10 mechanisms of heat production and loss. Thermoregulatory behavior *anticipates* hyperthermia, and the organism adjusts its behavior to avoid becoming hyperthermic: it removes layers of clothing, it goes for a cool swim,
15 etc. The organism can also respond to changes in the temperature of the body core, as is the case during exercise; but such responses result from the direct stimulation of thermoreceptors distributed widely within the central nervous
20 system, and the ability of these mechanisms to help the organism adjust to gross changes in its environment is limited.

Until recently, it was simply assumed that organisms respond to microwave radiation in the
25 same way that they respond to temperature changes that are caused by other forms of radiation. After all, the argument runs, microwaves are radiation and heat body tissues. Microwave irradiations at equivalent plane-wave
30 power densities of about 100 mW/cm² were presumed to produce "thermal" effects; irradiations within the range of 10 to 100 mW/cm² might or might not produce "thermal" effects; while effects observed at power densities
35 below 10 mW/cm² were assumed to be "nonthermal" in nature. Experiments have shown this to be an oversimplification. Fields as weak as 1 mW/cm² can be thermogenic. When the heat generated in the tissues by an imposed radio
40 frequency (plus the heat generated by metabolism) exceeds the heat-loss capabilities of the organism, the thermoregulatory system has been compromised.

This outdated theory ignores the fact that the
45 stimulus to a behavioral response is normally a temperature change that occurs at the surface of the organism. The thermoreceptors that prompt behavioral changes are located within the first millimeter of the skin's surface, but the energy of a
50 microwave field may be selectively deposited in deep tissues, effectively bypassing these thermoreceptors, particularly if the field is at near-resonant frequencies. The depth of penetration depends on the frequency of the
55 microwaves and the tissue type. Because lower frequencies penetrate deeper into the tissue, and there are few nerve endings in deeper-located parts of the body, the effects of the radio frequency waves (and the damage caused) may not be
60 immediately noticeable.

The lower frequencies at high power densities present a significant risk. The resulting temperature profile may well be a kind of reverse thermal gradient in which the deep tissues are
65 warmed more than those of the surface. Since the heat is not conducted outward to the surface to stimulate the appropriate receptors, the organism does not appreciate this stimulation in the same way that it does heating and cooling of the skin. In
70 theory, the internal organs of a human being or an animal could be quite literally cooked well-done before the animal even realizes that the balance of its thermomicroclimate has been disturbed.

The layers of the body can be approximated
75 as a thin layer of epidermis, dermis, adipose tissue (subcutaneous fat), and muscle tissue. At dozens of gigahertz, the radiation is absorbed in the top fraction to top few millimeters of skin. Muscle tissue is a much more efficient absorber than fat,
80 so at lower frequencies that can penetrate sufficiently deep, most energy gets deposited there. In a homogeneous medium, the energy/depth dependence is an exponential curve with the exponent depending on the frequency
85 and tissue. For 2.5 GHz, the first millimeter of muscle tissue absorbs 11% of the heat energy; the first two millimeters together absorb 20%. For lower frequencies, the attenuation factors are much lower, the achievable heating depths are
90 higher, and the temperature gradient within the tissue is lower.

Continue

21. According to the passage, low frequency radiation is most likely to heat the

A) epidermis.
B) dermis.
C) adipose tissue.
D) muscle tissue.

22. The author is primarily concerned with

A) showing that behavior is a more effective way of controlling body temperature than are innate mechanisms.
B) demonstrating that effects of microwave radiation on human tissue are different from those of other forms of radiation.
C) analyzing the mechanism by which an organism maintains its body temperature in a changing thermal environment.
D) discussing the importance of thermoreceptors in the control of the internal temperature of an organism.

23. The passage states that innate mechanisms for temperature regulation are

A) governed by thermoreceptors inside the body of the organism rather than at the surface.
B) a more effective means of compensating for gross changes in temperature than are behavioral strategies.
C) unlikely to be activated by temperatures deep in the body that are caused by microwaves.
D) activated when the organism determines that the temperature of the environment is changing.

24. The author suggests that the proponents of the theory that microwave radiation acts on organisms in the same way as other forms of radiation do based their conclusions primarily on

A) laboratory research.
B) unfounded guesswork.
C) controlled surveys.
D) direct observation.

25. Which of the following textual excerpts provides the best support for the correct answer to the previous question?

A) Lines 15–17 ("The organism . . . exercise")
B) Lines 17–20 ("such responses . . . system")
C) Lines 23–27 ("Until . . . radiation")
D) Lines 53–55 ("The depth . . . type")

26. In line 68, the word "appreciate" most nearly means

A) esteem.
B) prefer.
C) enjoy.
D) notice.

27. The author's strategy in lines 69–73 is to

A) introduce a hypothetical example to dramatize a point.
B) propose an experiment to test a scientific hypothesis.
C) cite a case study to illustrate a general contention.
D) produce a counterexample to disprove an opponent's theory.

28. In line 43, the word "compromised" most nearly means

A) agreed.
B) permitted.
C) endangered.
D) settled.

Continue

29. The author indicates that lower frequencies of microwave radiation at high power can be dangerous because

  A) upper layers of skin absorb the radiation and manifest symptoms similar to sunburn.
  B) deep tissues absorb more of the energy and the resulting heat is not conducted to the surface.
  C) most high-frequency microwave radiation is absorbed in the outermost layers of the skin.
  D) there are fewer nerve endings located in deeper parts of the body.

30. Which of the following pairs of excerpts from the passage provides the most complete explanation for the correct answer to the previous question?

  A) Lines 1–3 ("Behavior . . . temperature") and lines 11–15 ("Thermoregulatory . . . swim, etc.")
  B) Lines 29–36 ("Microwave . . . nature") and lines 38–43 ("When . . . compromised")
  C) Lines 62–65 ("The resulting . . . surface") and lines 78–82 ("Muscle . . . there")
  D) Lines 65–69 ("Since . . . skin") and lines 74–76 ("The layers . . . tissue")

Continue

Questions #31–41 are based on the following passage.

This passage is adapted from the speech "Is It a Crime for a Citizen of the United States to Vote?" by Susan B. Anthony.

Friends and Fellow Citizens: I stand before you tonight under indictment for the alleged crime of having voted at the last presidential election without having a lawful right to vote. It shall be
5 my work this evening to prove to you that in thus voting, I not only committed no crime, but, instead, simply exercised *my citizen's rights*, guaranteed to me and all United States citizens by the National Constitution, beyond the power of
10 any State to deny.

The preamble of the Federal Constitution says: "We, the people of the United States, in order to form a more perfect union, establish justice, insure *domestic* tranquility, provide for the
15 common defense, promote the general welfare, and secure the blessings of liberty to ourselves and our posterity." It was we, the people, not we, the white male citizens; but we, the whole people, who formed the Union. And we formed it, not to
20 give the blessings of liberty, but to secure them; not to the half of ourselves and the half of our posterity but to the whole people—women as well as men. And it is a downright mockery to talk to women of their enjoyment of the blessings of
25 liberty while they are denied the use of the only means of securing them provided by this government—the ballot.

For any State to make sex a qualification that results in the disfranchisement of one entire half
30 of the people is a violation of the supreme law of the land. By it the blessings of liberty are forever withheld from women and their female posterity. To them this government has no just powers derived from the consent of the governed. To
35 them this government is not a democracy. It is not a republic. It is a hateful oligarchy of sex. An oligarchy of learning, where the educated govern the ignorant, might be endured; but this oligarchy of sex, which makes father, brothers, husband,
40 sons, the oligarchs or rulers over the mother and sisters, the wife and daughters of every household—which ordains all men sovereigns, all women subjects—carries dissension, discord, and rebellion into every home of the nation.

45 But, it is urged, the use of the masculine pronouns he, his, and him, in all the constitutions and laws, is proof that only men were meant to be included in their provisions. If you insist on this version of the letter of the law, we shall insist that
50 you be consistent, and accept the other horn of the dilemma, which would compel you to exempt women from taxation for the support of the government, and from penalties for the violation of laws.

55 Though the words persons, people, inhabitants, electors, citizens, are all used indiscriminately in the national and state constitutions, there was always a conflict of opinion, prior to the war, as to whether they were
60 synonymous terms, as for instance:

"No person shall be a representative who shall not have been seven years a citizen, and who shall not, when elected, be an inhabitant of that state in which he is chosen. No person shall be a
65 senator who shall not have been a citizen of the United States, and an inhabitant of that state in which he is chosen."

But, whatever there was for a doubt, under the old regime, the adoption of the fourteenth
70 amendment settled that question forever, in its first sentence: "All persons born or naturalized in the United States and subject to the jurisdiction thereof, are citizens of the United States and of the state wherein they reside."

75 And the second settles the equal status of all persons—all citizens:

"No states shall make or enforce any law which shall abridge the privileges or immunities of citizens; nor shall any state deprive any person
80 of life, liberty, or property, without due process of law, nor deny to any person within its jurisdiction the equal protection of the laws."

The only question left to be settled now is: Are women persons? And I hardly believe any of
85 our opponents will have the hardihood to say we are not. Being persons, then, women are citizens; and no State has a right to make any law, or to enforce any old law, that shall abridge their privileges or immunities. Hence, every
90 discrimination against women in the laws of the States is today null and void.

Continue →

The 19th Amendment, also known as the Susan B. Anthony Amendment, was passed in 1920 and established universal women's suffrage; but even before its passage, women in the different states had various voting rights, as shown by the following graphic:

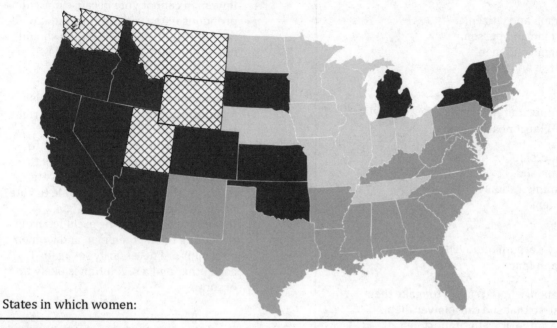

States in which women:

 had full voting rights before the 19th Amendment

 had full voting rights before the 19th Amendment and before statehood

could vote for president before the 19th Amendment

 gained voting rights with passage of the 19th Amendment

31. For the purpose of this speech, Anthony assumes the posture of a

A) defendant on trial in a court.
B) chair of a committee moderating a debate.
C) legislator arguing for a new law.
D) judge making a ruling at a trial.

32. Which of the following excerpts from the text most strongly supports the correct answer to the previous question?

A) Lines 1–7 ("I stand . . . *rights*")
B) Lines 17–19 ("It was . . . Union")
C) Lines 23–27 ("And it . . . ballot")
D) Lines 28–31 ("For any . . . land")

33. The word "oligarchy" (line 36) as used in this context refers to a government in which

A) only men of a certain status may hold positions of power in the government.
B) power is held by a few individuals who share a common characteristic.
C) the wealthy control power and exercise the functions of government.
D) a hereditary monarch has absolute power over the inhabitants of the country.

Continue

34. In paragraph six, Anthony quotes from the US Constitution in order to demonstrate the framers' ambiguous use of the terms

A) person and citizen.
B) woman and person.
C) woman and man.
D) citizen and man.

35. In the context of Anthony's speech, "regime" (line 69) most nearly means

A) leadership.
B) command.
C) administration.
D) system.

36. Anthony's argumentative strategy in paragraph four is to

A) challenge her accusers to make their case so that she can answer them.
B) cite authorities to support her interpretation of legal documents.
C) raise a possible objection to her position and offer a rebuttal.
D) demonstrate that the documents she cites are subject to different interpretations.

37. Which of the following best explains the dilemma to which Anthony refers in line 51?

A) If women cannot vote because masculine pronouns in the constitution and laws do not apply to them, then women should not be subject to other laws that use masculine pronouns.
B) When women are denied the right to vote on the basis of gender, then it is equally justifiable to deny men the right to vote on the basis of gender.
C) Once women are granted the right to vote, then it will no longer be legal to deny any individual the right to vote, even if that individual is not able to vote intelligently.
D) If women continue to be excluded from the voting booth, then men and women as groups are necessarily set against each other and a revolution is likely to occur.

38. Which of the following best exhibits the logical structure of Anthony's argument that she has a right to vote?

A) All persons are citizens; all citizens have the right to vote; women are persons; therefore, women have the right to vote.
B) All persons have the right to vote; all persons are citizens; women are citizens; therefore, women have the right to vote.
C) All citizens are persons; all persons have the right to vote; women are persons; therefore, women have the right to vote.
D) All women are persons; all citizens are persons; all citizens have the right to vote; therefore, women have the right to vote.

39. Which of the following excerpts proves the first premise of Anthony's argument, as set forth in the correct answer to the previous question?

A) Lines 61–62 ("No person . . . citizen")
B) Lines 64–67 ("No person . . . chosen")
C) Lines 71–73 ("All persons . . . citizens")
D) Lines 77–79 ("No states . . . citizens")

Continue

40. Anthony's main point in paragraph three is that

A) a government by men only creates dissension and instability rather than domestic tranquility.

B) educated persons of both genders should be the only people qualified to vote.

C) men are not uniquely qualified by their gender to make intelligent decisions in the voting booth.

D) the blessings of liberty extend to women even though they are not permitted to vote.

41. Which of the following conclusions can be most reliably drawn from the graphic?

A) Women in the southwestern states had voting rights even before statehood took effect or the 19th Amendment was passed.

B) Women in the southern states were denied the right to vote until the 19th Amendment was passed.

C) Women in the northeastern states could vote for president prior to the passage of the 19th Amendment.

D) Women in the upper-midwestern states enjoyed full voting rights once statehood had taken effect.

Continue

Questions #42–52 are based on the following passage.

The following passage is about the stratification of lakes.

Lake stratification is explained by the annual temperature cycle. In the spring, lakes commonly circulate from surface to bottom, resulting in a uniform temperature profile. This vernal mixing is
5 called the spring overturn. As surface temperatures warm further, the surface water layer becomes less dense than the colder underlying water, and the lake begins to stratify. This stratified condition exists throughout the
10 summer, and the increasing temperature differential between the upper and lower layers increases the stability (resistance to mixing) of the lake.

In the northern hemisphere, the water in
15 dimictic lakes mixes from the surface to the bottom twice each year. During the winter, they are covered by ice; and during the summer, they are thermally stratified, with temperature-derived density differences separating the warm surface
20 waters from the colder bottom waters.

The upper mixed layer of warm, low-density water is termed the epilimnion, while the lower, stagnant layer of cold, high-density water is termed the hypolimnion. The transitional zone
25 between the two is called the metalimnion. In this transitional zone, temperatures rapidly decline with depth, and the plane of maximum rate of decrease is called the thermocline. In general, the region in which the temperature gradient exceeds
30 1°C per meter is the thermocline.

As surface water temperatures cool in the fall, the density difference between isothermal strata (layers of similar temperature) decreases and lake stability is weakened. Eventually, wind-
35 generated currents are sufficiently strong to break down stratification and the lake circulates from surface to bottom (fall overturn). In warmer temperate regions, a lake may retain this completely mixed condition throughout the
40 winter, but in colder regions, particularly following the formation of ice, inverse stratification develops, resulting in winter stagnation.

In this condition, the densest water, at a
45 temperature of 4°C, constitutes the hypolimnion, which is overlain by less dense, colder water between 0°C and 4°C. The inversion is explained by the fact that freshwater is densest at 4°C. The difference in density is very small, so inverse
50 stratification results in only a minor density gradient just below the surface. Thus, the stability of inverse stratification is weak, and, unless the lake is covered by ice, it is easily disrupted by wind mixing.

55 During stratification, temperature variation can directly affect organisms as all life processes are temperature dependent. In aquatic environments, growth, respiration, reproduction, migration, mortality, and decay are all strongly
60 influenced by ambient temperature. Additionally, the thermocline acts as a barrier that suppresses many of the mass transport phenomena that are otherwise responsible for the vertical transport of water quality constituents in the lake. Slowing of
65 mass transport between the hypolimnion and the epilimnion produces sharply differentiated water quality between the strata. For example, if the dissolved oxygen transport rate across the thermocline is low relative to the dissolved
70 oxygen demand in the hypolimnion, vertical stratification occurs with respect to the dissolved oxygen concentration. As ambient dissolved oxygen concentrations in the hypolimnion decrease, the life functions of many organisms are
75 impaired.

Vertical stratification with respect to nutrients can also occur. In the euphotic zone (depth range at which sunlight is available), dissolved nutrients are converted to particulate
80 organic material through photosynthesis. Because the euphotic zone does not extend below the thermocline, this assimilation of dissolved nutrients lowers the ambient nutrient concentrations in the epilimnion. Subsequent
85 sedimentation of particulate algae and other organic matters then serves to transport the organically bound nutrients to the hypolimnion where they are released by decomposition. In addition, the vertical transport of the released
90 nutrients upward through the thermocline is suppressed by the same mechanisms that inhibit the downward transport of dissolved oxygen.

Continue ▶

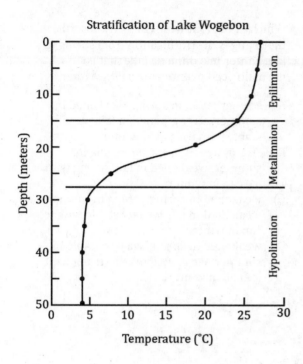

Stratification of Lake Wogebon

42. In the context of the passage, the term "vernal" (line 4) means

   A) overturn.
   B) autumn.
   C) cycle.
   D) spring.

43. It can be inferred that the "inverse stratification" (lines 41–42) is so called because

   A) a layer of warmer water is beneath a layer of colder water.
   B) a layer of colder water is beneath a layer of warmer water.
   C) the stability of the stratification is very weak.
   D) the wind can easily mix the layers, disrupting stratification.

44. Which of the following excerpts from the text best supports the correct answer to the previous question?

   A) Lines 31–34 ("As ... weakened")
   B) Lines 40–43 ("in colder ... stagnation")
   C) Lines 44–47 ("In this ... 4°C")
   D) Lines 51–54 ("Thus ... mixing")

45. The passage indicates that stratification can deplete the nutrients in the epilimnion because

   A) nutrients released by decomposition of sedimented organic material in the hypolimnion do not readily migrate upward across the thermocline.
   B) released nutrients that remain in the epilimnion are enriched by the process of photosynthesis in the euphotic zone.
   C) photosynthesis does not occur in the hypolimnion below the thermocline resulting in an oxygen surplus in the epilimnion.
   D) a build-up of nutrients in the hypolimnion does not produce an increase in organic activity because photosynthesis does not take place below the thermocline.

46. Which of the following excerpts from the text best supports the correct answer to the previous question?

   A) Lines 37–43 ("In warmer ... stagnation")
   B) Lines 67–72 ("For ... concentration")
   C) Lines 77–80 ("In the ... photosynthesis")
   D) Lines 88–92 ("In addition ... oxygen")

47. According to the passage, stratification can lead to decline in organic life because

   A) the ice cover on the lake traps most of the organic life in the epilimnion.
   B) the thermocline inhibits the vertical circulation of oxygen and nutrients.
   C) dissolved oxygen levels of cold, dense water are higher than those of warm, less dense water.
   D) organisms trapped in the epilimnion of a stratified lake cannot obtain dissolved oxygen.

Continue

48. According to the passage, the cycle of lake stratification is caused by

A) the melting of ice cover.
B) variation in wind velocity.
C) photosynthesis in the epilimnion.
D) seasonal temperature changes.

49. In context, the term "gradient" (line 51) refers to the

A) minimum possible value of a quantity.
B) imprecision in measurement of a quantity.
C) difference in value of a quantity.
D) maximum possible value of a quantity.

50. The author's primary purpose in the final two paragraphs is to explain the

A) cyclic nature of stratification.
B) adverse effects of stratification on aquatic life forms.
C) life cycle of aquatic life forms in dimictic lakes.
D) mechanisms by which stratification is formed and disrupted.

51. Based on the information provided in the passage, the thermocline for the lake shown in the graph is located at what depth?

A) 50 to 35 meters
B) 27.5 to 15 meters
C) 25 to 20 meters
D) 10 to 5 meters

52. Which of the following correctly describes the changes in stratification from spring to late winter in a dimictic lake that is normally iced over during cold weather?

A) strengthened in spring, weakened in summer, strengthened in fall, weakly stable with ice cap in winter.
B) strengthened in spring, strong in summer, weakened in fall, strong with ice cap in winter.
C) weakened in spring, strong in summer, weakened in fall, weakly stable with ice cap in winter.
D) weakened in spring, weakly stable in summer, weakened in fall, strong with ice cap in winter.

STOP

IF YOU FINISH BEFORE TIME IS CALLED, YOU MAY CHECK YOUR WORK ON THIS SECTION ONLY. DO NOT TURN TO ANY OTHER SECTION IN THE TEST.

SECTION 2—WRITING AND LANGUAGE

Time—35 minutes

44 items

> **DIRECTIONS:** Each set of questions is based on a passage. For some questions, think about how the passage could be revised to improve the expression of ideas. For other questions, think about how to edit the passage to correct sentence structure, usage, or punctuation errors. Passages or questions may be accompanied by a graphic such as a table or graph that you will consider while you make revising and editing decisions.
>
> Some questions reference an underlined word or phrase in the passage. Other questions refer to a location in the passage or to the passage as a whole.
>
> After reading each passage, choose the answer that improves the expression of ideas in the passage or conforms to standard English conventions. Many questions include a "NO CHANGE" answer choice. Choose that answer if you think the best choice is to leave the passage as it is. Answers are on page 244.

Continue ➜

Questions #1–11 are based on the following passage.

The History of Warfare

Warfare was the most complex, broad-scale, and demanding activity of pre-modernized people. The challenge of leading an army into battle—organizing, moving, and supporting troops—attracted the talents of the **1** most vigorous, most enterprising, most intelligent, and imaginative members of society. "Warrior" and "statesman" were virtually synonymous, and the military was one of the few professions in which an able, ambitious youth of humble origin could rise to the top. In the broader cultural context, war was accepted in the pre-modernized society as a part of the human condition, a mechanism of change, and an unavoidable, even noble, aspect of life. **2** The excitement and drama of war made it a vital part of literature and legends.

War has been one of the most persistent of human activities in the 80 centuries since humans settled into cities and became thereby **3** "civilized." In pre-modernized societies, successful warfare brought significant material **4** reward such as: the stored wealth of the defeated enemy, **5** having human slaves to do labor, natural resources, and productive agricultural land. The removal or destruction of a threat brought a sense of security, and power gained over others created pride and self-esteem.

1. A) NO CHANGE
   B) most vigorous, most enterprising, most intelligent and imaginative
   C) most vigorous, enterprising, most intelligent, and imaginative
   D) most vigorous, enterprising, intelligent, and imaginative

2. At this point, the author wishes to add a quotation to illustrate the pre-modern attitude toward war. Which of the following would best meet that goal?

   A) As the Roman poet Horace wrote, "It is sweet and fitting to die for one's country."
   B) As the American author John Steinbeck wrote, "War may sometimes be a necessary evil. But no matter how necessary, it is always an evil, never a good."
   C) As the American statesman Benjamin Franklin wrote, "There never was a good war or a bad peace."
   D) As Eurpides, the Ancient Greek dramitist, wrote, "The God of War hates those who hesitate."

3. The author places the word "civilized" in quotation marks in order to

   A) call attention to the fact that areas of wilderness and civilization can exist side-by-side.
   B) signal that the word is intended to have the opposite of its usual meaning.
   C) emphasize that pre-modernized peoples could gain significant wealth by war.
   D) disprove the contention that one's enemy is necessarily uncivilized.

4. A) NO CHANGE
   B) reward, for example:
   C) reward
   D) reward:

5. A) NO CHANGE
   B) having labor done by human slaves
   C) laboring to be done by human slaves
   D) human slave labor

Continue

Today, war is no longer confined to the battlefield and can now, with modern guidance systems on missiles, touch virtually every square meter of Earth. It no longer involves only the military but also spills over into civilian populations as well. Nuclear weapons have made a major war unthinkable. We are forced, [6] nevertheless, to think about the unthinkable because a large-scale nuclear war could come by accident or miscalculation. We must accept the [7] paradox of maintaining the capacity to fight a war so that we will never have to do so. [8]

War has also lost most of its utility in achieving the traditional goals of conflict. Control of territory carries with it the obligation to provide subject peoples with various administrative, health, educational, and other social services; such obligation outweighs the benefits of control. If the ruled population is racially, ethnically, or religiously different from the ruler, tensions and chronic unrest will exist, which further reduce the benefits and increase the cost of domination. Large populations no longer necessarily enhance state power and in the absence of high levels of economic development can impose severe burdens on food supply, employment, and the broad range of services expected from modern governments. The noneconomic security reasons for control of territory [9] has been progressively undermined by the advance of modern technology. The benefits of forcing another to nation to surrender

6. A) NO CHANGE
    B) moreover
    C) by the way
    D) at any rate

7. A) NO CHANGE
    B) theory
    C) assumption
    D) conclusion

8. The author wishes to add a sentence that offers an analogy to the changing effects of warfare. Which of the following would best accomplish that goal?

    A) Similarly, while the increased abundance of food has reduced the incidence of hunger and malnutrition, it has resulted in more obesity, diabetes, and other diseases.
    B) Likewise, technological advancements have produced labor-saving devices that now give us more leisure time to pursue other interests such as hobbies, sports, and other physical activities.
    C) Comparatively, greater educational opportunities have resulted in a more literate and skilled population, qualities that increase the nation's productivity and raise the standard of living for all.
    D) Similarly, advances in medicine and health care have produced treatments and cures for diseases that were once considered untreatable, leading to longer and more productive lives.

9. A) NO CHANGE
    B) have been
    C) has
    D) having been

Continue

10 it's wealth are vastly outweighed by the benefits of persuading that nation to produce and exchange goods and services. **11**

10.
A) NO CHANGE
B) its'
C) it
D) its

11. The author wishes to include a sentence that summarizes the final paragraph. Which of the following best accomplishes that purpose?

A) In brief, military conflicts are costly.
B) In brief, it is difficult to rule a defeated enemy.
C) In brief, security is much overrated.
D) In brief, conquering enemies no longer pays.

Questions #12–22 are based on the following passage.

Comparing Preventive and Curative Medicine

Asclepius was the god of medicine in ancient Greek mythology. He fathered two daughters: Panacea, goddess of universal remedy, and Hygeia, goddess of health, cleanliness, and sanitation. Asclepius was a son of Apollo and shares with Apollo the <u>**12** epithet</u> *Paean* (*Healer*). **13** <u>Today, a snake-entwined staff is the rod of Asclepius, a symbol of medicine.</u> Panacea and Hygeia gave rise to the dynasties of healers and hygienists, respectively, a division that characterizes training and clinical practice even today.

Preventive medicine has as its primary objective the maintenance and promotion of health. **14** <u>Having accomplished</u> its goals, preventive medicine controls environmental factors, for example, the purity of the municipal water supply or a region's air quality. Additionally, preventive medicine applies prophylactic measures against disease by actions such as immunization. Finally, **15** <u>it attempts</u> to motivate people to adopt healthful lifestyles through education.

For the most part, curative medicine has as its **16** <u>big</u> objective the removal of disease from the patient. Thus, diagnostic techniques are used to identify the presence and nature of the disease process. While it may be applied on a mass basis to screen out persons with preclinical disease, a diagnosis is usually not made until the patient appears with a complaint. Curative medicine applies treatment to the sick patient. In

12. A) NO CHANGE
B) nickname
C) moniker
D) handle

13. A) NO CHANGE
B) The rod of Asclepius, a snake-entwined staff, remains a symbol of medicine today.
C) Today, a snake-entwined staff is a symbol of medicine that is the rod of Asclepius.
D) A snake-entwined staff, which belonged to Asclepius, is today's symbol of medicine.

14. A) NO CHANGE
B) Already accomplishing
C) Accomplishing
D) To accomplish

15. A) NO CHANGE
B) they attempt
C) they attempts
D) one attempts

16. A) NO CHANGE
B) huge
C) major
D) immense

Continue

every case, treatment is individualized to the particular need of each patient. **17** <u>Initially,</u> curative medicine utilizes rehabilitation methodologies to return the treated patient to the best possible level of functioning.

18 The requirements for curative medicine call for clinically trained individuals who deal with patients on a one-to-one basis and **19** <u>who's</u> training is based primarily on an understanding of the biological, pathological, and psychological processes that determine an **20** <u>individuals</u> health and disease status. The locus for this training is the laboratory and clinic. Preventive medicine, on the other hand, calls for a very broad spectrum of professionals. Since their actions apply either to environmental factors or to the characteristics of population groups, their training takes place in a different type of laboratory or in the community.

[1] **21** <u>The economic differences between preventative medicine and curative medicine are well known.</u> [2] Sickness is a negative, nonproductive, and harmful **22** <u>state, health,</u> on the other hand, has a very high value. [3] To the extent that healthy members of the population are replaced by sick members, the economy is doubly burdened. [4] On balance, the cost of preventing disease is far lower than the cost of curing it.

17. A) NO CHANGE
    B) Instead
    C) For once
    D) Finally

18. Which of the following best introduces the main point of the paragraph?

    A) Curative medicine is more effective than preventive medicine.
    B) Treatment of a disease is more expensive than prevention.
    C) Preventive and curative technicians must be highly trained.
    D) Preventive and curative medicine require people with different qualifications.

19. A) NO CHANGE
    B) whose
    C) that
    D) which

20. A) NO CHANGE
    B) individual
    C) individual's
    D) individuals'

21. What is the best placement for this sentence in this paragraph?

    A) NO CHANGE (where it is now)
    B) after sentence 2
    C) after sentence 3
    D) after sentence 4

22. A) NO CHANGE
    B) state health,
    C) state. Health,
    D) state and, health

Continue

Questions #23–33 are based on the following passage.

The Origins of One Hypervelocity Star

NASA's Hubble Space Telescope has detected a hypervelocity star, a rare phenomenon, moving three times faster than our sun. **23** It is one of the fastest ever detected with a speed of 1.6 million miles per hour. Most of the 16 known hypervelocity stars are thought to be exiles from the heart of our galaxy. These exiled stars are rare in the Milky Way's population of 100 billion stars. For every 100 million stars in the galaxy, astronomers expect to find one hypervelocity star. This Hubble observation provides the first direct evidence that **24** the star originated in the Magellanic Cloud.

Astronomers originally thought the star was **25** evicted out of the Large Magellanic Cloud, a neighboring galaxy. Astronomers found a match between the exiled star's chemical makeup and the characteristics of stars in the Large Magellanic Cloud. The rogue star's position also is close to the neighboring galaxy, only 65,000 light-years away. **26** Using the Hubble Telescope to measure the runaway star's position and velocity, astronomers have now determined that the Milky Way's core was its starting point, and that raises a problem. Based on the speed and position of the star, **27** it would have to be 100 million years old to have **28** traveled the journey from the

23. A) NO CHANGE
B) It is one of the fastest with a speed of 1.6 million miles per hour ever detected.
C) With a speed of 1.6 million miles per hour, it is one of the fastest ever detected.
D) One of the fastest ever detected with a speed of 1.6 million miles per hour.

24. Which of the following is most strongly supported by the evidence presented in the next paragraph?

A) NO CHANGE
B) such a star originated in the center of the Milky Way.
C) the Milky Way contains hundreds of millions of stars.
D) the star's makeup is similar to those found in the Magellanic Cloud.

25. A) NO CHANGE
B) erupted
C) emitted
D) ejected

26. Which of the following best introduces the remainder of the paragraph?

A) This theory, however, has been proved wrong.
B) Most astronomers still favor this theory.
C) This makes the Magellanic Cloud the most likely source of origin.
D) Observations made by the Hubble have confirmed this theory.

27. A) NO CHANGE
B) they
C) one
D) we

28. A) NO CHANGE
B) journeyed
C) traveled the trip
D) made the travel

Continue

Milky Way's core. Yet its mass— 29 nine times our sun—and blue color 30 means that it should have burned out after only 20 million years—far shorter than the transit time it took to get to its current location.

[1] The answer to this seeming contradiction is that the star was most likely created in a cosmic misstep 100 million years ago. [2] Along with a pair of closely orbiting stars, it was the third outer member of a triple-star system that was traveling through the bustling center of our Milky Way galaxy. [3] As the pair rocketed away, they went on with normal stellar evolution: the more massive companion puffed up to become a red giant and enveloped its partner, and the two stars spiraled together, merging into a blue straggler, a relatively 31 young, massive star produced by the merger of two lighter-weight stars. [4] The galaxy's giant black hole captured the outer star, the momentum of this doomed star was transferred to the other two, and the duo was hurled out of the Milky Way. 32 33

29.
A) NO CHANGE
B) nine times that of our sun
C) our sun times nine
D) nine times more than our sun

30.
A) NO CHANGE
B) meaning
C) to mean
D) mean

31.
A) NO CHANGE
B) young massive
C) young, massive,
D) young massive,

32. In which of the following orders should the sentences in paragraph 3 be arranged in order to accurately reflect the sequence of events depicted in the graphic?

A) 1, 2, 3, 4 (NO CHANGE)
B) 1, 2, 4, 3
C) 1, 3, 2, 4
D) 1, 4, 2, 3

33. Is "freak accident" a suitable description of the formation of the hypervelocity star?

A) Yes, because the star was created due to an incident triggered by the triple-star system passing too close to the Milky Way's black hole.
B) Yes, because the discovery of the hypervelocity star by the Hubble telescope would not have occurred had it not been for a lucky observation.
C) No, because it is expected that on average a hypervelocity star will be found in every 100 million or so stars.
D) No, because the hypervelocity star was discovered only 65,000 light-years away from the Magellanic Cloud.

Triple-star System Passes Near Milky Way's Central Black Hole

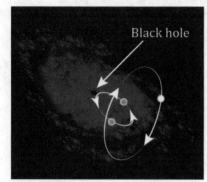

Triple-star system moves near black hole at center of Milky Way Galaxy.

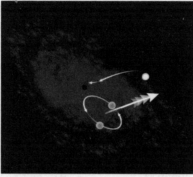

One star falls toward black hole; binary pair recoils and is expelled.

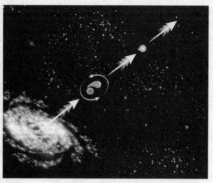

Binary merges to form blue straggler. Blue straggler travels away from galaxy.

Continue ➤

Questions #34–44 are based on the following passage.

James "Super Chikan" Johnson

The Mississippi Delta has been called the "birthplace of the blues." Many of the music's pioneers lived and performed throughout the region. While the music has changed since its early days, the blues are still important in the Delta culture. There are blues musicians living in most of the larger communities in the **34** region. Most notably, James "Super Chikan" Johnson of Clarksdale.

Johnson was born in 1951 in the small Delta community of Darling and grew up in rural towns around the area. Living in the country, his family kept chickens, **35** though Johnson spent time trying to understand the meaning of the noises they made. Soon, his friends and family began calling him "Chicken." Later, his speedy driving in his taxicab earned him a new **36** nickname: "Super Chikan."

His grandfather played the fiddle in local string bands, and one of his uncles, "Big" Jack Johnson, is an internationally known blues musician. Johnson's first musical effort was building and playing a diddly bow, a one-stringed instrument popular among Delta blues musicians. When he was thirteen, he got a **37** used guitar that had previously belonged to some else and learned the basics of the instrument from friends and family members. By the time he was in his early twenties, he was playing bass in local clubs

34. A) NO CHANGE
B) region most
C) region, most
D) region most,

35. A) NO CHANGE
B) while
C) and
D) when

36. A) NO CHANGE
B) nickname
C) nickname;
D) nickname.

37. A) NO CHANGE
B) used guitar previously belonging to someone else
C) previously used guitar that had belonged to someone else
D) used guitar

Continue

with his uncle Jack's band. Johnson <u>38</u> <u>had gone</u> on to play bass and guitar for a number of Delta blues bandleaders, including Frank Frost, Sam Carr, and Wesley Jefferson.

<u>39</u> <u>Later, while working as a truck driver, Johnson used the time on the road to write his own songs.</u> He recorded his first album as a bandleader, *Blues Come Home to Roost*, in 1997. On this recording, Johnson first showed <u>40</u> <u>up</u> his ability to blend the blues with a number of different musical styles, including country, funk, and rock. His lyrics also came from a unique perspective, providing both humorous and serious views of contemporary life in the Delta.

Since the success of his first record, Johnson has been performing <u>41</u> <u>by himself solo</u> and with his band, *The Fighting Cocks*, at festivals and clubs throughout the United States and Europe. He has also continued to release recordings at a steady pace. His most recent CD, *Chikan Supe*, <u>42</u> <u>was released,</u> on Clarksdale's Knockdown South Records.

38. A) NO CHANGE
B) had went
C) gone
D) went

39. The author is considering deleting this sentence. Should the author the delete the sentence?

A) No, because the sentence provides an interesting detail about Johnson's development as a musician.
B) No, because the sentence describes an essential link between Johnson's early and later careers as a driver.
C) Yes, because it was already mentioned that Johnson drove a taxicab when he was younger.
D) Yes, because Johnson's job driving a truck is not relevant to his musical career.

40. A) NO CHANGE
B) off
C) by
D) in

41. A) NO CHANGE
B) solo by himself
C) solo
D) alone by himself

42. A) NO CHANGE
B) was released;
C) were released
D) was released

Continue

43 He combines discarded guitar parts with old Army gas cans, creating "Chikantars," fully playable guitars that he now plays at many of his performances. He also makes cigar box guitars, diddley bows, and a variety of other instruments. Hand-painted by Johnson with detailed scenes of the Delta, these instruments are highly prized by collectors throughout the South.

Despite frequent international travel, "Super Chikan" remains firmly attached to his home state. He still performs in Clarksdale clubs on a regular basis and is a constant presence at music festivals around Mississippi. **44**

43. Which of the following sentences best introduces this paragraph?

A) In recent years, Johnson has been building his own guitars and other instruments.

B) The name "Chikantars" is a combination of the two words "chicken" and "guitar."

C) Cigar box guitars, built from wooden boxes, were made by musicians who could not afford manufactured instruments.

D) Johnson has several instruments and may play one or more of them during any given performance.

44. The author is thinking of deleting the final paragraph from the passage. If the paragraph is deleted, which of the following will be missing from the passage?

A) Johnson is from Clarksdale, Mississippi, and his nickname is "Super Chikan."

B) Johnson's handmade and painted musical instruments are highly collectible.

C) Johnson still plays in clubs and music festivals in and around his hometown.

D) Johnson has performed solo and with his band at locales in Europe.

STOP

IF YOU FINISH BEFORE TIME IS CALLED, YOU MAY CHECK YOUR WORK ON THIS SECTION ONLY. DO NOT TURN TO ANY OTHER SECTION IN THE TEST.

SECTION 3—MATH, NO CALCULATOR

Time—25 minutes

20 items

DIRECTIONS: For #1–15, solve each item and choose the correct answer choice. Then fill in the corresponding bubble on your answer sheet. For #16–20, solve each item and enter your answer in the grid on the answer sheet. Refer to the directions before #16 on how to enter your answers for these items. Use any available space for scratchwork. Answers are on page 244.

Notes:

(1) All expressions and equations represent real numbers unless otherwise indicated.

(2) Figures that accompany problems in this test are intended to provide information useful in solving the problems. They are drawn as accurately as possible EXCEPT when it is stated in a specific problem that the figure is not drawn to scale. All figures lie in a plane unless otherwise indicated.

(3) The domain of a given function f is the set of all real numbers x for which $f(x)$ is a real number unless otherwise indicated.

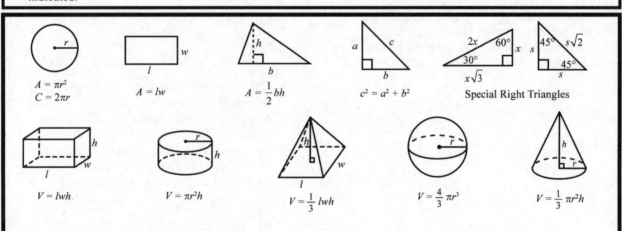

$A = \pi r^2$
$C = 2\pi r$

$A = lw$

$A = \frac{1}{2}bh$

$c^2 = a^2 + b^2$

Special Right Triangles

$V = lwh$

$V = \pi r^2 h$

$V = \frac{1}{3}lwh$

$V = \frac{4}{3}\pi r^3$

$V = \frac{1}{3}\pi r^2 h$

The number of degrees of arc in a circle is 360.

The sum of the measures in degrees of the angles of a triangle is 180.

The number of radians of arc in a circle is 2π.

Continue

1. A landscaper must load 38 bricks onto a truck. Given that she can carry at most 4 bricks at a time, what is the fewest number of trips that she must make to move all of the bricks from the brick pile onto the truck?

A) 8
B) 9
C) 10
D) 11

2. If $x + 1 + 2x + 2 + 3x + 3 = 6$, then $x = ?$

A) 0
B) 1
C) 2
D) 6

3. The cost of operating a coffee cart in the first year is $8,000 plus $0.50 for each cup of coffee. Assuming every coffee is sold for c dollars, which of the following expressions represents the number of coffees, n, that must be sold in the first year for the cart to break even?

A) $n = 8,000(c - 0.5)$
B) $n = 8,000 + c - 0.5$
C) $n = \dfrac{8,000}{c + 0.5}$
D) $n = \dfrac{8,000}{c - 0.5}$

4. If x, y, and z are consecutive integers, and $x > y > z$, then $(x - y)(x - z)(y - z) = ?$

A) –2
B) 0
C) 2
D) 4

5. Two 3D printer companies, M and N, are comparing their production records for a printed model. Printer M has already printed 120 models and can print 8 models per day. Printer N has printed only 80 models but can print 12 models per day. After how many days (in which both printers operate at maximum output) will the total number of models printed by Printer M equal to the total number of models printed by Printer N?

A) 4
B) 10
C) 12
D) 40

6. If a cube has a surface area of $54x^2$, what is its volume?

A) $9x^3$
B) $18x^3$
C) $27x^3$
D) $54x^3$

7. The low temperatures in City X for Monday through Friday are 20°C, 23°C, 24°C, x, and y, respectively. If the average (arithmetic mean) low temperature in City X for the week is 26°C and the low temperature on Thursday is three-fourths that of Friday, what is Thursday's low temperature?

A) 27°C
B) 30°C
C) 36°C
D) 63°C

Continue

Questions #8–9 refer to the following information.

For all positive integers n:

$$[n] = 2n \text{ if } n \text{ is even.}$$
$$[n] = 3n \text{ if } n \text{ is odd.}$$

8. $[3] \cdot [4] = ?$

A) $[12]$

B) $[18]$

C) $[36]$

D) $[72]$

9. If x is a prime number greater than 2, then $[x-1] = ?$

A) $3x$

B) $2x$

C) $3x - 3$

D) $2x - 2$

$$v = \$12{,}000\left(0.7^t\right)$$

10. The equation above is used to model the relationship between the value, v, of a car, and the number of years, t, elapsed since its purchase. According to the model, what is the meaning of the $12,000 in the equation?

A) The value of the car when purchased was $12,000.

B) The value of the car t years after its purchase is $12,000.

C) The increase in value of the car every year following its purchase.

D) The decrease in value of the car every year following its purchase.

11. Y years ago, Tom was three times as old as Julie was at the time. If Julie is now 20 years old, how old is Tom in terms of Y?

A) $60 - 2Y$

B) $60 - Y$

C) $60 + 2Y$

D) $30 - 2Y$

12. If x is an integer that is a multiple of both 9 and 5, which of the following must be true?

   I. x is equal to 45.

  II. x is a multiple of 15.

 III. x is odd.

A) I only

B) II only

C) II and III only

D) None of the statements must be true.

13. If the domain of the function $f(x) = x^2 - 4$ is all real numbers, what is the range?

A) All real numbers greater than –4.

B) All real numbers greater than or equal to –4.

C) All real numbers less than or equal to –4.

D) All real numbers greater than or equal to 4.

14. If the ordered pairs $(-3,-3)$, $(-2,2)$, and $(3,-3)$ are the vertices of a triangle, what is the area of the triangle?

A) 15

B) 16

C) 18

D) Cannot be determined from the information given

Continue ➤

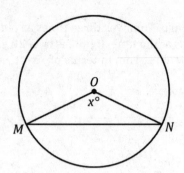

15. In the figure above, two points, M and N, are on the circle with center O and radius 1. If $\angle MON = x°$, what is the length of $\overline{MN}$?

A) $2\sin x$

B) $\sin\dfrac{x}{2}$

C) $2\cos\dfrac{x}{2}$

D) $2\sin\dfrac{x}{2}$

Continue

DIRECTIONS: For #16–20, solve each item and mark your answer on a special answer grid.

1. For each item, you should write your answer in the boxes at the top of each column and then fill in the ovals beneath each part of the answer you write.
2. Mark no more than one oval in any column.
3. Questions do not have negative answers.
4. Some problems have more than one possible answer. Grid only one answer.
5. See the first example below to grid mixed numbers.
6. See the last example below to grid decimal answers with more digits than the grid can accommodate.

Here are some examples:

Answer: 7/2 or 3.5	Answer: 325	Answer: 1/6, .166, or .167

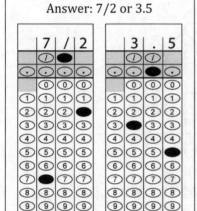

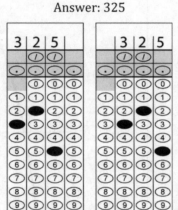

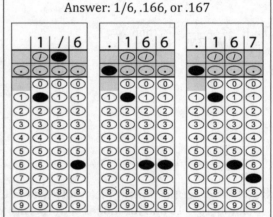

NOTE: A mixed number such as $3\frac{1}{2}$ must be gridded as 7/2 or as 3.5. If gridded as "31/2," it will be read as "thirty-one halves."

NOTE: Either position is correct.

NOTE: A decimal answer with more digits than the grid can accommodate must be truncated. A decimal such as $0.16\overline{6}$ must be gridded as .166 or .167. A less accurate value such as .16 or .17 will be scored as incorrect.

Continue ➤

16. Cyrus worked 8 hours on Monday. On each successive day, he worked half as long as he did on the previous day. How many total hours had he worked by the end of the day on Friday?

17. If $\dfrac{1}{2N} + \dfrac{1}{2N} = \dfrac{1}{4}$, then $N = ?$

18. The average (arithmetic mean) of a set of 10 numbers is 15 and the modes of the set are x, y, and z. If four of the 10 numbers are 4, $3(x+2)$, $3y-5$, and $3z$ and these four numbers are unique and are not equal to x, y, or z, what is the value of $x + y + z$?

19. What is the absolute value of the difference between the product and the sum of the roots of the quadratic equation $3x^2 - 2x - 1 = 0$?

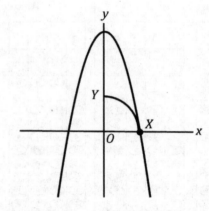

20. In the coordinate plane above, $\overset{\frown}{XY}$ is an arc of a circle with center O and point X lies on the graph of parabola $y = -x^2 + a$, where a is a constant. If the length of $\overset{\frown}{XY}$ is $\dfrac{3\pi}{2}$, what is the value of a?

S T O P

IF YOU FINISH BEFORE TIME IS CALLED, YOU MAY CHECK YOUR WORK ON THIS SECTION ONLY. DO NOT TURN TO ANY OTHER SECTION IN THE TEST.

SECTION 4—MATH, CALCULATOR

Time—55 minutes

38 items

DIRECTIONS: For #1–30, solve each item and choose the correct answer choice. Then fill in the corresponding bubble on your answer sheet. For #31–38, solve each item and enter your answer in the grid on the answer sheet. Refer to the directions before #31 on how to enter your answers for these items. Use any available space for scratchwork. Answers are on page 245.

Notes:

(1) All expressions and equations represent real numbers unless otherwise indicated.

(2) Figures that accompany problems in this test are intended to provide information useful in solving the problems. They are drawn as accurately as possible EXCEPT when it is stated in a specific problem that the figure is not drawn to scale. All figures lie in a plane unless otherwise indicated.

(3) The domain of a given function f is the set of all real numbers x for which $f(x)$ is a real number unless otherwise indicated.

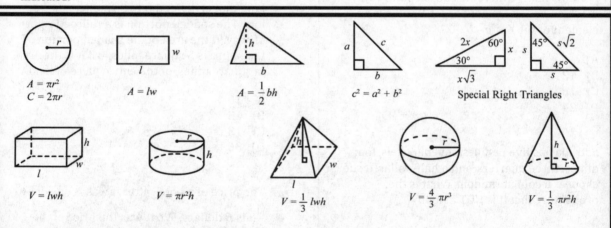

$A = \pi r^2$
$C = 2\pi r$

$A = lw$

$A = \frac{1}{2}bh$

$c^2 = a^2 + b^2$

Special Right Triangles

$V = lwh$

$V = \pi r^2 h$

$V = \frac{1}{3}lwh$

$V = \frac{4}{3}\pi r^3$

$V = \frac{1}{3}\pi r^2 h$

The number of degrees of arc in a circle is 360.

The sum of the measures in degrees of the angles of a triangle is 180.

The number of radians of arc in a circle is 2π.

Continue

1. Danielle sliced a pizza into sixths. She then sliced each slice into thirds. She served 4 of the small slices to Pete. In lowest terms, if T represents the whole pie, what fraction of the whole pizza did Pete have?

A) $\dfrac{T}{6}$

B) $\dfrac{2T}{9}$

C) $T - \dfrac{T}{18}$

D) $T - \dfrac{1}{3}$

2.
$$\text{Set } X = \{1, 2, 3, 4\}$$
$$\text{Set } Y = \{1, 2, 3, 4\}$$

For how many different ordered pairs (a, b) in which a is an element of set X and b is an element of set Y is $a - b > 0$?

A) 6
B) 12
C) 18
D) 24

3. Estrella has five pennies, seven nickels, four dimes, three quarters, and a half-dollar. If she chooses a coin at random, what is the probability that it is NOT a penny?

A) $\dfrac{1}{2}$

B) $\dfrac{3}{5}$

C) $\dfrac{3}{4}$

D) $\dfrac{4}{5}$

4. At Auburn Mills High, 80 percent of the graduating seniors go on to college. Of those, 75 percent will attend school in-state. If there are 150 graduating seniors in all, how many will attend college out-of-state?

A) 30
B) 38
C) 90
D) 120

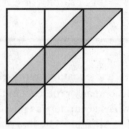

5. The figure above shows a square piece of land that is divided into 9 smaller square lots. The shaded portion is a railroad right-of-way. If the area of the shaded portion of the figure is 5 square miles, what is the area, in square miles, of the entire piece of land?

A) 10
B) 13
C) 18
D) 36

6. The price of a book, after it was reduced by $\dfrac{1}{3}$, is B dollars. What was the price of the book, in dollars, before the reduction?

A) $\dfrac{2B}{3}$

B) $\dfrac{6B}{5}$

C) $\dfrac{4B}{3}$

D) $\dfrac{3B}{2}$

Continue ►

7. A geologist is attempting to determine whether a rock sample is composed of iron meteorite, chondrite meteorite, magnetite, or basalt. The rock sample is in the shape of a rectangular prism and measures roughly 6 cm long, 3 cm wide, and 2.5 cm high. The rock sample has a mass of 150 grams. Based on this information and the table below, which type of rock is the sample?

$$\left(\text{Density} = \frac{\text{Mass}}{\text{Volume}}\right)$$

Common Rocks	Density
Iron meteorites	7–8 g/cm³
Chondrite meteorites	3–3.7 g/cm³
Magnetite	4.5–5 g/cm³
Basalt	< 3.0 g/cm³

A) Iron meteorite
B) Chondrite meteorite
C) Magnetite
D) Basalt

$$\frac{x+y}{2} = 1$$

$$ax + 2y = 10$$

8. In the system of linear equations above, a is a constant. If the system has no solution, what is the value of a?

A) $\dfrac{1}{10}$

B) $\dfrac{1}{2}$

C) 1
D) 2

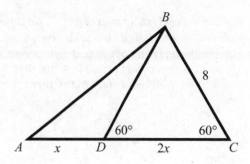

9. In $\triangle ABC$ above, what is the length of side $\overline{AC}$?

A) 8
B) 12
C) 18
D) 22

10. Avi donates $25 to a non-profit whose financial statements states that 1% of donations is spent on management and general oversight, 11% is spent on membership development and fundraising, and the remainder goes directly to program support. Brandon donates $30 to a different non-profit whose financial statements state that 2% of donations is spent on management and general oversight, 14% is spent on membership development and fundraising, and the remainder goes directly to program support. Which donation yields a larger amount that goes directly to program support, and by how much?

A) Avi's donation will yield a greater amount for program support, by $1.60.
B) Brandon's donation will yield a greater amount for program support, by $1.60.
C) Brandon's donation will yield a greater amount for program support, by $3.20.
D) Both donations will yield exactly the same amount for program support.

Continue

11. A student receives an average of 75 on three exams that are scored on a scale from 0 to 100 inclusive. If one of her test scores was 75, what is the lowest possible score that she could have received on any of the three tests?

A) 1
B) 25
C) 50
D) 75

Questions #12–13 refer to the following information.

A fish farm owner is increasing the size of the circular pool used for raising tilapia. He is considering two plans.

In Plan A, the radius of the pool is doubled, as shown in the figure below, in which O is the center of the new pool.

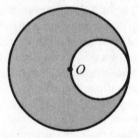

In Plan B, the radius of the pool is increased to 120% that of the original pool.

12. In the figure for Plan A, what is the ratio of the shaded area in the figure to the unshaded area in the figure?

A) $\dfrac{4}{1}$

B) $\dfrac{3}{1}$

C) $\dfrac{5}{2}$

D) $\dfrac{2}{1}$

13. If the farm owner chooses Plan B, what percentage of the surface of the old pool is the surface of the new pool?

A) 144%
B) 120%
C) 56%
D) 12%

14. Which of the following is the equation for the line that includes points $(-1,1)$ and $(7,5)$?

A) $y = \dfrac{x}{2} + \dfrac{3}{2}$

B) $y = \dfrac{x}{2} + \dfrac{2}{3}$

C) $y = \dfrac{x}{2} + 2$

D) $y = 2x + \dfrac{3}{2}$

Continue ➡

Questions #15–17 refer to the following information.

The graph below plots the calories and total grams of fat in nine items on the lunch menu at a fast food restaurant.

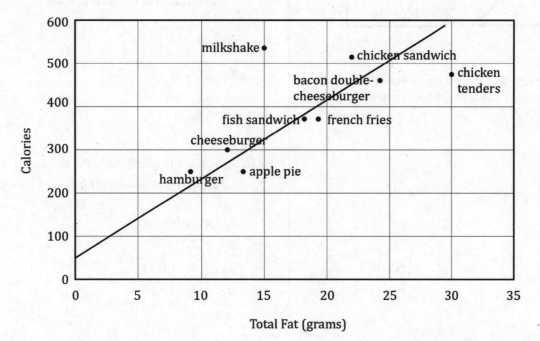

15. Which of the following is the median total fat content, in grams, of the nine fast food items shown on the graph?

A) 22
B) 19
C) 18
D) 16.5

16. Which of the following equations best represents the relationship between calories and total grams of fat represented by the line of best fit for the data?

A) $y = 20x - 50$

B) $y = -2x + 50$

C) $y = 20x + 50$

D) $y = x + 50$

17. Which of the following best approximates the total fat content, in grams, of a 325-calorie fast food item based on the line of best fit for the data?

A) 14
B) 20
C) 24
D) 28

Continue

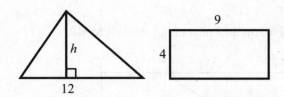

18. In the figures above, if the area of the rectangle is equal to the area of the triangle, then $h = $?

A) 3
B) 4
C) 6
D) 9

19. A chemist has 500 mL of 35% acid solution and 250 mL of 40% acid solution. If he mixes the two solutions together, what is the acid concentration of the final mixture?

A) $25\dfrac{1}{3}\%$

B) $36\dfrac{2}{3}\%$

C) 40%

D) 45%

20. Which of the following is the complete solution set to the equation $\left|y^2 - 5\right| - 4 = 0$?

A) $\{1,3\}$

B) $\{-1,1\}$

C) $\{-3,-1,0,1\}$

D) $\{-3,-1,1,3\}$

Continue

Questions #21–22 refer to the following information.

In 2011, 1.716×10^6 undergraduate degrees were awarded at US colleges and universities. The graph below shows the number of degrees awarded in each of the five most popular majors.

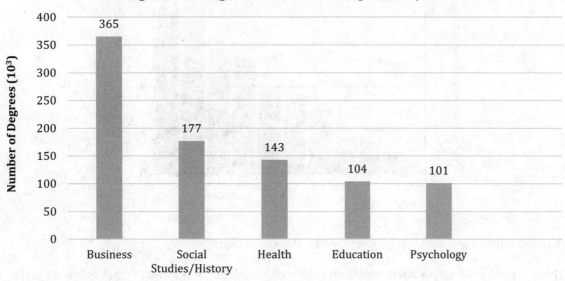

Undergraduate Degrees in Five Most Popular Majors, 2011

21. In 2011, approximately what percentage of undergraduate degrees awarded were in social studies/history?

A) 5%
B) 10%
C) 15%
D) 20%

22. In 2011, which of the following is closest to the ratio of degrees awarded in the five most popular undergraduate majors as compared with degrees awarded in all other undergraduate majors?

A) 2:1
B) 2:3
C) 1:2
D) 1:1

Continue

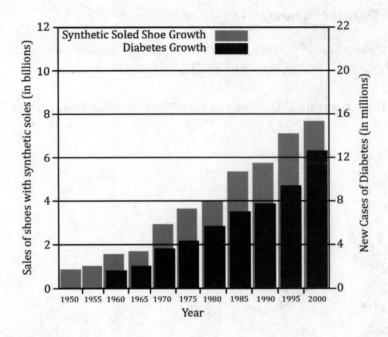

23. Which of the following statements is true based on the above graph?

A) There is neither correlation nor causation between the number of new cases of diabetes in the US population and the sales of synthetic soled shoes.

B) There is both a causal relationship and a positive correlation between the number of new cases of diabetes in the US population and the sales of synthetic soled shoes.

C) There is a causal relationship between the number of new cases of diabetes in the US population and the sales of synthetic soled shoes.

D) There is a positive correlation between the number of new cases of diabetes in the US population and the sales of synthetic soled shoes.

Continue

Questions #24–26 refer to the following information.

The radioactive half-life of a radioactive substance is the time it takes for one-half of the original sample to decay into its daughter product. The graph below shows the radioactivity decay curve for a sample of uranium-235 (U-235) and the growth curve for its daughter product lead-207 (PB-207), which is relatively stable and doesn't significantly decay in the time shown on the graph.

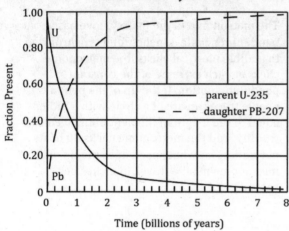

Radioactive Decay and Growth

24. The fraction of uranium-235 remaining after 2.5 billion years is approximately what percent of the fraction of uranium-235 remaining after 1.5 billion years?

A) 10%
B) 20%
C) 35%
D) 50%

25. Based on the given information, which of the following represents the amount of uranium-235 remaining after four half-lives if A_0 represents the amount at time $t = 0$?

A) $\dfrac{A_0}{16}$

B) $\dfrac{A_0}{4}$

C) $\dfrac{A_0}{2}$

D) $4A_0$

26. Which of the following correctly describes the relationship between the fraction of uranium-235 remaining and time, as shown in the graph?

A) negative linear
B) positive linear
C) exponential decay
D) exponential growth

27. Which of the following accurately describes the graph of the equations $y = -\dfrac{x}{2} + 3$ and $y = 4x + 6$?

A) The lines are parallel and do not intersect at any points.

B) The lines intersect once at $\left(-\dfrac{2}{3}, \dfrac{10}{3}\right)$.

C) The lines intersect once at $(0,3)$.

D) The lines intersect twice at $(0,3)$ and $\left(-\dfrac{2}{3}, \dfrac{10}{3}\right)$.

Continue ➤

$$8\,x$$
$$+\,x\,2$$
$$\overline{1\,y\,6}$$

28. The figure above shows a correctly performed addition problem, in which *x* and *y* each represent a single digit which may or may not be the same digit. Which of the following system of equations can be used to solve for the value(s) of *x* and *y*?

A) $2x = 6$; $x^2 + 8x = 106 + 10y$

B) $x + 2 = 6$; $80 + x = 10 + y$

C) $x + 2 = 6$; $8 + x = 10 + y$

D) $x + 2 = 6 + y$; $8 + x = 1y$

29. In the coordinate plane, the graph of which of the following lines is perpendicular to the graph of line $y = \dfrac{3}{2}x + 1$?

A) $y = \dfrac{3}{2}x - 1$

B) $y = \dfrac{3}{4}x + 1$

C) $y = -\dfrac{2}{3}x + 2$

D) $y = -\dfrac{3}{2}x - 1$

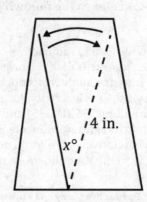

30. The metronome in the figure above has a pendulum needle 4 inches long synchronized to audible metrical clicks: the metronome clicks at each extreme of the constant pendulum motion. If the tip of the pendulum needle traces an arc of a circle with a radius equal to the length of the pendulum needle, $x = 30°$, and the metronome clicks 30 beats per minute, at what speed does the tip of the metronome needle travel, in inches per second?

A) $\dfrac{3\pi}{4}$

B) $\dfrac{\pi}{3}$

C) $\dfrac{\pi}{5}$

D) 20π

Continue

DIRECTIONS: For #31–38, solve each item and mark your answer on a special answer grid.

1. For each item, you should write your answer in the boxes at the top of each column and then fill in the ovals beneath each part of the answer you write.
2. Mark no more than one oval in any column.
3. Questions do not have negative answers.
4. Some problems have more than one possible answer. Grid only one answer.
5. See the first example below to grid mixed numbers.
6. See the last example below to grid decimal answers with more digits than the grid can accommodate.

Here are some examples:

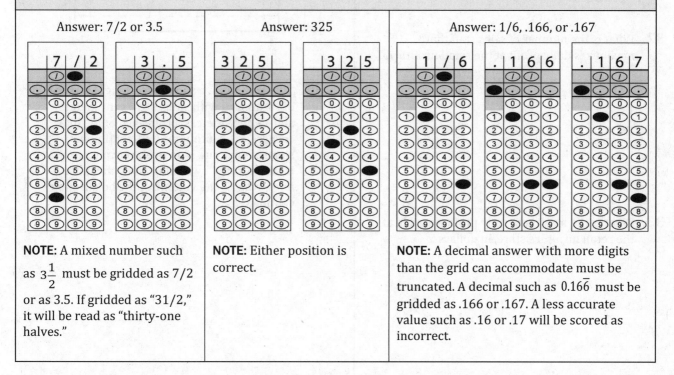

Answer: 7/2 or 3.5

Answer: 325

Answer: 1/6, .166, or .167

NOTE: A mixed number such as $3\frac{1}{2}$ must be gridded as 7/2 or as 3.5. If gridded as "31/2," it will be read as "thirty-one halves."

NOTE: Either position is correct.

NOTE: A decimal answer with more digits than the grid can accommodate must be truncated. A decimal such as $0.16\overline{6}$ must be gridded as .166 or .167. A less accurate value such as .16 or .17 will be scored as incorrect.

31. Rasheed can seal 50 envelopes in 1 minute and Tae-John can do the same job in 80 seconds. How many minutes (rounded to the nearest minute) will it take them to seal 500 envelopes if Rasheed seals the first 240 envelopes, then Tae-John seals envelopes for 4 minutes, and Rasheed then finishes the job?

Continue

Questions #32–34 refer to the following information.

At a retail furniture store, sales staff work in 8-hour shifts. The daily profit, y, in dollars, at the store is related to the number of sales staff working that day, x, according to the following equation:

$$y = -1,000x^2 + 4,000x + 2,000$$

32. What is the number of sales staff that maximizes daily profit at the retail furniture store?

33. What is the maximum daily profit possible at the retail furniture store, in dollars?

34. For the retail furniture store to keep profits above zero on a given day, what is the maximum number of sales staff that can work that day?

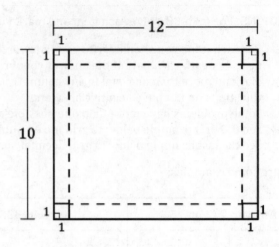

35. The figure above shows a rectangular piece of cardboard with sides of 10 centimeters and 12 centimeters. From each of the four corners, a 1 centimeter by 1 centimeter square is cut out. If an open rectangular box is then formed by folding along the dotted lines, what is the volume of the box in cubic centimeters?

Continue

Our Class Heights				
Aileen 56 in.	Azuany 60 in.	Elsa 55 in.	Meija 55 in.	Rio 59 in.
Aisha 52 in.	Carlos 56 in.	Estrella 56 in.	Monica 58 in.	Tae-John 59 in.
Alaina 58 in.	Charlie 54 in.	Fatima 56 in.	Radames 56 in.	Trevor 52 in.
Alli 51 in.	Cooper 57 in.	Flora 57 in.	Rasheed 59 in.	Yair 57 in.
Audrey 58 in.	Destiny 57 in.	Levie 58 in.	Revante 55 in.	Zephyr 58 in.

36. The figure above shows the data collected by Ms. Healy's and Ms. Powers' fourth grade class on height. What is the range of the data, in inches?

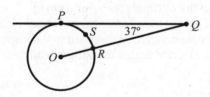

38. What is the positive solution for k in the equation $\left|k - \dfrac{1}{8}\right| = \left|\dfrac{1}{3} - \dfrac{1}{2}\right|$?

37. In the figure above, with O as the center of the circle, what is the measure, in degrees, of minor $\overset{\frown}{PSR}$?

STOP

IF YOU FINISH BEFORE TIME IS CALLED, YOU MAY CHECK YOUR WORK ON THIS SECTION ONLY. DO NOT TURN TO ANY OTHER SECTION IN THE TEST.

SECTION 5—ESSAY (OPTIONAL)

Time—50 minutes

1 essay prompt

DIRECTIONS: The essay measures your ability to read and understand a passage and write an essay that analyzes the passage. In your essay, demonstrate that you have carefully read the passage, write a clear and logical analysis, and use language precisely.

You have 50 minutes to read the passage and write an essay in response to the provided prompt. Sample essays are on page 268.

Read the passage below and think about how Geraldine S. Perry uses

- evidence (facts, examples, etc.) to support claims.
- reasoning to develop the passage and to connect claims and evidence.
- rhetorical or persuasive elements, such as language choices or emotional appeals, to increase the impact of the ideas expressed.

Adapted from "Raising Awareness of Sleep as a Healthy Behavior" by Geraldine S. Perry, DrPH, RDN; Susheel P. Patil, MD, PhD; and Letitia R. Presley-Cantrell, PhD. Originally posted in Preventing Chronic Disease, Volume 11, August 2013.

How Much Sleep Is Needed and Are We There?

The 2006 Institute of Medicine (IOM) report *Sleep Disorders and Sleep Deprivation* indicates that the average basal sleep needs of adults is approximately 7 to 8 hours per night, and the optimal sleep duration for adolescents is 9 hours per night. However, more than 35% of adults report getting fewer than 7 hours of sleep during a 24-hour period, and almost 70% of high school students report getting fewer than 8 hours of sleep on an average weeknight. Overall, about 15 million children in the United States do not get sufficient sleep.

Why Is Sleep a Public Health Issue?

Insufficient sleep has major health consequences for adults, adolescents, and young children. According to the Institute of Medicine Committee on Sleep Medicine and Research, strong evidence exists that, among adults, insufficient sleep has a significant effect on numerous health conditions, including chronic disease development and incidence. For instance, short sleep duration (less than 7 hours of sleep per night) and poor sleep quality are associated with cardiovascular morbidity and metabolic disorders such as glucose intolerance, which may lead to obesity, diabetes, heart disease, and hypertension. People who have short sleep duration are at 1.48 times greater risk of developing and dying of coronary heart disease than controls and 1.15 times more likely to have a stroke, according to a review and meta-analysis published by Cappuccio, Cooper, D'Elia, Strazzullo, and Miller. According to another study, children who experience short sleep duration are more likely to become obese than those who do not.

Insufficient sleep also affects immunologic function and development of mood disorders and is associated with depression; deficits in cognition, memory and learning; and reduced quality of life, according to the Institute of Medicine Committee on Sleep Medicine and Research. Adults who sleep fewer than 7 hours per night have greater difficulty concentrating, remembering, and performing other daily activities than those who sleep 7 to 9 hours a night, according to the CDCP. Children and adolescents who get insufficient sleep have impaired behavior, mood, and performance, according to another study.

One major consequence of insufficient sleep is daytime sleepiness, which reduces alertness and causes slow reaction time, leading to occupational and medical errors, workplace injuries, impaired driving, and motor vehicle accidents. In 2009, almost 5% of adults in 12 states reported that during the previous 30 days they had nodded off or fallen asleep while driving, according to the CDCP. In 2005, drowsy driving contributed to 100,000 motor vehicle accidents and 15,000 deaths.

The public health burden of sleep deprivation is enormous. There are substantial public health investments in all areas related to sleep, from obesity and other chronic conditions to motor vehicle accidents. Insufficient sleep, unlike other health risk factors such as smoking, excessive alcohol consumption, obesity, and physical inactivity, has historically received much less attention in the public health and clinical settings. Insufficient sleep is an important public health risk factor that would benefit from further investigation.

Lack of Awareness

Despite strong evidence of the relationship between insufficient sleep and health problems, most people are unaware of the amount of sleep they need, their level of sleep deprivation, and the negative impact of sleep deprivation on health. Because of lack of awareness, sleep is not commonly incorporated into public health approaches. In addition, many health care providers do not counsel their patients about healthy sleep habits, according to AJ Sorscher's study "How is your sleep: a neglected topic for health care screening." In that study, among 121 primary care clinics, only 43% included sleep-related questions on their screening batteries compared with 100% for smoking and alcohol, 93% for healthy eating, and 86% for physical activity. It is not clear why sleep is not included in health screenings, but it may be related to the clinician's lack of knowledge of the importance of sleep. In 2002, only 10% of primary care providers described their knowledge of sleep and sleep disorders as good.

Although little evidence exists on the effectiveness of sleep screening and counseling on sleep behavior, screening and counseling has been shown to improve the health behaviors of patients in other areas, such as dietary habits, smoking cessation, and physical activity. Therefore, giving providers information about screening and counseling for appropriate sleep time and needs could better equip primary care and public health professionals with the knowledge needed to screen and counsel patients to promote sleep as a healthy behavior. However, further investigation is needed on the effectiveness of sleep screening and sleep counseling.

Write an essay explaining how Geraldine S. Perry develops her argument that sleep deprivation is one of the biggest public health issues facing adults and children alike. In your essay, analyze how Perry uses one or more of the elements listed above (or other elements) to make her argument more logical and persuasive. Be sure to focus on the most relevant aspects of the passage.

Your essay should not discuss whether you agree with Perry's claims, but rather discuss how Perry develops her argument.

15SATC

Practice Test II

Outline

I. Section 1: Reading (pp. 111–125)

II. Section 2: Writing and Language (pp. 126–139)

III. Section 3: Math, No Calculator (pp. 140–146)

IV. Section 4: Math, Calculator (pp. 147–157)

V. Section 5: Essay (Optional) (pp. 158–159)

DIRECTIONS

Practice Test II includes five test sections: Reading, Writing and Language, Math, No Calculator, Math, Calculator, and the optional Essay. Calculator use is permitted on the Math, Calculator section only.

Cambridge offers several services for schools utilizing our practice tests. Ask your teacher whether your school has decided to send your answers to Cambridge for scoring or to score your answers at your school. If Cambridge is scoring your test, you will use a Scantron™ form provided by your teacher, or you will enter your answers online. If your school is scoring your test, you may use a Scantron™ form provided by your teacher, or you may write your answers on paper.

If you are entering your test answers on a Scantron™ form, please be sure to include the following information on the Scantron™:

Book and edition	*The Practice Book, 13th Edition*
Practice Test Form Code	**15SATC**

If you are only completing a single section of this practice test, make sure to also include the following information:

Subject	**Reading, Writing and Language,** or **Math**
Section Number	**Section 1**, **2**, **3** or **4**

The items in each test section are numbered and the multiple-choice answers are lettered. The Scantron™ form has numbered rows that correspond to the items on the test. Each row contains lettered ovals to match the answer choices for each item on the test. Each numbered row has a corresponding item on the test.

For each multiple-choice item, first decide on the best answer choice. Then, locate the row number that corresponds to the item. Next, find the oval in that row that matches the letter of the chosen answer. Then, use a soft lead pencil to fill in the oval. DO NOT use a ballpoint pen. For each student-produced response item on the math test sections, decide on the correct answer. Then, locate the SPR grid that corresponds to the item. Write your answer in the top of the grid and use a soft lead pencil to fill in each corresponding oval. DO NOT use a ballpoint pen.

Mark only one answer for each item. If you change your mind about an answer choice, thoroughly erase your first mark before marking your new answer.

Note that only responses marked on your Scantron™ form or written on your paper will be scored. Your score on each test will be based only on the number of items that are correctly answered during the time allowed for that test. You will not be penalized for guessing. Therefore, it is in your best interest to answer every item on the test, even if you must guess.

On the Essay, write your response to the prompt using the essay response sheets or loose-leaf paper provided by your teacher. (Note that the Writing Test is optional.)

You may work on each test only during the time allowed for that test. If you finish a test before time is called, use the time to review your answer choices or work on items about which you are uncertain. You may not return to a test on which time has already been called, and you may not preview another test. You must lay down your pencil immediately when time is called at the end of each test. You may not for any reason fill in or alter ovals for a test after time has expired for that test. Violation of these rules will result in immediate disqualification from the exam.

SECTION 1—READING

Time—65 minutes

52 items

DIRECTIONS: Each passage or pair of passages is followed by a set of items. Choose the best answer to each question based on what is stated or implied in the passage or passages and in any accompanying graphics. Answers are on page 271.

Questions #1–10 are based on the following passage.

The passage is adapted from Kate Chopin's "Ma'ame Pélagie."

When the war began, there stood on Côte Joyeuse an imposing mansion of red brick, shaped like the Pantheon. A grove of majestic live-oaks surrounded it.

5 Thirty years later, only the thick walls were standing, with the dull red brick showing here and there through a matted growth of clinging vines. The huge round pillars were intact; so, to some extent, was the stone flagging of hall and portico.
10 There had been no home so stately along the whole stretch of Côte Joyeuse. Everyone knew this, as they knew it had cost Philippe Valmet sixty thousand dollars to build, way back in 1840. No one was in danger of forgetting that fact, so long as
15 his daughter Pélagie survived. She was a queenly, white-haired woman of fifty. "Ma'ame Pélagie," they called her, though she was unmarried, as was her sister Pauline, a child in Ma'ame Pélagie's eyes; a child of thirty-five.

20 The two lived alone in a three-roomed cabin, almost within the shadow of the ruin. They lived for a dream, for Ma'ame Pélagie's dream, which was to rebuild the old home.

It would be pitiful to tell how their days were
25 spent to accomplish this end, how the dollars had been saved for thirty years and the picayunes hoarded, and yet, not half enough gathered! But Ma'ame Pélagie felt sure of twenty years of life before her, and counted upon as many more for
30 her sister. And what could not come to pass in twenty—in forty—years?

Often, on pleasant afternoons, the two would drink their black coffee, seated upon the stone-
flagged portico whose canopy was now the blue
35 sky of Louisiana. They loved to sit there in the silence, with only each other and the sheeny, prying lizards for company. They talked of the old times and planned for the new, light breezes stirring the tattered vines high up among the
40 columns where owls nested.

"We can never hope to have all just as it was, Pauline," Ma'ame Pélagie would say. "Perhaps the marble pillars of the salon will have to be replaced by wooden ones, and the crystal candelabra left
45 out. Should you be willing, Pauline?"

"Oh, yes, Sesoeur, I shall be willing." It was always, "Yes, Sesoeur," "No, Sesoeur," or "Just as you please, Sesoeur," with poor little Mam'selle Pauline. For what did she remember of that old
50 life and that old splendor? Only a faint gleam here and there, the half-consciousness of a young, uneventful existence, and then a great crash. That meant the nearness of war, the revolt of slaves, confusion ending in fire and flame through which
55 she was borne safely in the strong arms of Pélagie and carried to the log cabin, which was still their home. Their brother, Léandre, had known more of it all than Pauline, and not so much as Pélagie. He had left the management of the big plantation,
60 with all its memories and traditions, to his older sister, and had gone away to dwell in cities. That was many years ago. Now, Léandre's business frequently required him to take long journeys from home, and his motherless daughter was
65 coming to stay with her aunts at Côte Joyeuse.

They talked about it, sipping their coffee on the ruined portico. Mam'selle Pauline was terribly excited; the flush that throbbed into her pale, nervous face showed it, and she locked her thin
70 fingers in and out incessantly.

Continue ➡

"But what shall we do with La Petite, Sesoeur? Where shall we put her? How shall we amuse her? Ah, Seigneur!"

"She will sleep upon a cot in the room next
75 to ours," responded Ma'ame Pélagie, "and live as we do. She knows how we live, and why we live; her father has told her. She knows we have money and could squander it if we chose. Do not fret, Pauline; let us hope La Petite is a true Valmet."

80 Then Ma'ame Pélagie rose with stately deliberation and went to saddle her horse, for she had yet to make her last daily round through the fields. She threaded her way slowly among the tangled grasses toward the cabin.

85 The coming of La Petite, bringing with her as she did the pungent atmosphere of an outside and dimly known world, was a shock to these two, who were living their dream-life. The girl was as tall as her aunt Pélagie, with dark eyes that
90 reflected joy as a still pool reflects the light of stars; her rounded cheek was tinged like the pink crepe myrtle. Mam'selle Pauline kissed her and trembled. Ma'ame Pélagie looked into her eyes with a searching gaze, which seemed to seek a
95 likeness of the past in the living present.

And they made room between them for this young life.

1. It can be inferred that the Valmet mansion was

A) destroyed during a war.
B) built by the Valmet sisters.
C) designed by La Petite's father.
D) begun but never finished.

2. In the context of line 26, "picayunes" means

A) household belongings.
B) years of effort.
C) coins of little value.
D) heirloom jewelry.

3. The author uses "whose canopy was now the blue sky of Louisiana" (lines 34–35) to emphasize that the

A) Valmet house was once the most elegant home on the Côte Joyeuse.
B) portico of the Valmet house no longer has a roof.
C) Valmet sisters both drank their coffee without milk.
D) afternoon is an especially beautiful time in Louisiana.

4. The author implies that the plan to rebuild the Valmet house is

A) dependent on Léandre's daughter.
B) mainly the vision of Ma'ame Pélagie.
C) endorsed equally by Pélagie, Léandre, and Pauline.
D) a dream shared jointly by Pélagie and Léandre.

5. Which of the following textual excerpts provides the strongest support for the correct answer to the previous question?

A) Lines 16–19 ("Ma'ame Pélagie . . . thirty-five")
B) Lines 35–40 ("They loved . . . nested")
C) Lines 46–49 ("Oh, yes . . . Pauline")
D) Lines 57–58 ("Their brother . . . Pélagie")

6. The phrase "made room between them for this young life" in lines 96–97 means that

A) the Valmet house required more years to reconstruct than planned.
B) La Petite was required to sleep in the cabin with the sisters.
C) La Petite was much younger looking than either sister had imagined.
D) the sisters accepted the newly arrived Petite into their home.

Continue

7. It can be inferred from paragraph 7 (lines 46–65) that Pauline treated her sister Pélagie

  A) deferentially.
  B) condescendingly.
  C) abruptly.
  D) insincerely.

8. In line 79, Pélagie uses the phrase "a true Valmet" to mean someone who

  A) shares her vision of the family's social and economic position.
  B) will be honest and obey the instructions given her by her aunts.
  C) has endured the hardship of the Valmet family over the years.
  D) prefers living on the Côte Joyeuse to traveling in large cities.

9. Pauline regards the expected arrival of Léandre's daughter with

  A) trepidation.
  B) resignation.
  C) indifference.
  D) enthusiasm.

10. As it is used in line 81, "deliberation" means

  A) intensity.
  B) eagerness.
  C) resolve.
  D) uncertainty.

Continue ➡

Questions #11–21 are based on the following passages.

Many US honey bee populations have recently been threatened by Colony Collapse Disorder, a phenomenon that causes bees to abandon their queen and their hive. These passages discuss the possible causes of CCD.

Passage 1

Honey bees are essential crop pollinators, and are responsible for more than $15 billion in increased crop value each year. Recently, honey bees have been under serious pressure from a
5 mystery problem: Colony Collapse Disorder (CCD). Beekeepers have reported losses of 30 to 90 percent of their hives. While colony losses are not unexpected, especially over the winter, this magnitude of loss is unusually high. The main
10 features of CCD are very low numbers of adult bees in the hive, a live queen, honey still in the hive, and the presence of immature bees.

According to a study from Harvard's School of Public Health, the probable cause of CCD is
15 pesticides, specifically two widely used neonicotinoids: imidacloprid and clothianidin. The research was conducted by Dr. Chengsheng Lu, associate professor of environmental exposure biology at Harvard, and the results were published
20 in the *Bulletin of Insectology*.

Dr. Lu studied 18 bee colonies in three locations. Researchers separated the six colonies at each location into three groups—one treated with imidacloprid, one with clothianidin, and one
25 untreated. The result was that in 6 of the 12 colonies that were treated with neonicotinoids, bees died at elevated rates and fled the hives, exhibiting symptoms of Colony Collapse Disorder.

There was a steady decline in the size of all of
30 the colonies during the beginning of winter, a decline that is typical among hives during the colder months in New England. Beginning in January 2013, bee populations in the control colonies began to increase as expected, but
35 populations in the neonicotinoid-treated hives continued to decline. By April 2013, 6 out of 12 of the neonicotinoid-treated colonies were lost, with abandoned hives that are typical of CCD. Only one of the control colonies was lost, apparently to an
40 infestation of *Nosema ceranae*, a common intestinal parasite.

Exposure to imidacloprid and clothianidin affected the winterization of healthy colonies and subsequently led to CCD. This observation
45 suggests the impairment of honey bee neurological functions, specifically memory, cognition, or behavior, to be the results of chronic sub-lethal neonicotinoid exposure.

Passage 2

Honey bees, which are a critical link in US
50 agriculture, have been under serious pressure from a mystery problem: Colony Collapse Disorder (CCD). Following the collapse of the colony, a live queen remains with honey in the hive and immature bees are still present, but no
55 adult bees are left, only dead bee bodies. CCD is only one of several major dangers threatening honey bees, but the syndrome captured the imaginations of certain elements of the press following the announcement that a connection
60 had been made between CCD and pesticides. The *Boston Globe*, *The New Yorker*, *Motherjones*, *The Guardian*, *Salon* and others ran stories citing the research conducted by Dr. Chensheng Lu under the auspices of the Harvard School of Public
65 Health, in which neonicotinoids are blamed for CCD. As one writer put it, neonicotinoids were the "smoking gun" that killed the bees.

A more careful examination of Lu's research shows that there was a rush to judgment. In the
70 first place, Dr. Lu himself is not an expert on insects—much less bees—and many reputable journals in the United States declined to publish his findings. The paper was finally printed in an obscure Italian journal called the *Bulletin of*
75 *Insectology*, a publication of little importance. There are many more expert researchers who have reached far more conservative conclusions who might have been cited, but the press was excited by the dramatic story line that evil
80 manufacturers were killing innocent bees with nasty chemicals for their own profits, and a thin scientific veneer that dressed up the simplistic story line made it perfect for public consumption.

One of the central problems with Lu's
85 conclusion—and much of the reporting—is that despite the colony problems, the global bee population has remained remarkably stable since the widespread adoption of neonicotinoids in the late 1990s. The United Nations reports that the
90 number of hives has actually risen over the past

Continue ➤

15 years to more than 80 million colonies, a record, as neonicotinoids usage has soared.

Then, a closer examination of Lu's methodology shows striking flaws in the
95 experimental setup. Bees are ordinarily fed a supplemental diet of high fructose corn syrup, and Lu spiked their diet with either imidacloprid or clothianidin in hopes of mimicking field conditions. In reality, Lu fed his bees
100 concentrations of chemicals that were 135 parts per billion compared with concentrations found in ordinary applications of 1 to 3 parts per billion. Given the strength of this toxic cocktail, it is a wonder that Lu's bees survived as long as they did.
105 What Lu proved was only something we have known all along: you can kill bees using a sufficiently powerful poison.

Managed Honey Colonies (1991–2008)

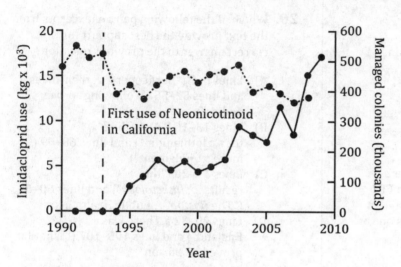

11. The primary purpose of Passage 1 is to

A) convince readers that scientific research proves the need to limit the use of neonicotinoids as pesticides.
B) present evidence that honey bees are economically important to the agricultural sector of the economy.
C) report on an experiment that seems to establish that neonicotinoids cause honey bee Colony Collapse Disorder.
D) praise Dr. Lu for research that discovered the "smoking gun" that has caused the death of honey bee colonies.

12. Lines 29–41 primarily describe the

A) scientific methodology of Dr. Lu's experiment.
B) results of Dr. Lu's scientific experiment.
C) political implications of Dr. Lu's experiment.
D) importance of using the scientific methods.

13. In context, "auspices" (line 64) most nearly means

A) influence.
B) control.
C) sponsorship.
D) opinion.

14. According to Passage 1, a decrease in the number of bees in colonies during the start of winter cold is

A) proof that neonicotinoids are harmful.
B) typical of the life cycle of the hive.
C) a sign that disease agents are present.
D) unusual except in regions of New England.

Continue

15. Given the definition of CCD provided in paragraph 1 of Passage 1, Dr. Lu's findings, as reported in paragraphs three and four, show the hives exhibited

A) all of the symptoms associated with CCD.
B) some but not all of the symptoms associated with CCD.
C) none of the symptoms associated with CCD.
D) all but one of the symptoms associated with CCD.

16. In context, "sub-lethal" (line 48) means

A) not sufficient to kill.
B) ineffective amount.
C) insignificant quantity.
D) extremely concentrated dosage.

17. The attitude of the author of Passage 2 toward the authors of the articles on CCD that appeared in the publications listed in lines 61–62 can best be described as one of

A) contempt.
B) sympathy.
C) indifference.
D) compassion.

18. The main point of the final paragraph of Passage 2 is that

A) several publications incorrectly reported Dr. Lu's findings.
B) Dr. Lu's experimental setup was fatally flawed.
C) CCD can be triggered by small dosages of neonicotinoids.
D) field conditions are very difficult to simulate in a laboratory setting.

19. The authors of the two passages mainly *disagree* about the

A) value of honey bees to US agriculture.
B) defining characteristics of Colony Collapse Disorder.
C) motivation for reporting done by the media.
D) validity of the conclusions reached by Dr. Lu.

20. Which of the following pairs of excerpts from the text provide the best support for the correct answer to the previous question?

A) Lines 6–7 ("Beekeepers . . . their hives") and lines 52–55 ("Following . . . bee bodies")
B) Lines 13–16 ("According to . . . clothianidin") and lines 68–69 ("A more . . . judgment")
C) Lines 19–20 ("the results . . . *Insectology*") and lines 60–65 ("The *Boston* . . . Public Health")
D) Lines 29–32 ("There was . . . New England") and lines 105–107 ("What Lu proved . . . poison")

21. Which of the following conclusions implied by the data in the graph would most strongly support the conclusion that imidacloprid is not a cause of CCD?

A) Prior to the introduction of imidacloprid, the number of managed honey bee colonies was approximately zero but grew to almost 300,000 by 2004.
B) From 1994 to 2003, the number of managed honey bee colonies remained almost constant even as the use of imidacloprid increased.
C) Following the introduction of imidacloprid, the number of managed honey bee colonies declined at approximately the same rate as the increase in imidacloprid usage.
D) Both the amount of imidacloprid used and the number of managed honey bee colonies remained virtually constant during the years 1994 to 2010.

Continue

Questions #22–31 are based on the following passage.

This passage explores the history and influences of the Nuevo Mexicanos *or* Hispanos *of New Mexico and southern Colorado.*

Beginning with the establishment of the Spanish colony in 1598, the *Nuevo Mexicanos* of northern New Mexico and southern Colorado, or *Hispanos*, as they call themselves, developed a
5 distinctive regional culture. Once the fabled mineral wealth of the region turned out to be a legend, the principal reason for the Spanish Crown to maintain the colony was the large population of natives, who represented a substantial harvest of
10 souls for the Church. However, the overzealous Franciscan fathers entrusted with the project outlawed Kachina dances by the Pueblo Indians and ordered the destruction of traditional masks, prayer sticks, and effigies. The total and ruthless
15 suppression of the indigenous religion led to the 1680 Pueblo Revolt, which totally restored native religion. Following the Revolt, political power remained distributed among the individual pueblos until 1692, when the Spanish
20 reconquered them one by one. Differences were set aside as the Pueblos and the Spanish American settlers united to defend their communities from the attacks of nomadic tribes.

After the devastating Comanche wars ended
25 with the treaty of 1786, the frontiers of the colony became safe enough for settlement. Since the protective alliance with the Pueblo was no longer necessary to survive, *Hispano* settlers moved beyond Taos Valley looking for new lands to graze
30 their flocks. The enterprising villagers were familiar with the rigors of frontier life and had always been responsible for their own welfare, the defense of their communities, and even the sustenance of their religious traditions.

35 Since the few priests that came to New Mexico were assigned to the Pueblo missions, settlers only rarely enjoyed their services. In the last quarter of the eighteenth century, this institutional void was filled by the appearance of a
40 lay religious organization whose social and cultural influence became the hallmark of the nineteenth century in the region. The organization was known as *Los Hermandad Piadosa de Nuestro Padre Jesús Nazareno* (Pious Brotherhood of Our
45 Father Jesus the Nazarene) and, less formally, as the *Penitentes,* or Brotherhood.

The *Penitentes* fulfilled the same functions that confraternities, sodalities, and religious volunteer associations did all over Latin America.
50 In frontier areas like New Mexico, they became central to the very survival of the communities they served. The *Penitente* brothers led saint's day festivities, Lenten and Holy Week services, rosaries, prayer vigils, wedding ceremonies, and
55 wakes for the dead on a year-round basis in their *moradas.* With the permission of their mothers and wives, boys and young men joined the *Penitentes* and learned to respect the moral and civic authority of the leadership of the
60 confraternity. The *Hermanos*, as they called themselves, were involved in resolution of disputes, allocation of water, and virtually all group decisions. They also saw to it that families in need or distress were provided for. As the
65 strongest organization at the village level, they became the basis for organized participation in the political process and formed effective voting blocs during elections.

The origins of the Brotherhood are still a
70 mystery. Some scholars have emphasized similarities with the Third Order of Saint Francis, especially since New Mexico is a Franciscan province. Others theorize that the organization arrived fully developed from southern Spain, since
75 there are similar confraternities with the same name in the area of Seville. The *Hermanos* are dedicated to self-sacrifice and observe penitential devotions that are widespread in Spain and Spanish America.

80 Feeling culturally and politically threatened by the *Hermanos*, American newcomers to New Mexico condemned and sensationalized the Brotherhood. The Archdiocese of Sante Fe attempted unsuccessfully to suppress the
85 brotherhood in the latter part of the nineteenth century, driving the membership underground. It is for this reason that Los *Penitentes* are sometimes described as a "secret society." In 1948, after ostracizing the brotherhood for years,
90 the American Catholic church finally made its peace with the *Hermanos* and has since formally recognized the contributions and leadership of the Brotherhood. After a decline in membership after World War II and into the 1960s, the Brotherhood
95 experienced a resurgence in the 1980s and 1990s.

Continue

22. The author implies that the Spanish government was originally interested in the Northern New Mexico and southern Colorado region for its

A) agricultural potential.
B) mineral resources.
C) grazing lands.
D) large population.

23. Which of the following textual excerpts most strongly supports the correct answer to the previous question?

A) Lines 2–5 ("the *Nuevo Mexicanos* . . . regional culture")
B) Lines 5–7 ("the fabled . . . a legend")
C) Lines 28–30 ("*Hispano* settlers . . . flocks")
D) Lines 30–34 ("The enterprising . . . traditions")

24. The author implies that the members of the *Penitentes* were

A) ordained members of the priesthood.
B) un-ordained members of a lay community.
C) settlers who moved beyond the Taos Valley.
D) priests assigned to Pueblo missions.

25. Which of the following textual excerpts provides the most support for the correct answer to the previous question?

A) Lines 30–34 ("The enterprising . . . traditions")
B) Lines 37–42 ("In the last quarter . . . in the region")
C) Lines 50–52 ("In frontier . . . they served")
D) Lines 52–56 ("The *Penitente* . . . *moradas*")

26. In context, "sodalities" (line 48) means

A) tribes.
B) communities.
C) priesthoods.
D) settlements.

27. The author of the selection would most likely say that the 1680 Pueblo Revolt was attributable to

A) the desire by *Nuevo Mexicanos* to acquire farmland for themselves outside of the Taos Valley.
B) the inability of the *Hermanos* to preserve civic order within the Pueblos of Taos Valley.
C) the failure of the Spanish Crown to reassert its central authority after arrival of the Franciscan fathers.
D) abuse suffered by the indigenous peoples at the hands of the Franciscan friars.

28. When discussing the origin of the Brotherhood, the author mentions confraternities with a similar name near Seville to indicate that the Brotherhood may have

A) developed in the New Mexico province.
B) had its origins in southern Spain.
C) originally been founded as a political party.
D) started in New Mexico and spread to Spain.

29. In context, "enterprising" (line 30) means

A) wealthy.
B) resourceful.
C) business-oriented.
D) indigenous.

30. It can be inferred from the passage that in the New Mexico area, water was

A) in plentiful supply.
B) controlled by the Crown.
C) a scarce natural resource.
D) available only to the wealthy.

Continue

31. The author would be most likely to characterize the *Hispano* settlers of northern New Mexico and southern Colorado as

A) self-reliant.
B) unreliable.
C) hostile.
D) changeable.

Continue

Questions #32–41 are based on the following passage.

This passage explores the definition and effects of drought.

Drought can be defined as a lack of water, but this unadorned definition obscures many complexities. The most important is that drought is a characteristic of a time, not of a place. A place
5 can be dry or wet, but droughts occur in given locations over time. For example, the Sonoran Desert may have a lack of water for many purposes, but conceptually it has just the right amount of water for the Sonoran Desert, though
10 occasionally even the Sonoran Desert experiences droughts. Wet places, like the coastal rain forests in Washington State, also experience droughts when there is an unusually dry summer. Consistently dry seasons would not merit the
15 designation of "drought" in and of themselves; however, variations in how dry or long the dry season is from year to year are relevant. In places like the Western United States, where there is a coincidence of the dry season with the growing
20 season every year, it does not make sense to frame summer as a "drought" so much as to note the seasonal aridity of the location.

Although drought is generally defined from a climatic perspective (precipitation levels that are
25 much lower than the annual average), short-term moisture fluctuations can also produce drought conditions. A wet period followed by a dry spell, for instance, may not constitute a "drought" relative to long-term averages, but the lack of
30 water to meet the temporarily increased demand by additional vegetation produced during the wet period would nonetheless represent a meaningful drought. From the perspective of plants that have thrived during the wet period, the normal dry
35 spell following has a drought effect. The effect of such a drought can be significant; for example, there is an increased fire risk in rangeland ecosystems where wet springs can produce an overabundance of fine fuels from invasive annual
40 grasses.

Most of the indices used to define drought are tied to common meteorological measurements, like precipitation and temperature, because these are widely available
45 with relatively long records. The long records make it possible to compare particular precipitation amounts or water-balance estimates to the local climatological distribution, in essence gauging risk or probability levels of current
50 meteorological events. The meteorologically-based indices are commonly applied for drought forecasting based on weather forecasts, given that weather is the most fundamental driver and also the most fundamental uncertainty in drought
55 estimation.

Hydrologic, agricultural, and socioeconomic drought are filters used to highlight how meteorological drought affects human demands and values for water, ranging from food
60 production to electrical power production, recreation, and wildlife management. Generally, the context is economic, although environmental benefits of water are recognized as well. They also frame different time scales of response to
65 meteorological forcing. Most of these drought types frame drought as an event. In this framing, a drought is a type of disturbance, or even disaster, with a distinct occurrence. This framing is particularly relevant to crops of limited lifespan,
70 seasonal cycles of water demand (municipal supply, hydropower demand, water-oriented recreation), and other activities where short-term interruptions in water supply are economically relevant (e.g., manufacturing). Lack of water is
75 considered a drought usually only when water requirements for human uses cannot be met. It is most commonly thought of in terms of the harm it can induce. It is broadly seen as one of the most potentially severe natural disasters in terms of
80 either human lives or capital loss because it covers large areas and can lead to famine for large populations. The emphasis on human impact is central in drought reporting as well. Specialists report on droughts by tallying impacts, or
85 instances in which individuals or weather services mention the effects of a drought. For example, agricultural impacts include crop damage, cost of water resource development, and lack of water for fisheries and horticulture. Increased total impacts
90 indicate increased disturbance of human activity.

Continue ▶

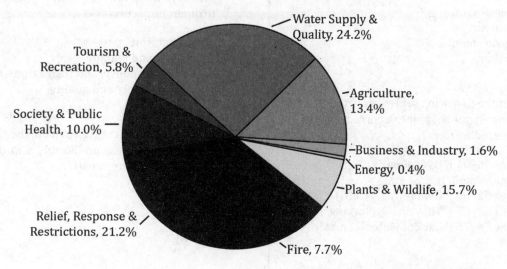

Impacts Associated with a Typical Drought

Water Supply & Quality, 24.2%

Tourism & Recreation, 5.8%

Society & Public Health, 10.0%

Agriculture, 13.4%

Business & Industry, 1.6%

Energy, 0.4%

Plants & Wildlife, 15.7%

Relief, Response & Restrictions, 21.2%

Fire, 7.7%

Total Impacts: 218

32. The author writes primarily to

A) disprove a theory.
B) announce a discovery.
C) refute a conclusion.
D) clarify a definition.

33. In context, the word "unadorned" (line 2) means

A) accurate.
B) useful.
C) simple.
D) unattractive.

34. The author states that "the Sonoran Desert . . . has just the right amount of water for the Sonoran Desert" (lines 6–9) to show that

A) a seasonal dry spell can precipitate a drought in any climate.
B) an area can experience a drought without the occurrence of lack of water.
C) a prolonged dry period does not necessarily create desert conditions.
D) a normal lack of water in an arid region should not be termed a drought.

35. Which of the following best explains why an abnormal wet period can create a fire risk?

A) Surplus moisture is absorbed by the soil during a wet period and remains for the grasses to use during the dry period.
B) Wet conditions stimulate excessive growth that cannot be sustained during the dry period and so become dry fuel.
C) Abnormally wet conditions affect only non-native plants while dry conditions affect both native and invasive species.
D) An abnormal wet period suppresses the growth of native species allowing the non-native plants to thrive during a subsequent dry period.

36. According to the passage, weather information like precipitation and temperatures is useful for drought forecasting because

A) detailed records have been kept for a long time.
B) forecasting weather entails considerable uncertainty.
C) drought events can have significant effects on humans.
D) the data are easily understood by most people.

Continue

37. In context, "driver" (line 53) means

    A) determinant.
    B) chauffeur.
    C) measurement.
    D) weather.

38. Which of the following sentences provides the strongest support for the correct answer to the preceding item?

    A) Lines 56–61 ("Hydrologic . . . management")
    B) Lines 61–63 ("Generally . . . well")
    C) Lines 63–65 ("They also . . . forcing")
    D) Lines 74–76 ("Lack of water . . . met")

39. With which of the following statements about *drought* as a scientific concept would the author be most LIKELY to agree?

    A) As a scientific concept, *drought* is objective and must have the same definition in all contexts.
    B) As a scientific concept, *drought* is defined more by human need than by objective measurements.
    C) *Drought* is a word that has different definitions depending on the time and place to which it is applied.
    D) While the meaning of *drought* varies by time and region, "shortage of water" has a constant meaning.

40. According to the chart provided, the category that accounted for the greatest number of drought impacts was

    A) agriculture.
    B) plants and wildlife.
    C) relief, response, and restrictions.
    D) water supply and quality.

41. According to the chart provided, the number of reported impacts on "Society & Public Health" was approximately

    A) 5.
    B) 10.
    C) 22.
    D) 30.

Continue

Questions #42–52 are based on the following passage.

This passage explores the authorship of the poem commonly known as "The Night Before Christmas."

"A Visit from St. Nicholas," more commonly known from its first line as "The Night Before Christmas," is a poem first published anonymously in New York's *Troy Sentinel* on December 23,
5 1823, and attributed to Clement Clarke Moore, a professor of Oriental and Greek Literature, in 1837. In that year, Moore claimed authorship and explained that the poem had originally been written for his children and later sent, without his
10 knowledge, to the newspaper by a housekeeper. The poem was included in an anthology of Moore's work in 1844. It seems indisputable that the poem first appeared on December 23, 1823, in the *Troy Sentinel*, that the manuscript originated
15 in Moore's home, and that the person giving the poem to the newspaper, without Moore's knowledge, believed that it had been written by Moore.

In 1859, however, 26 years after the poem
20 first appeared in print, the children of Major Henry Livingston, Jr., who was born in Poughkeepsie in 1748, claimed to have heard the poem recited by their father as early as 1807— sixteen years before the poem's original
25 publication and 37 years before Moore claimed authorship. The Livingston family also claimed to have found a copy of the poem with edits in Livingston's hand in their father's desk. There is no evidence that Livingston himself ever claimed
30 authorship of the poem. No print record has ever been found with Livingston's name attached to it. The manuscript claimed to have been found by Livingston's family was allegedly destroyed in a house fire. Moore, however, personally made
35 copies of the poem in his own hand as favors for family members and friends.

Like Moore, Livingston was an amateur poet with several publishing credits to his name. Unlike Moore, who wrote only one other poem in
40 anapestic form, the meter of "A Visit," Livingston frequently used the anapest. In fact, Livingston was apparently in the habit of writing a holiday poem for his children each Christmas using anapest verse. Many of them borrowed language
45 and form from Christopher Anstey, an English poet who died in 1805, and so resemble "A Visit."

But there is also considerable evidence in the poem to support Moore's authorship: lighthearted, spontaneous-sounding mixed iambs and anapests,
50 exclamation marks, the rare use of "all" as an adverb, syncopation, and familial affection. In any case, Livingston might have been likelier to employ a style, but this does not mean that Moore never did so.

55 Setting aside direct testimony of authorship and the analysis of form, an intriguing bit of evidence is names given in the poem, as originally published, to two of Saint Nicholas' reindeer: *Dunder* and *Blixem*. The names are Dutch for
60 *thunder* and *lightning*. Moore did not speak Dutch; Livingston's mother, however, was Dutch.

As intriguing as this point may be, it ignores the then-fashionable Knickerbocker movement which sought to find in everything associated with
65 New York a Dutch beginning. It would have been consistent with the prevailing style for the *Troy Sentinel* editor to change the German *Donder* and *Blitzen* to the Dutch equivalents. In fact, later emendations to the poem, in Moore's own hand,
70 changed the names back to the original *Donder* and *Blitzen*.

Moore's close friendship with the author Washington Irving, who was closely associated with the Knickerbocker trend, may also help to
75 explain any other Dutch elements that are found in "A Visit." But the Dutch influence proves much more. The Livingston family now claims that the poem was written by Henry Livingston around 1808. But the poem clearly reflects the later
80 influence of Washington Irving, the New York Historical Society, and the Knickerbocker movement, which date the poem to 1822, consistent with all the other evidence that Moore penned the classic verse.

85 To be charitable to the Livingston family, perhaps the most likely explanation for the seemingly conflicting evidence is the unreliability of human memory. Assuming that Livingston read to his children a special verse written in anapestic
90 meter each year, it would not be inconceivable that a quarter of a century later, the then-adult children would have a recollection of the meter and Christmas theme. Upon hearing "A Visit," the topical and stylistic similarities would make it
95 easy to conflate "A Visit" and the holiday poems by their father.

Continue

42. The author mentions Moore's friendship with Washington Irving in order to show that "A Visit" was probably written around:

A) 1807
B) 1822
C) 1837
D) 1859

43. The primary purpose of the passage is to

A) evaluate the poetic merit of "A Visit."
B) examine the social setting of the first publication of "A Visit."
C) assess the evidence for the authorship of "A Visit."
D) compare the features of "A Visit" to other poems written by Livingston.

44. The fact that Moore's housekeeper submitted "A Visit" to the newspaper without Moore's knowledge helps to explain why

A) the poem was written in a meter seldom used by Moore.
B) Moore did not make a claim of authorship at the time.
C) "A Visit" has Dutch features even though Moore was not Dutch.
D) the manuscript supposedly written by Livingston could not be found.

45. The author regards the evidence for Livingston's authorship presented in the third paragraph as

A) indisputable.
B) inconclusive.
C) irrelevant.
D) complete.

46. Which of the following sentences best supports the correct answer to the preceding question?

A) Lines 37–38 ("Like Moore . . . his name")
B) Lines 41–44 ("In fact . . . anapest verse")
C) Lines 44–46 ("Many of them . . . resemble 'A Visit'")
D) Lines 51–54 ("In any case . . . did so")

47. It can be inferred that the author of the passage believes that *Dunder* and *Blixem* were names

A) used by Moore in his original manuscript.
B) inserted by Moore into a later version.
C) chosen by an editor at the *Troy Sentinel.*
D) selected by Livingston, who knew Dutch.

48. In context, "emendations" (line 69) means

A) objections.
B) corrections.
C) deletions.
D) inquiries.

49. The author's attitude toward the claim of the Livingston heirs to have once been in possession of a copy of "A Visit" handwritten by Livingston can best be described as

A) inquisitive.
B) defensive.
C) insightful.
D) skeptical.

50. Which of the following sentences most strongly supports the correct answer to the preceding item?

A) Lines 28–30 ("There is no evidence . . . of the poem")
B) Lines 30–31 ("No print record . . . attached to it")
C) Lines 32–34 ("The manuscript claimed . . . house fire")
D) Lines 34–36 ("Moore, however . . . and friends")

51. In context, "conflate" (line 95) means

A) confuse.
B) plagiarize.
C) approve.
D) remember.

Continue

52. In the final paragraph, the author attempts to

A) reconcile the conflicting theories by proposing a third.

B) show that Moore, rather than Livingston, wrote "A Visit."

C) correct a longstanding misconception about "A Visit."

D) excuse the Livingstons' claim as an honest mistake.

STOP

IF YOU FINISH BEFORE TIME IS CALLED, YOU MAY CHECK YOUR WORK ON THIS SECTION ONLY. DO NOT TURN TO ANY OTHER SECTION IN THE TEST.

SECTION 2

SECTION 2—WRITING AND LANGUAGE

Time—35 minutes

44 items

DIRECTIONS: Each set of questions is based on a passage. For some questions, think about how the passage could be revised to improve the expression of ideas. For other questions, think about how to edit the passage to correct sentence structure, usage, or punctuation errors. Passages or questions may be accompanied by a graphic such as a table or graph that you may refer to while making revising and editing decisions.

Some questions reference an underlined word or phrase in the passage. Other questions refer to a location in the passage or to the passage as a whole.

After reading each passage, choose the answer that improves the expression of ideas in the passage or conforms to standard English conventions. Many questions include a "NO CHANGE" answer choice. Choose that answer if you think the best choice is to leave the passage as it is. Answers are on page 272.

Questions #1–11 are based on the following passage.

Professional Sports: Beyond the Fantasy

Many people dream of becoming professional athletes. Few people, however, make a full-time living from sports. And when they do, they often have short careers with little job security.

[1] There is about 14,900 jobs for professional athletes, and the pay varies greatly. The best athletes compete in events that are broadcast on national television and earn [2] big bucks. Though the highest-paid athletes earn almost $190,000 yearly, [3] the median annual salary is about $40,000, and the lowest-paid athletes earn less than $18,000 a year.

Being a professional athlete involves more than showing up for the match or game. Athletes spend many hours each day practicing under the guidance of a sports instructor or a coach. They work regularly with strength trainers to gain muscle and stamina and to prevent injury. Many athletes push their bodies to the limit during both practice and play, so a major career-ending injury is always a risk. [4] Even minor injuries may put a player at risk of being replaced.

1. A) NO CHANGE
   B) There are about
   C) About
   D) Though there are about

2. A) NO CHANGE
   B) scads of money
   C) large salaries
   D) a lot of dinero

3. The author is considering deleting the underlined part of the sentence. If the underlined part of the sentence is deleted, what will be the effect on the passage?

   A) Deleting the underlined part will have no effect because the author supplies the same information later in the passage.
   B) Deleting the underlined part will have no effect because the passage is primarily about the best professional athletes.
   C) Deleting the underlined part will remove information that helps the reader to understand that most professional athletes are not paid large salaries.
   D) Deleting the underlined part will permit the reader to compare the compensation of the highest-paid athletes to that of the lowest-paid athletes.

4. The author uses the word *even* to

   A) emphasize that minor as well as major injuries can end an athlete's career.
   B) distinguish the ways in which professional athletes train for different risks.
   C) show that it is likely that most athletes will eventually be injured.
   D) prove that most professional athletes train and compete on a rigorous schedule.

Continue

5 Competition at all levels is extremely intense and job security is always in question. Athletes usually train throughout the year in order to maintain excellent form and technique and remain in peak physical condition. At the professional level, athletes get very little downtime.

Professional athletes typically develop their skills by playing the sport at lower levels. For most team sports, athletes **6** competed in high school and collegiate athletics or on club teams. **7** Other athletes may learn the sport by taking private or group lessons, such as gymnastics or tennis. It typically takes many years of practice and experience to become a professional athlete.

For most aspiring athletes, turning professional is a major advancement. A few will begin to compete on a regular basis almost immediately, while **8** another may spend time as a reserve in order to gain experience. In some sports, such as baseball, athletes often begin their professional career on a minor league team before moving up to the major leagues. Professional athletes advance in a sport by displaying superior **9** performance, in turn, they earn progressively higher salaries.

5. Which of the following is the best way of combining the two sentences?

   A) Because competition at all levels is extremely intense and job security is always in question, athletes
   B) Competition at all levels is extremely intense and job security is always in question, but athletes
   C) Competition at all levels being extremely intense and job security always in question, so athletes
   D) Competition at all levels is extremely intense and job security is always in question when athletes

6. A) NO CHANGE
   B) compete
   C) had competed
   D) will compete

7. A) NO CHANGE
   B) Otherwise, athletes may learn the sport, either gymnastics or tennis, by taking private or group lessons.
   C) Other athletes who take private or group lessons may learn a sport such as gymnastics or tennis.
   D) Other athletes may learn a sport such as gymnastics or tennis by taking private or group lessons.

8. A) NO CHANGE
   B) others
   C) one another
   D) some other

9. A) NO CHANGE
   B) performance in turn,
   C) performance, and, in turn,
   D) performance and in turn,

Continue ▶

Employment for athletes and sports competitors is **10** <u>projected into the future to grow 7 percent over the next ten years</u>, slower than the average for all occupations. Thus, very few high school or college athletes will become professional athletes. In a major sport, such as men's basketball, only about 1 in 12,000 high school athletes make it to the professional level. **11**

10. A) NO CHANGE
B) projected to grow into the future over the next ten years by 7 percent
C) growing into the future 7 percent over the next ten years
D) projected to grow 7 percent over the next ten years

11. Which of the following sentences best summarizes the main point of the final paragraph?

A) The number of talented young men and women who dream of becoming sports superstars is much greater than the number of openings.
B) For those who are not skilled enough to compete professionally, there are other jobs in professional sports such as coaching.
C) Professional athletics is like most other professions including law and business: the better you are, the more you earn.
D) Even if a high school athlete is unable to advance to a higher level, competing in a team sport can be a rewarding experience.

Continue

Questions #12–22 are based on the following passage.

Big Expectations for the Big Top

    12 I was born in the little town of Kinderhook, New York, in 1847. At an early age, I 13 was itchy to go into show business. School didn't interest me a bit. I hated books. I wasn't interested in reading about what 14 someone else did, or where they went, or what they saw. I wanted 15 to be seeing things, to be going places, and to do things myself, and I couldn't think of any better way to satisfy my ambition than to join up with a circus. My family was determined that I should be a doctor, like my father. But when I got older, I was able to get my own way and left home to join a circus. I stayed with circuses for nearly sixty years, though studying to be a doctor for a short time gave me the nickname "Doc."

    I've been asked to draw a comparison between the modern circus 16 and the past. Well, there just isn't any comparison. The circus of today really seems to be the stupendous, gigantic, colossal exhibition that the advance 17 billing and the

12. The writer is thinking of deleting the first sentence. What would be the effect on the essay as whole?

    A) The reader would not know that there were important differences between early circuses and later ones.
    B) The reader would lack any reference point for determining the approximate time covered by the essay.
    C) The reader would not understand that the narrator wanted to be a part of a circus even when he was young.
    D) The reader would have no information about the differences between audiences of difference eras.

13. A) NO CHANGE
    B) had a hankering
    C) had a craving
    D) desired

14. A) NO CHANGE
    B) they
    C) others
    D) one

15. A) NO CHANGE
    B) to be doing, to be going, and to be seeing things
    C) to see, to go, and to do things
    D) to see things, to go places, and to do things

16. A) NO CHANGE
    B) and those of the past.
    C) and the circus of the past.
    D) and the past circus.

17. A) NO CHANGE
    B) billing, and
    C) billing the
    D) billing; the

Continue

18 barkers, spielers, and grinders claim it to be. The old-time circus was a puny forerunner of the mammoth aggregations now on the road. The circus your grandfather went to see as a boy was nothing more than a variety show or vaudeville under canvas. Almost all the acts could be put on in an ordinary theater of that time. **19** Can you imagine the Ringling Brothers' B & B show of today trying to squeeze itself into any theater or auditorium?

The people who work for circuses today are all trained specialists. **20** The old-time trouper was a jack-of-all-trades who could shoe a horse, clown, drive horses, lay out canvas, and fill in anywhere except aerial acrobatics.

18. Is the author's use of the terms "barkers," "spielers," and "grinders" appropriate?

A) No. The terms are imprecise and likely to mislead the reader.
B) No. The terms are obscure and likely to be unfamiliar to the modern reader.
C) Yes. The terms are apparently those that are used in the circus business to describe those positions.
D) Yes. The terms help the author to create an impression of the circus of a bygone era.

19. The question is one that

A) the author answers in greater detail in the remainder of the passage.
B) has already been adequately answered in the first two paragraphs.
C) needs no answer as it is should obvious to the ordinary reader.
D) the author expects the reader to research further in order to find an answer.

20. The author is thinking of revising this sentence to:

The old-time trouper was a jack-of-all-trades who could shoe a horse, clown, drive horses, lay out canvas, and fill in anywhere except aerial acrobatics and, believe it or not, many of the old-timers could even double in acrobatics.

The effect of the revision would be to

A) repeat information that has already been stated earlier in the sentence.
B) provide another example of the versatility of the old-time trouper.
C) define for the reader the status of the aerial acrobat in the circus hierarchy.
D) demonstrate that circuses of old required large numbers of workers to put on the show.

Continue

The circus has always been an innovative enterprise. New technology and inventions were adopted as soon as they became feasible. <u>For example,</u> 21 Also, the circus was always ahead of everyone else in lighting equipment. When stores and business places were still using tallow dips for light, the circus was using calcium flares bright enough to blind you. The pressure gaslights used by circuses in the early part of this century were intensely brilliant by contrast with the lights of the average town.

Yes, the circus of today is bigger and better in every way than circuses of even twenty-five years ago. Youngsters today, however, aren't as wide-eyed and amazed at what they see at a circus 22 <u>than</u> they were twenty-five years ago. So many marvelous things go on all the time today that children probably expect more from a circus now than it's humanly possible to give.

21. Which of the following, when inserted to complete the sentence, would provide the strongest support for the main point of this paragraph?

A) in 1872, P.T. Barnum's circus began to travel by rail, enabling it to transport massive amounts of equipment, hundreds of animals, and larger tents with more seats.
B) in 1882, Al Ringling was performing as a juggler and acrobat when he and his four younger brothers joined together to form the Ringling Brothers circus, one of the most successful circuses ever.
C) in 1882, P.T. Barnum purchased the largest African elephant in captivity, Jumbo, which travelled with the circus until its death three years later.
D) in 1886, Adam Forepaugh entered the circus business, but his success ended twenty years later because he was notoriously greedy and corrupt.

22. A) NO CHANGE
B) then
C) as
D) when

Continue

Questions #23–33 are based on the following passage.

No Free Rein for Free Speech

[1]

[1] 23 <u>One of the group of amendments known as the Bill of Rights, under the First Amendment to the Constitution citizens are allowed</u> to disseminate and be exposed to a wide range of opinions and views. [2] It is intended to ensure a free exchange of ideas, even if the ideas exchanged are unpopular. [3] Freedom of speech encompasses not only the spoken and written word, but non-verbal communication, such as sit-ins, art, photographs, films, and advertisements. [4] Under the First Amendment's provisions, the 24 <u>media—including television, radio, and the web, are</u> free to distribute a wide range of news, facts, opinions, and pictures. [5] The amendment protects the 25 <u>speaker, it</u> also protects the person who receives the information. [6] The right to read, hear, see, and obtain different points of view is a First Amendment right as well.

[2]

[1] The right to free speech, however, is not absolute. The US Supreme Court has ruled that 26 <u>limited speech is something that the government may sometimes do</u>. [2] The government can ban libel (the communication of false statements about a person that may injure his or her reputation), obscenity, fighting words, and words that present a clear and present danger to the nation and its people.

23. A) NO CHANGE
    B) One of the group of amendments known as the Bill of Rights, citizens are allowed under the First Amendment to the Constitution
    C) The First Amendment to the Constitution, which is known as the Bill of Rights, allows citizens
    D) One of the group of amendments known as the Bill of Rights, the First Amendment to the Constitution allows citizens

24. A) NO CHANGE
    B) media—including television, radio, and the web are
    C) media—including television, radio, and the web—are
    D) media, including television, radio, and the web are

25. A) NO CHANGE
    B) speaker it
    C) speaker, and it
    D) speaker, who

26. A) NO CHANGE
    B) sometimes the government may do limited speech
    C) the government may sometimes limit speech
    D) sometimes limiting speech may be done by the government

Continue ➡

[3]

[1] In the case of *Schenck v. United States*, in a unanimous opinion written by Justice Oliver Wendell Holmes, Jr., the Supreme Court held that the First Amendment did not protect speech encouraging men to resist induction into the armed services during wartime. [2] The Court said that attempts made by speech or writing could be punished like other attempted crimes. [3] To justify **27** it's conclusion, the Court cited special circumstances: "when a nation is at war, many things that might be said in time of peace are such a hindrance to its effort that their utterance will not be endured so long as men fight." [4] In other words, the Court held, the circumstances of wartime **28** allowing greater restrictions on free speech than would be allowed during peacetime, if only because new and greater dangers are present. **29**

[4]

[1] The opinion's most famous and most often quoted passage of the decision is: "The most stringent protection of free speech would not protect a man in falsely shouting fire in a theatre and causing a panic." [2] The phrase "shouting fire in a crowded theater" has since become a **30** popular metaphor used often by many people for the dangers of free speech.

27. A) NO CHANGE
    B) its
    C) its'
    D) they're

28. A) NO CHANGE
    B) allow
    C) were allowing
    D) would be allowed

29. The case of *Schenck v. United States* is used by the author to illustrate which of the following exceptions to free speech mentioned in paragraph 3?

    A) Libel
    B) Obscenity
    C) Fighting words
    D) Words presenting a clear and present danger

30. A) NO CHANGE
    B) popular metaphor
    C) well-known metaphor used often by many
    D) widely accepted metaphor used often by many people

Continue

[5]

[1] In addition to restricting speech under exigent circumstances, the government also may regulate speech by limiting the time, place, or manner in which it is made. [2] 31 <u>Despite</u> some restrictions on its scope, the First Amendment protection of free speech is one of the broadest of any industrialized nation and plays 32 <u>an important and very critical</u> role in American government. 33

31. A) NO CHANGE
B) Because of
C) Including
D) In addition to

32. A) NO CHANGE
B) an important and critical
C) a very critical
D) a critical

33. The author is considering adding the following sentence to the essay:

For example, the government may require activists to obtain a permit before holding a large protest rally on a public street.

The most appropriate place for the sentence would be:

A) First paragraph, following sentence 2.
B) First paragraph, following sentence 3.
C) Third paragraph, following sentence 3.
D) Final paragraph, following sentence 1.

Continue

Questions #34–44 are based on the following passage.

Fueling the Natural Gas Campaign

[1]

There are good reasons for replacing coal with natural gas for electrical generation. The technology is very efficient, because it makes maximum use of the energy in the fuel through a two-step generating process that captures waste heat that would otherwise be lost. The new gas-fired plants were constructed in the 1990s and [34] subsequently after that date were built around the latest design of combustion turbines—a specialized form of the same kind of technology used in a jet engine.

[2]

[1] Gas plants can be built [35] relatively quick and cheap. [2] [36] It costs roughly half as much as a coal-fired plant and can be built in about two to three years from ground-breaking to operation. [3] This compares to about five to six years to build a coal plant. [4] The combined cycle technology of new gas plants is suitable for relatively small-scale and modular construction. [5] Plants can be economically built at unit sizes of about 100 megawatts, and larger projects can be constructed by adding units in a building block fashion over time. [6] [37] Coal plants, in contrast, are generally economical only at a unit size of several hundred megawatts.

34. A) NO CHANGE
    B) after that subsequent date
    C) subsequently
    D) subsequently and after that date

35. A) NO CHANGE
    B) relative quick and cheap
    C) relatively quickly, cheaply
    D) relatively quickly and cheaply

36. A) NO CHANGE
    B) It has cost
    C) They cost
    D) They were costing

37. What would be the most effective location for the underlined sentence in paragraph 2?

    A) Where it is now (NO CHANGE)
    B) After sentence 1
    C) After sentence 2
    D) After sentence 3

Continue ➤

[3]

Natural gas plants generally produce **38** less harmful environmental effects than coal-fired plants. Newer gas plants produce fewer air emissions than coal plants, in part because of the nature of the fuel and, in part, because of the greater efficiency of the technology. For example, natural gas, when burned, inherently emits about half as much carbon dioxide as coal. However, because combined-cycle plants are more efficient than typical existing coal plants in converting fuel into **39** electricity, the difference in emissions is greater when measured in terms of CO_2 released per megawatt-hour of electricity produced. By this measure, a modern combined-cycle gas plant emits only about 40% of the CO_2 per megawatt-hour as much as a typical existing coal **40** plant's.

[4]

From the 1990s into this century, gas-fired power plants have constituted the vast majority of new generating capacity built in the United States. ("Capacity" is a measure of the potential instantaneous electricity output from a power plant, usually measured in megawatts or kilowatts. "Generation" is the actual amount of electricity produced by the plant over a period of time, usually measured in megawatt-hours or kilowatt-hours.) Minimal new coal plant capacity was constructed, and **41** the growing of nuclear plant capacity was limited to upgrades to existing plants.

38. A) NO CHANGE
    B) lesser
    C) fewer
    D) the less

39. A) NO CHANGE
    B) electricity the
    C) electricity; the
    D) electricity. The

40. A) NO CHANGE
    B) plant does
    C) plant's emissions
    D) plant's emissions do

41. A) NO CHANGE
    B) growth of
    C) grown
    D) the growing

Continue

[5]

Right now, the United States has a large, underutilized base of advanced technology, gas-burning power plants. Although natural gas is the largest source of generating capacity, it trails far behind coal as a source of actual electricity generation. In 2007, coal accounted for 49% of all electricity produced, compared to 21% for natural gas, 20% for nuclear power, and 6% for hydroelectric generation. **42** **43** **44**

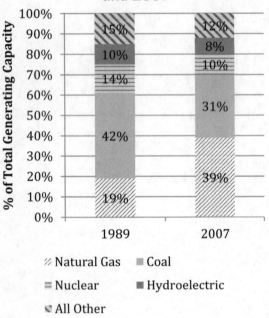

Shares of Total Generating Capacity by Energy Source, 1989 and 2007

42. Which of the following sentences, when added as the last sentence of the essay, would best summarize the author's argument?

A) There are many unused natural gas plants that could produce electricity while reducing the construction and environmental costs of coal-powered plants.
B) Thus, the amount of electricity produced by gas can be greatly increased with existing capacity, achieving considerable cost savings and reducing adverse environmental effects.
C) As a consequence, coal is an important fuel for generating electricity and could become even more important in the future if it is possible to reduce its environmental impact.
D) Accordingly, the government should act to require a shift away from coal with its cost and harmful effects on the environment to gas, nuclear power, and other energy sources.

43. According to the graph, which type of generating plant accounted for the greatest percent of total generating capacity in 1989?

A) Natural Gas
B) Coal
C) Nuclear
D) All Other

Continue

44. The author is thinking of referring to the graph to support the claim that in 2007 plants powered by natural gas produced more electricity that those powered by coal. Does the data in the graph support this claim?

A) Yes, because the bar for 2007 clearly shows that natural gas powered plants accounted for 39% of electricity produced while coal powered plants accounted for only 31%.

B) Yes, because the bar showing electricity produced by coal is approximately 70% while the bar for natural gas is less than 40%.

C) No, because the bar provides data for electricity generated by nuclear power, hydroelectric power, and other forms of power in addition to coal and natural gas.

D) No, because the graph provides information about the capacity of electrical generating plants using various sources of power, not about electricity generated.

STOP
**IF YOU FINISH BEFORE TIME IS CALLED, YOU MAY CHECK YOUR WORK ON THIS
SECTION ONLY. DO NOT TURN TO ANY OTHER SECTION IN THE TEST.**

SECTION 3—MATH, NO CALCULATOR

Time—25 minutes

20 items

DIRECTIONS: For #1–15, solve each item and choose the correct answer choice. Then fill in the corresponding bubble on your answer sheet. For #16–20, solve each item and enter your answer in the grid on the answer sheet. Refer to the directions before #16 on how to enter your answers for these items. Use any available space for scratchwork. Answers are on page 272.

Notes:

(1) All expressions and equations represent real numbers unless otherwise indicated.

(2) Figures that accompany problems in this test are intended to provide information useful in solving the problems. They are drawn as accurately as possible EXCEPT when it is stated in a specific problem that the figure is not drawn to scale. All figures lie in a plane unless otherwise indicated.

(3) The domain of a given function f is the set of all real numbers x for which $f(x)$ is a real number unless otherwise indicated.

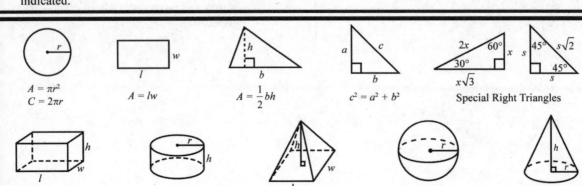

$A = \pi r^2$
$C = 2\pi r$

$A = lw$

$A = \frac{1}{2}bh$

$c^2 = a^2 + b^2$

Special Right Triangles

$V = lwh$

$V = \pi r^2 h$

$V = \frac{1}{3}lwh$

$V = \frac{4}{3}\pi r^3$

$V = \frac{1}{3}\pi r^2 h$

The number of degrees of arc in a circle is 360.

The sum of the measures in degrees of the angles of a triangle is 180.

The number of radians of arc in a circle is 2π.

---

1. Which of the following expressions is the same as "3 less than the product of 4 and x"?

   A) $4x - 3$
   B) $3x - 4$
   C) $4(x - 3)$
   D) $3 - 4x$

2. $\dfrac{10^3 \left(10^5 + 10^5\right)}{10^4} = ?$

   A) $2\left(10^2\right)$
   B) $2\left(10^4\right)$
   C) 10^6
   D) $2\left(10^9\right)$

Continue ▶

3. If $x^3 > x^2$, then which of the following could be the value of x?

A) $-\dfrac{1}{2}$

B) $\dfrac{1}{2}$

C) 1

D) $\dfrac{3}{2}$

4. The sum of three consecutive even integers is 156.

If n is the least of the three integers, which of the following equations represents the information given in the statement above?

A) $3n + 6 = 156$
B) $3n + 4 = 156$
C) $3n + 3 = 156$
D) $3n + 2 = 156$

$$(-3x^2 y - xy^2 + 2xy) - (-3xy + 2x^2 y - 5xy^2)$$

5. Which of the following is equivalent to the expression above?

A) $xy(5 - y)$
B) $xy(x - 6y - 1)$
C) $xy(-5x + 4y + 5)$
D) $x^2 y(7 - 3y^2)$

6. At the Speed Shuttle Company, the possible starting salary, s, in dollars, for new bus drivers is represented by the inequality $|s - 28{,}600| \le 3{,}500$. Which of the following is NOT true?

A) The maximum starting salary is $32,100.
B) The minimum starting salary is $28,600.
C) The average possible starting salary is $28,600.
D) The range in starting salaries is as much as $7,000.

$$f(x) = x(2x + 3)(x - 1)(x^2 - 1)$$

7. The graph of the equation above has how many distinct zeros?

A) One
B) Two
C) Three
D) Four

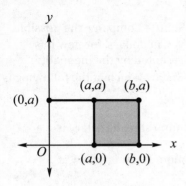

8. In the figure above, what is the area of the shaded portion, expressed in terms of a and b?

A) $a(b-a)$

B) $a(a-b)$

C) $b(a-b)$

D) $b(b-a)$

9. Which of the following is the solution set for the equation $\dfrac{6}{(x+3)(x-3)} = \dfrac{1}{x-3} + \dfrac{1}{x+3}$?

A) {}

B) {6,1}

C) {3}

D) {−3,3}

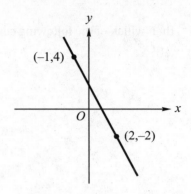

10. The graph above represents which of the following equations?

A) $y = -\dfrac{3}{2}x - 2$

B) $y = -2x + 2$

C) $y = \dfrac{2}{3}x + 3$

D) $y = x + 2$

11. The relation defined by the set of ordered pairs {(0,3), (2,1), (3,0), (−1,2), (0,5), and (−2,5)} is NOT a function. Eliminating which of the following ordered pairs will result in a set of ordered pairs that is a function?

A) (−1,2)

B) (0,3)

C) (2,1)

D) (3,0)

Continue

12. Which of the following correctly shows the graph of $y = \left| x^2 - 3 \right|$?

A)

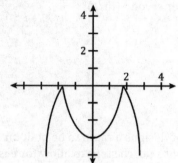

B)

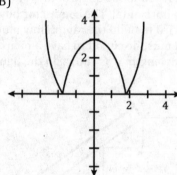

C)

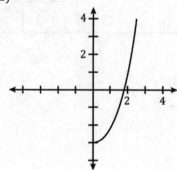

D)

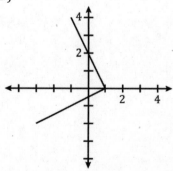

Questions #13–14 refer to the following information.

The kinetic energy, *KE*, of an object traveling at velocity *v* is modeled by the equation $KE = \frac{1}{2}mv^2$, where *m* is the mass of the object.

13. Which of the following graphs best represents the relationship between the kinetic energy of an object and its velocity?

A)

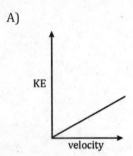

B)

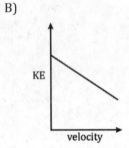

C)

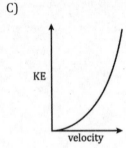

D)

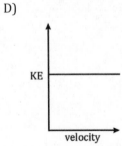

14. If an object has a mass of 2,000 grams and a kinetic energy of 120 joules (1 J = $1\ \dfrac{kg \cdot m^2}{s^2}$), what is the velocity of the object, in meters per second (m/s)?

A) $8\sqrt{5}$

B) $4\sqrt{10}$

C) $2\sqrt{30}$

D) 1

15. A contractor designs a ramp to be built on top of a client's porch steps to allow for easy access with a wheelbarrow. The height of the top step is 6 feet and the angle of the ramp is 35° with the horizontal. The contractor buys a 12-foot board to build the ramp. How much of the board must he cut off to have a board of the correct length, *x*, as shown in the figure below?

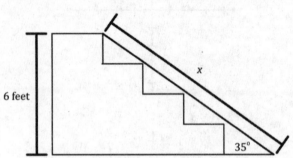

A) $12(\sin 35°)$

B) $12 - \dfrac{\sin 35°}{6}$

C) $12 - 6\sin 35°$

D) $12 - \dfrac{6}{\sin 35°}$

Continue

DIRECTIONS: For #16–20, solve each item and mark your answer on a special answer grid.

1. For each item, you should write your answer in the boxes at the top of each column and then fill in the ovals beneath each part of the answer you write.
2. Mark no more than one oval in any column.
3. Questions do not have negative answers.
4. Some problems have more than one possible answer. Grid only one answer.
5. See the first example below to grid mixed numbers.
6. See the last example below to grid decimal answers with more digits than the grid can accommodate.

Here are some examples:

Answer: 7/2 or 3.5	Answer: 325	Answer: 1/6, .166, or .167

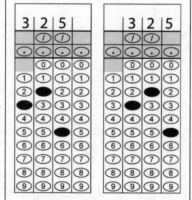

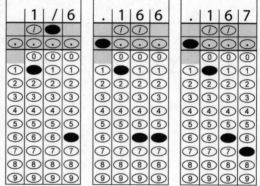

NOTE: A mixed number such as $3\frac{1}{2}$ must be gridded as 7/2 or as 3.5. If gridded as "31/2," it will be read as "thirty-one halves."

NOTE: Either position is correct.

NOTE: A decimal answer with more digits than the grid can accommodate must be truncated. A decimal such as $0.16\overline{6}$ must be gridded as .166 or .167. A less accurate value such as .16 or .17 will be scored as incorrect.

16. If $\frac{3}{4}$ of x is 36, what is the value of $\frac{1}{3}$ of x?

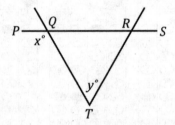

17. In the figure above, $\overline{QT} = \overline{QR}$. If $x = 120$, then $y = ?$

18. If $x < 0$, $y < 0$, $|x - 2| = 6$, and $|y + 8| = 10$, what is the value of $x - y$?

19. What is the value of $3i^4 + 2i^2 + 10$? (Note: $i = \sqrt{-1}$)

$$k(x) = \frac{2}{(x+2)^2 - \dfrac{x+2}{2} - 3}$$

20. Let m and n represent the values of x for which the function k above is undefined. What is the value of $m - n$?

Continue ▶

SECTION 4

SECTION 4—MATH, CALCULATOR

Time—55 minutes

38 items

DIRECTIONS: For #1–30, solve each item and choose the correct answer choice. Then fill in the corresponding bubble on your answer sheet. For #31–38, solve each item and enter your answer in the grid on the answer sheet. Refer to the directions before #31 on how to enter your answers for these items. Use any available space for scratchwork. Answers are on page 273.

Notes:

(1) All expressions and equations represent real numbers unless otherwise indicated.

(2) Figures that accompany problems in this test are intended to provide information useful in solving the problems. They are drawn as accurately as possible EXCEPT when it is stated in a specific problem that the figure is not drawn to scale. All figures lie in a plane unless otherwise indicated.

(3) The domain of a given function f is the set of all real numbers x for which $f(x)$ is a real number unless otherwise indicated.

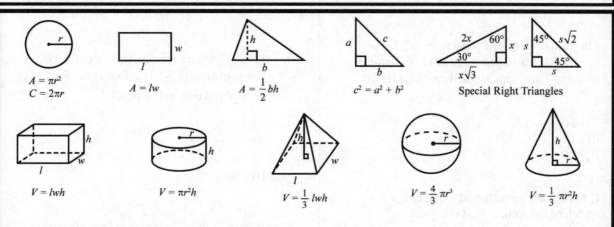

$A = \pi r^2$
$C = 2\pi r$

$A = lw$

$A = \frac{1}{2}bh$

$c^2 = a^2 + b^2$

Special Right Triangles

$V = lwh$

$V = \pi r^2 h$

$V = \frac{1}{3}lwh$

$V = \frac{4}{3}\pi r^3$

$V = \frac{1}{3}\pi r^2 h$

The number of degrees of arc in a circle is 360.

The sum of the measures in degrees of the angles of a triangle is 180.

The number of radians of arc in a circle is 2π.

1. If n is a multiple of 3, which of the following is also a multiple of 3?

   A) $2+n$
   B) $2-n$
   C) $2n+1$
   D) $2n+3$

2. A certain mixture of gravel and sand consists of 2.5 kilograms of gravel and 12.5 kilograms of sand. What percent of the mixture, by weight, is gravel?

   A) 10%
   B) $16\frac{2}{3}\%$
   C) 25%
   D) $33\frac{1}{3}\%$

3. The sum of Tom and Herb's age is 22. The sum of Herb and Bob's age is 17. The sum of Bob and Tom's age is 15. How old is Herb?

   A) 7
   B) 10
   C) 12
   D) 15

4. If x and y are negative integers, and $x > y$, which of the following is the greatest?

   A) $-(xy)^2$
   B) xy
   C) x^2y
   D) $x+y$

5. To mail a letter costs x cents for the first ounce and y cents for every additional ounce. Which of the following equations can be used to determine the cost, C, in cents to mail a letter that weighs w ounces?

   A) $C = x + y(w-1)$
   B) $C = x(w-y)$
   C) $C = x(w-1) + y(w-1)$
   D) $C = x + wy$

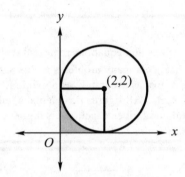

6. In the figure above, the center of the circle has coordinates $(2,2)$. What is the area of the shaded portion of the figure?

   A) $2-\pi$
   B) $4-\pi$
   C) $8-2\pi$
   D) $8-\pi$

7. If $2^x = 16$ and $x = \frac{y}{2}$, then $y = ?$

   A) 8
   B) 6
   C) 4
   D) 3

Continue

8. If $12 + x = 36 - y$, then $x + y = ?$

A) -48
B) -24
C) 24
D) 48

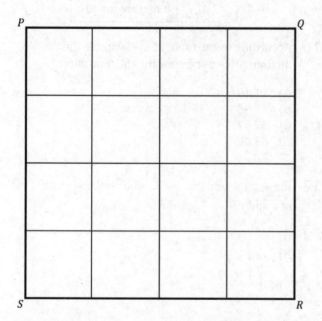

9. Two security guards, Jane and Ed, patrol the perimeter of a square fenced area *PQRS* shown in the map above, with side lengths of 400 yards. Starting at corner *P* at 8:00 p.m., Jane walks around the fence in a clockwise direction while Ed walks around the fence in a counterclockwise direction. If it takes exactly 10 minutes for each guard to walk from one corner to the next, how far apart, along the perimeter of the fence, are the two guards at 11:30 p.m.?

A) 0 yards
B) 200 yards
C) 400 yards
D) 800 yards

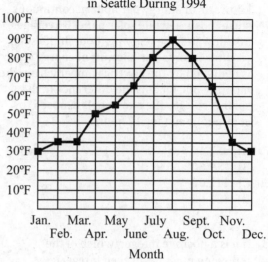

Average Noon Temperatures in Seattle During 1994

10. The above graph depicts the average monthly noon temperatures in Seattle during 1994. Which of the following is true of the temperatures?

 I. The average (arithmetic mean) is greater than 50°F.
 II. The median is greater than 50°F.
 III. The mode is greater than 50°F.

A) I only
B) II only
C) I and II only
D) I, II, and III

11. If $x^2 - y^2 = 3$ and $x - y = 3$, then $x + y = ?$

A) 1
B) 2
C) 3
D) 9

Continue

12. Solar panel A stores an average of 40 kilowatts of energy per hour of continuous sun exposure, while solar panel B averages 50 kilowatts of energy per hour. If the solar credit is 2 cents per kilowatt of energy stored is deducted by the electric company from the monthly bill, what is the difference in the solar credit for the two panels exposed to continuous sun for 12 hours?

A) $2.40
B) $9.60
C) $12.00
D) $21.60

13. If n is a positive integer, which of the following must be an even integer?

A) $3n+1$
B) $3n+2$
C) n^2+1
D) n^2+n

1 mil = 0.001 inch

1 inch = 2.54 centimeters

14. A sheet of plastic is 2 mils thick. Based on the information given above, approximately how thick is the sheet of plastic in centimeters?

A)　　0.005
B)　　0.05
C)　　500
D) 5,000

15. In a certain group of 36 people, 18 people have hats and 24 people have sweaters. If 6 people have neither hats nor sweater, how many people have both hats and sweaters?

A) 30
B) 24
C) 12
D) 8

WIRE	COST
A	2 meters for $6
B	4 meters for $10
C	5 meters for $7
D	8 meters for $10

16. According to the table above, what is the median price per meter for the four wires?

A) $1.40
B) $1.95
C) $2.97
D) $3.00

17. If $x=b+4$ and $y=b-3$, what is b in terms of x and y?

A) $x+y-1$
B) $x+y+1$
C) $\dfrac{x+y+1}{2}$
D) $\dfrac{x+y-1}{2}$

18. If $\Delta(x)=x+1$ and $\nabla(x)=x-1$, then which of the following is equal to $\Delta(3)\cdot\nabla(5)$?

A) $\Delta(12)$
B) $\Delta(14)$
C) $\nabla(17)$
D) $\nabla(20)$

19. $|-3|\cdot|2|\cdot\left|\dfrac{1}{2}\right|+(-4)=?$

A) −1
B) 0
C) 1
D) 4

Continue

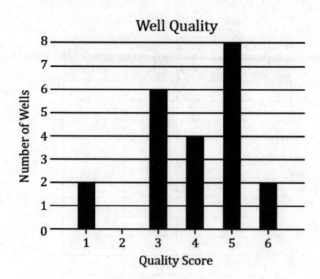

Well Quality

20. A recent survey of a city's municipal water wells rated the water quality of the 22 wells on a six-point scale, with 6 representing the best water quality and 1 representing the poorest water quality. The 22 water well quality reports are summarized in the histogram above. If the city plans on opening three additional wells, the average water quality of the three of the new wells must be at least which value in order for the average water quality of all 25 wells to be at least 4?

A) 2
B) 3
C) 4
D) 5

21. What are the values for which $\dfrac{x(x+3)}{(x-1)(x+2)}$ is undefined?

A) −2 only
B) 1 only
C) −2 and 1 only
D) −3, −2, and 1

22. The product flow through a manufacturing facility is modeled by the solution set of two inequalities in the coordinate plane, as shown by the shaded region in the figure below.

Which of the following system of inequalities model the product flow?

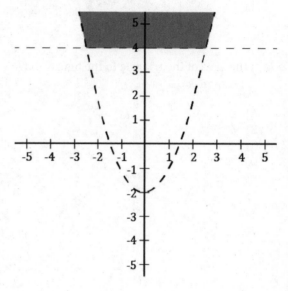

A) $y<4$ and $y>x^2+2$
B) $x>4$ and $y>x^2-2$
C) $y<4$ and $y<x^2-2$
D) $y>4$ and $y>x^2-2$

Continue

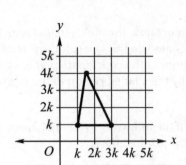

23. If the area of the triangle in the figure above is 12, then $k = ?$

A) 1
B) 2
C) 3
D) 4

DROP HEIGHT (FEET)	DROP TIME (SECONDS)
2	0.7
4	0.8
6	1.0
8	1.3
10	1.5
12	1.6
14	1.7
16	1.8
18	1.9
20	2.0

24. A student uses a very tall vacuum tube with near-zero air resistance attached to a dispenser that releases small metal balls of equal mass from heights that increase by two feet with each trial. The time required for each ball to fall through the vacuum tube to ground level is recorded and shown in the table above. Which of the following graphs best represents the relationship between the height from which the ball is dropped and the time it takes to reach ground level?

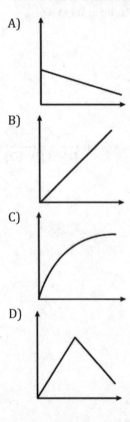

A)

B)

C)

D)

Continue

25. The figure above shows nine tiles with single-digit numbers painted on them. If *xy* is the product of the value of any two tiles selected at random, what is the probability of $xy = 0$?

A) $\dfrac{5}{6}$

B) $\dfrac{5}{7}$

C) $\dfrac{1}{6}$

D) $\dfrac{1}{7}$

26. A sourdough bread recipe calls for dry ingredients comprised of 2 cups of flour, 3 teaspoons of sugar, and $2\dfrac{1}{4}$ teaspoons of salt to be added to the starter sponge. After thoroughly mixing the ingredients, a baker realizes that she accidentally added 3 cups of flour to the dry ingredients instead of 2 cups. To correct her error, she removes $\dfrac{1}{3}$ of the dry ingredients. Approximately how much sugar and salt, respectively, must be added to the dry ingredients to maintain the correct ratio of flour to sugar to salt in the final mix of dry ingredients to be added to the starter sponge?

A) $\dfrac{1}{3}$ teaspoon sugar and $\dfrac{9}{4}$ teaspoon salt

B) 1 teaspoon sugar and $\dfrac{3}{4}$ teaspoon salt

C) 1 teaspoon sugar and $\dfrac{1}{6}$ teaspoon salt

D) $\dfrac{9}{4}$ teaspoon sugar and 1 teaspoon salt

27. Which graph below represents the solution set for the equation $y = 3(x + 2)$?

A)

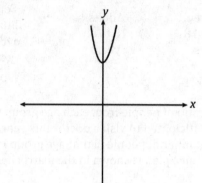

B)

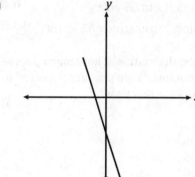

C)

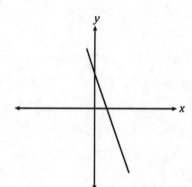

D)

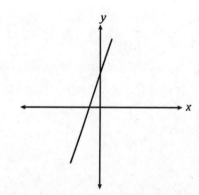

Continue

28. The number of patients belonging to a group insurance plan is shown in the matrix below:

Children, under 18 years	Adults, 18 to 65 years	Senior Citizens, over 65 years
125	75	150

The ratio of people from each age group who are anticipated to visit a doctor this year to the number of people in that age group in the insurance plan is shown in the matrix below:

Children, under 18 years	$\begin{bmatrix} 0.60 \\ 0.40 \\ 0.90 \end{bmatrix}$
Adults, 18 to 65 years	
Senior Citizens, over 65 years	

Based on the matrices, how many people in the group insurance plan are expected to visit a doctor this year?

A)   75
B)   105
C)   135
D)   240

SCHOOL MEAL PRICES

	Breakfast	Lunch	Milk
Elementary School	$1.00	$2.10	$0.50
Middle School	$1.25	$2.60	$0.50
High School	$1.50	$3.00	$0.50

29. A family has three children: one in elementary school, one in middle school, and one in high school. This year, the family buys breakfasts, lunches, and milks for each child. Each child eats a school lunch twice as often as breakfast and milk with every breakfast and lunch. If x is the number of breakfasts, then which of the following expresses the total cost, in dollars, for the children's school meals this year?

A) $23.65x$
B) $20.90x$
C) $18.92x$
D) $9.73x$

30. If the area of a square inscribed in a circle is 16 cm^2, what is the probability that a dart will land outside of the square but inside of the circle?

A) $8(\pi - 2)$

B) $1 + \dfrac{\pi}{2}$

C) $\dfrac{\pi}{2}$

D) $1 - \dfrac{2}{\pi}$

Continue

DIRECTIONS: For #31–38, solve each item and mark your answer on a special answer grid.

1. For each item, you should write your answer in the boxes at the top of each column and then fill in the ovals beneath each part of the answer you write.
2. Mark no more than one oval in any column.
3. Questions do not have negative answers.
4. Some problems have more than one possible answer. Grid only one answer.
5. See the first example below to grid mixed numbers.
6. See the last example below to grid decimal answers with more digits than the grid can accommodate.

Here are some examples:

Answer: 7/2 or 3.5

Answer: 325

Answer: 1/6, .166, or .167

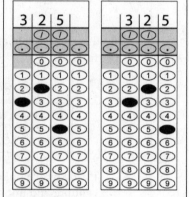

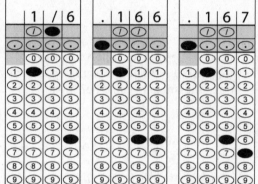

NOTE: A mixed number such as $3\frac{1}{2}$ must be gridded as 7/2 or as 3.5. If gridded as "31/2," it will be read as "thirty-one halves."

NOTE: Either position is correct.

NOTE: A decimal answer with more digits than the grid can accommodate must be truncated. A decimal such as $0.16\overline{6}$ must be gridded as .166 or .167. A less accurate value such as .16 or .17 will be scored as incorrect.

Continue

31. In a certain country, $\frac{2}{5}$ of the population has blue eyes. How many people would you have to look at to be sure that you have at least 50 with blue eyes, assuming that your sample has blue-eyed people in the same ratio as the general population?

32. The average of seven different positive integers is 12. What is the greatest that any one of the integers could be?

33. In Company A, 50 percent of the employees are women. In Company B, 40 percent of the employees are women. If Company A has 800 employees, and Company B has half that number, how many more women are employed at Company A than at Company B?

34. The contents of an aquarium habitat are as follows:

Spotted snakes	4
Striped snakes	6
Unmarked snakes	10

If snakes are pulled out of the aquarium at random and not replaced, what is the minimum number of snakes that must be pulled out to guarantee that two of every type snake have been selected?

Continue

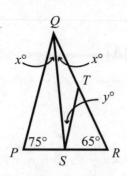

Note: Figure not drawn to scale.

35. In $\triangle PQR$ above, if $\overline{PQ} \parallel \overline{ST}$, then $y = ?$

ESTIMATED TIME OF CLEANING		
Room	Number	Time per Room
Bedroom	4	20 minutes
Bathroom	2	30 minutes
Kitchen	1	t minutes
Living Area	4	25 minutes
Garage	1	75 minutes

36. The table above shows the estimated time by area needed to clean a house. If the entire house takes 6 hours to clean, how many minutes does it take to clean the kitchen?

$$m = \frac{\$400,000}{(0.8)(\$500,000)} L - \$2,000 \text{, where } L \leq \$400,000$$

$$n = \frac{\$350,000}{(0.8)\$500,000} L - \$1,000 \text{, where } L \leq \$350,000$$

37. K'Nya is comparing property insurance quotes for her home, which has a value of $500,000. The first quote has a policy limit of $400,000 and a $2,000 deductible. The second quote has a policy limit of $350,000 and a $1,000 deductible. If K'Nya's property were damaged and the loss L were determined to be $150,000, what would be the difference in the two payouts, m and n, in dollars?

38. If the y-intercept of a line is -10 and it passes through the point $(3, -4)$, what is the x-intercept of the line?

STOP
IF YOU FINISH BEFORE TIME IS CALLED, YOU MAY CHECK YOUR WORK ON THIS SECTION ONLY. DO NOT TURN TO ANY OTHER SECTION IN THE TEST.

SECTION 5—ESSAY (OPTIONAL)

Time—50 minutes

1 essay prompt

DIRECTIONS: The essay measures your ability to read and understand a passage and write an essay that analyzes the passage. In your essay, demonstrate that you have carefully read the passage, write a clear and logical analysis, and use language precisely.

You have 50 minutes to read the passage and write an essay in response to the provided prompt. Sample essays are on page 296.

Read the passage below and think about how Roosevelt uses

- evidence (facts, examples, etc.) to support claims.
- reasoning to develop the passage and to connect claims and evidence.
- rhetorical or persuasive elements, such as language choices or emotional appeals, to increase the impact of the ideas expressed.

Adapted from 26th US President Theodore Roosevelt's speech, "Conservation as a National Duty," given in 1908 to the Conference of Governors.

1 Every step of the progress of mankind is marked by the discovery and use of natural resources previously unused. Without such progressive knowledge and utilization of natural resources, population could not grow, nor industries multiply, nor the hidden wealth of the earth be developed for the benefit of mankind.

2 From the beginnings of civilization, on the banks of the Nile and the Euphrates, the industrial progress of the world has gone on slowly. But of late the rapidity of the process has increased at such a rate that more space has been actually covered during the century and a quarter occupied by our national life than during the preceding six thousand years.

3 When this country was founded, coal was known only as a useless black stone. Water was practically the only source of power, and this power was used only in the most primitive fashion. Wood was practically the only fuel, and forests were regarded as obstructions to settlement and cultivation.

4 Since then our knowledge and use of the resources have increased a hundred-fold. Indeed, the growth of this Nation by leaps and bounds makes one of the most striking and important chapters in the history of the world. Its growth has been due to the rapid development, and alas that it should be said, to the rapid destruction, of our natural resources.

5 The Constitution of the United States grew in large part out of the necessity for united action in the wise use of our natural resources. The enormous consumption of these resources, and the threat of imminent exhaustion of some of them, due to reckless and wasteful use, once more calls for common effort, common action.

6 The mere increase in our consumption of coal during 1907 over 1906 exceeded the total consumption in 1876, the Centennial year. This is a striking fact: Thirty years went by, and the mere surplus of use of one year

over the preceding year exceeded all that was used in 1876—and we thought we were pretty busy people even then.

7   The time has come to inquire seriously what will happen when our forests are gone, when the coal, the iron, the oil, and the gas are exhausted, when the soils shall be further impoverished and washed into the streams, polluting the rivers. These questions do not relate only to the next century or to the next generation. We should exercise foresight now, as the ordinarily prudent man exercises foresight in conserving and wisely using the property which contains the assurance of well-being for himself and his children.

8   The natural resources I have enumerated can be divided into two distinguished classes accordingly as they are or are not capable of renewal. The minerals do not and cannot renew themselves. Therefore in dealing with the coal, the oil, the gas, the iron, the metals, all that we can do is to try to see that they are wisely used. The exhaustion is certain to come in time.

9   The second class of resources consists of those which can not only be used in such manner as to leave them undiminished for our children, but can be improved by wise use. The soil, the forests, the waterways come in this category. In dealing with the soil and its products man can improve on nature by compelling the resources to renew and reconstruct themselves.

10 We are coming to recognize as never before the right of the Nation to guard its own future in the essential matter of natural resources. As a people we have the right and the duty to protect ourselves and our children against the wasteful development of our natural resources.

11 Finally, let us remember that the conservation of our natural resources, though the gravest problem of today, is but part of another and greater problem to which this Nation is not yet awake, but to which it will awake in time, and with which it must hereafter grapple if it is to live—the problem of national efficiency, the patriotic duty of insuring the safety and continuance of the Nation. When the People of the United States consciously undertake to raise themselves as citizens to the highest pitch of excellence in private, State, and national life, and to do this because it is the first of all the duties of true patriotism, then and not till then the future of this Nation, will be assured.

Write an essay explaining how Theodore Roosevelt develops his argument that the United States must prioritize the conservation of natural resources. In your essay, analyze how Roosevelt uses one or more of the elements listed before the passage (or other elements) to make his argument more logical and persuasive. Be sure to focus on the most relevant aspects of the passage.

Your essay should not discuss whether you agree with Roosevelt's claims but rather discuss how he develops his argument.

15SATD

Practice Test III

Outline

I. **Section 1:** Reading (pp. 163–178)

II. **Section 2:** Writing and Language (pp. 179–192)

III. **Section 3:** Math, No Calculator (pp. 193–198)

IV. **Section 4:** Math, Calculator (pp. 199–210)

V. **Section 5:** Essay (Optional) (pp. 211–212)

DIRECTIONS

Practice Test III includes five test sections: Reading, Writing and Language, Math, No Calculator, Math, Calculator, and the optional Essay.. Calculator use is permitted on the Math, Calculator section only.

Cambridge offers several services for schools utilizing our practice tests. Ask your teacher whether your school has decided to send your answers to Cambridge for scoring or to score your answers at your school. If Cambridge is scoring your test, you will use a Scantron™ form provided by your teacher, or you will enter your answers online. If your school is scoring your test, you may use a Scantron™ form provided by your teacher, or you may write your answers on paper.

If you are entering your test answers on a Scantron™ form, please be sure to include the following information on the Scantron™:

Book and edition	*The Practice Book, 13th Edition*
Practice Test Form Code	**15SATD**

If you are only completing a single section of this practice test, make sure to also include the following information:

Subject	**Reading, Writing and Language, or Math**
Section Number	**Section 1, 2, 3 or 4**

The items in each test section are numbered and the multiple-choice answers are lettered. The Scantron™ form has numbered rows that correspond to the items on the test. Each row contains lettered ovals to match the answer choices for each item on the test. Each numbered row has a corresponding item on the test.

For each multiple-choice item, first decide on the best answer choice. Then, locate the row number that corresponds to the item. Next, find the oval in that row that matches the letter of the chosen answer. Then, use a soft lead pencil to fill in the oval. DO NOT use a ballpoint pen. For each student-produced response item on the math test sections, decide on the correct answer. Then, locate the SPR grid that corresponds to the item. Write your answer in the top of the grid and use a soft lead pencil to fill in each corresponding oval. DO NOT use a ballpoint pen.

Mark only one answer for each item. If you change your mind about an answer choice, thoroughly erase your first mark before marking your new answer.

Note that only responses marked on your Scantron™ form or written on your paper will be scored. Your score on each test will be based only on the number of items that are correctly answered during the time allowed for that test. You will not be penalized for guessing. Therefore, it is in your best interest to answer every item on the test, even if you must guess.

On the Essay, write your response to the prompt using the essay response sheets or loose-leaf paper provided by your teacher. (Note that the Writing Test is optional.)

You may work on each test only during the time allowed for that test. If you finish a test before time is called, use the time to review your answer choices or work on items about which you are uncertain. You may not return to a test on which time has already been called, and you may not preview another test. You must lay down your pencil immediately when time is called at the end of each test. You may not for any reason fill in or alter ovals for a test after time has expired for that test. Violation of these rules will result in immediate disqualification from the exam.

SECTION 1—READING

Time—65 minutes

52 items

> **DIRECTIONS:** Each passage or pair of passages is followed by a set of items. Choose the best answer to each question based on what is stated or implied in the passage or passages and in any accompanying graphics. Answers are on page 299.

Questions #1–10 are based on the following passage.

The following passage is from Caroline M.S. Kirkland's The Schoolmaster's Progress, *originally published in 1844.*

Master William Horner came to our village to the school when he was about eighteen years old: tall, lanky, straight-sided, and straight-haired, with a mouth of the most puckered and solemn kind.
5 His figure and movements were those of a puppet cut out of shingle and jerked by a string; and his address corresponded very well with his appearance, a prim mouth never giving way before a laugh.

10   Truly he had a grave time that first winter. The rod of power was new to him, and he felt it his "duty" to use it more frequently than might have been thought necessary by those upon whose sense the privilege had palled. Tears and sulky
15 faces, and impotent fists doubled fiercely when his back was turned, were the rewards of his conscientiousness.

    Let it not be supposed that Master Horner was of a cruel and ogrish nature. Such souls there
20 may be, among those endowed with the awful control of the ferule*, but they are rare in the fresh and natural regions we describe. It is, we believe, where young gentlemen are to be crammed for college, that the process of hardening heart and
25 skin together goes on most vigorously. He was sadly brow-beaten during his first term of service by a great broad-shouldered lout of some eighteen years, who thought he needed a little more "schooling," but at the same time felt quite
30 competent to direct the manner and measure of his attempts.

    "You'd ought to begin with large-hand, Joshua," said Master Horner to this youth.

    "What should I want coarse-hand for?" said
35 the disciple, with great contempt; "coarse-hand won't never do me no good. I want a fine-hand copy."

    The master looked at the infant giant and did as he wished.

40   At another time, Master Horner, having had a hint from someone more knowing than himself, proposed to his elder scholar to write after dictation, expatiating at the same time quite floridly (the ideas having been supplied by the
45 knowing friend), upon the advantages likely to arise from this practice, and saying, among other things,

    "It will help you, when you write letters, to spell the words good."

50   "Pooh!" said Joshua, "spellin' ain't nothin'; let them that finds the mistakes correct 'em. I'm for everyone's havin' a way of their own."

    "How dared you be so saucy to the master?" asked one of the little boys, after school.

55   "Because I could lick him, easy," said the hopeful Joshua, who knew very well why the master did not undertake him on the spot.

    Can we wonder that Master Horner determined to make his empire good as far as it
60 went? In any case, the students were glad when working time came round again, and the master went home to help his father on the farm.

    Among the uneducated there is so high a respect for bodily strength, that it is necessary for
65 the schoolmaster to show, first of all, that he possesses this inadmissible requisite for his place.

Continue →

The rest is more readily taken for granted. Brains he *may* have—a strong arm he *must* have: so he proves the more important claim first. We must
70 therefore make all due allowance for Master Horner, who could not be expected to overtop his position so far as to discern at once the philosophy of teaching.

The following autumn Master Horner came
75 again, dropping among us as quietly as the faded leaves, and awakening at least as much serious reflection. Would he be as self-sacrificing as before, postponing his own ease and comfort to the public good, or would he have become more
80 sedentary, and less fond of circumambulating the school-room with a switch over his shoulder? But here he was, and all the broader-chested and stouter-armed for his labors in the harvest-field. Our schoolmaster entered upon his second term
85 with new courage and invigorated authority. Even Joshua was civil.

*A ferule is a ruler used to administer punishment for minor infractions.

1. The author describes Master Horner's demeanor during his first term as

   A) very understanding and usually sympathetic.
   B) relentlessly severe and very stern.
   C) generally serious but occasionally jovial.
   D) eternally vigilant but always fair-minded.

2. Which of the following phrases from the first paragraph provides the best support for the correct answer to the preceding question?

   A) Line 2 (about eighteen years old)
   B) Line 3 (tall, lank, straight-sided, and straight-haired)
   C) Line 6 (cut out of shingle and jerked by a string)
   D) Lines 8–9 (a prim mouth never giving way before a laugh)

3. In context, *address* (line 7) means

   A) location of residence.
   B) manner of speaking.
   C) oration given in public.
   D) style of clothing.

4. The author uses the word *rewards* (line 16) to express

   A) irony because the students disliked Master Horner's conscientiousness.
   B) regret that Master Horner found it necessary to discipline students.
   C) surprise that Master Horner used the rod to corporally discipline students.
   D) enthusiasm for the style of teaching brought to the school by Master Horner.

5. The author theorizes about teachers at college preparatory schools (lines 21–25) in order to

   A) support the claim that Master Horner's background did not make him unusually cruel.
   B) justify the behavior of teachers who teach at schools that prepare students for higher education.
   C) familiarize the reader with the required procedures for entering the teaching profession.
   D) highlight the advantages of a summer spent doing physical labor in the outdoors.

6. The author uses the phrase *infant giant* (line 38) to express that

   A) Master Horner and Joshua are the same age, 18 years old.
   B) Joshua is physically developed but mentally immature.
   C) a teacher is in a position of authority over the students.
   D) Joshua is one of the more accomplished students in the class.

Continue ➤

7. Which of the following best explains the change in Joshua's behavior from the first term to the second?

A) Master Horner completed his college studies, thus acquiring additional authority.
B) Master Horner was physically stronger when he returned to teach in the second term.
C) Joshua's classmates cautioned him against challenging the authority of the teacher.
D) Both Joshua and Master Horner were a year older and therefore more mature.

8. The attitude of the author toward Master Horner's shortcomings as a teacher can best be described as

A) insensitive.
B) condescending.
C) understanding.
D) approving.

9. The author states that a teacher is most likely to impress people who are not well educated by a

A) confident method of speaking.
B) show of physical strength.
C) friendly, engaging personality.
D) threatening physical posture.

10. If the story were continued, the author would most likely describe

A) how the children in the school grew up, graduated, and went out into the world.
B) the ways in which Master Horner matured as a teacher and his effect on students.
C) Master Horner's relationship with his father and his summers on the family farm.
D) efforts by the community to replace Master Horner, who was considered unreasonably strict.

Continue ➤

Questions #11–21 are based on the following passages.

The following passages discuss the migratory habits and population trends of monarch butterflies in two regions.

Passage 1

The familiar orange and black wings of the monarch butterfly (*Danaus plexippus*) are seen in the northern United States from the Rockies to the Atlantic Ocean throughout the summer months.
5 Each fall, these eastern monarchs undertake a long migration to central Mexico where they overwinter.

The best available estimate for the population is extrapolated from the land area of
10 the overwintering sites. Assuming 50 million monarchs occur per hectare, the highest population estimate was for the winter of 1996–97, with more than one billion individual butterflies spread among twelve sites. The most
15 recent, in 2013, was exceptionally low at 0.67 hectares occupied, which represents a 90% decline from the 1994–2013 average. Across the range of the species, populations remain stable, so that the species is not in immediate danger of
20 extinction, but the eastern subspecies is critically imperiled.

The monarch, as with all butterflies, undergoes complete metamorphosis. Eggs are laid on milkweed leaves, and after three to five days
25 the caterpillar hatches. It will eat milkweed as it grows and molts. After ten to fourteen days, the caterpillar pupates and spends nine to fourteen days as a chrysalis. When fully developed, the adult butterfly will emerge from the pupal case
30 and fly off to search for nectar, mate, and (if female) lay its own eggs.

In the summer, adults live two to six weeks. Migrating monarchs live all winter, approximately six to nine months, as reproductively inactive
35 adults in dense clusters on oyamel fir trees in cool, high-elevation forests in Mexico. With reduced metabolic rates in the cold climate, monarchs live off of their lipid reserves and do not feed again until February. Monarchs that survive the winter
40 fly north in spring. When they reach areas with milkweed, they mate and lay eggs. Their offspring move further north and successive generations populate the entire eastern range by June or July.

The main factor in the decline of eastern
45 monarchs is the loss of the milkweed, on which the monarch larvae feed exclusively, due to changes in agricultural practices, specifically, the widespread adoption of genetically modified, herbicide-tolerant corn and soybeans and use of the
50 herbicide glyphosate on these crops. Additional threats to milkweed habitat include excessive roadside mowing, development, reforestation, and insecticide use. Restoring milkweed habitat is the most important measure for the conservation and
55 management of the eastern monarch.

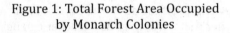

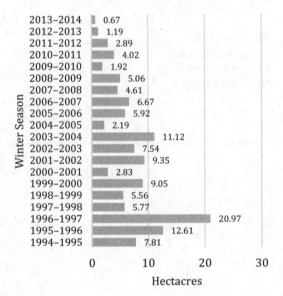

Figure 1: Total Forest Area Occupied by Monarch Colonies

Winter Season	Hectacres
2013–2014	0.67
2012–2013	1.19
2011–2012	2.89
2010–2011	4.02
2009–2010	1.92
2008–2009	5.06
2007–2008	4.61
2006–2007	6.67
2005–2006	5.92
2004–2005	2.19
2003–2004	11.12
2002–2003	7.54
2001–2002	9.35
2000–2001	2.83
1999–2000	9.05
1998–1999	5.56
1997–1998	5.77
1996–1997	20.97
1995–1996	12.61
1994–1995	7.81

Passage 2

Monarch butterflies that live west of the Rockies overwinter in forested groves on the Pacific coast. Mild environmental conditions provide the microclimate that monarchs require
60 to survive. The majority of these sites are at low elevations (below 60–90 meters), within 2.4 km of the Pacific Ocean or San Francisco Bay (where these water bodies moderate temperatures), and in shallow canyons or gullies. Many groves occur
65 on slopes that are oriented to the south, southwest, or west, which offer the most favorable solar radiation exposure and wind shelter.

Continue ➤

Almost all overwintering monarchs are in reproductive diapause and remain in this state
70 until late-February or March when they will leave their overwintering habitat and again breed, spreading out across interior California and several western states. Breeding habitat is characterized by the presence of milkweeds, the
75 broadly distributed *A. fascicularis* (narrow-leaved milkweed) and *A. speciosa* (showy milkweed) used by monarch larvae for food.

To fuel their migration, adults forage from a wide variety of plant species for nectar, which
80 they convert into lipids. Monarchs metabolize these lipid reserves as an energy source for winter survival. As monarchs breed and disperse, they produce multiple generations during the spring and summer. They are most abundant in the Great
85 Basin from June to August but still occur in the Great Basin in September and, to a lesser extent, October.

The monarch's overwintering range has contracted in recent years due to urban and other
90 development, and monarchs are rarely found overwintering in the far northern or southern extremes of their overwintering range. In 1997, there were more than 1.2 million monarchs over-wintering in California (or an average of 12,232
95 monarchs per site monitored), but by 2014 there were only about 234,000 monarchs counted (an average of 1,268 monarchs per site). This represents a decline of 81% from the 1997 high and a 48% decline from the 18-year average. The
100 population is categorized as vulnerable to imperiled.

Increasing drought conditions associated with ongoing climate change are the most likely cause of decreases in monarch population size.
105 The severity of the drought in key monarch breeding states (California, Arizona, Nevada, and Oregon) explains the variation in monarch population: The multi-year drought reduced the diversity of milkweed and monarch nectar sources
110 at a landscape scale. Future climate scenarios pre-dict that drought severity in arid and semi-arid mid-latitude areas of temperate western North America will increase, suggesting that the population decline is likely to continue.

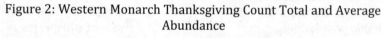

Figure 2: Western Monarch Thanksgiving Count Total and Average Abundance

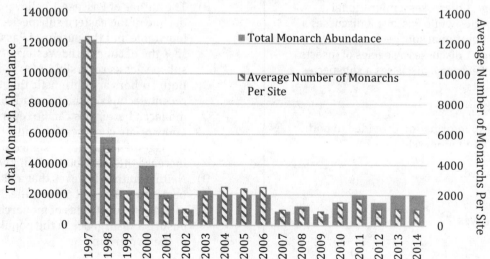

Continue

11. As it is used in line 69, *reproductive diapause* refers to a period during which the insect does not

A) breed.
B) feed.
C) migrate.
D) congregate.

12. Which of the following is true of both the eastern and western monarch populations?

A) The adults overwinter in high-elevation forests.
B) The caterpillars feed only on species of milkweed.
C) Adult monarchs are reproductively active in winter.
D) Adult butterflies live on average six to nine months.

13. Which of the following best contrasts the predominant organizing principles of the two passages?

A) Passage 1 discusses the eastern monarch while Passage 2 discusses the western monarch.
B) Passage 1 discusses an endangered species while Passage 2 discusses a species with a stable population.
C) Passage 1 discusses a migrational subspecies while Passage 2 discusses a non-migrational subspecies.
D) Passage 1 discusses a species of insects while Passage 2 discusses a subspecies of insects.

14. According to information provided in both passages, adult monarchs feed on

A) milkweed.
B) lipids.
C) nectar.
D) tree leaves.

15. The phrase *complete metamorphosis* (line 23) refers to the transformation of

A) an egg to a caterpillar.
B) an egg to a chrysalis.
C) an egg to an adult.
D) a pupa to an adult.

16. The author of Passage 2 attributes the decline in the western monarch population to

A) increased demand placed on western water resources by humans.
B) reduced diversity of milkweed and nectar sources caused by drought.
C) destruction of monarch overwintering habitat by urban development.
D) declining concentrations of adult monarchs in the overwintering range.

17. Which of the following best describes the authors' attitudes toward the decline of the monarch populations discussed?

A) The author of Passage 1 believes that the decline of the eastern subspecies can be reversed by conservation and management, but the author of Passage 2 sees the continued decline of the western subspecies as inevitable.
B) The author of Passage 1 believes that the decline of the eastern subspecies is inevitable, but the author of Passage 2 sees the decline of the western subspecies as reversible.
C) Both authors are optimistic that the recent declines in the populations of monarch butterflies can be reversed by appropriate conservation and management policies designed to increase the availability of milkweed.
D) Neither author believes that a plan can be devised that will protect the migratory subspecies of monarchs and ensure a resurgence in the populations of the two groups.

Continue

18. According to the information provided in Passage 2, western monarchs overwinter in close proximity to the coast because

A) sea-level is the only altitude for the continued survival of the monarch species.
B) the coastline helps to define the extreme western-most boundaries of the migratory trek.
C) enormous quantities of moisture are required to nourish the milkweed on which they feed.
D) large bodies of water help to maintain temperatures within a range conducive to survival.

19. Based on the information provided in Passage 1, the most important step for increasing the population of the eastern monarchs would be to

A) expand the overwintering range for eastern monarchs in the high-elevation forests of Mexico.
B) plant more acreage of genetically modified corn and soybeans as food sources for monarchs.
C) return open lands to wildflowers in order to provide nectar for adult eastern monarchs.
D) control pesticides and herbicides in order to increase the availability of milkweed plants.

20. The data provided in Figure 1 support the claim of Passage 1 about the magnitude of the decline in the eastern population only with the additional assumption that

A) the density of monarchs at overwintering sites is about 50 million per hectacre.
B) the greatest threat to milkweed is the increased reliance on genetically modified corn and soybeans.
C) adult eastern monarchs live approximately six to nine months before migrating north to breed.
D) roadside mowing, development, reforestation, and insecticides do not endanger monarchs.

21. The data in the graph in Figure 2 most directly supports which of the claims made in Passage 2?

A) Lines 60–62 ("The majority of [western monarch overwintering] sites are at low elevations (below 60–90 meters), within 2.4 km of the Pacific Ocean or San Francisco Bay.")
B) Lines 88–89 "The monarch's overwintering range has contracted in recent years.")
C) Lines 92–94 ("In 1997, there were more than 1.2 million monarchs overwintering in California.")
D) Line 102–104 ("Increasing drought conditions associated with ongoing climate change are the most likely cause of decreases in monarch population size.")

Continue

Questions #22–32 are based on the following passage.

The following passage is from a government report released in 2016 shortly after Supreme Court Justice Antonin Scalia's death.

Supreme Court Justice Antonin Scalia was a strong advocate of *originalism*, an approach to constitutional interpretation which insists that the Constitution's meaning should be drawn from
5 how its text was originally understood. In the wake of the constitutional revolution of the Warren and Burger Courts, Justice Scalia complained that the Supreme Court had too often based its constitutional rulings not on the original
10 meaning of the Constitution, but on broad principles such as defining "fundamental values," tempting judges to infuse the Constitution with their own "political values." For Justice Scalia, originalism, by establishing a historical
15 requirement separate from the preferences of an individual judge, restrained the unelected judiciary. Justice Scalia's originalism was perhaps most famously displayed in the Court's 2008 decision striking down the District of Columbia's
20 ban on handguns, in part, because the Court viewed the Second Amendment as originally understood to protect an individual right to possess firearms regardless of any connection with an existing militia.

25 In his interpretation of statutes, Justice Scalia advocated an interpretative method known as *textualism*. This method interprets statutes based on their text and structure, rather than through external evidence of the intent or purpose of the
30 Congress that enacted the statute. Focusing on the text of the statute, he refused to consider legislative history materials—such as committee reports, reports of congressional hearings, and records of congressional debates.

35 Other justices have disagreed with Justice Scalia's view on legislative history materials. They have used such materials to inform their understanding of a statute's meaning or the legislature's purpose. Justice Scalia, however,
40 noted that "the only language that constitutes 'a Law' is the text of the enacted statute." He was also concerned that legislative history materials are neither written by legislators nor considered by them when voting on bills, a view which may
45 not be entirely accurate for certain types of

legislative history materials. In addition, he feared that if legislative history materials were to be used, judges could select the materials that support their preferred policy positions, in much
50 the same manner as a person "walking into a crowded cocktail party and looking over the heads of the guests to pick out [his] friends."

Unlike some other supporters of textualism, Justice Scalia even objected to the use of
55 legislative history materials to confirm text-based interpretations of statutes. He argued that such use provides a "false and disruptive lesson in the law." He was, however, willing to consider legislative history materials to determine the
60 meanings of particular words based on their contexts.

Justice Scalia's general objections to the use of legislative history materials impacted other justices. In certain majority opinions that Justice
65 Scalia joined, "liberal" justices seem to have opted not to rely upon legislative history materials because of Justice Scalia's well-known opposition to the use of such materials. And commentators have noted the greater use of dictionaries and
70 lesser reliance on legislative history in the 1988–1989 term, when Justice Scalia was part of the Court, when compared to the 1981 term when he was not on the Court.

Both aspects of Justice Scalia's
75 jurisprudence—advocating originalism and his textualism—show his preference for judicial restraint and his belief about the proper role of the courts in the constitutional framework. His preferences reveal a reaction to the more recent
80 popular approaches to constitutional and statutory interpretation, which characterize judges as playing an active role in effecting the law's purposes in changed circumstances. Questions have been raised about the extent to
85 which Justice Scalia was less active in his approach than his colleagues on the Court, but Justice Scalia shaped the manner in which his colleagues on the Court and others approach the interpretation of a legal text, particularly his focus
90 on the ordinary meaning of words and his general skepticism about the value of historical context.

Continue

Supreme Court Decisions
(Scalia and Court)
2010–2011

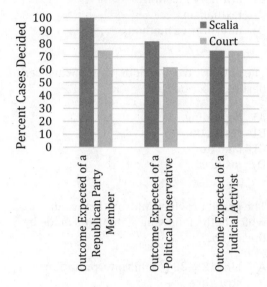

22. In the first paragraph, the author is primarily concerned with

A) identifying some key differences between the opinions of Justice Scalia and those of other justices.
B) explaining the concept of originalism and identify Justice Scalia with that legal tradition.
C) criticizing the Warren and Burger Courts for too often deciding cases on political values.
D) demonstrating how fundamental and political values can lead a justice to the wrong decision.

23. The Fourteenth Amendment to the Constitution, which contains the phrase "equal protection of the law," took effect in 1868. Justice Scalia would most likely have interpreted that phrase

A) according to the intention of the drafters of the amendment.
B) in reference to the underlying purpose of the amendment.
C) according to the usual meaning of the words in 1868.
D) using the words as they were used in 1789 when the Constitution was adopted.

24. Which of the following statements provides the strongest support for the correct answer to the preceding question?

A) Lines 1–5 ("Supreme Court . . . understood")
B) Lines 30–34 ("Focusing . . . debates")
C) Lines 39–41 ("Justice Scalia . . . statute")
D) Lines 58–61 ("He was . . . contexts")

25. The author uses the 2008 Supreme Court decision on handguns (lines 17–24) to

A) refute the contention that Scalia sometimes deviated from the doctrine of originalism.
B) demonstrate that some Supreme Court justices were influenced by Scalia's reasoning.
C) illustrate the general claim that Scalia interpreted text according to its original meaning.
D) define certain key terms in the Constitution according to their meanings in a modern context.

26. In the quotation in lines 50–52, Justice Scalia intends for "friends" to mean

A) statutes.
B) other justices.
C) legislators.
D) helpful sources.

Continue

27. The impact of Justice Scalia's thinking on the Court can best be described as

    A) inconsequential.
    B) influential.
    C) predictable.
    D) ineffectual.

28. Which of the following mentioned in the passage provides the strongest support for the correct answer to the preceding question?

    A) The decision in the DC handgun case
    B) Justice Scalia's refusal to consider legislative history
    C) The reliance on dictionaries when Justice Scalia was on the Court
    D) The insistence on judicial restraint by Justice Scalia and others

29. According to the passage, Justice Scalia was even stricter in his textualism than others in that he

    A) insisted on using dictionaries and other reference materials to establish the ordinary meaning of words.
    B) rejected the use of legislative history even to support a decision based on the plain text.
    C) considered legislative history to understand the context in which the text was formulated.
    D) disagreed with "liberal" justice about the wisdom of using legislative history in majority opinions.

30. In context, *jurisprudence* (line 75) means

    A) legal philosophy.
    B) ordinary meaning.
    C) textualism.
    D) interpretive method.

31. The author's treatment of Justice Scalia can best be described as

    A) degrading.
    B) respectful.
    C) laudatory.
    D) insincere.

32. The graph provides information to support which of the following statements made by the author?

    A) Lines 25–28 ("In his interpretation . . . structure")
    B) Lines 31–34 ("he refused . . . debates")
    C) Lines 65–68 ("'liberal' justices . . . materials")
    D) Lines 84–86 ("Questions . . . court")

Continue

Questions #33–42 are based on the following passage.

The following passage presents a position on the consumption of raw milk.

Many Americans have adopted a "back to nature" philosophy about food, including the naive notion that minimally processed products are necessarily safer and more nutritious. Raw milk
5 currently enjoys the uncritical support of many in this group, and, increasingly, specialty shops and farmers' markets are offering raw milk and products made from it. Its appeal is enhanced by urban myths and popular misconceptions about
10 the supposed nutritional and health benefits of raw milk.

Most of the milk sold in the United States is pasteurized, a process during which the milk is heated to 161°F for 15 seconds to kill harmful
15 bacteria. The term "raw milk" refers to milk that comes straight from the cow. Proponents of the consumption of raw milk insist that the milk sold at the local supermarket is a chemically altered substance, heat-pasteurized simply to prolong
20 shelf life. The resultant low-enzyme activity, it is argued, makes pasteurized milk difficult to digest, the altered fat content renders the vitamins and minerals difficult to absorb, and the residual drugs and antibiotics pose a threat to human health. On
25 top of this, consumers of raw milk claim, naturally occurring beneficial bacteria have been destroyed.

According to its supporters, raw milk is an incredibly complex whole food, complete with digestive enzymes and its own antiviral,
30 antibacterial, and anti-parasitic mechanisms. It is full of both fat and water-soluble vitamins, a wide range of minerals and trace elements, all eight essential amino acids, more than 60 enzymes, and CLA—an omega-6 fatty acid with impressive
35 effects on everything from insulin resistance to cancer to cardiovascular disease. Raw milk, it is claimed, actually helps protect against allergic reactions and boosts the immune system.

In reality, none of the claims made by the
40 raw milk advocates withstand scientific scrutiny. Raw milk is not safer or better than pasteurized milk, and pasteurization is the one method available to almost guarantee that the milk we drink is safe.

45 Pasteurization has minimal impact on milk's nutritional quality. Typical cow's milk contains about 3 to 4% milk fat, with 97.5% of the fat existing as triglycerides. Pasteurized milk has essentially the same fat composition. Minerals are
50 stable under pasteurization conditions and there is minimal change in their concentrations after pasteurization. Thus, raw milk is not nutritionally superior to pasteurized milk.

The two major groups of milk protein are
55 casein (about 80%) and whey proteins (about 20%), and the protein quality of pasteurized milk is not different from that of raw milk. Therefore, it is not surprising that pasteurization does not change the allergenicity of milk. The concentration
60 of immunoglobulins in cow's milk is low, typically about 0.6–1.0 mg/ml. At these low concentrations, cow immunoglobulins, when consumed directly from milk, are physiologically insignificant to humans.

65 There are no beneficial bacteria in raw milk for gastrointestinal health. Probiotic microorganisms must be of human origin in order to have an impact on human health, and bacteria in raw milk are typically not of human origin.
70 Bacteria present in raw milk are from infected udders, the dairy environment (e.g., manure), and contaminated milking equipment. High bacteria counts in raw milk only indicate poor animal health and poor farm hygiene.

75 The image of a seemingly happy, germ-free dairy cow in a pristine bucolic setting ready to produce bacteria-free milk is just clever advertising. Dairy farming is a dirty business. Teats and udders of cows inevitably become
80 soiled while they are lying in stalls or when allowed in muddy barnyards. Used bedding has been shown to harbor large numbers of microorganisms. Improperly cleaned equipment and storage surfaces harbor bacteria.
85 Consumption of non-pasteurized milk, organic or not, has been associated with serious illnesses caused by several pathogens. From 2007 to 2012, a total of 81 outbreaks associated with non-pasteurized milk were reported from 26 states.
90 These outbreaks resulted in 979 illnesses and 73 hospitalizations. Luckily, no deaths were reported.

Continue

33. In line 10, *supposed* means

   A) speculative.
   B) unpredictable.
   C) unprovable.
   D) unlikely.

34. The author's attitude toward those who advocate using raw milk can best be described as

   A) dismissive bordering on contemptuous.
   B) puzzled, nearly mystified.
   C) cool and almost indifferent.
   D) sympathetic but not supportive.

35. According to the passage, advocates of raw milk believe that milk processors use pasteurization to

   A) replace minerals, enzymes, and other properties removed from milk by processing.
   B) conceal the effects of unhealthy farm conditions on the quality of milk.
   C) prevent consumers from receiving the health benefits of unprocessed milk.
   D) create a more stable product that can be sold for a greater period of time.

36. Which of the following best summarizes the main claim presented in lines 39–91?

   A) Raw milk and products made from it are not pasteurized and so are consistent with a "back to nature" approach to food.
   B) Raw milk is not nutritionally superior to pasteurized milk and poses health risks that can be avoided by pasteurization.
   C) Pasteurization kills harmful bacteria and is therefore effective in preventing outbreaks of foodborne illnesses.
   D) The "back to nature" movement encourages dietary practices that expose its adherents to unnecessary risks.

37. In lines 45–53, the comparison of the fat composition of raw and pasteurized milk undermines the claim that pasteurization

   A) increases the allergenicity of milk and weakens the immune system.
   B) destroys naturally occurring beneficial bacteria found in milk.
   C) interferes with the absorption of both vitamins and minerals.
   D) reduces the effectiveness of antibacterial and anti-parasitic mechanisms.

38. In line 76, *pristine* means

   A) minimal.
   B) healthful.
   C) pure.
   D) rural.

39. The author implies that the allergenicity of milk is caused by

   A) milk proteins.
   B) microorganisms.
   C) bacteria.
   D) unsanitary conditions.

40. The author mentions the 0.6–1.0 mg/ml concentration of immunoglobulins in cow's milk to show that

   A) the bacteria in cow's milk are dangerous to humans.
   B) levels are too low to affect the human immune system.
   C) pasteurized milk is not nutritionally inferior to raw milk.
   D) cows that produce organic milk are not healthier than other cows.

Continue ▶

41. According to the passage, in order for probiotic microorganisms to benefit humans the bacteria must

    A) originally come from a human source.
    B) be destroyed by the process of pasteurization.
    C) be within a certain range of concentration.
    D) remain on equipment surfaces after decontamination.

42. The primary purpose of the final paragraph is to

    A) correct an impression created by potentially misleading advertising.
    B) persuade the reader that the health risks of raw milk are minimal.
    C) illustrate techniques used by advertisers to mislead consumers.
    D) dramatize the health benefits of consuming organically produced raw milk.

Continue ➤

Questions #43–52 are based on the following passage.

The following passage discusses the US and Spanish Boards of Inquiry into the sinking of the Maine *in 1898.*

On February 16, 1898, the *New York World* newspaper hit the streets a little after 3 a.m. carrying the headline, "USS *Maine* Blown Up in Havana Harbor." The 5 a.m. special edition added
5 "*World* Staff Correspondent Cables It Is Not Known Whether Explosion Occurred on or Under the *Maine*"—in other words, whether the incident was an accident or sabotage. It would be up to a naval court of inquiry to establish the cause of the
10 explosion, but if it had been a Spanish mine, then war with Spain would quickly follow.

The Spanish government feared this possibility and immediately proposed a joint, US-Spanish investigation into the cause of the sinking.
15 The United States declined. The Spanish board convened almost immediately and identified spontaneous combustion of coal in a bunker adjacent to the munition stores as the likely cause of the explosion. Additional observations
20 supported this conclusion, including the lack of a column of water that would have been seen had a mine been the cause of the explosion, calm waters making it unlikely that a mine would have been detonated by contact, and the lack of dead fish
25 that would be found killed by an explosion in the water. These conclusions were not reported at that time by the American press.

The United States convened its own Board of Inquiry. The Secretary of the Navy had the option
30 of selecting the members personally but instead, he fell back on protocol and assigned the commander–in–chief of the North Atlantic Squadron to do so. The commander produced a list of junior line officers for the board. The fact
35 that the officer proposed to be court president was junior to the captain of the *Maine* would have prevented the board from effectively inquiring whether the ship was lost by the negligence of her captain. Eventually, however, an officer more
40 senior to the *Maine's* captain was appointed.

The Board of Inquiry did not make use of many technically qualified experts. It relied

heavily on the testimony of Captain Sigsbee, the commander of the *Maine* at the time of the sinking,
45 who couched his answers to the Board's questions evasively in terms such as "It was our invariable custom . . . ." or "I cannot now state specifically." In other words, Captain Sigsbee provided little, if any, direct testimony about conditions that might
50 have caused the explosion.

The board concluded that the *Maine* had been blown up by a mine, which, in turn, caused the explosion of her forward magazines. They reached this conclusion based on the fact that the
55 majority of witnesses stated that they had heard two explosions and that that part of the keel was bent inward. The board declined, however, to speculate as to who might have been responsible for the placement of the explosive device.

60 The Navy's Chief Engineer was not asked for his views, but he suspected that the cause of the disaster was a magazine explosion. Many ships, including the *Maine*, had coal bunkers located next to magazines that stored ammunition, gun shells,
65 and gunpowder. Only a bulkhead separated the bunkers from the magazines. If the coal, by spontaneous combustion, overheated, the ammunition was at risk of exploding. In fact, fires from coal bunkers were frequent occurrences.
70 From 1894 to 1908, more than 20 coal bunker fires were reported on US naval ships. Additionally, the *Maine* took on bituminous coal, which was particularly subject to spontaneous combustion.

75 The *New York Journal* and the *New York World* gave the *Maine* intense press coverage, but employed tactics that would later be labeled "yellow" journalism, exaggerating and distorting information and sometimes even fabricating news.
80 For a week, the *Journal* devoted a daily average of eight and a half pages to the event. Its editors offered a reward of $50,000 "for the conviction of the criminals who sent 258 American sailors to their deaths." The American public, already
85 agitated over reported Spanish atrocities in Cuba, was increasingly agitated. The Spanish-American War began in April 1898, two months after the sinking, to the rallying cry, "Remember the *Maine*! To Hell with Spain!"

Continue

43. The author implies that the membership originally proposed for the US Board of Inquiry was selected to ensure that

   A) the possibility of an internal explosion was never seriously considered.
   B) expert testimony on all theories of the sinking was provided to the board.
   C) the Spanish government would not be able to influence the board's decision.
   D) the New York newspapers would be satisfied that the hearing was fair.

44. Which of the following statements provides the strongest support for the correct answer to the preceding question?

   A) Lines 12–14 ("The Spanish . . . sinking")
   B) Lines 34–39 ("The fact . . . captain")
   C) Lines 41–42 ("The Board . . . experts")
   D) Lines 57–59 ("The board . . . device")

45. It can be inferred that the findings of the Spanish Board of Inquiry were not reported by the American press because

   A) the press had already decided that the cause of sinking was an enemy mine.
   B) the US Board of Inquiry had not yet published its findings.
   C) Spain suppressed the findings of the board to avoid a war with the United States.
   D) publicity given to the findings would have unfairly damaged Captain Sigsbee's reputation.

46. The primary purpose of lines 60–74 is to

   A) explain how warships of the time were constructed.
   B) demonstrate that spontaneous combustion is an unanticipated event.
   C) convince the reader that the Spanish government was behind the sinking.
   D) present an alternative to the enemy mine theory.

47. The author mentions that bituminous coal is prone to spontaneous combustion in order to

   A) strengthen the implication that the cause of the explosion was internal.
   B) support the point that the American press distorted the facts of the incident.
   C) minimize the importance of the expert opinion of the Navy's Chief Engineer.
   D) cast doubt on the credibility of the testimony of the *Maine's* captain.

48. The author regards the start of the Spanish-American War as

   A) unwarranted.
   B) justified.
   C) premature.
   D) moral.

49. In context, *magazines* (line 64) means

   A) libraries.
   B) periodicals.
   C) living quarters.
   D) storage bins.

50. In context, *yellow* (line 78) means

   A) current.
   B) sensational.
   C) unbiased.
   D) empirical.

51. The author implies that the Spanish government proposed a joint inquiry into the sinking of the *Maine* because government officials

   A) knew that a mine caused the explosion.
   B) wished to avoid a war with the United States.
   C) were aware of various atrocities in Cuba.
   D) hoped to draw the United States into a war.

Continue

52. Which of the following statements provides
the strongest support for the correct answer
to the preceding question?

A) Lines 12–14 ("The Spanish . . . sinking")
B) Lines 15–19 ("The Spanish . . .
   explosion")
C) Lines 51–53 ("The board . . . magazines")
D) Lines 86–89 ("The Spanish-American
   War . . . Spain!")

STOP

**IF YOU FINISH BEFORE TIME IS CALLED, YOU MAY CHECK YOUR WORK ON THIS
SECTION ONLY. DO NOT TURN TO ANY OTHER SECTION IN THE TEST.**

SECTION 2—WRITING AND LANGUAGE

Time—35 minutes

44 items

DIRECTIONS: Each set of questions is based on a passage. For some questions, think about how the passage could be revised to improve the expression of ideas. For other questions, think about how to edit the passage to correct sentence structure, usage, or punctuation errors. Passages or questions may be accompanied by a graphic such as a table or graph that you may refer to while making revising and editing decisions.

Some questions reference an underlined word or phrase in the passage. Other questions refer to a location in the passage or to the passage as a whole.

After reading each passage, choose the answer that improves the expression of ideas in the passage or conforms to standard English conventions. Many questions include a "NO CHANGE" answer choice. Choose that answer if you think the best choice is to leave the passage as it is. Answers are on page 300.

Questions #1–11 are based on the following passage.

From Flight to Novel Fame

    A plane crashes in the remote Sahara. Miraculously, the pilot survives and meets a boy wearing a flowing scarf, 1 which he calls "the little prince." While the pilot repairs the plane, he chats with his 2 new acquaintance he has just met and learns of the prince's remarkable journey from his home on asteroid B-612. Since its publication in 1943, *The Little Prince*, written by Antoine de Saint-Exupéry, has charmed readers with its inventive 3 story whimsical watercolors, and philosophical insights. 4

    5 Saint-Exupéry's lifelong plan was to become an architect. He tried and failed to gain admission to the French naval academy, studied architecture but did not earn a degree, and spent several months in Paris working odd jobs before finally joining the French army in 1921. He was transferred to the French Air Force, trained as a pilot, and finally 6 they assigned him to the 34th Aviation regiment. After a plane crash in which he was seriously injured, Saint-Exupéry left military service.

1. A) NO CHANGE
    B) who
    C) whom
    D) that

2. A) NO CHANGE
    B) new acquaintance
    C) newly just met acquaintance
    D) new, just met acquaintance

3. A) NO CHANGE
    B) story, whimsical
    C) story, whimsically
    D) story and whimsical

4. The author wants the reader to understand that *The Little Prince* is a fictional story. Which of the following phrases, if deleted from paragraph 1, would make it difficult for the reader to reach that conclusion?

    A) in the remote Sahara
    B) Miraculously
    C) wearing a flowing scarf
    D) home on asteroid B-612

5. Which choice most effectively introduces paragraph 2?

    A) NO CHANGE
    B) As a young man, Saint-Exupéry did not have definitive career plans.
    C) As an aspiring author, Saint-Exupéry hoped to publish fictional stories.
    D) Saint-Exupéry spent his youth traveling from city to city.

6. A) NO CHANGE
    B) he was assigned
    C) assigned him
    D) assigned

Continue ➤

In 1926, Saint-Exupéry joined Aéropostale, the French air mail service. He spent the next few years flying mail between France and North [7] Africa. In his free time, he wrote stories. His first novel, *Southern Mail*, chronicled his time flying the Casablanca–Dakar mail route, while the second, *Night Flight*, recounted his tenure with Aeroposta Argentina. Both novels feature almost mystical descriptions of flying, along with philosophical musings on life and love. *Night Flight* became an international best-seller and made Saint-Exupéry a literary star.

Saint-Exupéry continued to fly. In 1935, while attempting to break the speed record from Paris to Saigon, he crashed in the Egyptian desert. He survived but nearly [8] died of dehydration from a lack of water. [9] A Bedouin caravan found him and delivered him by camel back to a French outpost. The event is recounted in *Wind, Sand, and Stars*, mixed with reflections on the dangers of flying and meditations on heroism, friendship, and the meaning of life. The French Academy awarded *Wind, Sand, and Stars* the Grand Prize for Fiction.

7. A) NO CHANGE
   B) Africa, in his free time, he wrote stories
   C) Africa, in his free time he wrote stories
   D) Africa, in his free time, he writing stories

8. A) NO CHANGE
   B) died, dehydrated from a lack of water
   C) died from dehydration and a lack of water
   D) died of dehydration

9. The author is thinking of deleting this sentence. If the author deletes the sentence, readers will not learn

   A) what caused Saint-Exupéry's plane to crash.
   B) how Saint-Exupéry was rescued from the desert.
   C) about the main themes of *Wind, Sand, and Stars.*
   D) why Saint-Exupéry was piloting a plane across the Sahara.

Continue ➤

After World War II broke out, Saint-Exupéry relocated to New York City, where he became a leading voice of the French expatriate community. In November 1942, he secured a spot with a Free French Air Force unit based in Algeria. [10] Initially rejected for combat duty because he was too old, General Eisenhower, the Allied commander, put him back in the cockpit. On July 31, 1944, Saint-Exupéry departed Corsica in an unarmed P-38 on a photographic mission. He never returned. In 1998, a fisherman recovered a bracelet bearing the names of Saint-Exupéry and his wife; the bracelet was attached to fabric that might have been a flight suit. In 2000, a diver in the area discovered the wreckage of an unarmed P-38 on the floor of the Mediterranean Sea. [11]

10. A) NO CHANGE
B) Initially rejected for combat duty, because he was too old,
C) Saint-Exupéry was initially rejected for combat duty because he was too old, but
D) Initially Saint-Exupéry was rejected for combat duty because he was too old,

11. Which of the following sentences provides the best conclusion for the final paragraph?

A) The wreckage discovered was certainly that of the plane flown by Saint-Exupéry.
B) The debris located by the diver was most likely from the plane piloted by Saint-Exupéry.
C) Both Saint-Exupéry and his wife were aboard the P-38 when it crashed into the water.
D) The plane flown by Saint-Exupéry was shot down by enemy fire and crashed into the sea.

Continue

Questions #12–22 are based on the following passage.

Getting Around in a Gig Economy

[1]

The *gig economy* is on-demand commerce that matches providers to consumers on a job-by-job (gig) basis. In the basic business model, a gig worker enters into a formal agreement with an on-demand company for the company to represent the worker in the gig market. The company, which specializes in particular kinds of work such as home repair, transportation, or even personal shopping, promotes the services, assigns the providers, and handles the financial transactions, collecting money from the client and paying the provider. The company <u>12 retains, a portion</u> of the client's payment as compensation for acting as an intermediary.

[2]

[1] Uber is a company that offers transportation. [2] <u>13 In the expected anticipation of using</u> the service, potential clients download and install the Uber app to a smartphone. [3] A client then uses the app to request a transportation service for a ride from point A to point B. [4] The company locates an available car in <u>14 its</u> database, dispatches the driver to the pick-up point, and <u>15 then it confirms</u> the identity and time of arrival of the provider to the client. [5] The driver conveys the client to the destination, and the client is automatically billed by credit or debit card. [6] <u>16 The driver is paid by the company.</u> <u>17</u>

12.
A) NO CHANGE
B) retains a portion
C) retains a portion,
D) retains, a portion,

13.
A) NO CHANGE
B) In expected anticipation of using
C) In anticipation of the expected utilization
D) In anticipation of using

14.
A) NO CHANGE
B) its'
C) it's
D) they're

15.
A) NO CHANGE
B) then it confirmed
C) confirming
D) confirms

16. The author is thinking of moving the underlined sentence to another place in the same paragraph. Which is the best place for the underlined sentence?

A) Where it is now
B) After sentence 1 in paragraph 2
C) After sentence 2 in paragraph 2
D) After sentence 3 in paragraph 2

17. The author is thinking of deleting paragraph 2. If the author deletes the paragraph, the passage will no longer

A) demonstrate that the gig economy is very similar to the traditional.
B) give a specific example of the operation of a gig economy company.
C) outline the basic principles of a gig economy company's business plan.
D) discuss the economic efficiencies obtainable by specializing in one service.

Continue

[3]

On-demand companies usually classify providers as independent contractors and not **18** employees. This arrangement is usually being made explicit in the formal agreement governing the provider-company relationship. Additionally, on-demand companies discourage providers from accepting work outside the platform from certain clients.

[4]

On-demand companies control, maintain, and protect **19** its brand. Some on-demand businesses condition provider participation upon passing a background check and having certain credentials. Most reserve the right to terminate the relationship if the work delivered does not meet company-defined standards of quality and professionalism.

[5]

[1] The gig economy can be viewed as an expansion of classical freelance work (i.e., self-employed workers who generate income through a series of jobs and projects). [2] To the extent that gig-economy workers are viewed as independent contractors, gig jobs differ from **20** employment back in the day in important ways. [3] A gig worker may not enjoy the protections of various state and federal employment laws nor benefits provided by such laws. [4] **21** On the other hand, the flexibility of gig jobs is seen by gig providers as a real advantage of the relationship, an advantage sufficient to offset the benefits of a traditional employer-employee relationship that are lost in the gig economy. **22**

18. A) NO CHANGE
B) employees, an arrangement usually
C) employees, this arrangement is usually
D) employees, and this arrangement is usually being

19. A) NO CHANGE
B) its brands
C) their brand
D) their brands

20. A) NO CHANGE
B) old timey employment
C) old fashioned employment
D) traditional employment

21. A) NO CHANGE
B) By the same token,
C) Similarly,
D) In fact,

22. The author is thinking of adding the following sentence to the final paragraph.

> Gig workers also usually do not receive employer-provided benefits such as paid sick leave, health insurance, and retirement packages.

It should be placed:

A) at the beginning of the paragraph
B) after sentence 1 in the final paragraph
C) after sentence 2 in the final paragraph
D) after sentence 3 in the final paragraph

Continue

Questions #23–33 are based on the following passage.

Are GM Crops Safe to Eat?

Plants with desirable characteristics have been cultivated for thousands of years by conventional breeding methods. Traits are selected, combined, and propagated by repeated sexual crossings over numerous generations—a long process, taking up to 15 years to produce new varieties. Genetic engineering dramatically accelerates this process. Transgenic plants, also called Genetically Modified or GM plants, are those that **23** <u>have been</u> altered using recombinant DNA technology. The principle crops grown are soybeans, corn, and cotton, and the acreage planted with these GM crops is increasing. **24**

23. A) NO CHANGE
B) has been
C) is
D) was

24. The data provided in the graph most strongly supports which of the points made in the first paragraph?

A) Plants with desirable characteristics have been cultivated for thousands of years.
B) Conventional breeding methods take up to 15 years to produce new varieties.
C) The principle transgenic crops are soybeans, corn, and cotton.
D) The acreage planted with GM soybeans, corn, and cotton is increasing.

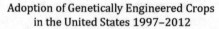

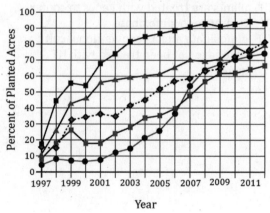

Adoption of Genetically Engineered Crops
in the United States 1997–2012

HT Soybeans
HT Cotton
Bt Cotton
HT Corn
Bt Corn

Continue

In the context of agriculture, Bt refers to plants that have been genetically engineered to contain *Bacillus thuringiensis*. When a susceptible insect tries to feed on a transgenic crop expressing the Bt protein, [25] they stop feeding and die. Herbicide tolerance (HT) refers to plants treated with genes that confer tolerance to glufosinate. By inserting these HT genes into a plant's [26] genome: herbicides that are [27] traditionally toxic to conventional crop cultivars can be sprayed on fields without damage to transgenic crops [28] while destroying weeds.

25. A) NO CHANGE
    B) the insect stopped feeding and died
    C) the insect stops feeding and dies
    D) stopping feeding and dying

26. A) NO CHANGE
    B) genome; herbicides
    C) genome, herbicides
    D) genome. Herbicides

27. A) NO CHANGE
    B) historically
    C) usually
    D) in practice

28. The author is thinking of deleting the underlined part of the sentence. If the underlined part is deleted, the paragraph will no longer explain how

    A) *Bacillus thuringiensis* kills insects that attack GM crops.
    B) HT genes work with herbicides to control weeds.
    C) plants are treated with genes to confer tolerance to glufosinate.
    D) glufosinate affects conventional cultivars that have not been treated with HT genes.

Continue

29 Are GM foods safe for consumers to eat? GM crops are tightly regulated by the Food and Drug Agency, the Environmental Protection Agency, and the US Department of Agriculture. GM plants undergo extensive safety testing prior to commercialization. Foods derived from GM crops have been consumed by hundreds of millions of people across the world for more than fifteen years, with no reported ill effects or legal cases related to human health, despite many of the consumers coming from that most litigious of countries, the USA. **30**

Additionally, there is little research to suggest that GM crops **31** have the potential to possibly be toxic to humans. The most damning evidence is a 1999 study claiming that rats fed with GM potatoes suffered damage to gut mucosa. However, the Royal Society has since stated that the study was flawed in many respects and that no conclusions should be drawn from it.

Is there any theoretical reason to believe that GM crops might be harmful when consumed? The presence of foreign DNA sequences in food *per se* poses no intrinsic risk to human health. All foods contain significant amounts of DNA and RNA, which we **32** have consumed every day. Plus, the potential toxicity of the protein expressed in a GM food is an essential component of the safety assessment that must be conducted before the GM food enters the food supply.

29. Which of the following questions would provide the best transition from the first part of the passage to the second?

A) NO CHANGE
B) Will GM foods be accepted by consumers?
C) Are GM foods likely to replace conventional cultivars?
D) Are GM foods as nutritious as conventional varieties?

30. The author is concerned that the reasoning of the last sentence of the third paragraph may not be clear. Which of the following parenthetical notes, if added to the end of the paragraph, would most clarify the logic of the sentence?

A) (If there were injuries caused by GM foods, there would be lots of litigation.)
B) (Many personal injury lawsuits are decided in favor of the defendant.)
C) (If someone died from eating GM food, the family could bring suit.)
D) (One famous lawsuit involved a container of yogurt with a bug in it.)

31. A) NO CHANGE
B) have the possible potential to be toxic
C) have a possible toxic potential to be harmful
D) are potentially toxic

32. A) NO CHANGE
B) are consuming
C) were consuming
D) consume

Continue ➤

Potential allergenicity to the novel gene product is another common concern, but allergies to non-GM foods such as soft-fleshed [33] <u>fruit, potatoes</u>, and soy are widespread. Clearly, new varieties of crops produced by either GM techniques or conventional breeding both have the potential to be allergenic. There is no reason to fear that GM foods pose any additional risks.

33. A) NO CHANGE
B) fruit potatoes
C) fruit; potatoes
D) fruit. Potatoes

Continue

Questions #34–44 are based on the following passage.

Is the Electoral College the People's Choice?

The president and vice-president of the United States are chosen indirectly by a group of persons elected by American voters. These officials are known as electors, and 34 the whole ball of wax is referred to as the electoral college. Established in 1787 as one of several compromises in the Constitution, 35 some political theorists have criticized the electoral college as an undemocratic anachronism, while others have praised it as a pillar of political stability and American federalism. Absent a constitutional amendment, this system will likely continue to govern US presidential elections 36 for the time being into the foreseeable future.

34. A) NO CHANGE
    B) in the big picture it's
    C) in the overall scheme of things
    D) the institution as a whole

35. A) NO CHANGE
    B) they have been criticized by some political theorists as an undemocratic anachronism and praised by others
    C) some political theorists who have criticized the electoral college as an undemocratic anachronism, while others have praised
    D) the electoral college has been criticized by some political theorists as an undemocratic anachronism and praised by others

36. A) NO CHANGE
    B) for the time being into the future
    C) for the foreseeable future
    D) into the foreseeable future as time being

Continue ▶

The electoral college has delivered the people's choice in 53 of 57 elections, but in four instances it has chosen presidents who received fewer popular votes than their major opponents. Three occurred in the 19th century, in the elections of 1824, 1876, and 1888. The elections in 1824 and 1876 of candidates who received fewer popular votes than their leading opponents revealed the weaknesses of the system. It led to constitutional crises in both instances and brought the nation to the brink of civil disturbance. Most recently, in the presidential election of 2000, George W. Bush narrowly won the electoral vote and the presidency but with fewer popular votes than his major opponent, Al Gore, Jr. This event, sometimes referred to as an electoral college 37 "misfire," continues to influence American political discourse more than a decade later. In the contentious political atmosphere of contemporary presidential elections, another misfire, a tie vote in the electoral college, the failure of any candidate to receive a majority of electoral votes, or an extremely close election—in either popular or electoral votes— 38 arguably lead to an acrimonious and protracted political struggle or even a constitutional crisis.

37. The author is considering providing a definition for "misfire." Which of the following, when inserted following "misfire," would best help the reader to understand the meaning of that term as the author is using it?

A) "misfire" because the election was not held according to the schedule required by the Constitution,
B) "misfire" because the electoral college chose a candidate who did not receive the majority of the popular vote
C) "misfire" to acknowledge that political events are inherently unpredictable and can produce odd results
D) "misfire" because the resulting civil turmoil nearly resulted in armed conflict in the streets

38. A) NO CHANGE
B) arguably leads
C) could arguably lead
D) led

Continue

The electoral college system has demonstrated both durability and adaptability during more than two centuries of government under the Constitution. [39] Although the constitutional elements have remained largely unchanged since ratification of the Twelfth Amendment, the electoral college has never worked as the founders planned. The historical record reveals that they intended it to be an [40] indirect, deliberative selection process, carefully filtered from political considerations, with the degree of voter participation left to the discretion of the state legislatures. [41] Consequently, it accommodated the demands of an increasingly democratic and political party–dominated presidential election system, ultimately evolving into an improvised yet enduring assemblage of constitutional provisions, [42] state laws, political party practices, and traditions. [43] [44]

39. A) NO CHANGE
B) The
C) Its
D) Although their

40. A) NO CHANGE
B) indirect deliberative
C) indirect; deliberative
D) indirect—deliberative

41. A) NO CHANGE
B) Naturally
C) Instead
D) At last

42. A) NO CHANGE
B) laws of the states, political
C) state laws political
D) states, laws, political

43. Assuming that each of the sentences below makes a factually accurate statement, which sentence, when added to the end of the last paragraph of the passage, would best summarize the overall development of the passage?

A) While this arrangement may not work as the founders intended, it has elected the presidential candidate who had the greatest public support in 53 of 57 elections under the Constitution—a success rate of 92.8%.
B) While public opinion has consistently and historically favored direct popular election, electoral college reform does not appear to be an urgent public issue at present.
C) Given the stringent requirements faced by all proposed constitutional amendments, the electoral college system seems likely to remain in place.
D) There is little support in Congress for reforming the electoral college system, and this lack of enthusiasm for change is paralleled by the lack of progress of the National Popular Vote Initiative.

Continue ➤

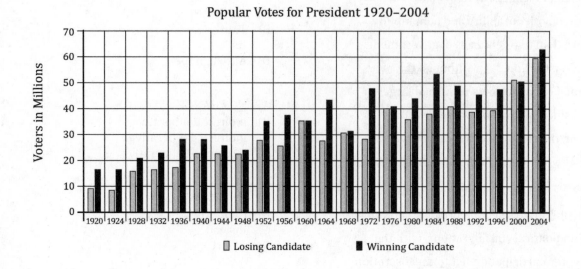

Popular Votes for President 1920–2004

Legend: ☐ Losing Candidate   ■ Winning Candidate

44. The data provided in the graph best support which of the following conclusions stated in the passage?

A) The electoral college system has demonstrated both durability and adaptability during more than two centuries of government under the Constitution.

B) The electoral college has delivered the people's choice in 53 of 57 elections, but in four instances it has chosen presidents who received fewer popular votes than their major opponents.

C) The elections in 1824 and 1876 of candidates who received fewer popular votes than their leading opponents revealed the weaknesses of the system and led to constitutional crises in both instances and brought the nation to the brink of civil disturbance.

D) Most recently, in the presidential election of 2000, George W. Bush narrowly won the electoral vote and the presidency but with fewer popular votes than his major opponent, Al Gore, Jr.

STOP
IF YOU FINISH BEFORE TIME IS CALLED, YOU MAY CHECK YOUR WORK ON THIS SECTION ONLY. DO NOT TURN TO ANY OTHER SECTION IN THE TEST.

SECTION 3

SECTION 3—MATH, NO CALCULATOR

Time—25 minutes

20 items

DIRECTIONS: For #1–15, solve each item and choose the correct answer choice. Then fill in the corresponding bubble on your answer sheet. For #16–20, solve each item and enter your answer in the grid on the answer sheet. Refer to the directions before #16 on how to enter your answers for these items. Use any available space for scratchwork. Answers are on page 300.

Notes:

(1) All expressions and equations represent real numbers unless otherwise indicated.

(2) Figures that accompany problems in this test are intended to provide information useful in solving the problems. They are drawn as accurately as possible EXCEPT when it is stated in a specific problem that the figure is not drawn to scale. All figures lie in a plane unless otherwise indicated.

(3) The domain of a given function f is the set of all real numbers x for which $f(x)$ is a real number unless otherwise indicated.

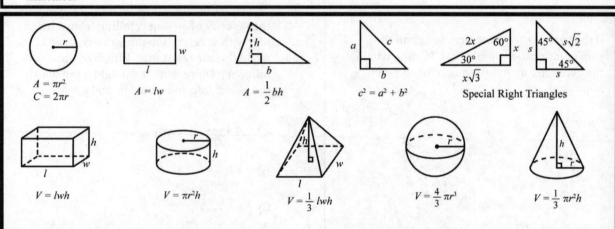

$A = \pi r^2$
$C = 2\pi r$

$A = lw$

$A = \frac{1}{2}bh$

$c^2 = a^2 + b^2$

Special Right Triangles

$V = lwh$

$V = \pi r^2 h$

$V = \frac{1}{3} lwh$

$V = \frac{4}{3} \pi r^3$

$V = \frac{1}{3} \pi r^2 h$

The number of degrees of arc in a circle is 360.

The sum of the measures in degrees of the angles of a triangle is 180.

The number of radians of arc in a circle is 2π.

Continue

1. The product of x and 5 is equal to one-half of the sum of $3x$ and 3.

   Which of the following equations correctly expresses the relationship described above?

   A) $5x = \dfrac{3(3x)}{2}$

   B) $5x = 2(3x+3)$

   C) $5x = \dfrac{3x+3}{2}$

   D) $\dfrac{x}{5} = \dfrac{3x+3}{2}$

2. If $x+2=7$ and $x+y=11$, then $y=?$

   A) 2
   B) 4
   C) 6
   D) 9

3. If the sum of three numbers is $4x$ and the sum of four other numbers is $3x$, then what is the average (arithmetic mean) of all seven numbers?

   A) $7x$
   B) x
   C) $\dfrac{x}{7}$
   D) 7

4. If $f(x) = -2x^2 + 2$, then $f(3) = ?$

   A) 16
   B) 4
   C) −4
   D) −16

5. Which of the following expressions does NOT equal $w(x+y+z)$?

   A) $w(xy) + w(yz)$
   B) $wx + wy + wz$
   C) $wx + w(y+z)$
   D) $w(x+y) + wz$

6. $(-3x)^3 \left(\dfrac{-3x^{-3}}{27} \right) = ?$

   A) 3
   B) 9
   C) 27
   D) $27x^3$

$$v = \sqrt{2gh}$$

7. The equation above can be used to calculate the velocity of an object falling from a height of h with acceleration due gravity, g, and negligible air resistance. Which of the following represents the height from which the object falls in terms of v and g?

   A) $h = \dfrac{v}{2g}$

   B) $h = \dfrac{v^2}{2g}$

   C) $h = \dfrac{v}{\sqrt{2g}}$

   D) $h = \dfrac{\sqrt{v}}{2g}$

8. A cube has edges of length s. Which of the following represents the distance from any vertex to the center of the cube?

   A) $\dfrac{s\sqrt{3}}{2}$

   B) $\dfrac{s\sqrt{2}}{3}$

   C) $s\sqrt{2}$

   D) $s\sqrt{3}$

Continue ➤

Questions #9–11 refer to the following information.

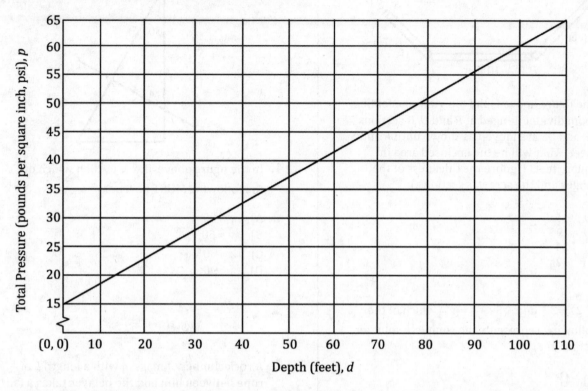

The graph above displays the total pressure, p, in pounds per square inch (psi), on a scuba diver at a depth of d feet below the water surface. Total pressure is a measure of both atmospheric pressure and water pressure.

9. What does the slope of the line in the graph represent?

A) The depth of the scuba diver below the water surface
B) The maximum total pressure on a scuba diver at a depth of 110 feet below the water surface
C) The increase in total pressure on a scuba diver for each additional foot closer to the water surface
D) The increase in total pressure on a scuba diver for each additional foot of depth below the water surface

10. At which of the following depths will the diver experience a total pressure of 40 psi?

A) 33 feet
B) 40 feet
C) 41 feet
D) 56 feet

11. Which of the following represents the relationship between d and p?

A) $p = 15d$

B) $p = \dfrac{9d}{20} + 15$

C) $d = 15p + \dfrac{20}{9}$

D) $p = 0.6d + 15$

Continue

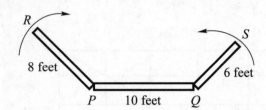

12. The figure above is the top view of a folding room divider, hinged at *P* and *Q*. If sections *PR* and *QS* are moved as shown until *R* and *S* meet, what will be the enclosed area in square feet? (Ignore the thickness of the hinges and the screen's sections.)

A) 12
B) 6π
C) 24
D) 12π

13. If $2^x = 32$ and $\sqrt{5x} + 4 = y^2$, which of the following represents the complete solution set for *y*?

A) {}
B) {3}
C) {9}
D) {−3,3}

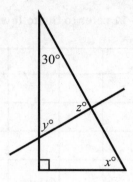

14. In the figure above, if $x < y$, then which of the following MUST be true?

A) $x \le 60$
B) $y = 60$
C) $z = 90$
D) $z < 90$

$$mg(H + s) = \frac{k}{2L}s^2$$

15. A rock climber of mass *m* with a length *L* of rope between him and the belayer takes a fall of length *H*. The rope, held statically in place by the belayer, stretches a maximum amount *s* in stopping the fall, derived using the equation above, where *g* is the acceleration due to gravity and *k* is a constant. Which of the following correctly expresses *s* in terms of *m*, *g*, *H*, and *L*?

A) $s = mg + \sqrt{-m^2g^2 + 2kmg(H/L)}$

B) $s = \dfrac{mg}{k/L} + \sqrt{mg + 2kmg(H/L)}$

C) $s = \dfrac{mg \pm \sqrt{(mg)^2 + 2kmg(H/L)}}{k/L}$

D) $s = \dfrac{mg + \sqrt{(mg)^2 + 2kmg(H/L)}}{k/L}$

Continue ►

DIRECTIONS: For #16–20, solve each item and mark your answer on a special answer grid.

1. For each item, you should write your answer in the boxes at the top of each column and then fill in the ovals beneath each part of the answer you write.
2. Mark no more than one oval in any column.
3. Questions do not have negative answers.
4. Some problems have more than one possible answer. Grid only one answer.
5. See the first example below to grid mixed numbers.
6. See the last example below to grid decimal answers with more digits than the grid can accommodate.

Here are some examples:

Answer: 7/2 or 3.5	Answer: 325	Answer: 1/6, .166, or .167

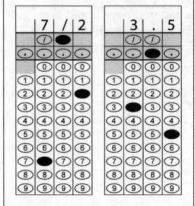

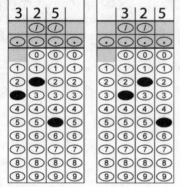

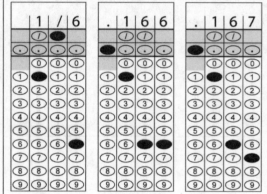

NOTE: A mixed number such as $3\frac{1}{2}$ must be gridded as 7/2 or as 3.5. If gridded as "31/2," it will be read as "thirty-one halves."

NOTE: Either position is correct.

NOTE: A decimal answer with more digits than the grid can accommodate must be truncated. A decimal such as $0.16\overline{6}$ must be gridded as .166 or .167. A less accurate value such as .16 or .17 will be scored as incorrect.

Continue

16. If $x = 2$, then $x^2 - 2x = ?$

17. If $6 \le x \le 30$, $3 \le y \le 12$, and $2 \le z \le 10$, then what is the least possible value of $\dfrac{x + y}{z}$?

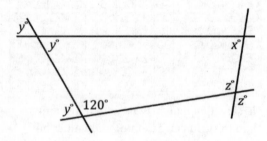

Note: Figure not drawn to scale.

18. In the figure above, $z = x$, then $x = ?$

19. If x and y are two different positive integers and $x^3 y^2 = 200$, then $xy = ?$

$$x = 6y - 2$$

$$a(y + 3) = x - b$$

20. In the system of equations above, a and b are constants. If the system has an infinite number of solutions, what is the value of $|a - b|$?

STOP

IF YOU FINISH BEFORE TIME IS CALLED, YOU MAY CHECK YOUR WORK ON THIS SECTION ONLY. DO NOT TURN TO ANY OTHER SECTION IN THE TEST.

SECTION 4—MATH, CALCULATOR

Time—55 minutes

38 items

DIRECTIONS: For #1–30, solve each item and choose the correct answer choice. Then fill in the corresponding bubble on your answer sheet. For #31–38, solve each item and enter your answer in the grid on the answer sheet. Refer to the directions before #31 on how to enter your answers for these items. Use any available space for scratchwork. Answers are on page 301.

Notes:

(1) All expressions and equations represent real numbers unless otherwise indicated.

(2) Figures that accompany problems in this test are intended to provide information useful in solving the problems. They are drawn as accurately as possible EXCEPT when it is stated in a specific problem that the figure is not drawn to scale. All figures lie in a plane unless otherwise indicated.

(3) The domain of a given function f is the set of all real numbers x for which $f(x)$ is a real number unless otherwise indicated.

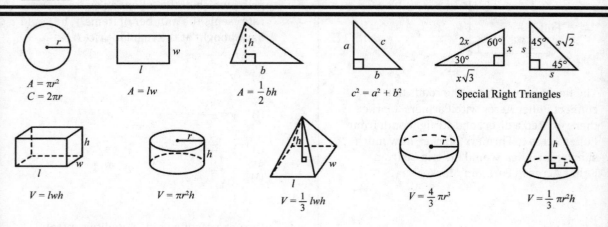

$A = \pi r^2$
$C = 2\pi r$

$A = lw$

$A = \dfrac{1}{2}bh$

$c^2 = a^2 + b^2$

Special Right Triangles

$V = lwh$

$V = \pi r^2 h$

$V = \dfrac{1}{3}lwh$

$V = \dfrac{4}{3}\pi r^3$

$V = \dfrac{1}{3}\pi r^2 h$

The number of degrees of arc in a circle is 360.

The sum of the measures in degrees of the angles of a triangle is 180.

The number of radians of arc in a circle is 2π.

Continue →

1. If the average (arithmetic mean) of 5, 5, 10, 12, and x is equal to x, what is the value of x?

A) 6
B) 8
C) 10
D) 12

2. If $x^2 + 2x + 1 = 0$, what are all the possible values of x?

A) −1 only
B) 2 only
C) −1 and 1 only
D) −1 and 2 only

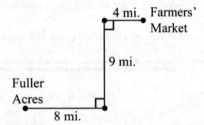

3. The figure above shows the roads that connect Fuller Acres with Farmers' Market. If there existed a direct and straight path from Fuller Acres to Farmers' Market, how much shorter, in miles, would the trip be from Fuller Acres to Farmers' Market?

A) 3
B) 4
C) 6
D) 8

4. Originally, a group of 11 students was supposed to equally share a cash prize. If 1 more student is added to the group and the 12 students share the prize equally, then each new share is worth what fraction of each original share?

A) $\dfrac{1}{12}$

B) $\dfrac{1}{11}$

C) $\dfrac{10}{11}$

D) $\dfrac{11}{12}$

5. During a sale, three of a certain item can be purchased for the usual cost of two of the items. If John buys x of the items at the sale price, which of the following expressions represents the number of items, y, he could have bought at the regular price?

A) $y = \dfrac{2x}{3}$

B) $y = \dfrac{3x}{2}$

C) $y = \dfrac{2}{3} + x$

D) $y = 3x + 2$

6. During a certain shift, a quality control inspector inspects 6 out of every 30 items produced. What was the ratio of inspected items to uninspected items during that shift?

A) 6:1
B) 5:1
C) 1:4
D) 1:5

Continue

7. If $\dfrac{13t}{7}$ is an integer, which one of the following CANNOT be t?

A) −91
B) −77
C) 3
D) 70

8. If $\dfrac{x+y}{x} = 4$ and $\dfrac{y+z}{z} = 5$, what is the value of $\dfrac{x}{z}$?

A) $\dfrac{1}{3}$

B) $\dfrac{3}{4}$

C) $\dfrac{4}{3}$

D) 3

9. On Monday, Juan withdraws $\dfrac{1}{2}$ of the money in his savings account. On Tuesday, he withdraws another \$60, leaving $\dfrac{1}{5}$ of the original amount in the account. How much money was originally in Juan's savings account?

A) \$300
B) \$200
C) \$150
D) \$120

Having X and Y	10
Having X but not Y	30
Having Y but not X	40
Having neither X nor Y	20

10. The table above gives the distribution of two genetic characteristics, X and Y, in a population of 100 subjects. What is the ratio of the number of people having characteristic X to the number of people having characteristic Y?

A) 1:3
B) 2:3
C) 4:5
D) 3:2

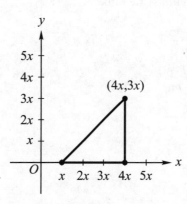

11. In the figure above, if the area of the triangle is 54, then $x = ?$

A) $3\sqrt{3}$
B) 3
C) $2\sqrt{3}$
D) $\sqrt{3}$

12. A 10,000-bushel shipping compartment is being filled with grain by a pipe at a constant rate. After 20 minutes, the container is filled to 40 percent of its capacity. After another 15 minutes, the container will be filled to what percent of its capacity?

A) 70%

B) $66\dfrac{2}{3}\%$

C) 60%
D) 55%

Continue

13. A bowling team has 5 members, 40 percent of whom averaged over 230 this fall. Of those team members who averaged more than 230, 50 percent had scores averaging 250 or better. How many people had scores averaging below 250?

A) One
B) Two
C) Three
D) Four

14. A tank contains g gallons of water. Water flows into the tank by one pipe at the rate of m gallons per minute, and water flows out by another pipe at the rate of n gallons per minute. If $n > m$, how many minutes will it take to empty the tank?

A) $\dfrac{g-m}{n}$

B) $\dfrac{g}{n-m}$

C) $\dfrac{g}{m-n}$

D) $\dfrac{n-g}{m}$

15. A training seminar offers x course choices for the morning session, y choices for the lunch roundtable discussion, and z choices for the afternoon session. Which of the following expressions represents the number of different seminar course schedules, consisting of a morning session, a lunch roundtable, and an afternoon session, that are possible?

A) $x + y + z$
B) xyz
C) $3(xyz)$
D) x^{y+z}

16. If $\dfrac{x}{y} = -1$, then $x + y = ?$

A) -2
B) -1
C) 0
D) 1

Continue

Questions #17–18 refer to the following information.

The graph below shows the density of frozen and liquid freshwater at standard atmospheric pressure as a function of temperature.

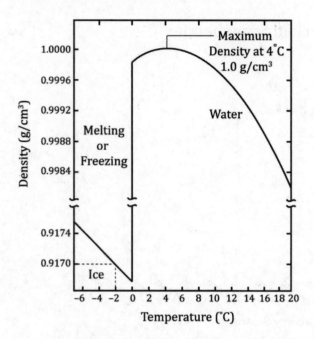

17. According to the graph, what is the difference in density between water at its maximum density and ice at −2°C?

A) 0 g/cm³
B) 0.083 g/cm³
C) 0.83 g/cm³
D) 3 g/cm³

18. Which of the following illustrations of a freezing freshwater lake is best supported by the information in the graph?

A)

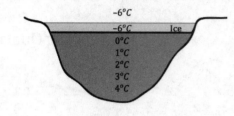

B)

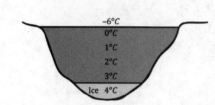

C)

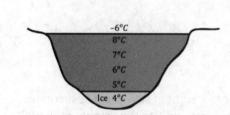

D)

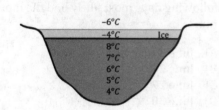

Continue

Questions #19–21 refer to the following information.

A strawberry farm charges $4.25 per quart of pre-picked strawberries (picked the day before they are sold) and $1.65 per pound of u-picked strawberries (picked the day they are sold). The weight of fresh strawberries per quart varies based on size and rainfall prior to picking. The graph below shows the average weight, in pounds, of pre-picked strawberries per quart each day during strawberry season.

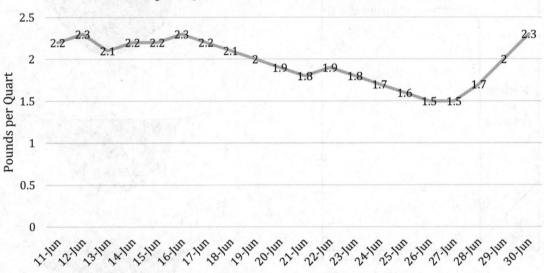

19. If the weight of strawberries increases proportionally to the amount of rainfall in the previous 24 hours, which of the following days most likely had the most rain?

A) June 21
B) June 26
C) June 27
D) June 30

20. Approximately what percentage of the maximum weight is the range of the weight of strawberries?

A) 35%
B) 25%
C) 10%
D) 5%

21. A jam recipe calls for 5 cups of crushed strawberries (equivalent to 5 pounds of strawberries) to produce eight half-pint jars of jam. What is the difference in price (in dollars) between pre-picked and u-picked strawberries sold on June 27 for the amount required to make a dozen pints of strawberry jam? (1 quart = 2 pints = 4 cups; 1 cup = 8 ounces)

A) $9.25
B) $10.50
C) $17.75
D) $24.00

Continue

22. For the numbers a, b, c, and d, the average (arithmetic mean) is twice the median. If $a < b < c < d$, $a = -2c$, $b = 0$, and $d = nc$, what is the value of n?

A)   5
B)   0
C)   −3
D)   −5

23. For a graph of the equation

$\sqrt{(x-2)^2 + (y-(-1))^2} = 3$, which of the following corresponds to the value −1 in the equation?

A)   A line drawn through the center of the circle parallel to the y-axis intersects the x-axis at −1.
B)   The radius of the circle is −1.
C)   A line drawn through the center of the circle parallel to the x-axis intersects the y-axis at −1.
D)   A line drawn through the center of the circle perpendicular to the x-axis intersects the y-axis at −1.

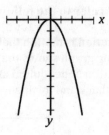

24. The graph of $y = -x^2$ is shown above. Which of the following is the graph of $y = (x-1)^2 + 2$?

A)

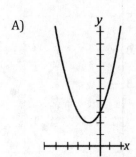

B)

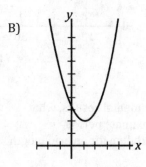

C)

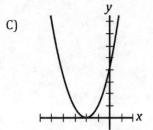

D)

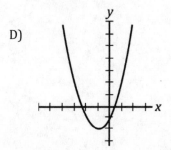

Continue

Questions #25–27 refer to the following information.

Simple harmonic motion is motion that is periodic and can be described by a frequency of oscillation, or period. The following graph shows the results of an experiment designed to measure the period, T, of a pendulum as a function of pendulum arm lengths, l. The period is defined as the time necessary for the pendulum to swing back and forth once.

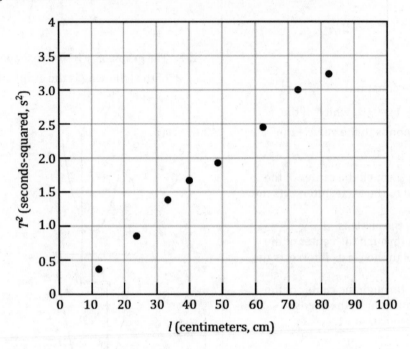

25. Based on the experimental results, what would be the approximate period, in seconds, of the pendulum for an arm length of 100 cm?

A) 1
B) 2
C) 4
D) 5

26. Which of the following is the line of best fit for the data?

A)

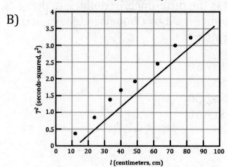

B)

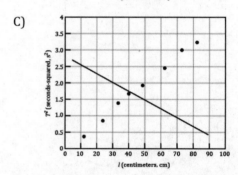

C)

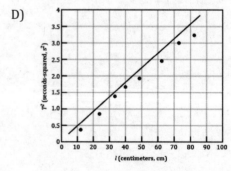

D)

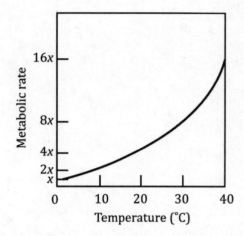

27. When the period of the pendulum is $\sqrt{2}$ seconds, what is the approximate arm length of the pendulum, in centimeters?

A)   33
B)   48
C)   62
D)   100

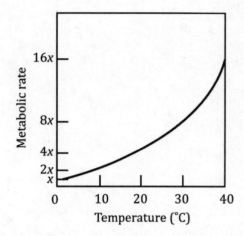

28. The graph above illustrates the effect of increased temperature on the metabolic rate in an aquatic ectotherm *Daphnia magna*, the water flea. Which of the following best represents the relationship between metabolic rate, R, and temperature, T, as illustrated in the graph?

A) $R = x(2)^{T/10}$

B) $R = 2x^{T}$

C) $R = 2T^{x}$

D) $R = 2(T + x)$

Continue ➤

Questions #29–30 refer to the following information.

For the Great Spell Check at Emerson Elementary, each child signs up sponsors who pledge a child at least $5 for participating plus five cents, ten cents, or twenty-five cents per word spelled correctly. Cooper signs up s sponsors, one-third of whom pledge five cents, one-fourth of whom pledge ten cents, and the remainder of whom pledge a quarter per word spelled correctly.

29. Which of the following represents the total amount t, in dollars, raised by Cooper in the fundraiser if he spells c words correctly?

A) $c\left(5+\dfrac{7s}{48}\right)$

B) $s\left(5+\dfrac{7c}{48}\right)$

C) $5c+\dfrac{7s}{48}$

D) $c(5+0.4s)$

30. Assume Cooper signs up 25 sponsors ($s=25$) and spells 72 words correctly ($c=72$). Maya signs up 50 sponsors, each pledging $5 plus ten cents per word spelled correctly, and spells 55 words correctly. What is the difference, in dollars, in the amounts raised by Cooper and Maya in the fundraiser?

A) $137.50
B) $87.25
C) $37.50
D) $17.00

Continue

DIRECTIONS: For #31–38, solve each item and mark your answer on a special answer grid.

1. For each item, you should write your answer in the boxes at the top of each column and then fill in the ovals beneath each part of the answer you write.
2. Mark no more than one oval in any column.
3. Questions do not have negative answers.
4. Some problems have more than one possible answer. Grid only one answer.
5. See the first example below to grid mixed numbers.
6. See the last example below to grid decimal answers with more digits than the grid can accommodate.

Here are some examples:

Answer: 7/2 or 3.5	Answer: 325	Answer: 1/6, .166, or .167

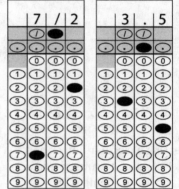

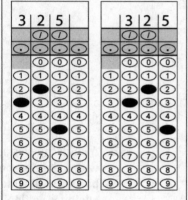

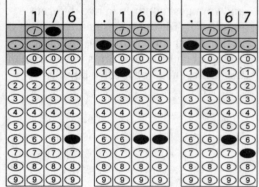

NOTE: A mixed number such as $3\frac{1}{2}$ must be gridded as 7/2 or as 3.5. If gridded as "31/2," it will be read as "thirty-one halves."

NOTE: Either position is correct.

NOTE: A decimal answer with more digits than the grid can accommodate must be truncated. A decimal such as $0.16\overline{6}$ must be gridded as .166 or .167. A less accurate value such as .16 or .17 will be scored as incorrect.

---

31. If 2 pounds of coffee make exactly 7 pots of coffee, how many pots of coffee can be made from a 10-pound bag of coffee?

32. If $(x + y)^2 = (x - y)^2 + 4$, then $xy = ?$

Continue ➡

AGE DIFFERENCE FOR CHILDREN IN FIVE FAMILIES				
Family	Oldest	Age	Youngest	Age
LaTours	Joan	15	Ed	12
Pickett	Harold	17	Claire	8
Thibault	Rene	16	Henri	3
Barber	Fred	9	Gloria	7
Newcomb	Danny	12	Syd	8

33. The table above shows the ages for the oldest and youngest children in five different families. If "Difference" is defined as the age of the oldest child minus the age of the youngest child, then what is the median of the "Difference" for the five families?

34. What is the smallest of 5 consecutive integers if the sum of the integers is 55?

35. After trimming, a sapling has $\frac{9}{10}$ of its original height. If it must grow $\frac{9}{10}$ of a foot to regain its original height, what was the original height of the sapling, in feet?

36. In right triangle ABC, $\overline{AB}$ is congruent to $\overline{BC}$. What is the value of $\frac{\sin A}{\cos C}$?

37. If $f(x) = 2x - 5$ and $g(x) = x - 2$, for what value of x does $f(x-1) = g(x+2)$?

38. A landscaper is creating a circular flower bed with a diameter of 12 feet and wants to add a border of flexible landscape edging. The edging is sold in 4-foot lengths. What is the minimum number of whole edging lengths that need to be purchased to encircle the bed? (Ignore the thickness of the edging.) ($\pi \approx 3.14$)

STOP

IF YOU FINISH BEFORE TIME IS CALLED, YOU MAY CHECK YOUR WORK ON THIS SECTION ONLY. DO NOT TURN TO ANY OTHER SECTION IN THE TEST.

SECTION 5—ESSAY (OPTIONAL)

Time—50 minutes

1 essay prompt

DIRECTIONS: The essay measures your ability to read and understand a passage and write an essay that analyzes the passage. In your essay, demonstrate that you have carefully read the passage, write a clear and logical analysis, and use language precisely.

You have 50 minutes to read the passage and write an essay in response to the provided prompt. Sample essays are on page 323.

Read the passage below and think about how Lindsey uses

- evidence (facts, examples, etc.) to support claims.
- reasoning to develop the passage and to connect claims and evidence.
- rhetorical or persuasive elements, such as language choices or emotional appeals, to increase the impact of the ideas expressed.

Adapted from Rebecca Lindsey's article "Tropical Deforestation," published on earthobservatory.nasa.gov in March 2007.

1 Stretching out from the equator on all Earth's land surfaces is a wide belt of forests of amazing diversity and productivity. Tropical forests include dense rainforests, seasonally moist forests, and drier, more open woodlands. Tropical forests of all varieties are disappearing rapidly as humans clear the natural landscape. Although deforestation meets some human needs, it also has profound consequences, including social conflict, extinction of plants and animals, and climate change—challenges that aren't just local, but global.

2 Although tropical forests cover only about 7 percent of the Earth's dry land, they probably harbor about half of all species on Earth. As people clear large areas of tropical forests, entire species are vanishing. In addition to the species lost when an area is totally deforested, the plants and animals in the forest that remains also become increasingly vulnerable to extinction. Changes in the types of trees, plants, and insects that can survive in the fragments rapidly reduce biodiversity in the remaining forest.

3 The genetic diversity of tropical forests is the deepest end of the planetary gene pool. Hidden in the genes of plants, animals, fungi, and bacteria that have not even been discovered yet may be cures for cancer and other diseases or the key to improving the yield and nutritional quality of foods. Finally, genetic diversity in the planetary gene pool is crucial for the resilience of all life on Earth to rare but catastrophic environmental events.

4 When people clear the forests, carbon stored in the wood returns to the atmosphere, enhancing the greenhouse effect and global warming. Undisturbed tropical forests may be nearly neutral with respect to carbon, but deforestation is currently a source of carbon to the atmosphere and has the potential to turn the tropics into an even greater source. Forest regrowth and crops recapture some carbon, but overall, deforestation is a source of atmospheric carbon dioxide and therefore a contributor to global warming.

5 Although subsistence activities have dominated agriculture-driven deforestation in the tropics to date, large-scale commercial activities are playing an increasingly significant role. On the southern margin of the

Amazon, in the state of Mato Grosso, Brazil, huge expanses of rainforest are being cleared by industrial producers.

6 Brazil led the world in terms of total deforested area between 1990 and 2005. The country lost 163,436 square miles of forest, roughly the size of California. Rounding out the top five tropical countries with the greatest total area of deforestation were Indonesia, Sudan, Myanmar, and the Democratic Republic of Congo.

7 Although tropical forests are largely confined to developing countries, they aren't just meeting local or national needs; economic globalization means that the needs and wants of the global population are bearing down on them as well. Direct causes of deforestation are agricultural expansion, wood extraction and infrastructure expansion such as road building and urbanization.

8 Strategies for preserving tropical forests can operate on local to international scales. On a local scale, governments and non-governmental organizations are working with forest communities to encourage low-impact agricultural activities, such as shade farming, as well as the sustainable harvesting of non-wood forest products such as rubber, cork, produce, or medicinal plants. Parks and protected areas that draw tourists can provide employment and educational opportunities for local people as well as stimulating related service-sector economies.

9 For tropical forests to survive, governments must develop realistic scenarios for future deforestation that take into account what scientists already know about the causes and consequences of deforestation. Although deforestation in the tropics is rapid and widespread, some people are making an increasing effort to mitigate potential disaster. Sustainable harvesting of native plants, shade farming, nature preserves, and management by indigenous peoples are techniques that help maintain a vital resource.

10 Finally, on the national and international scale, an increasing value in the global marketplace for products that are certified as sustainably produced or harvested may provide incentives for landowners to adopt more forest-friendly practices, and for regional and national governments to create and enforce forest-preservation policies. Direct payments to tropical countries for the ecosystem services that intact tropical forest provide, particularly for carbon storage to offset greenhouse gas emissions, are likely to become an important international mechanism for sustaining tropical forests as more countries begin to seriously tackle the problem of global warming.

Write an essay explaining how Lindsey develops her argument that global strategies that preserve tropical rainforests and combat deforestation must be implemented. In your essay, analyze how Lindsey uses one or more of the elements listed before the passage (or other elements) to make her argument more logical and persuasive. Be sure to focus on the most relevant aspects of the passage.

Your essay should not discuss whether you agree with Lindsey's claims but rather discuss how she develops her argument.

Appendix A:
Answers and Explanations

READING QUIZZES

Reading Quiz I (p. 3)

1. **(A)** *Reading/Social Studies/Vocabulary.* The word "nomological" will not be familiar to most students. The item illustrates, however, that it is possible to use the context in which the word appears to arrive at a good guess as to its meaning. In this case, the Hempel model views history as a science and claims that it can produce conclusions that can be logically deduced from laws. These two elements, logic and laws, are the heart of the theory. Since "deductive-nomological" is intended to describe this view, and since deduction describes the "logical" element, we can infer that "nomological" describes the "law-like" element.

2. **(D)** *Reading/Social Studies/Vocabulary.* The burden of Passage A is that it is not reasonable to expect historical explanations to be as good as scientific explanations because there are so many variables that must be taken into account. However, according to the author of Passage A, if it were possible to capture and account for all the variables, then a scientifically valid historical conclusion could be drawn—the "if" being an "adequately articulated" set of empirical laws. Thus, in this case, the phrase means "sufficiently detailed," (D).

3. **(C)** *Reading/Social Studies/Application.* In the third paragraph of Passage A, the author notes that history may seem to be different from the Natural Sciences because it does not allow for laboratory experiments. Then, the author mentions a series of revolutions. We can infer that the author thinks that a series of observed historical events can confirm a hypothesis in the same way that a series of laboratory experiments can.

4. **(B)** *Reading/Social Studies/Explicit Detail.* Toward the end of the third paragraph, the author of Passage A specifically states that it is "difficult to find a sufficiently large number of revolutions" to test the validity of a scientific hypothesis, (B). While (A) is true, it does not respond to the question asked. (C) and (D) are both incorrect since they are not mentioned in Passage A.

5. **(C)** *Reading/Social Studies/Voice.* In the third paragraph, the author argues that historical explanations would seem more scientific if data from other disciplines were incorporated into its explanations. To use the example of a revolution, we might expect that a "complete" historical explanation might include information from psychology about something such as a "frustration threshold." For example, the average person is ready to revolt when the standard of living drops by 25 percent. So, the author apparently believes that these disciplines are able to provide reliable data.

6. **(B)** *Reading/Social Studies/Main Idea.* The burden of the author's argument is to demonstrate that history, when properly understood, is as much a science as physics or chemistry.

7. **(B)** *Reading/Social Studies/Explicit Detail.* Passage B mentions *Verstehen* in the third paragraph as the technique that is used by historians to get at the "inside" of an event—the "why," or the motives and intentions, of the actors, (B). (A) is incorrect because "understanding" would not apply to the "outside" or physical aspect of an event. As for (C), while psychology and sociology study intentions and motives, they do not employ *Verstehen*. Rather, those disciplines emulate the hard sciences. (D) is incorrect since the whole point of *Verstehen* is that historical laws simply do not exist.

8. **(D)** *Reading/Social Studies/Application.* The author of Passage A argues that both human actions and strictly physical events are governed by scientific laws; the author of Passage B argues that human actions are not governed by scientific laws, though purely physical events are. Thus, despite their disagreement, both authors would share the intuition that purely physical events are law-like.

9. **(D)** *Reading/Natural Sciences/Explicit Detail.* All electromagnetic waves, including radio waves and radar waves, travel at 300,000 kilometers per second, or the speed of light (lines 21–22). Frequency, (A), which is measured in cycles per second, (C), and wavelength, (B), are different for different electromagnetic waves.

10. **(D)** *Reading/Natural Sciences/Application.* Line 36 states: $\text{wavelength} = \dfrac{\text{speed}}{\text{frequency}}$ and line 45 states that 1 megahertz = 1,000,000 cycles per second. Thus, 3,000 megahertz = 3,000,000,000 cycles per second.

    Therefore, $\dfrac{300,000 \text{ km/sec}}{3,000,000,000 \text{ cps}} = 0.0001 \text{ km}$, or 0.1 m, (D).

11. **(D)** *Reading/Natural Sciences/Explicit Detail.* Lines 16–18 state that radar waves "are not deflected by atmospheric layers and therefore always travel in a straight line—in all weather, both day and night." Thus, radar can track an airplane traveling at supersonic speeds, (A); in any atmospheric condition, (B); or above the atmosphere, since radar is unaffected by the atmosphere itself, (C). However, since radar waves travel in a straight line, they cannot be used to locate an airplane flying below the horizon, (D).

12. **(C)** *Reading/Natural Sciences/Explicit Detail.* Lines 13–14 state that "the time it takes for the signal to return indicates the distance to the object." This is possible because the speed of electromagnetic waves, including radar, is constant, (C).

13. **(D)** *Reading/Natural Sciences/Explicit Detail.* The equation relating frequency and wavelength is given in line 36: $\text{wavelength} = \dfrac{\text{speed}}{\text{frequency}}$. Therefore, as wavelength increases, frequency decreases; conversely, as frequency increases, wavelength decreases. This describes an inverse relationship between the two variables, (D).

14. **(C)** *Reading/Natural Sciences/Explicit Detail.* According to the table, a television signal has a wavelength of 1 meter, (C). All of the other choices have much shorter wavelengths.

15. **(A)** *Reading/Natural Sciences/Application.* If microwaves penetrate the ionosphere while radio waves cannot, then this indicates that any signals with shorter wavelengths than microwaves can penetrate the ionosphere. Therefore, X-rays must also penetrate the ionosphere, since X-rays have wavelengths that are shorter than microwaves, (A).

16. **(B)** *Reading/Natural Sciences/Explicit Detail.* According to the table, visible light rays have much longer wavelengths than do cosmic rays. Therefore, as indicated by the wavelength equation (line 36), the frequency of visible light is lower than the frequency of cosmic rays, (B).

17. **(B)** *Reading/Natural Sciences/Application.* Since "radar waves detect objects by their varying densities" (lines 15–16), it is the difference in air mass densities that allows meteorologists to employ weather radar, (B). Although radar travels in straight lines, (A); in all conditions, (C); and at the speed of light, (D), these factors are not as crucial as density.

18. **(B)** *Reading/Natural Sciences/Application.* According to the passage, radar can be used to find the distance to an object because radar waves travel at a fixed rate. Therefore, if the distance to an object can be determined from an echo in a similar fashion, sound waves must also travel at a fixed rate, (B).

Reading Quiz II Brain Buster (p. 8)

1. **(D)** *Reading/Social Studies/Main Idea.* The author begins by stating that the Agricultural Adjustment Act of 1933 was declared unconstitutional; then, the author describes the administration's reaction to that decision. Specifically, the author details the difficulties of the administration in working out a second and permanent agricultural policy, the Agricultural Adjustment Act of 1938. This development is correctly described by (D). (A) is wrong for two reasons. First, the author doesn't really analyze the connection between changes in the weather and fluctuations in farm prices. Second, the connection is only a part of the overall discussion. (B) is wrong because, while the reader might learn something about farmers during the Great Depression, this is not the *author's* purpose in writing the passage. Finally, (C) is wrong because, while the passage might be used to argue that Roosevelt's policy had some weaknesses, finding weaknesses is not the main point of the passage.

2. **(A)** *Reading/Social Studies/Vocabulary.* The author explains that many farmers who otherwise supported Roosevelt refused to participate in voluntary production control programs. Thus, they were favorable toward Roosevelt but not entirely committed. The best choice to describe this shifting attitude is *wavering*.

3. **(D)** *Reading/Social Studies/Explicit Detail.* The phrase "according to" identifies this as an Explicit Detail item, and the item stem includes the thought-reverser "EXCEPT," so the correct choice is NOT explicitly stated in the passage. (A) and (C) are mentioned in the second paragraph. (B) is developed in the final paragraph. Only (D) is not mentioned in the passage: while the passage states that the administration wanted a bill that would not be struck down, it does not indicate that constitutional concerns were an impediment to the bill's passage.

4. **(A)** *Reading/Social Studies/Implied Idea.* The word "implies" identifies this as an Implied Idea item, so the correct answer is not directly stated in the passage but is inferable. In the final paragraph, the author describes the sequence of events that led to the passage of the 1938 legislation, and he shows how Roosevelt used the changing economic conditions to his advantage. In this discussion, the author implies that the changing economic conditions were a critical factor in the passage of the bill. Therefore, (A) is the best choice. (B) is wrong because, while the author does state that some farm groups were displeased with the new bill, as it was written primarily by members of the Farm Bureau, it is not inferable that the Secretary of Agriculture was blamed for this. (C) is wrong because it represents a confused reading of the passage: the author never states why the 1933 Act was voided but later does say that it was the new legislation (which would finally become the 1938 Act) that was written by members of the Farm Bureau. (D) is wrong because the Soil Conservation and Domestic Allotment Act, not the CCC (Commodity Credit Corporation), encouraged farmers to take their land out of production.

5. **(D)** *Reading/Social Studies/Textual Evidence.* The excerpt makes it clear that large harvests resulted in agricultural surpluses. With a glut on the market, prices began to fall, and farmers panicked. The pressure on farmers produced a demand for government action, and Roosevelt was able to extract various concessions in return for that action.

6. **(B)** *Reading/Social Studies/Implied Idea.* In the third paragraph, the author states that *since* ten members of the Committee of Eighteen were members of the American Farm Bureau Federation, the bill was labeled a Farm Bureau Bill and opposed by the Farmer's Holiday Association (FHA). Therefore, it is inferable that the Farmer's Holiday Association opposed the American Farm Bureau Federation, (B). (A) is wrong because, while the passage does state that the bill was not, at first, strongly supported by Roosevelt, the author does not give that as the reason for the opposition to the bill by the Farmer's Holiday Association. (C) is wrong because, while the passage does state that some groups opposed the bill for the reason given in (C), the author does not give this as the reason for the FHA's opposition; in fact, it seems more likely that the FHA would favor a bill for farmers even if it did entail government spending. (D) is wrong because, while the author does mention that opponents of the bill charged that it favored large-scale farmers, the passage does not imply that this was the reason for the FHA's opposition.

7. **(B)** *Reading/Social Studies/Textual Evidence.* The excerpt explains that the Committee of Eighteen was dominated by the American Farm Bureau Federation, which prompted outcry and opposition from the competing Farmer's Holiday Association.

8. **(D)** *Reading/Social Studies/Implied Idea.* Under Wallace's plan, the Commodity Credit Corporation (CCC) would grant farmers loans that could be repaid in the future when the grain was sold. It is inferable that the loans were intended to be a substitute for the revenue generated by the immediate sale of the grain. So, in essence, the loan simply postponed the farmer's sale of grain and eventual financial gain. (A) is wrong because the loan in no way provided an incentive to take land out of production. If anything, when guaranteed some sort of a return, farmers would have an incentive to increase acreage. (B) is wrong because the passage does not mention the successful enactment of a mandatory soil conservation program. (C) is wrong because the passage states that Roosevelt made the granting of loans through the CCC contingent upon Congress's willingness to support the AAA, not the farmer's willingness.

9. **(A)** *Reading/Social Studies/Voice.* Eliminate (D) because the tone of the passage is neutral. The first words of the remaining choices seem correct. One might describe the passage as scholarly, objective, or analytical. Eliminate (B), however, because the author doesn't offer a negative assessment of the policies; and eliminate (C) because the tone of the passage is not abrasive. Therefore, by the process of elimination, (A) is the correct choice. Indeed, "appreciative" is supported by the author's reference to Roosevelt's "adroit" political maneuver (Line 61), which indicates that the author appreciates the significance of that move.

10. **(B)** *Reading/Social Studies/Vocabulary.* The final paragraph describes how Roosevelt took advantage of market conditions to exact from farmers the concessions he wanted. This type of political maneuvering is described by the author as "adroit," meaning skillful.

11. **(B)** *Reading/Social Studies/Data Presentations.* The line for 1937 shows prices dropping precipitously in the summer of 1937, almost to the point in December where they reach the lows of 1933.

12. **(A)** *Reading/Social Studies/Voice.* The passage is mostly describes the theories of Burnham. However, the author's tone shifts dramatically in the last paragraph. In the final paragraph, the author harshly criticizes Burnham for being hypocritical.

13. **(B)** *Reading/Social Studies/Explicit Detail.* The methodological weakness in Burnham's argument, according to the author, is the uncritical reliance on the assumption that existing conditions would continue to exist into the indefinite future. This myopia caused Burnham to overlook important developments that would ultimately prove his theory false.

14. **(D)** *Reading/Social Studies/Textual Evidence.* As discussed above, the weakness in Burnham's approach was to assume that existing conditions would continue to hold. The excerpt cited by (D) specifically makes this point.

15. **(A)** *Reading/Social Studies/Implied Idea.* The author states that most thinkers identify three political entities, beginning with the individual, and consider society an embodiment of the individual and the state a logical outgrowth of the individual and the society. Burnham inverts that sequence and theorizes that the state is the logical beginning and individuals are merely parts of the state, (A).

16. **(A)** *Reading/Social Studies/Explicit Detail.* The phrase "According to" identifies this as an Explicit Detail item, so the correct choice is explicitly stated in the passage (lines 35–40). (B) and (C) are both wrong because, while mentioned in the passage, they are not mentioned in the second paragraph where the author talks about the end of history. (D) is wrong because it is not stated in the passage. Therefore, (A) is the best choice: apparently, what the author means is that history will end because there will no longer be any change; instead, the state will prescribe certain forms to which individuals must conform.

17. **(C)** *Reading/Social Studies/Main Idea.* (C) is the best choice: the author describes Burnham's theories and then criticizes them. (A) is wrong because the author does not present his own vision. (B) is wrong because, although the author mentions the fact that Burnham's predictions were false, this observation is only a part of his criticism of Burnham's views. (D) is wrong because the author never mentions Burnham's literary style.

18. **(C)** *Reading/Social Studies/Vocabulary.* The author states that Burnham inverts traditional political theory. Whereas traditional thinkers, such as John Locke, believed that the individual first existed in a state of nature and then entered into society and only later created the state, Burnham argued that individuals have never existed outside of society and the state. (Note: Burnham would likely say that so-called survivalists do not constitute a counter-example, as these individuals existed first in society and state and only later declared themselves outside.)

19. **(B)** *Reading/Social Studies/Implied Idea.* Burnham paints a very dark vision of the future, a future in which the means of production are controlled by a managerial elite and the majority of people would be under harsh autocratic rule.

20. **(B)** *Reading/Social Studies/Textual Evidence.* The excerpt provided by (B) summarizes nicely the dark vision of Burnham: an autocracy even more extreme than that in Stalin's Russia. The author goes on into the next paragraph to develop this notion in greater detail, and a couple of sentences there also provide good support for our conclusion. But, of course, those were not offered to us as answer choices.

21. **(A)** *Reading/Social Studies/Vocabulary.* In the final paragraph, the author accuses Burnham and, indeed, the British intelligentsia of a very grave moral weakness. According to the author, the ultimate goal of Burnham and the other intelligentsia was to dismantle egalitarian socialism and create a new hierarchical society in which they were at the top.

22. **(B)** *Reading/Natural Sciences/Main Idea.* One of the striking features about the passage is that the author does not first produce a contention and then offer facts to support it. Rather, the author's method is to produce the facts and then ask what conclusions might be drawn, (B). (A) is wrong because the author is not arguing for a single conclusion but is instead working toward a conclusion by exploring data. (C) is wrong for the same reason as (A): the author does answer some objections along the way, but that is not the main purpose. (D) is wrong because, while the final paragraph does seem to be a sort of challenge, there is a lot more going on in the passage than (D) suggests.

23. **(A)** *Reading/Natural Sciences/Explicit Detail.* How do we know that the meteor is from Mars? The answer is found in the first paragraph, which states that oxygen isotopes found in the group of meteorites match the analysis of the Martian atmosphere. Therefore, (A) is the best choice. As for the remaining choices, while they mention ideas from the passage, each of them proves something different; many serve as evidence of microorganisms rather than as evidence of where the meteorite originated.

24. **(A)** *Reading/Natural Sciences/Explicit Detail.* This is an Explicit Detail item. All of the ideas given are mentioned in the passage, but (B), (C), and (D) all provide evidence that ALH84001 may show signs of life. As for (B), the PAHs, while possibly produced by inorganic processes, might have been produced by living matter. As for (C) and (D), the odd deposits suggest chemical processes. (A), however, suggests only that the rock came from Mars, not that it contains signs of extinct life.

25. **(B)** *Reading/Natural Sciences/Explicit Detail.* The passage states that the carbonate deposits might have come from inorganic processes (lines 27–29), but they seem more likely to have been deposited by a microorganism (lines 37–39). Similarly, the PAHs are different from the byproducts of ordinary combustion (lines 41–44), but, according to the author, they might conceivably be the result of inorganic reactions (lines 46–48).

26. **(A)** *Reading/Natural Sciences/Development.* This item asks about the connection between the two ideas mentioned in the stem and the larger argument. Why does the author mention gravitation and space? Well, there are some shapes in the meteorite that seem to be bacteria, or at least they have the right shape, but they are very, very small compared to any bacteria we actually know. So, the author suggests that the unique conditions on Mars (weaker gravitational field) and the conditions in the rock (small spaces) might mean that the bacteria would be small.

27. **(C)** *Reading/Natural Sciences/Vocabulary.* The author uses the word "form" several times in this part of the passage and contrasts morphology with size. Morphology is shape or structure.

28. **(D)** *Reading/Natural Sciences/Application* The author seems to be inclined toward the view that the scientific evidence is at least consistent with the possibility of life on Mars. Of course, the author does not go so far as to say that the data conclusively proves the existence of life on Mars, but, on balance, that would seem to be the author's view.

29. **(D)** *Reading/Natural Sciences/Textual Evidence.* The argument offered by the author is really pretty weak, but there is no mistaking its structure. The author says, in essence, "No one has yet disproved my argument, so it must be correct."

30. **(B)** *Reading/Natural Sciences/Vocabulary.* At this point in the passage, the author is referring to the amounts or quantities of PAHs found on objects that have fallen to earth.

31. **(C)** *Reading/Natural Sciences/Data Presentations.* Given the conditions found today on Mars (see table), H_2O would be found to the right of the vertical dividing line for ice and well below pressure at which H_2O would exist as a liquid. In that region, H_2O is ice.

WRITING AND LANGUAGE QUIZZES

Writing and Language Quiz I (p. 17)

Passage I

1. **(B)** *Writing and Language/Standard English Conventions/Grammar and Usage/Pronoun Usage.* The original sentence is incorrect because the pronoun "one" does not agree with its antecedent "most people." (B) corrects this problem. (C) is wrong because, like the original, it uses a singular pronoun, not a plural one. Additionally, "that" should be used instead of "which" since the introduced material specifies the type of crime. Finally, (D) is wrong because it creates a shifting point of view.

2. **(C)** *Writing and Language/Standard English Conventions/Grammar and Usage/Diction.* The contraction of "it is" is written as "it's." "Its" is a possessive pronoun, therefore (A) is incorrect. (B) is wrong because "they," which is plural, is intended to refer to "a certain crime," which is singular.

3. **(B)** *Writing and Language/Expression of Ideas/Strategy/Effective Transitional Sentence.* "Moreover" is not a logical transitional word choice. It signals a continuation of a thought, while the author clearly implies a contrast. (B) makes the appropriate correction by using "however" to signal a contrast. (C) is wrong for the same reason that the original sentence is wrong. (D) is wrong because "therefore" is used to signal a logical deduction rather than a contrasting idea.

4. **(A)** *Writing and Language/Expression of Ideas/No Change.* The original sentence is correct; "odd" logically functions to demonstrate that the "confidence scheme" would not normally be viewed as the worst crime.

5. **(C)** *Writing and Language/Standard English Conventions/Sentence Structure/Fragments.* The underlined portion of the original sentence creates a sentence fragment. "Although" is a subordinate conjunction used to introduce a dependent clause, and a dependent clause is not a complete sentence. (C) corrects this problem by replacing "although" with the coordinate conjunction "but" and creates a correctly punctuated compound sentence. (B) eliminates the sentence fragment problem but makes the mistake of illogical subordination. The intended meaning of the original sentence requires that the second idea (the crime is heartless) has the same emphasis as the first idea (the crime is nonviolent). However, "though" is used to introduce a subordinate idea. (D) eliminates the fragment problem and creates a proper compound sentence in which the two ideas are given equal importance, but it is incorrect since "and" signals a similarity of ideas.

6. **(A)** *Writing and Language/Standard English Conventions/No Change.* The original sentence is correct. (B) is wrong because "it" does not agree with its plural antecedent, "con artists." Both (C) and (D) are awkward. Additionally, (C) is wrong because "its" does not have an antecedent. (D) is also wrong because the possessive pronoun "their," not the objective pronoun "them," must modify the gerund.

7. **(C)** *Writing and Language/Standard English Conventions/Punctuation/Commas.* The original sentence is incorrect because the punctuation disrupts the parallel direct objects "honesty and trust." (C) appropriately punctuates the sentence. (B) fails to eliminate the incorrect punctuation. As for (D), a comma is necessary to set off the parenthetical phrase describing honesty and trust.

8. **(C)** *Writing and Language/Standard English Conventions/Punctuation/Commas.* The original sentence runs together two ideas: "simplistic" and "almost infantile." (C) correctly separates them with a comma.

9. **(D)** *Writing and Language/Expression of Ideas/Style/Idiomatic Expression* The use of "on account of" to indicate a causal relationship is informal usage and unacceptable in standard written English. (B) fails to correct the error and creates an awkward sentence. (C) is awkward and substitutes another unacceptable phrase ("owing to"). (D) expresses the correct causal relationship by using the word "because."

10. **(D)** *Writing and Language/Standard English Conventions/Sentence Structure/Faulty Parallelism.* The original underlined portion is incorrect because it does not maintain the parallel structure of the sentence. The auxiliary verb "can" governs the other verbs in the sentence, so the form of the verb "to dangle" must be parallel to both "win" and "talk." Only (D) provides the necessary verb form.

11. **(C)** *Writing and Language/Standard English Conventions/Grammar and Usage/Sequence and Verb Tense.* The use of the future tense in the original sentence conflicts with the other present tense verbs in the paragraph. (B) is wrong because the use of the infinitive verb form eliminates the only conjugated verb in the clause, thus reducing the clause to a fragment. (D) is wrong because "is" is singular and does not agree with the plural noun "targets."

12. **(B)** *Writing and Language/Standard English Conventions/Grammar and Usage/Pronoun Usage.* The underlined material in parentheses is not incidental to the passage's development—it has the same status as "the primary targets . . . are the elderly and women." Therefore, it should be incorporated into the main body of the passage. Additionally, it is not clear whether "they" refers to women, criminals, or the elderly. The use of "con artists" in (B) corrects this ambiguity.

13. **(A)** *Writing and Language/Expression of Ideas/Strategy/Data Presentation.* (A) does a very nice job of showing that the traditional demographics for con games have changed. It uses information from the graph to show that men and women are equally likely to be targeted, and it shows that the number of victims over 60 is actually less than the number in the age ranges between 20 and 59.

14. **(D)** *Writing and Language/Expression of Ideas/Strategy/Data Presentation.* (D) does an excellent job of responding to the question. The writer wants to identify the group that was monetarily hurt the worst, and that would be males under the age of 20. That group had the fewest members but suffered the greatest loss. The other choices focus on the number of complaints filed, not the greatest monetary loss.

15. **(D)** *Writing and Language/Expression of Ideas/Strategy/Data Presentation.* The stem notes that the declines in reports for 2012 and 2013 might lead one to question whether internet fraud will continue to increase. (D) analyzes the data to reach the opposite conclusion: we've had dips before, but each time the numbers started increasing again.

16. **(A)** *Writing and Language/Expression of Ideas/Strategy/Main Idea.* (B), (C), and (D) are assertions that can be empirically verified. (A), on the other hand, expresses an opinion.

17. **(A)** *Writing and Language/Expression of Ideas/Organization/Passage-Level Structure.* A striking feature of the passage is its generality. An example or two would help the reader appreciate the points that the author makes.

18. **(C)** *Writing and Language/Expression of Ideas/Strategy/Appropriate Supporting Material.* A specific example of how a con game preys on and breaks a person's trust would strengthen the author's argument.

Passage II

19. **(D)** *Writing and Language/Expression of Ideas/Style/Conciseness*. The underlined material is irrelevant to the discussion of the character of Elizabeth; it should be deleted.

20. **(C)** *Writing and Language/Standard English Conventions/Grammar and Usage/Subject-Verb Agreement and Sequence and Verb Tense*. The original sentence is incorrect because the verb "is" is singular and must be plural to agree with "splendor and pleasure." In addition, the past tense is needed in order to agree with the other past tense verbs in the passage.

21. **(D)** *Writing and Language/Standard English Conventions/Sentence Structure/Fragments*. The original sentence is incorrect because the material following "age" creates a fragment. Additionally, the comma after "even" is incorrect because "even" is intended to be a part of the parenthetical phrase "even to old age." (B) is wrong because the use of the present tense conflicts with the past tense verbs in the rest of the paragraph. (C) also fails because it is in the present tense and because a second comma is required after "age" to complete the parenthetical expression. (D) is correct because its verb is in the past tense and because the parenthetical expression is correctly set off by two commas.

22. **(C)** *Writing and Language/Standard English Conventions/Grammar and Usage/Pronoun Usage*. The original sentence is incorrect because the object pronoun "whom," not "who," is required (she outwitted "them," not "they"). (B) is wrong because the pronoun "that" should not be used to refer to people. (D) is wrong because "whom," not "who," is required, and the past progressive tense is awkward.

23. **(A)** *Writing and Language/Expression of Ideas/No Change*. The original sentence is correct. The underlined phrase should not be omitted since it describes an important trait of Elizabeth's character. Therefore, (D) is wrong. (B) and (C) are awkward.

24. **(A)** *Writing and Language/Standard English Conventions/No Change*. The original sentence is correct. (B) is wrong because it is not idiomatic. (C) is wrong because the tense is incorrect; it suggests that Elizabeth was "being" before and up to the time the statesmen saw her. The original sentence indicates that she was "being" Elizabeth at the same time they saw her. Additionally, omitting the gerund changes the meaning of the sentence. (D) suggests "far" in the sense of distance, which makes little sense in this context.

25. **(B)** *Writing and Language/Standard English Conventions/Grammar and Usage/Diction*. The idiomatic form of comparison in English is "as . . . as," (B).

26. **(A)** *Writing and Language/Expression of Ideas/No Change*. The original sentence is correct. The other choices are needlessly wordy or awkward.

27. **(B)** *Writing and Language/Standard English Conventions/Grammar and Usage/Verb Tense*. The original sentence is incorrect because the past perfect tense is wrong and because the past participle should be "become," not "became." (C) is wrong because it suggests an ongoing state of affairs, but the sentence intends that the transformation occurred and was completed at a certain point in time. (D) is wrong because the switch to the present tense creates a conflict of tenses. (B) correctly provides the past tense.

28. **(A)** *Writing and Language/Standard English Conventions/No Change*. The original sentence is correct. All the other choices are wrong because they are not idiomatic. In English, the correct phrasing is to say that someone has "superiority over" someone or that someone is "superior to" someone.

29. **(C)** *Writing and Language/Standard English Conventions/Grammar and Usage/Diction*. The original sentence is incorrect because "more nobler" is not idiomatic since "nobler" is already the comparative form of the adjective. (B) is wrong because the comma illogically separates the noun from its corresponding prepositional phrase. (D) fails to correct the original error and suffers from the same punctuation defects as (B). (C) correctly omits "more" and does not include a comma.

30. **(C)** *Writing and Language/Standard English Conventions/Sentence Structure/Run-On Sentences.* The original sentence is incorrect because it is a run-on sentence. The comma after "genius" is not enough to separate the two independent clauses—it is preferable to start a new sentence.

31. **(D)** *Writing and Language/Standard English Conventions/Sentence Structure/Faulty Parallelism.* The original sentence is incorrect because it fails to preserve the sentence's parallel construction. (B) is wrong because it changes the meaning of the sentence. It implies that Elizabeth endeavored to keep her throne and to keep England out of war because she wanted to restore civil and religious order. (C) is wrong because it does not maintain the parallelism of the sentence. (D) correctly preserves the sentence's parallel construction.

32. **(A)** *Writing and Language/Expression of Ideas/Organization/Passage-Level Structure.* The passage is a discussion of Elizabeth's character. Some biographical background might have provided the reader with a context in which to place the later discussion.

33. **(B)** *Writing and Language/Expression of Ideas/Strategy/Audience.* Since the passage is a discussion of Elizabeth's character, the information was most likely excerpted from a biographical information source.

34. **(B)** *Writing and Language/Expression of Ideas/Strategy/Appropriate Supporting Material.* The passage speaks in general terms about Elizabeth's character. Some specific examples of her dual nature would help the reader appreciate what the author means by those descriptions.

Writing and Language Quiz II Brain Buster (p. 25)

1. **(C)** *Writing and Language/Standard English Conventions/Sentence Structure/Faulty Parallelism.* The sentence should read: "for her luminous beauty, for her acclaimed acting ability, and for her humanitarian work with organizations." (B) fails to address the problem of parallelism. Additionally, "humanitarian organizations work" is awkward. (D) fails because it does not replicate the "for her…" structure used by the first two elements in the series.

2. **(C)** *Writing and Language/Standard English Conventions/Sentence Structure/Incomplete Split Constructions.* The problem with the original is the improperly completed split construction: "as great or greater…than." (C) corrects this by substituting "at least as great…as," which is logically equivalent to "as great as or greater than." (B) fails to correct the original error. (D) changes the meaning of the original with the phrase "can be," which implies a state of affairs contingent upon some unstated event or factor.

3. **(D)** *Writing and Language/Standard English Conventions/Sentence Structure/Misplaced Modifiers.* The original contains an ambiguity. It is not clear whether "caused by" is supposed to modify "increase" or "churn"; consequently, the reader must work to determine whether it is the churn or the increase in the churn that is the problem that results from the greater customer willingness to switch providers. Of course, it is the increase that is caused by customer willingness to switch, and you will likely figure this out for yourself; but, in general, a properly written sentence should not require so much work of the reader. (D) is better because it avoids the ambiguity. (B) is wrong because it fails to remove the ambiguity and introduces a new error. (B) implies that the offers switch the providers rather than provide a reason to switch. (C) corrects the error of the original but introduces a new problem: does "dramatic" modify "churn" or "increase"?

4. **(C)** *Writing and Language/Standard English Conventions/Grammar and Usage/Verb Tense.* The original sentence contains two similar errors. First, the use of the present participle "originating" fails to show that

the action of "originating" is completed and in the past. To reflect the correct sequence of events, the sentence should use a verb to show past action. Second, there is an error of diction. To show bloodlines, the sentence needs the word "descended," not "descending." "Descending" used here suggests the dog is walking down a staircase. (B) makes the first correction but not the second. (D) makes both needed changes, but the way in which the first change is made changes the intended meaning of the original sentence. (D) implies that it is "the water spaniel" that "originated in ancient times in the Mediterranean area," but in the original, this phrase modifies "Bichon Frisé." Only (C) makes both needed changes without introducing another error.

5. **(B)** *Writing and Language/Standard English Conventions/Sentence Structure/Faulty Parallelism.* In the original, the phrase "after drawing trumps" cuts off the remainder of the sentence from the main body of the sentence, so "was able…" has no clear logical connection with any other element in the sentence. The sentence intends, however, for "was able…" to be the third element in a series of parallel verbs: "ruffed," "sloughed," and "was able to score." The "and" in (B) provides the logical connection to bring the orphan phrase back into the sentence. "And" creates a compound verb consisting of the three elements just mentioned.

6. **(D)** *Writing and Language/Standard English Conventions/Grammar and Usage/Verb Tense.* The original contains two errors. One, the use of "discovering" suggests that "discovering" is intended to be an adjective modifying "Lincoln," but the speaker really intends for "discovering" to be a verb showing some action taken by Lincoln. Two, the use of "has" creates an illogical sequence of verb tenses by implying that the action of the Yankee peddler began before Lincoln's act of discovering but continued through that time of discovery. (B) changes the order of the elements in the sentence but doesn't correct either error. (C) corrects the second error but not the first. Only (D) corrects both errors adequately.

7. **(D)** *Writing and Language/Standard English Conventions/Grammar and Usage/Adjectives versus Adverbs* and *Sentence Structure/Unintended Meanings.* The original sentence contains two errors. First, "inadvertent" is intended to modify the action of leaving the portfolio, so the adverb "inadvertently" is needed. Second, the use of "including" illogically implies that the uncompleted sketches were examples of watercolors. (B) corrects the first error but not the second. (C) corrects the first error but not the second and introduces yet another problem: "containing" seems to modify "bus." Thus, (C) implies that it was the bus that contained the art and not the portfolio. Only (D) corrects both the errors of the original without introducing any new problems.

8. **(B)** *Writing and Language/Expression of Ideas/Style/Clarity of Meaning.* The difficulty with the original is that two ideas are run together in the underlined portion in such a way that the significance of neither is clear. Some device—a word, a phrase, or punctuation—needs to be used to separate those two ideas and make clear their significance. (B) does this with the word "or." (C) fails to separate the ideas clearly; plus, it changes the meaning of the original. And (D) is wrong because the resulting sentence would lack parallel structure.

9. **(C)** *Writing and Language/Expression of Ideas/Style/Conciseness.* The original sentence runs together two ideas and is needlessly wordy. (C) correctly contrasts the two ideas –that the authors were brought up in one language but wrote their books in another– and eliminates the excess verbiage. (B) is wrong because it introduces an illogical verb tense, and (D) is needlessly wordy.

10. **(B)** *Writing and Language/Standard English Conventions/Grammar and Usage/Subject-Verb Agreement* and *Expression of Ideas/ Style/Idiomatic Expression.* The original sentence is incorrect because the verb "have" does not agree with the subject "relationship." Additionally, it is not idiomatic to say "the relationship of x and y." The correct expression is "the relationship of x to y." (C) corrects that mistake but introduces a logical error. It now says that the warnings jeopardize health. (D) is awkward and not idiomatic.

11. **(D)** *Writing and Language/Standard English Conventions/Sentence Structure/Misplaced Modifiers.* This sentence is afflicted by the notorious dangling modifier. As written, the sentence implies that the "prima ballerina" was thrown onto the stage by the adoring fans. To avoid this ambiguity, the modifier should be placed closer to what it modifies, "the bouquets." Only (C) and (D) make any attempt to correct the placement of the modifier. (C) attempts to correct the sentence by moving what is modified, but the resulting sentence is awkward. (D) is a better choice. (D) not only solves the problem of the dangling modifier, but it is also a more direct way of rendering the thought.

12. **(A)** *Writing and Language/Standard English Conventions/No Change.* The original is correct as written. The problem with both (B) and (C) is that the use of "could" implies that there is an event that might have occurred, but did not occur, that would have made the Battle of Fort Ann the most significant event: the battle could have been the most significant event if only something else had happened. (D) is wrong because it is unclear what "that" is referring to: the Battle of Fort Ann or the Revolutionary War.

13. **(B)** *Writing and Language/Standard English Conventions/Sentence Structure/Problems of Coordination and Subordination* and *Unintended Meanings.* The original is wrong because the coordinating conjunction "and" does not create a logical connection between the two ideas that are expressed. In this case, the writer intends to say that poor driving conditions did not result in any car accidents even though one might have expected accidents to occur. So, a contrast must be made between the two ideas (what was expected and what actually occurred). The coordinating conjunction "but" provides the necessary contrast.

14. **(B)** *Writing and Language/Standard English Conventions/Grammar and Usage/Faulty or Illogical Comparisons.* The original contains a faulty comparison. It seems to compare the movie industry in India with the United States. (D) does not address this problem; (B) and (C) do. But (C) is wrong because "on account of" is not an acceptable alternative to "because."

15. **(D)** *Writing and Language/Standard English Conventions/Sentence Structure/Problems of Coordination and Subordination.* The problem with the original is that the relationship between the two clauses is upside-down. The author means to express a causal connection in which the dropped baton is the cause and the failure to qualify is the effect. (D) makes the needed correction.

16. **(A)** *Writing and Language/Expression of Ideas/No Change.* The original is correct as written; the other choices introduce idiomatic expression errors or change the intended meaning of the original. (B) is wrong because "released new worm" is not idiomatic. (C) is wrong for the same reason and for the additional reason that the change in the order of words in the latter part of the underlined segment changes the meaning of the original. And (D) is wrong because "on account of" is not an acceptable substitute for "because."

17. **(D)** *Writing and Language/Expression of Ideas/Style/Clarity of Meaning.* The original is wrong because it is illogical. It compares sanitation workers to other city agencies instead of to other city workers. (B) repeats this error and adds a new one. The possessive case is needed when a pronoun modifies the "-ing" form of verbs. Therefore, "their being underpaid," not "them being underpaid," is correct. (C) repeats the illogical comparison. So, (D) is the correct answer choice.

18. **(C)** *Writing and Language/Standard English Conventions/Sentence Structure/Misplaced Modifiers.* The original contains a misplaced modifier. As written, the sentence implies that it was the failure of the Crusades that learned of the fall of Constantinople. Each of the other choices corrects this error. (B), however, is wrong because the placement of the final clause is incorrect. (What is "which" intended to modify?) (D) changes the intended meaning of the original. (D) implies that Christian Europe reached its realization while ignoring earlier defeats, but the original means to say that Christian Europe only then realized that the Crusades had failed.

19. (D) *Writing and Language/Expression of Ideas/Style/Idiomatic Expression* and *Clarity of Meaning*. The original has two faults. "Insofar as" is used incorrectly, and "a good bargain" and "less than a dollar a pound" are too loosely connected. Only (D) corrects both faults.

20. (D) *Writing and Language/Expression of Ideas/Style/Idiomatic Expression* and *Clarity of Meaning*. The original contains two errors. First, the phrase "more percentage" is not idiomatic. The correct idiom is "greater percentage" or "higher percentage." Second, the original creates an illogical comparison between the population of Boston and other cities. (B) fails to eliminate either error and introduces a new mistake. Without "other," the sentence seems to include Boston itself in the comparison. (C) eliminates the incorrect idiom but introduces a new one: "greater…as." Only (D) corrects both errors in the original sentence.

MATH: MULTIPLE-CHOICE QUIZZES

Math: Multiple-Choice Quiz I (p. 29)

No Calculator

1. **(D)** *Math: Multiple-Choice/Coordinate Geometry/Slope of a Line.* The graph of $f(x)$ includes the points $(3,5)$ and $(7,7)$, so the slope of the line is: $m = \dfrac{y_2 - y_1}{x_2 - x_1} = \dfrac{7-5}{7-3} = \dfrac{2}{4} = \dfrac{1}{2}$.

2. **(D)** *Math: Multiple-Choice/Algebra/Creating, Expressing, and Evaluating Algebraic Equations and Functions.* For the model to be within the height requirements, his or her height, x, must be within 70 ± 2 inches. Therefore, $70 - 2 < x \Rightarrow -2 < x - 70$ and $x < 70 + 2 \Rightarrow x - 70 < 2$, which combined is the same as $-2 < x - 70 < 2 \Rightarrow |x - 70| < 2$.

   Alternatively, you can easily determine that the models height must be between 68 and 72 inches. Therefore, simply plug these two numbers into each answer choice to see which yields true statements for both.

3. **(A)** *Math: Multiple-Choice/Algebra/Solving Algebraic Equations or Inequalities with One Variable/Equations Involving Exponents.* Rewrite $\sqrt{5}$ as $5^{\frac{1}{2}}$ and use the common base 5: $5^6 = \left(5^{\frac{1}{2}}\right)^{-4x} \Rightarrow 5^6 = 5^{-2x}$. Since the bases are the same, the exponents are equivalent: $6 = -2x \Rightarrow x = -3$ and $5^x = 5^{-3} = \dfrac{1}{5^3}$.

4. **(A)** *Math: Multiple-Choice/Algebra/Solving Quadratic Equations and Relations.* Solve the quadratic equation by factoring: $x^2 + 3x - 18 = 0 \Rightarrow (x - 3)(x + 6) = 0$. So, $x - 3 = 0 \Rightarrow x = 3$ or $x + 6 = 0 \Rightarrow x = -6$. Since $2m = x$, the possible values of m are $2m = 3 \Rightarrow m = \dfrac{3}{2}$ and $2m = -6 \Rightarrow m = -3$.

5. **(B)** *Math: Multiple-Choice/Geometry/Circles.* To find the length of an arc in the circle, use the proportion $\dfrac{\text{central angle}}{360} = \dfrac{\text{arc length}}{\text{circumference}}$. Find the circumference of the circle: $C = 2\pi r = 2\pi(18) = 36\pi$. Next, find the arc length: $\dfrac{40}{360} = \dfrac{x}{36\pi} \Rightarrow 1{,}440\pi = 360x \Rightarrow 4\pi = x$.

Calculator

1. **(D)** *Math: Multiple-Choice/Algebra/Solving Algebraic Equations or Inequalities with One Variable/Equations Involving Rational Expressions.* Solve the given equation for x: $\dfrac{x}{x+3} = \dfrac{3}{4} \Rightarrow 4x = 3x + 9 \Rightarrow x = 9$.

2. **(C)** *Math: Multiple-Choice/Algebra/Manipulating Algebraic Expressions.* Simply substitute 10 for k:

$$\frac{k^2}{20} + k = \frac{10^2}{20} + 10 = \frac{100}{20} + 10 = 15.$$

3. **(B)** *Math: Multiple-Choice/Problem Solving and Advanced Arithmetic/Multi-Step Problem Solving Items.* Let T be the total number of pages in the assignment: $\left(T - \dfrac{T}{2} \right) - 3 = 6 \Rightarrow \dfrac{T}{2} = 9 \Rightarrow T = 18$.

Alternatively, "test-the-test," beginning with (C): if the assignment was 24 pages, then the student had 12 left after the first day and 9 left after the second day. Since 9 pages is too many, try (B) next: $\dfrac{1}{2}(18) = 9$, and $9 - 3 = 6$. Therefore, the answer is (B).

4. **(B)** *Math: Multiple-Choice/Data Interpretation/Bar, Cumulative, and Line Graphs and Statistics/Measures of Center and Spread/Averages.* The total period shown in the graph is four months (there are five data points, but the total period covered in the graph is four months long). The average monthly change was $\dfrac{-1\ \mu g/L + 2\ \mu g/L + 1\ \mu g/L + 0.5\ \mu g/L}{4\ \text{months}} = \dfrac{2.5\ \mu g/L}{4\ \text{months}} = 0.625\ \mu g/L$ per month.

5. **(D)** *Math: Multiple-Choice/Algebra/Solving Simultaneous Equations and Creating, Expressing, and Evaluating Algebraic Equations and Functions.* Write the given ratios as equations: $\dfrac{a}{b} = \dfrac{1}{5}$, $\dfrac{b}{c} = \dfrac{3}{2}$, and $\dfrac{2a + c}{c} = \dfrac{8}{w}$. The item stem asks for w, so $w = \dfrac{8c}{2a + c}$. Using the first two equations, rewrite both a and c in terms of the common variable b: $a = \dfrac{b}{5}$ and $c = \dfrac{2b}{3}$. Therefore, $w = \dfrac{8\left(\dfrac{2b}{3} \right)}{2\left(\dfrac{b}{5} \right) + \dfrac{2b}{3}} = \dfrac{\dfrac{16}{3}b}{b\left(\dfrac{2}{5} + \dfrac{2}{3} \right)} = \dfrac{\dfrac{16}{3}}{\dfrac{2(3) + 2(5)}{15}} =$

$\dfrac{\dfrac{16}{3}}{\dfrac{16}{15}} = \dfrac{15}{3} = 5$.

6. **(D)** *Math: Multiple-Choice/Problem Solving and Advanced Arithmetic/Common Problem Solving Items/Percentages.* To calculate the total number of patients that experienced either an increase or no change in blood pressure while taking the placebo, first add the number of patients who took the placebo with no blood pressure change to the number of patients who took the placebo with an increase in blood pressure, yielding $994 + 404 = 1,398$. To compute the percentage, divide 1,398 by the total number of patients taking the placebo: $\dfrac{1,398}{1,500} = 0.932 = 93.2\%$.

7. **(C)** *Math: Multiple-Choice/Problem Solving and Advanced Arithmetic/Common Problem Solving Items/Ratios and Probability/Arithmetic Probability.* The total number of patients who experienced a decrease in blood pressure is 954. The total number of patients given the drug is 1,500. There are 852 patients who experienced a decrease in blood pressure *and* who were given the drug. Therefore, the total number of patients who experienced a decrease in blood pressure or were given the drug is $1,500 + 954 - 852 = 1,602$. Thus, the probability is $\dfrac{1,602}{3,000}$.

8. **(B)** *Math: Multiple-Choice/Coordinate Geometry/Graphs of Polynomial Functions.* The equation $y = ax^b$, where a is negative and b is positive, corresponds to many different graphs. If b is even, the negative a causes the graph of y to look like a downward parabola. If b is odd, the negative a causes the graph of y to look like a mirror reflection of an odd function. But in every variation, the y-intercept will always be the origin: $y = a(0)^b = 0$. Thus, eliminate (A) and (C). And only the scatterplot in (B) can be modeled by this equation; (D) shows no correlation.

9. **(C)** *Math: Multiple-Choice/Algebra/Solving Algebraic Equations or Inequalities with One Variable/Equations Involving Radical Expressions.* Solve the given equation for E:

$$v = \sqrt{\frac{2(E - mgh)}{m}} \Rightarrow v^2 = \frac{2(E - mgh)}{m} \Rightarrow \frac{mv^2}{2} = E - mgh \Rightarrow E = \frac{mv^2}{2} + mgh \text{. Since the second term is the}$$

object's potential energy (mgh), the first term is the kinetic energy: $\frac{1}{2}mv^2$.

10. **(D)** *Math: Multiple-Choice/Algebra/Solving Quadratic Equations and Relations.* Using the discriminant to evaluate the roots is much faster than solving the quadratic formula (or completing the square) to evaluate the roots. Plug the coefficients from the given equation ($a = 1$, $b = -7$, and $c = 14$) into the discriminant of the quadratic formula: $b^2 - 4ac = (-7)^2 - 4(1)(14) = 49 - 56 = -7$. Since -7 is negative and not a perfect square, the roots will be imaginary, unequal, and irrational. You can also use the quadratic equation, though

it's a slower solution than just checking the discriminant: $x = \dfrac{-(-7) \pm \sqrt{(-7)^2 - 4(1)(14)}}{2(1)} = \dfrac{7 \pm \sqrt{49 - 56}}{2} =$

$\dfrac{7 \pm \sqrt{-7}}{2} = \dfrac{7 \pm i\sqrt{7}}{2}$, which are imaginary, unequal, and irrational.

Math: Multiple-Choice Quiz II Brain Buster (p. 34)

No Calculator

1. **(C)** *Math: Multiple-Choice/Algebra/Creating, Expressing, and Evaluating Algebraic Equations and Functions/ Functions as Models.* Rewrite the function in slope-intercept form: $m(t) = \dfrac{t}{10} + 10$, This equation means

that a graph of m (in grams) versus t (in hours) has a slope of $\dfrac{1}{10}$ grams per hour and a y-intercept of 10 grams. The mass of the caterpillar increases from an initial 10 grams at $t = 0$ by 0.1 gram every hour. An increase of 0.1 grams is only equal to 1% after the first hour, when the initial mass is 10 grams. After that, the percentage is less, since the overall weight increases. Therefore, only statements (II) and (III) are true.

2. **(C)** *Math: Multiple-Choice/Algebra/Solving Simultaneous Equations.* A quick look at the answer choices suggests rewriting the equations in slope-intercept form before solving the system of equations:

$$3y - 15 = 2x \Rightarrow 3y = 2x + 15 \Rightarrow y = \frac{2}{3}x + 5 \text{ and } -\frac{2}{3}x + y = 6 \Rightarrow y = \frac{2}{3}x + 6 \text{. Since the two equations have the}$$

same slope but difference y-intercepts, the lines are distinct and parallel—there is no solution to the system of equations.

3. **(D)** *Math: Multiple-Choice/Algebra/Solving Simultaneous Equations.* First, rewrite each inequality in slope-intercept form: $-y+x>1 \Rightarrow -y>-x+1 \Rightarrow y<x-1$ and $3y+6x\le-2 \Rightarrow 3y\le-6x-2 \Rightarrow y\le-2x-\frac{2}{3}$. The boundary line for $y<x-1$ has a positive slope and must be dashed (the line itself is not included in the inequality), which eliminates (A). The boundary line for $y\le-2x-\frac{2}{3}$ has a negative slope and must be solid (the line itself is included in the inequality), which eliminates (C). The solution to the system of inequalities includes the area that satisfies both $y<x-1$ (the half-plane below $y=x-1$) and $y\le-2x-\frac{2}{3}$ (the half-plane below $y=-2x-\frac{2}{3}$), which corresponds to the shaded area in (D).

4. **(B)** *Math: Multiple-Choice/Algebra/Solving Quadratic Equations and Relations.* Use the quadratic formula:

$$x=\frac{-b\pm\sqrt{b^2-4ac}}{2a}=\frac{-4\pm\sqrt{4^2-4(1)(6)}}{2(1)}=\frac{-4\pm\sqrt{16-24}}{2}=\frac{-4\pm\sqrt{-(4)(2)}}{2}=-2\pm i\sqrt{2}.$$

5. **(D)** *Math: Multiple-Choice/Algebra/Solving Algebraic Equations or Inequalities with One Variable/Equations Involving Radical Expressions.* Substitute 5 for m in the equation and isolate the radical: $\sqrt{x+5}=x-1$. Square both sides (doing so potentially introduces an extraneous solution, so all solutions must be checked) and simplify: $\left(\sqrt{x+5}\right)^2=(x-1)^2 \Rightarrow x+5=(x-1)(x-1)=x^2-2x+1 \Rightarrow x=x^2-2x-4 \Rightarrow 0=x^2-3x-4$.

Factor the quadratic expression: $0=x^2-3x-4=(x-4)(x+1)$. In order for the equation to hold true, one or both of the factors must equal 0: $x=4$ and/or $x=-1$. Test both of these solutions in the original equation, First, $\sqrt{x+5}=x-1 \Rightarrow \sqrt{4+5}\overset{?}{=}4-1 \Rightarrow \sqrt{9}=3$, so 4 is a solution. Second,

$\sqrt{x+5}=x-1 \Rightarrow \sqrt{-1+5}\overset{?}{=}-1-1 \Rightarrow \sqrt{4}=-2 \Rightarrow 2\ne-2$, so -1 is not a solution. The complete solution set of the equation is $\{4\}$.

Calculator

1. **(B)** *Math: Multiple-Choice/Problem Solving and Advanced Arithmetic/Common Problem Solving Items/Percentages and Algebra/Solving Simultaneous Equations.* The question asks what percentage of the subtotal the group pays to the waiter as a tip. First, determine the amount of the subtotal. The group paid $235.95 with 6 percent tax and a $29.25 tip, so subtract the tip from the total paid: $235.95-$29.25=$206.70. Now determine the subtotal by omitting the tax: $1.06x=$206.70 \Rightarrow x=195.

Finally, calculate the percentage of the subtotal the group paid as a tip: $\frac{$29.25}{$195}=\frac{x\%}{100\%} \Rightarrow x=15$. The group tipped 15%.

2. **(A)** *Math: Multiple-Choice/Coordinate Geometry/The Coordinate System and Geometry/Triangles/Pythagorean Theorem.* A figure isn't provided, so draw one that includes the given points:

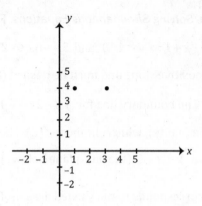

Since the area of the square is 2, the two given points must be at the ends of the diagonal of the square. (If the given points were at the ends of the same side of the square, the area would be $2 \times 2 = 4$.) The orientation of the square must be as follows:

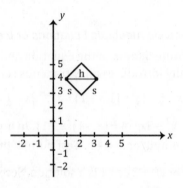

The length of the diagonal is equal to the length of the hypotenuse of the two $45° - 45° - 90°$ triangles that comprise the square. From the graph, the length of the hypotenuse is $3 - 1 = 2$. Use the Pythagorean theorem to determine the side length of the square: $h^2 = s^2 + s^2 \Rightarrow 2^2 = 2s^2 \Rightarrow s = \sqrt{2}$.

3. **(D) *Math: Multiple-Choice/Coordinate Geometry/The Coordinate System* and *Graphs of Linear Equations* and *Slope-Intercept Form of a Linear Equation*.** Use substitution to solve. The two equations are $y = x - 1$

   and $y = -2x$, so substitute $-2x$ for y in the first equation: $y = x - 1 \Rightarrow -2x = x - 1 \Rightarrow -3x = -1 \Rightarrow x = \dfrac{1}{3}$. Now

   solve for y, using either equation: $y = -2x \Rightarrow y = -2\left(\dfrac{1}{3}\right) = -\dfrac{2}{3}$. In this case, x is positive and y is negative,

   meaning the solution is in Quadrant IV:

	y	
II		I
x negative		x positive
y positive		y positive
		x
x negative		x positive
y negative		y negative
III		IV

Alternatively, graph the lines:

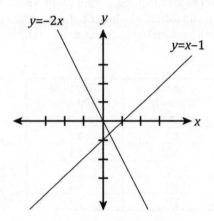

The lines intersect in Quadrant IV.

4. **(D)** *Math: Multiple-Choice/Coordinate Geometry/Transformations and Their Effects on Graphs of Functions.*
In the original equation, the slope is 2. The new line is shifted down 2 units and to the right 3 units, which doesn't affect the slope. Eliminate (A) because it has a negative slope and eliminate (B) because the slope is $\frac{1}{2}$. To shift $y = 2x - 1$ down 2 units means each y-value of the line (the output of the function) is decreased by 2: $y' = y - 2 = 2x - 1 - 2 = 2x - 3$. To shift $y' = 2x - 3$ to the right 3 units means each x-value of the line (the input of the function) is decreased by 3: $y'' = y'(x - 3) = 2(x - 3) - 3 = 2x - 6 - 3 = 2x - 9$. The graph in (D) has a y-intercept of -9 and a slope of 2.

If you forgot how transformations work, your knowledge of the slope-intercept form of linear equations and their graphs is enough to know that shifting $2x - 1$ down 2 units and to the right 3 units places it in a position to have a greater negative y-intercept than the original line, so the answer must be (D):

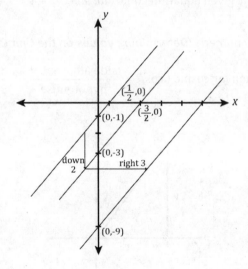

5. (D) *Math: Multiple-Choice/Coordinate Geometry/Graphs of Quadratic Equations and Relations.* The stopping distances increase for increases in speed, so the relationship is one of growth, which eliminates (B) and (C). According to the table, the difference in stopping distances increases for each successive increase in speed of 20 km/hr, so the relationship is not linear, which eliminates (A). Therefore, (D) is the correct answer.

Speed (kilometers per hour)	Stopping Distance (meters)	
40	10	11
60	21	15
80	36	19
100	50	23
120	78	

6. (A) *Math: Multiple-Choice/Statistics/Measures of Center and Spread/Averages and Median.* The original mean (average) is $\dfrac{10+2(12)+13+2(16)+17+18+21}{9}=15$. The original median is the middlemost value, or 16. Adding another tulip 14 inches tall to the data set will reduce the average to slightly below 15. The new median will be between 14 and 16 inches, or 15 inches. So, the mean will change less than the median.

7. (B) *Math: Multiple-Choice/Algebra/Manipulating Algebraic Expressions/Manipulating Expressions Involving Exponents.* Ignore the given equation for now and simplify the second term in the expression $3^y\left(\sqrt[3]{9^{3x/2}}\right)$ using the rules for working with exponents and radicals: $\sqrt[3]{9^{3x/2}}=9^{\frac{3x/2}{3}}=9^{\frac{x}{2}}$. Rewrite it using the same base as the first term 3^y: $9^{\frac{x}{2}}=(3^2)^{\frac{x}{2}}=3^{2\left(\frac{x}{2}\right)}=3^x$. The given expression simplifies to $3^y(3^x)$, which is the same as 3^{y+x}. This is where the given equation comes in: since $x+y=5$, $3^{y+x}=3^5$.

8. (D) *Math: Multiple-Choice/Trigonometry/Determining Values on the Unit Circle.* Since $\dfrac{\pi}{2}<\theta<\pi$, the angle is in Quadrant II. Use the definition for cosine ($\cos\theta=\dfrac{\text{side adjacent }\theta}{\text{hypotenuse}}=-\dfrac{3}{5}$) to construct a triangle in Quadrant II:

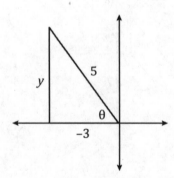

Use the Pythagorean theorem to find the missing side of the triangle: $5^2 = y^2 + (-3)^2 \Rightarrow$

$y^2 = 25 - 9 = 16 \Rightarrow y = 4$. (Or, recognize that the triangle is a 3-4-5 triangle.) The definition for sine is

$\sin\theta = \dfrac{\text{side opposite } \theta}{\text{hypotenuse}}$. Therefore, $\sin\theta = \dfrac{4}{5}$.

9. **(D)** *Math: Multiple-Choice/Algebra/Solving Algebraic Equations or Inequalities with One Variable/Equations*

Involving Rational Expressions. The area of a triangle is $\dfrac{bh}{2}$, where b is the base and h is the height:

$12x^2 + x - 6 = \dfrac{(3x-2)b}{2} \Rightarrow b = \dfrac{24x^2 + 2x - 12}{3x - 2}$. Use polynomial long division to simplify:

$$
\begin{array}{r}
8x + 6 \\
3x-2 \overline{\smash{\big)}\, 24x^2 + 2x - 12} \\
\underline{-(24x^2 - 16x)} \\
18x - 12 \\
\underline{-(18x - 12)} \\
0
\end{array}
$$

Therefore, the length of the base of the triangle is $8x + 6$.

10. **(D)** *Math: Multiple-Choice/Statistics/Measures of Center and Spread and Common Data*
Representations/Histograms and Data Interpretation/Drawing Inferences. In the corrected histogram, the sum of the first two columns would be $110 + 75 = 185$ and the sum of the last two columns would remain $70 + 52 = 112$. The middle column now has 178, so the median will fall in the middle column, which is 3 days. This eliminates (A), since the item is a thought-reverser and the correct choice is NOT necessarily true. Before calculating the possible range of the mean again, let's look at the other choices. The original mode is the bar with the greatest number of students: "2 days." Recall that the right endpoint of histogram ranges is not included. The corrected mode is 3 days, which eliminates (B). As for (C), since the bar with the greatest number of students is now the middle bar rather than the second bar, the corrected mean must be greater than the uncorrected mean. By the process of elimination, the correct choice must be (D). Indeed,

calculating the new mean shows it to be $\dfrac{1(75) + 2(110) + 3(178) + 4(70) + 5(52)}{595} = \dfrac{1{,}369}{595} = 2.3$ days, so (D) is

not true.

MATH: STUDENT-PRODUCED RESPONSES QUIZZES

Math: Student-Produced Responses Quiz I (p. 41)

No Calculator

1. **(2)** *Math: Student-Produced Responses/Algebra/Creating, Expressing, and Evaluating Algebraic Equations and Functions.* Let R be Ray's age now and C be Cindy's age now: $R = C + 10$. Then in 8 years: $R + 8 = 2(C + 8)$. Substituting for R: $(C + 10) + 8 = 2(C + 8) \Rightarrow C + 18 = 2C + 16 \Rightarrow C = 2$.

2. **(8)** *Math: Student-Produced Responses/Algebra/Creating, Expressing, and Evaluating Algebraic Equations and Functions/Function Notation.* Perform the indicated operations: $2 \otimes 3 = 2(3) + 3 = 9$ and $z \otimes 1 = z(1) + 1$. Since $2 \otimes 3 = z \otimes 1$, $9 = z + 1 \Rightarrow z = 8$.

Calculator

1. **(0)** *Math: Student-Produced Responses/Algebra/Creating, Expressing, and Evaluating Algebraic Equations and Functions* and *Solving Simultaneous Equations.* Set up the averages: $\dfrac{4 + 5 + x + y}{4} = 6 \Rightarrow$

   $9 + x + y = 24 \Rightarrow x + y = 15$ and $\dfrac{x + z + 8 + 9}{4} = 8 \Rightarrow x + z + 17 = 32 \Rightarrow x + z = 15$. Now, subtract the first equation from the second to eliminate the x variable:

   $$\begin{array}{r} x + z = 15 \\ -(x + y = 15) \\ \hline z - y = 0 \end{array}$$

2. **(130)** *Math: Student-Produced Responses/Geometry/Triangles/Pythagorean Theorem.*

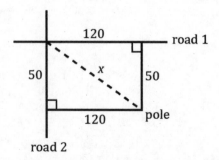

   Using the Pythagorean theorem: $x^2 = (50)^2 + (120)^2 = 2,500 + 144,000 = 169,000 \Rightarrow x = 130$. Alternatively, you can skip using the Pythagorean theorem all together if you recognize that the triangle is a multiple of the Pythagorean triple 5-12-13.

3. **(30)** *Math: Student-Produced Responses/Geometry/Lines and Angles.* When two parallel lines are cut by a transversal, opposite exterior angles are equal. And the sum of the angles in a straight line is $180°$. Therefore, $y = 4x$ and $y + 2x = 180 \Rightarrow 4x + 2x = 180 \Rightarrow 6x = 180 \Rightarrow x = 30$.

Math: Student-Produced Responses Quiz II Brain Buster (p. 46)

No Calculator

1. **(3)** *Math: Student-Produced Responses/Algebra/Solving Algebraic Equations or Inequalities with One Variable/Equations Involving Exponents.* Apply the rules of exponents to rewrite each term with the same base: $2^{x+1} = 4^{x-1} \Rightarrow 2^{x+1} = (2^2)^{x-1} = 2^{2x-2}$. Now, with similar bases, the exponents can be directly compared: $x + 1 = 2x - 2 \Rightarrow x = 3$.

2. **(21, 22, 23, 24, 25, 26, 27, 28, 29)** *Math: Student-Produced Responses/Coordinate Geometry/Graphs of Quadratic Equations and Relations.* The graph of $f(x) = x^4 - 4x^3 + 10x^2 + 45x + k$ must equal k for $x = 0$. Therefore, k is the y-intercept, which according to the graph is between -20 and -30. The value of $|k|$ must be an integer between 20 and 30.

Calculator

1. **(9)** *Math: Student-Produced Responses/Coordinate Geometry/Transformations and Their Effects on Graphs of Functions.* To shift $y = 2x - 1$ down 2 units means each y-value of the line (the output of the function) is decreased by 2: $y' = y - 2 = 2x - 1 - 2 = 2x - 3$. To shift $y' = 2x - 3$ to the left 6 units means each x-value of the line (the input of the function) is increased by 6: $y'' = y'(x + 6) = 2(x + 6) - 3 = 2x + 12 - 3 = 2x + 9$. The graph has a y-intercept of 9.

2. **(18)** *Math: Student-Produced Responses/Algebra/Solving Algebraic Equations or Inequalities with One Variable/Equations Involving Radical Expressions.* Raise both sides of the equation to the fourth power and solve for x: $\left(\left((x+7)^2 \right)^{\frac{1}{4}} \right)^4 = 5^4 \Rightarrow (x+7)^2 = 5^4 \Rightarrow x + 7 = \pm 5^2 \Rightarrow x = -32$ and $x = 18$. The only valid answer is 18 since the answer grid accommodates only positive numbers.

3.   **(2, 3)** *Math: Student-Produced Responses/Coordinate Geometry/Graphs of Polynomial Functions.* If the function $f(x) = k$ has four real solutions, then the line $y = k$ passes through the function four times. Draw horizontal lines on the graph that correspond to integer values of k:

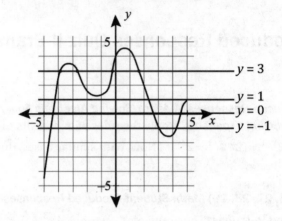

Only $y = k = 2$ and $y = k = 3$ passes through the function four times.

ESSAY QUIZ

Above Average Response

Access to technology is no longer limited to scientists, researchers, or those with large bank accounts. We no longer need entire rooms to house a single computer, and we have more information than we can imagine at our fingertips. With the invention of the smartphone, Michael Bloomberg claims in his address to the University of North Carolina at Chapel Hill, we launched ourselves into a technological revolution. Bloomberg's address outlines how a revolution that started small is "now being led by the masses." He justifies this claim by providing a glimpse into the places where technology is being developed, and by inspiring his audience to realize that they, too, have the opportunity to take part in this technological revolution.

Bloomberg begins his argument by describing how technology is evolving all around us, and not just in the offices and laboratories of a few elite individuals or companies. Cities and universities are places where technological advances are routinely made. Colleges and universities have the opportunity to join forces with other institutions across the globe to create new applied science and engineering campuses. These campuses will result in more researchers and innovators that emerge from colleges and universities. These graduates will then go on to make discoveries in the world of technology and, as Bloomberg notes, "if those discoveries happen in New York City, the companies that spin off from them will start in New York City." Bloomberg's specific example of New York City's partnership with universities around the world illustrates the vast global impact of technological developments. Readers are meant to be amazed at the expansive development of technological progress, and the specific examples of institutions (cities, universities, companies) help demonstrate the broad extent of the channels of development.

It is not just those in the fields of applied sciences or engineering that will make technological discoveries and advances. Bloomberg explains to his audience that many of them, whether they are business, finance, journalism, or pre-med majors, will be a part of the discoveries that shape the technological revolution. While the influence of these different groups will be different, they all have their own part to play in the development. Finance majors will help with funding, journalism majors will publish articles about new technological advances, and lawyers will aid in creating patents. There is an opportunity for anyone and everyone to take part in. Bloomberg makes his speech relevant to a diverse audience and simultaneously demonstrates the universal applicability of the technological revolution's impact by addressing a wide variety of majors and careers. This earns him interest and support from a broader audience and works especially well in this particular context because, at a college graduation, he is addressing students of all majors and making his message relevant to them and an optimistic one as they embark on their career paths.

Bloomberg also makes an ethical appeal to his audience by emphasizing technology's humanitarian potential. In his address, Bloomberg reminds his audience that the technological revolution will not only make our lives more convenient, but will also help to be "our most powerful weapon in the fight against poverty and disease—it will be our most powerful weapon in the fight against repression and intolerance." This ethical appeal can convince an even broader range of people of Bloomberg's argument for the impact of technology; those who may not have the opportunity to be involved in it or benefit in immediately tangible ways from it (through income or profit, perhaps) will still experience its benefits through the improvement of society, culture, and living conditions for all. This appeal is uniquely effective because those people in particular who actually suffer from poverty, disease, repression, and intolerance may now be moved by Bloomberg's claim if they hadn't been convinced before. Here, Bloomberg strategically and successfully persuades by appealing to people's emotions and morals (and cleverly, to the idealism of graduating college students).

While Bloomberg begins his address with the mention of one invention, the smartphone, his inspirational description of the opportunities available to new college graduates and the effects that technology can have on the world drives home his point that we are in the midst of a technological revolution. Those who wish to take part need only explore the endless number of opportunities available to make discoveries and advances in this revolution.

Assessment of the Essay

Reading: This response demonstrates thorough comprehension of the source text through its use of strategically positioned paraphrases and direct support from the text (*Finance majors will help with funding, journalism majors will publish articles about new technological advances, and lawyers will aid in creating patents*). The writer succinctly summarizes the main proposal of Bloomberg's speech (*With the invention of the smartphone, Michael Bloomberg claims in his address to the University of North Carolina at Chapel Hill, we launched ourselves into a technological revolution. Bloomberg's address outlines how a revolution that started small is "now being led by the masses"*). The writer then constructs tight, focused paragraphs revolving around and offering support for how Bloomberg develops this claim. The response is free of inaccuracies in interpretation. Overall, the response exhibits higher-level reading proficiency.

Analysis: This response offers a perceptive, acute analysis of the source text and exhibits mature comprehension of the analytical task. The writer demonstrates observant attention to Bloomberg's audience and understands how the elements of his speech apply to his audience in the context of his purpose with the argument (*Here, Bloomberg strategically and successfully persuades by appealing to people's emotions and morals (and cleverly, to the idealism of graduating college students)*). The writer tackles key points of analysis: what contribution these strategies make to the overall argument (*this ethical appeal can convince an even broader range of people of Bloomberg's argument for the impact of technology*); the reason they are included (*Bloomberg makes his speech relevant to a diverse audience*); and the characteristics that make them effective (*This . . . works especially well in this particular context because, at a college graduation, he is addressing students of all majors and making his message relevant to them and an optimistic one as they embark on their career paths*). Overall, this response exhibits advanced analytical skill.

Writing: The response is characterized by a strong command of language and skillful organization. It advances an unambiguous central claim (*With the invention of the smartphone, Michael Bloomberg claims in his address to the University of North Carolina at Chapel Hill, we launched ourselves into a technological revolution. Bloomberg's address outlines how a revolution that started small is "now being led by the masses"*), and develops this claim clearly through three main points expounded in three tightly focused and sufficiently detailed body paragraphs. The writer varies the sentence structure and strategically chooses certain words and phrases (*tangible, channels of development, idealism*) in order to make the writing flow smoothly and convey ideas with precision. This response exhibits advanced writing skill and a strong grasp over the principles of written English.

Below Average Response

Technology is all around us. Pretty much everyone has some kind of technology like a computer or a phone. The best invention as far as technology goes is the smartphone. It is literally a computer that you can take with you everywhere and it fits in your pocket. This is considered a technology revolution. Michael Bloomberg talks about it in his speech and how it is going to be a revolution in the world of technology and not just in the United States like places like New York City. The reason why this is is because there are a lots of universities where people can study technology and everyone can help with making new technology not just those people who are "computer nerds." I am going to explain why this is a technology revolution.

There is a technology revolution going on because of the smartphone and this is because there are lots of universities in the US where students can learn about technology. They can learn about it in Boston Massachusetts and Austin Texas or their own university where they go to school. These places are taking the smartphone and making it so much more than just a phone they are making it technology that is revolutionary. Also they don't have to be majoring in computer science or something with technology. You can still learn about technology even if you are studying business or something other than computers.

Also, its not just the computer nerds who are doing things with technology. Like I mentioned before, people who are majoring in business or education can still do thing with technology. Teachers can teach their students about the new technology that is coming out and people who work for newspapers can write stories about the new technology that we have. People who are lawyers will also get involved, and it makes it pretty much a game for anyone. You don't even need to be involved in making technology to make a difference.

Technology is going to be a weapon against poverty, disease, repression and intolerance, and that is what makes it so revolutionary. I am not sure how this is going to happen and Michael Bloomberg does not explain it but I believe it is true because look at all the things technology can do. We basically carry a computer around in our pocket all day long and we can look up whatever information we need. It is all at our fingertips. I am sure that because technology is so powerful it will be revolutionary and help us to help the poor and figure out cures for diseases.

The technology revolution is a real thing and it all starts with the smartphone. It is possible that someday we will have something much better and more advanced than the smartphone, and that is what will help us to cure disease and help people. People who are graduating from college have the best chance at getting jobs dealing with technology and making new discoveries like the smartphone.

Assessment of the Essay

Reading: This disorganized response reflects little comprehension of the source text, lacking a clear focus and misunderstanding Bloomberg's central claim. Moreover, it does not ground its assertions in the source text and consists of sweeping generalizations unsupported by the text (*People who are graduating from college have the best chance at getting jobs dealing with technology and making new discoveries like the smartphone*). The response does not attempt to make logical inferences, but rather resorts to filling in gaps with the writer's own opinion (*Technology is going to be a weapon against poverty, disease, repression and intolerance, and that is what makes it so revolutionary. I am not sure how this is going to happen and Michael Bloomberg does not explain it but I believe it is true because look at all the things technology can do*). Overall, this essay displays a superficial understanding of Bloomberg's speech.

Analysis: This response misses the point of the analytical task. It takes a stance on the issue (agrees with Bloomberg), rather than analyzing the elements of Bloomberg's argument (*I am going to explain why this is a technology revolution*). The writer identifies points of evidence that Bloomberg uses to persuade his audience (*Like I mentioned before, people who are majoring in business or education can still do thing with technology*), but does not assess how this evidence functions within the context of Bloomberg's argument. The writer neither explains why Bloomberg is concerned with certain points nor attempts to understand whether or not these points are effective and why they are or are not. Overall, the response exhibits weak analytical skill.

Writing: The response demonstrates loose cohesion and weak grasp over the conventions of written English. There are frequent grammatical errors that interrupt the flow of the response (*These places are taking the smartphone and making it so much more than just a phone they are making it technology that is revolutionary*). Many sentences are rambling and do not contribute to the thesis in a meaningful way (*We basically carry a computer around in our pocket all day long and we can look up whatever information we need. It is all at our fingertips*). The point of view switches sporadically (*Also they don't have to be majoring in computer science or something with technology. You can still learn about technology even if you are studying business or something other than computers*). The response lacks a clear introduction, and the conclusion strays from the original thesis (*It is possible that someday we will have something much better and more advanced than the smartphone, and that is what will help us to cure disease and help people*). Overall, this essay exhibits below-average writing proficiency.

PRACTICE TEST I

Answer Key

DIRECTIONS: For items answered <u>correctly</u>, circle the answer, then check any corresponding shaded box(es). Total the number of circled answers to determine the raw score for the test section. Total the number of checkmarks for each of the subscores and cross-test scores to determine each raw subscore and raw cross-test score.

Section 1: Reading (p. 59)

#	Answer	WC (Subscore)	CE (Subscore)	S (Cross-Test)	H/S (Cross-Test)
1.	D	■			
2.	B	■			
3.	C				
4.	D		■		
5.	C				
6.	B		■		
7.	A				
8.	B				
9.	C				
10.	D				
11.	B				■
12.	B	■			
13.	C				
14.	D		■	■	
15.	B				■
16.	A		■		
17.	B				■
18.	A				■

#	Answer	WC (Subscore)	CE (Subscore)	S (Cross-Test)	H/S (Cross-Test)
19.	B				■
20.	B				■
21.	D			■	
22.	B			■	
23.	A			■	
24.	B			■	
25.	C		■		
26.	D	■			
27.	A				
28.	C	■			
29.	B			■	
30.	C		■	■	
31.	A				■
32.	A		■		
33.	B	■			
34.	A				■
35.	D				■
36.	C				■

#	Answer	WC (Subscore)	CE (Subscore)	S (Cross-Test)	H/S (Cross-Test)
37.	A				■
38.	A				■
39.	C		■		■
40.	A				■
41.	B				■
42.	D				■
43.	A			■	
44.	C		■	■	
45.	A			■	
46.	D		■	■	
47.	B			■	
48.	D			■	
49.	C	■			
50.	B				■
51.	C			■	
52.	C			■	

Raw Score: _____ /52

Section 2: Writing and Language (p. 75)

	Subscores		Cross-Test Scores	
	WC	CE	S	H/S
1. D				
2. A				▓
3. B	▓			▓
4. D				
5. D				
6. A				▓
7. A	▓			
8. A		▓	▓	
9. B				
10. D				
11. D		▓	▓	
12. A	▓			
13. B				
14. D				
15. A				

	Subscores		Cross-Test Scores	
	WC	CE	S	H/S
16. C	▓			
17. D				
18. D		▓		
19. B				
20. C				
21. A		▓		
22. C				
23. C				
24. B			▓	▓
25. D	▓		▓	
26. A	▓			
27. A				
28. B	▓		▓	
29. B				
30. D				

	Subscores		Cross-Test Scores	
	WC	CE	S	H/S
31. A				
32. B			▓	
33. A			▓	
34. C				
35. C				
36. A				
37. D	▓			
38. D				
39. A		▓		
40. B				
41. C	▓			
42. D				
43. A		▓		
44. C				

Raw Score: _____ /44

Evidence-Based Reading and Writing Subscores

Words in Context (WC): _____ /18   Command of Evidence (CE): _____ /18

Section 3: Math—No Calculator (p. 87)

	Cross-Test Scores	
	S	H/S
1. C		
2. A		
3. D		
4. C		
5. B		▓
6. C		
7. A	▓	

	Cross-Test Scores	
	S	H/S
8. C		
9. D		
10. A		▓
11. A		
12. B		
13. B		
14. A		

		Cross-Test Scores	
		S	H/S
15. D			
16. 15.5, 31/2			
17. 4			
18. 29			
19. 1			
20. 9			

Section 4: Math—Calculator (p. 93)

	Cross-Test Scores				Cross-Test Scores				Cross-Test Scores	
	S	H/S			S	H/S			S	H/S
1. B			14. A				27. B			
2. A			15. C				28. C			
3. C			16. C				29. C			
4. A			17. A				30. B			
5. C			18. C				31. 11			
6. D			19. B	▓		32. 2			▓
7. B	▓		20. D			33. 6000			▓
8. D			21. B		▓	34. 4			▓
9. B			22. D		▓	35. 80			
10. C		▓	23. D	▓		36. 9			
11. C	▓		24. D	▓		37. 53			
12. B	▓		25. A	▓		38. 7/24			
13. A			26. C	▓					

Math Raw Score (total of calculator and no-calculator sections): _____ /58

Cross-Test Scores (All four test sections)

Science (S): _____ /35   History/Social Studies (H/S): _____ /35

Explanations

Section 1: Reading

Questions #1–10

1. **(D)** (p. 60) *Reading/Literary Fiction/Vocabulary.* Although "mean" has several different meanings, Robin's description of the place as a "low hovel" makes it clear that in this context the word means "shabby" or "run-down."

2. **(B)** (p. 60) *Reading/Literary Fiction/Vocabulary.* Robin is walking down the street and sees someone moving "in advance" of him. "In advance," in this context, means "up ahead" or simply "ahead."

3. **(C)** (p. 60) *Reading/Literary Fiction/Implied Idea.* Throughout the passage, Robin asks a series of people (a stranger on the street, the innkeeper, the night watchman, and a man at the foot of the church building) how to find his relative, Major Molineux. Each of them either denies knowing him or evades the question. All the while, Robin believes that Major Molineux is an important person in the town. In the final paragraph, however, we learn that Major Molineux has been disgraced.

4. **(D)** (p. 60) *Reading/Literary Fiction/Textual Evidence.* The fact that Major Molineux has fallen into disgrace is supported in the final paragraph when Robin learns that his kinsman has been tarred and feathered by the townspeople.

5. **(C)** (p. 60) *Reading/Literary Fiction/Implied Idea.* The man at the foot of the church building says that he is familiar with the name Molineux, that the Major will pass by where they are standing, and that he is curious to see Robin and Major Molineux. The fact that the man knows Molineux will pass by indicates that he is aware of Molineux's fate and knows the route that the mob of people will take. Also, it can be inferred that Major Molineux's fate will be a surprise to Robin since the man at the foot of the church building is interested in witnessing their meeting.

6. **(B)** (p. 60) *Reading/Literary Fiction/Textual Evidence.* The fact that the man at the foot of the church building is aware that Major Molineux has been tarred and feathered is best supported by his knowledge that the Major will pass by the place where he and Robin are sitting.

7. **(A)** (p. 61) *Reading/Literary Fiction/Development.* The third paragraph from the end of the passage provides details of Robin's relationship to Major Molineux. Major Molineux and Robin's father are cousins. Molineux, who from his appearance during a visit a few years ago to Robin's family appeared to be a very prosperous person, had suggested that Robin could benefit from his oversight. So, a couple of years later Robin goes to town to meet his kinsman. Then, as already discussed in the explanation to item #3, Robin asks a series of people how to find his relative, and each of them either denies knowing the Major or is unclear. In fact, they even become hostile toward Robin; and at the end of the passage we learn that the reason for this hostility is that Major Molineux has done something that has caused him to be tarred and feathered by the townspeople.

8. **(B)** (p. 61) *Reading/Literary Fiction/Implied Idea.* It's the name "Major Molineux" that disturbs both the innkeeper and the others in the inn. The animosity suddenly directed toward Robin comes as a result of his mention of and association with that name.

9. **(C)** (p. 61) *Reading/Literary Fiction/Explicit Detail.* According to the last sentence in the first paragraph, Robin headed into the town with a light step and an eager eye, so the best description of Robin's state of mind upon entering the town is one of "anticipation."

10. **(D)** (p. 61) *Reading/Literary Fiction/Implied Idea.* . There is a wonderful irony in Robin's thinking, for he concludes that the stranger whom he has accosted is an out-of-towner who is unfamiliar with the town, its people, and its convention. Of course, this describes Robin, who has no idea where he is, how to find Major Molineux, or if it is good manners to grab the coat of a total stranger.

Questions #11–20

11. **(B)** (p. 63) *Reading/Social Studies/Implied Idea.* In the fourth paragraph of Passage 1, the author states that there is no crisis of judicial activism. Based on that statement, it can be inferred that the author would find claims of judicial activism exaggerated, (B).

12. **(B)** (p. 63) *Reading/Social Studies/Vocabulary.* In line 52, the author of Passage 2 states that the doctrine of judicial review does not mean that the courts have a monopoly on the power to deem an act

unconstitutional. The author then explains that both Congress and the president have a similar power. So, we can infer that "monopoly" in this context means "exclusive control."

13. **(C)** (p. 63) *Reading/Social Studies/Implied Idea.* In the second paragraph of Passage 1, the author describes the ways in which a law must be scrutinized by each branch of government. And in the second paragraph of Passage 2, the author states that not only the courts but also Congress and the president have an obligation to determine the constitutionality of a law.

14. **(D)** (p. 63) *Reading/Social Studies/Textual Evidence.* As noted in the explanation to item #12, both authors write that each branch has an obligation to test the constitutionality of laws: the Congress when it enacts them, the president when he or she either vetoes or enforces them, and the courts when they evaluate them.

15. **(B)** (p. 63) *Reading/Social Studies/Implied Idea.* The author of Passage 1 seems to find the basis for judicial review in the oath taken by all members of the government to uphold the Constitution. This interpretation seems to make the three branches equal, giving a final say to the Supreme Court since it is the last to decide on the issue. The author of Passage 2, on the other hand, starts out by saying that this is not an adequate foundation for the doctrine and goes on to cite both Marshall and Hamilton as authorities.

16. **(A)** (p. 63) *Reading/Social Studies/Textual Evidence.* As noted in the explanation to item #14, the author of Passage 2 believes that the basis for judicial review goes beyond the obligation of the judges to support the Constitution. This doctrine is explicitly stated in lines 42–45.

17. **(B)** (p. 63) *Reading/Social Studies/Vocabulary.* In most contexts, the word "vex" means "to annoy" or "to irritate." The author here does not intend the usual meaning. In this context, "vexing" takes on a shade of that meaning: "difficult." The question posed in the passage is a difficult one because it is not easy to say whose view should prevail in case of conflict.

18. **(A)** (p. 64) *Reading/Social Studies/Development.* The author cites Marshall and Hamilton as authorities on the Constitution (Marshall being the first Chief Justice of the Supreme Court and Hamilton being one of the authors of *The Federalist Papers*) and does so to support the contention that judicial review is not just the courts' obeying of the Constitution, but is a more expansive doctrine that requires them to assess the constitutionality of laws.

19. **(B)** (p. 64) *Reading/Social Studies/Explicit Detail.* In the fifth paragraph of Passage 2, the author states that Jefferson pardoned those convicted under the Sedition Act on grounds that courts had already rejected. In other words, the people convicted had already argued to the courts that the Act was unconstitutional, and those courts rejected the argument. The author explains that Jefferson, however, was exercising an inherent power of the executive branch: granting pardons. The author's reasoning is that since the executive had won the convictions in the first place, it was later free to undo that result since it was giving up only what it had won.

20. **(B)** (p. 64) *Reading/Social Studies/Main Idea.* . In paragraph three of Passage 1, the author states that losing the doctrine of judicial review would be "unfortunate," and in the last paragraph of Passage 2, that author cites Jefferson and Jackson to emphasize the value of judicial review.

Questions #21–30

21. **(D)** (p. 66) *Reading/Natural Sciences/Explicit Detail.* According to the last paragraph, lower frequency radiation is able to penetrate more deeply and so would likely deposit its energy in muscle tissue.

22. **(B)** (p. 66) *Reading/Natural Sciences/Main Idea.* The main point of the passage is to demonstrate that the effects of microwave radiation on human tissue are different from those of other forms of radiation, (B). As for (A), while the author does explain the importance of behavior response in humans for the regulation of body temperature, this point is made to introduce the outdated theory based on the assumption that organisms respond to microwave radiation in the same way that they do to other forms of radiation. As for (C) and (D), the author's main point does not involve either the analysis of a *particular* mechanism or the discussion of the *specific* importance of thermoreceptors, respectively.

23. **(A)** (p. 66) *Reading/Natural Sciences/Explicit Detail.* . In the opening sentence, the author establishes that there are two general responses available to warm-blooded animals for regulating body temperature: behavior and innate mechanisms. The author goes on to state that when the organism responds to changes in temperature in the core of the body (the second type of response), these changes are triggered by thermoreceptors that are distributed throughout the central nervous system (inside the body of the organism).

24. **(B)** (p. 66) *Reading/Natural Sciences/Implied Idea.* . In the first sentence of the second paragraph, the author remarks that proponents of the generally accepted theory (which treats microwave radiation like other forms of radiation) simply *assumed* that one type of radiation would have the same thermal effect as other types of radiation would.

25. **(C)** (p. 66) *Reading/Natural Sciences/Textual Evidence.* As discussed in the explanation to item #21, the outdated theory took it for granted that microwaves behave like other forms of radiation. The passage goes on to explain that this idea is wrong. In lines 23–27, the author specifically states that the only support for this erroneous belief was assumption.

26. **(D)** (p. 66) *Reading/Natural Sciences/Vocabulary.* The word "appreciate" often means "to like" or "to be pleased by," but that meaning is out of place here. Rather, the author uses the word to mean "notice."

27. **(A)** (p. 66) *Reading/Natural Sciences/Development.* . In the lines indicated, the author states that it is possible that an organism could be cooked by microwave radiation (because the radiation penetrates into the core) before it even realizes its temperature is rising. The verb tense here ("could") clearly indicates that the author is introducing a hypothetical possibility; additionally, the author uses the phrase "in theory." Given the shocking nature of the example, we should conclude that the author has introduced it to dramatize a point.

28. **(C)** (p. 66) *Reading/Natural Sciences/Vocabulary.* The most common meaning of the word "compromise" is "reach an agreement in which each side gives up something," but that meaning is not appropriate here. Rather, the author intends a less common meaning: "endanger."

29. **(B)** (p. 67) *Reading/Natural Sciences/Implied Idea.* . In the fourth paragraph, the author begins by stating that microwaves at lower frequencies and high power pose a "significant risk." In this paragraph, the author notes that the resulting temperature profile may be a reverse thermal gradient in which the inside is warmer than the surface. But you also need information to explain why the low frequency microwaves heat

the inside, and you can find that information in the final paragraph: lower frequencies penetrate to the deep muscle tissue, which absorbs more efficiently than does fat so most energy is found at that level.

30. **(C)** (p. 67) ***Reading/Natural Sciences/Textual Evidence.*** A complete explanation of the phenomenon requires a couple of facts, both of which are provided in the explanation to item #26: that there is a reverse thermal gradient in which the inside is warmer than the surface and that the lower frequency microwaves penetrate the body and heat the muscle tissue, which absorbs energy more efficiently than fat.

Questions #31–41

31. **(A)** (p. 69) ***Reading/Social Studies/Voice.*** In the first sentence, Susan B. Anthony says, "I stand before you tonight under indictment for the alleged crime." A person under indictment for a supposed crime is a defendant on trial. So, (A) is the correct answer choice.

32. **(A)** (p. 69) ***Reading/Social Studies/Textual Evidence.*** Anthony opens her speech by stating that she is under indictment for fraudulently voting in the most recent federal election and is, therefore, a criminal defendant. After the opening statement, she goes on to say that she will prove that she has committed no crime and is in fact well within her rights as a citizen.

33. **(B)** (p. 69) ***Reading/Social Studies/Vocabulary.*** An oligarchy is a form of government in which those few who hold power share and are made eligible to govern by a common characteristic such as wealth or lineage. Anthony here refers to the United States as an oligarchy of sex, meaning that the qualifying characteristic for holding office is that one is male.

34. **(A)** (p. 70) ***Reading/Social Studies/Development.*** Anthony has a small problem with the presentation of argument (see #38). The original Constitution was not always clear about terms like "person" and "citizen." She handles this problem by acknowledging the ambiguity and then goes on to say the ambiguity was resolved by the fourteenth amendment. The two terms that appear in the excerpt from the original Constitution are "person" and "citizen."

35. **(D)** (p. 70) ***Reading/Social Studies/Vocabulary.*** "Regime" could mean any of the four things offered by the choices, but in this particular case, Anthony uses "regime" to mean "the old way of thinking," that is, before the fourteenth amendment. So "system" is the best choice.

36. **(C)** (p. 70) ***Reading/Social Studies/Development.*** The fourth paragraph begins with "but, it is urged," referring to objections that Anthony's opponents might raise. Then she proceeds to answer the possible objection by pointing out that the argument places the opponents in a dilemma.

37. **(A)** (p. 70) ***Reading/Social Studies/Development.*** Anthony anticipates a possible objection to her position: the Constitution and other laws use masculine pronouns, which means that the provisions of the documents were meant to apply only to men. Anthony's response is that women should therefore not have to pay taxes or otherwise be subject to the constraints of laws since such laws are described using masculine pronouns.

38. **(A)** (p. 70) ***Reading/Social Studies/Development.*** This question requires you to abstract from the passage and exhibit the formal or logical structure of Anthony's argument. In lines 71–74, Anthony quotes the Fourteenth Amendment to establish the first premise of the argument that all persons born or naturalized in the United States are citizens. Then in lines 77–79, she further quotes the Amendment to establish the premise that all citizens have the right to vote (no law shall abridge the privileges or immunities of citizens). Once she has established that all persons who are citizens have the right to vote, she needs only answer the question "Are women persons?" And the answer to that question, she believes, is obvious.

39. **(C)** (p. 70) *Reading/Social Studies/Textual Evidence.* The language of the first sentence of the Fourteenth Amendment clearly states that all persons born or naturalized in the United States are citizens both of the United States and of the state where they live.

40. **(A)** (p. 71) *Reading/Social Studies/Main Idea.* The third paragraph is an independent argument that is quite persuasive, even though it technically does not belong in Anthony's criminal defense. In this paragraph, she argues that a government restricted in its participation to men can only introduce instability because women, excluded from the vote, perceive the government and its laws as oppressive.

41. **(B)** (p. 71) *Reading/Social Studies/Data Presentations.* The map shows several interesting things. Note that the western states generally granted full voting rights to women prior to the 19th amendment. In four of those states, women had full voting rights not only before the passage of the 19th Amendment but also before these territories were granted statehood. These four states, however, do not represent the southwestern region, so (A) can be eliminated. Notice that states in the south and along the eastern seaboard granted women the right to vote only after the 19th Amendment was ratified. So (B) is the correct answer choice.

Questions #42–52

42. **(D)** (p. 73) *Reading/Natural Sciences/Vocabulary.* According to the passage, the vernal mixing takes place in the spring. So, "vernal" must mean "spring."

43. **(A)** (p. 73) *Reading/Natural Sciences/Implied Idea.* In paragraph five, the passage explains that freshwater is densest at a temperature of 4°C. Thus, water between 0°C and 4°C is colder but less dense. Since denser water sinks, the warmer layer is beneath the colder layer, an inversion of the usual order.

44. **(C)** (p. 73) *Reading/Natural Sciences/Textual Evidence.* Lines 44–47 provide the description for inverse stratification that is laid out in the explanation to item #39.

45. **(A)** (p. 73) *Reading/Natural Sciences/Explicit Detail.* In the final paragraph, the author explains how stratification can reduce the nutrients needed in the epilimnion. Photosynthesis occurs in the epilimnion so organisms are consuming nutrients. While the organisms live, the nutrients are bound up in the organisms. When the organisms die, they sink to the bottom of the lake and decompose, so the nutrients are released. If the water circulates from bottom to top, the nutrients are carried back to the epilimnion for reuse. But when the lake is stratified, there is no movement across the thermocline, so the nutrients are trapped in the hypolimnion. Eventually, organisms use up the nutrients in the epilimnion because there is no resupply from the bottom.

46. **(D)** (p. 73) *Reading/Natural Sciences/Textual Evidence.* . As already described in the explanation to item #41, when the lake is stratified, there is no movement across the thermocline, so the nutrients are trapped in the hypolimnion. This process is stated explicitly in lines 88–92.

47. **(B)** (p. 73) *Reading/Natural Sciences/Explicit Detail.* According to the last two paragraphs, stratification poses a threat to lake life because the dissolved oxygen in the upper layer cannot cross the thermocline to

the bottom so life on the bottom cannot carry on respiration. Additionally, after an organism dies, sinks to the bottom, and decomposes, the released nutrients cannot rise to the top, so life there has nothing to eat.

48. **(D)** (p. 74) *Reading/Natural Sciences/Explicit Detail.* In the very first sentence of the passage, the author states that the lake stratification is explained by changes in temperature.

49. **(C)** (p. 74) *Reading/Natural Sciences/Vocabulary.* In the sentence in which "gradient" is used, the author notes that the difference in density is very small so the gradient is minor. "Gradient," therefore, must mean "difference."

50. **(B)** (p. 74) *Reading/Natural Sciences/Main Idea.* As already mentioned in the explanation to item #43, the last two paragraphs discuss how stratification poses a threat to lake life: the thermocline barrier disrupts the vertical transport of both dissolved oxygen and the nutrients released from dead organisms. So, (B) is the correct answer choice.

51. **(C)** (p. 74) *Reading/Natural Sciences/Data Presentations.* For this item, use the process of elimination. (A) and (D) can be eliminated because the passage states that the thermocline is located within the metalimnion layer. (B) can be eliminated because the passage distinguishes the thermocline from the metalimnion. (Theoretically, the two could coincide, in which case the graph would show a line of constant slope between the top and bottom of the metalimnion.) So, (C) is the correct answer choice. The author defines the thermocline as the "plane of maximum rate of decrease." From 20 to 25 meters, this change of depth of 5 meters is associated with a temperature change from just under 20°C to approximately 7.5°C, or a little greater than 10°C.

52. **(C)** (p. 74) *Reading/Natural Sciences/Explicit Detail.* According to paragraph one, after the spring mixing, warm summer temperatures cause the lake to stratify, and as temperatures continue to warm and remain warm, the stratification becomes increasingly stable. Then, according to paragraph four, cool fall temperatures disrupt the stratification and cause mixing. In the winter, the lake will either remain mixed or will stratify inversely.

Section 2: Writing and Language

Passage 1

1. **(D)** (p. 76) *Writing and Language/Standard English Conventions/Sentence Structure/Faulty Parallelism.* This item tests sentence structure. The problem with the original is that the lack of a "most" before "imaginative" disrupts the parallelism of the series. The problem can be solved by inserting another "most." Yes, you would have the repetition of "most," but it would not necessarily be needless repetition. A writer may choose that route in order to provide emphasis to each element in the series. Or, as the correct answer does, the "most" can be position in front of the entire series so that it modifies each of the four elements— more concise, less dramatic. Remember, the test would never ask for students to choose between two good alternatives, so only one or the other of those would be used as a choice.

2. **(A)** (p. 76) *Writing and Language/Expression of Ideas/No Change.* The author is looking for a quotation that will echo the pre-modern attitude toward war that is described in the immediately preceding sentence. According to that sentence, war in pre-modernized times was considered "unavoidable" and even "noble." The idea that dying for one's country ("war") is sweet ("noble") and fitting ("unavoidable") best meets the author's goal.

3. **(B) (p. 76) *Writing and Language/Expression of Ideas/Style/Tone.*** The author places the word "civilized" in quotes in order to alert the reader that something unusual is taking place. In this case, the author is using the word ironically to call attention to the fact that the so-called "civilized" humanity who settled into cities 8,000 years ago has been consistently at war all that time.

4. **(D) (p. 76) *Writing and Language/Standard English Conventions/Punctuation/Colons.*** In this case, it is used to introduce a series. The original is wrong, however, because the phrase "such as," which may also be used to introduce a series, is superfluous. So, (D) is the correct answer choice. Note that using the phrase "such as" without the colon would also result in a correct construction, but this is not one of the options.

5. **(D) (p. 76) *Writing and Language/Standard English Conventions/Sentence Structure/Faulty Parallelism.*** The original is wrong because it is not parallel to the other elements in the series. As written, the elements are presented as so: "enemy," "having . . . slaves," "natural resources," and "land." In order to correct this problem, "having human slaves to do labor" should be changed to "human slave labor." So, (D) is the correct answer choice.

6. **(A) (p. 77) *Writing and Language/Expression of Ideas/No Change.*** In this sentence, "nevertheless," which means "in spite of that," is a conjunctive adverb. It is used to signal a relationship of opposition or contrast between the preceding sentence and the sentence in which it appears. In this case, it effectively sets up an idea against the idea that precedes it: a major war is unthinkable; "nevertheless," we must think about it.

7. **(A) (p. 77) *Writing and Language/Expression of Ideas/No Change.*** A paradox is a statement that contradicts itself. Our need to maintain the capacity for war as a means to preserving peace is certainly a self-contradictory idea.

8. **(A) (p. 77) *Writing and Language/Expression of Ideas/No Change.*** The author wants to effectively make his or her point by providing an example that is analogous to the changing effects of warfare. As described in the paragraph, with advances in warfare (nuclear weapons that make traditional war unthinkable) come side-effects (the mass destruction that can come from a nuclear war brought on by accident or miscalculation). So, the advance of techniques in warfare has created a situation in which war becomes more dangerous. Analogously, while the abundance of food has reduced hunger, it has been accompanied by a rise in diet-related illnesses.

9. **(B) (p. 77) *Writing and Language/Standard English Conventions/Grammar and Usage/Subject-Verb Agreement.*** The original is wrong because the singular verb "has been" does not agree with the plural subject of the sentence ("reasons"). Instead, the plural verb "have been" is required.

10. **(D) (p. 78) *Writing and Language/Standard English Conventions/Grammar and Usage/Pronoun Usage.*** The original is wrong because the contraction "it's" is inappropriate in this context. The author intends to show possession (of "wealth"), so the singular possessive pronoun "its" is required.

11. **(D) (p. 78) *Writing and Language/Expression of Ideas/Strategy/Main Idea.*** In the final paragraph, the author discusses several disadvantages to controlling a conquered territory, such as the cost of providing and administering government services to a conquered enemy. In summary, it no longer makes financial sense to conquer and rule because the costs outweigh the benefits.

Passage 2

12. **(A)** (p. 79) *Writing and Language/Expression of Ideas/Style/Precision.* An epithet is a descriptive phrase so closely associated with a person's nature or character that it becomes a part of one of the names by which that person is called (e.g., Philip the Tall or Henry the Navigator). In this context, "epithet" not only provides the author's intended meaning, but it also expresses the appropriately formal tone of the passage.

13. **(B)** (p. 79) *Writing and Language/Expression of Ideas/Organization/Sentence-Level Structure.* The original is wrong because it is awkward and imprecise. As written, it seems to say that a snake-entwined staff used to have a different name and symbolic meaning than what it does today. Instead, the author means to suggest that the rod was associated with health and medicine in ancient times and express that it remains a symbol of medicine today. (B) best captures this idea, making the description of the rod itself a non-essential element of the sentence.

14. **(D)** (p. 79) *Writing and Language/Standard English Conventions/Sentence Structure/Unintended Meanings.* The original is wrong because it suggests that the objective of preventive medicine has already been met. What the author intends to say is that the maintenance and promotion of health is an ongoing concern. So, "to accomplish" this objective, preventive medicine takes certain actions and measures.

15. **(A)** (p. 79) *Writing and Language/Standard English Conventions/Grammar and Usage/Pronoun Usage.* This item tests pronoun reference. The referent (antecedent" of "it") is found in an earlier sentence, making the item a bit more difficult than a similar item in which both the pronoun and the referent are contained in the same sentence. Students must search the previous sentence or sentences to learn that "it" refers "preventive medicine."

16. **(C)** (p. 79) *Writing and Language/Expression of Ideas/Style/Tone.* The original is wrong because it inappropriately uses the concept of size to refer to something that cannot be measured in that way (an objective). "Major," which means "important," is the correct word choice.

17. **(D)** (p. 80) *Writing and Language/Expression of Ideas/Strategy/Effective Transitional Sentence.* The logical structure of the paragraph consists of a general statement followed by five supporting points. Since the five points do not necessarily require any sequential arrangement, "initially" is inappropriate in this context. However, since the related sentence is the fifth and final point, "finally" is certainly acceptable and is in fact the best of the remaining answer choices. "Instead" and "for once" result in meanings that are not intended by the author.

18. **(D)** (p. 80) *Writing and Language/Expression of Ideas/Strategy/Main Idea.* In the fourth paragraph, the author explains that curative medicine requires clinically trained practitioners (presumably doctors, nurses, physician assistants, etc.) while preventive medicine requires people who deal with environmental factors and communities (presumably engineers and specialized technicians who work in areas such as water supply, pollution, etc.). (D) nicely summarizes this explanation.

19. **(B)** (p. 80) *Writing and Language/Standard English Conventions/Grammar and Usage/Pronoun Usage.* "Who's" is a contraction for "who is" and is inappropriate in this context. Instead, the possessive pronoun "whose" is required to refer to the plural noun "individuals" and indicate that they possess "training."

20. (C) (p. 80) *Writing and Language/Standard English Conventions/Punctuation/Apostrophes.* Just as with the previous item, this item deals with possession; in this case, however, the issue is one of correct apostrophe use when creating a possessive noun. Since the author intends to refer to the health and disease status of an individual, the singular possessive of "individual" ("individual's") is required.

21. (A) (p. 80) *Writing and Language/Expression of Ideas/No Change.* The underlined sentence states that there are economic differences between preventive and curative medicine. The remainder of the paragraph develops this point: sickness is nonproductive but health has a high value; a sick population is a greater economic burden than is a healthy population; and the cost of prevention is lower than the cost of curing. So, the underlined sentence makes a good topic sentence.

22. (C) (p. 80) *Writing and Language/Standard English Conventions/Sentence Structure/Comma Splices.* The problem with the original is that it results in a commas splice (two independent clauses joined together with only a comma). The different ways to solve this problem are to insert a coordinating conjunction immediately after the comma, replace the comma with a semicolon, or create two sentences by using the appropriate end-stop punctuation. (C) uses the third of these approaches to address the comma splice.

Passage 3

23. (C) (p. 81) *Writing and Language/Standard English Conventions/Sentence Structure/Misplaced Modifiers.* The original is wrong because the misplacement of the modifier "with a speed of 1.6 million miles per hour" changes the author's intended meaning. As written, the sentence seems to illogically say that the speed was used to detect the star or that the star is one of the fastest of those stars detected that have a speed of 1.6 million miles per hour. (C) solves the problem by placing the modifier close to what it is intended to modify: "it" (the star).

24. (B) (p. 81) *Writing and Language/Expression of Ideas/Strategy/Appropriate Supporting Material.* What do the observations made by Hubble prove? The answer to this question is contained in the second paragraph. At first, astronomers thought that the star originated in the Large Magellanic Cloud, but the Hubble evidence has proven this to be wrong; the star actually originated in the Milky Way.

25. (D) (p. 81) *Writing and Language/Expression of Ideas/Style/Precision.* The original is wrong because the word "evicted" does not have the meaning required in this context. "Ejected," which means "violently thrown out," is the correct word choice.

26. (A) (p. 81) *Writing and Language/Expression of Ideas/No Change.* As already described in the explanation to item #25, the second paragraph states how the astronomers' original theory of the star's origin in the Large Magellanic Cloud was disproven by the Hubble evidence. The original theory precedes the location in the paragraph designated by this item, and the description of the Hubble findings immediately follows this location. So, (A) is the correct answer choice. The remaining answer choices suggest that the original theory was correct.

27. (A) (p. 81) *Writing and Language/Standard English Conventions/No Change.* This item asks whether or not the underlined pronoun is used unambiguously. The original is correct. "It" clearly refers to "star." Each of the other choices disrupts that clear, unambiguous connection.

28. **(B)** (p. 81) *Writing and Language/Expression of Ideas/Style/Conciseness.* The problem with the original is that it is needlessly wordy. The phrase "traveled the journey" is essentially redundant, so either "traveled" or "journeyed" will suffice.

29. **(B)** (p. 82) *Writing and Language/Standard English Conventions/Grammar and Usage/Faulty or Illogical Comparisons.* The original suffers from a faulty comparison. The underlined portion tries to compare the star's mass with nine of our suns. By inserting the pronoun "that," which refers to "mass," (B) corrects the mistake: the star's mass is nine times that (the mass) of our sun.

30. **(D)** (p. 82) *Writing and Language/Standard English Conventions/Grammar and Usage/Subject-Verb Agreement.* The subject of the sentence is the compound "mass . . . and blue color," so a plural verb is required.

31. **(A)** (p. 82) *Writing and Language/Standard English Conventions/No Change.* This question turns on a fairly subtle point of punctuation. In this sentence, the adjectives "young" and "massive" both modify the noun "star." Two such adjectives are referred to as coordinate adjectives and need to be separated by either a comma or a coordinating conjunction. The original is correct because the two adjectives are separated by a comma. Without the comma, "young" would seem to modify "massive." Note that using the coordinating conjunction "and" in this context would also be correct ("young and massive star").

32. **(B)** (p. 82) *Writing and Language/Expression of Ideas/Strategy/Data Presentation.* The sequence of events depicted in the graphic is: triple-star system travels through Milky Way galaxy (sentence 2), black hole captures one star and the other two stars are expelled (sentence 4), and two expelled stars continue to evolve into a blue straggler (sentence 3).

33. **(A)** (p. 82) *Writing and Language/Expression of Ideas/Strategy/Main Idea.* In the final paragraph, the author refers to the formation of the star (which was triggered by the triple-star system passing too close to the Milky Way's black hole) as a "cosmic misstep." So, for this reason, "freak accident" is a suitable description of the hypervelocity star's formation.

Passage 4

34. **(C)** (p. 84) *Writing and Language/Standard English Conventions/Sentence Structure/Fragments.* The original is wrong because it results in a sentence fragment: "Most notably James "Super Chikan" Johnson of Clarksdale." This construction lacks a main verb. A fragment can be solved by either providing a main verb or joining the construction to an already complete sentence. (C) takes the second approach.

35. **(C)** (p. 84) *Writing and Language/Standard English Conventions/Sentence Structure/Problems of Coordination and Subordination.* The original suffers from faulty subordination. The author does not really intend to make the second clause dependent upon the first and certainly does not intend to create a contrast between the two ideas. (C) solves the problem by using the coordinating conjunction "and" to indicate that the two ideas are of equal importance.

36. **(A)** (p. 84) *Writing and Language/Standard English Conventions/No Change.* Colons can be used to signal that a detail or a further explanation will follow. Here, the author uses the colon to good effect, introducing James Johnson's new nickname: "Super Chikan."

37. **(D)** (p. 84) *Writing and Language/Expression of Ideas/Style/Conciseness.* Since the adjective "used" implies that the guitar was "previously owned," the verbiage following "used guitar" is redundant and should be eliminated.

38. **(D)** (p. 85) *Writing and Language/Standard English Conventions/Grammar and Usage/Verb Tense.* The problem with the original is that the past perfect verb "had gone" is inconsistent with the past tense verbs used elsewhere in the paragraph. The past perfect suggests that Johnson playing with other Delta bluesmen preceded some other event, but no other event is described in the sentence. (D) solves the problem by using the simple past tense verb "went."

39. **(A)** (p. 85) *Writing and Language/Expression of Ideas/No Change.* The underlined sentence provides an interesting detail about Johnson's life and is entirely consistent with painting a compelling backstory to Johnson's career: Johnson talked to chickens, drove a cab, played homemade instruments, and wrote music while driving a truck.

40. **(B)** (p. 85) *Writing and Language/Expression of Ideas/Style/Idiomatic Expression.* The original is wrong because the preposition "up" is not idiomatic in this context. The author intends to say that Johnson "showed off" his musical abilities.

41. **(C)** (p. 85) *Writing and Language/Expression of Ideas/Style/Conciseness.* Just as with item #37, this item suffers from redundancy. "Solo," of course, means "by oneself" or "alone."

42. **(D)** (p. 85) *Writing and Language/Standard English Conventions/Punctuation/Commas.* The problem with the original is that the comma immediately following "released" disrupts the logical flow of the sentence. (D) solves the problem by simply eliminating the comma.

43. **(A)** (p. 86) *Writing and Language/Expression of Ideas/No Change.* This question is asking for a topic sentence to introduce the remainder of the paragraph. (A) is the best option, as this paragraph provides details about the instruments that Johnson makes by hand.

44. **(C)** (p. 86) *Writing and Language/Expression of Ideas/Organization/Passage-Level Structure.* (A), (B), and (D) are all mentioned earlier in the passage. While the author does mention in the third paragraph that Johnson played in local clubs when he was young, the idea that he *still* plays in hometown clubs is only mentioned in the last paragraph. So, (C) is the correct answer choice.

Section 3: Math—No Calculator

1. **(C)** (p. 88) *Math: Multiple-Choice/Problem Solving and Advanced Arithmetic/Multi-Step Problem Solving Items.* Since $38 \div 4 = 9$, with a remainder of 2, the landscaper must make 9 trips carrying 4 bricks and an additional trip with the last 2 bricks, for a total of 10 trips.

2. **(A)** (p. 88) *Math: Multiple-Choice/Algebra/Solving Algebraic Equations or Inequalities with One Variable/Simple Equations.* Solve the given equation for x:
$$x + 1 + 2x + 2 + 3x + 3 = 6 \Rightarrow 6x + 6 = 6 \Rightarrow 6x = 0 \Rightarrow x = 0.$$

3. **(D) (p. 88)** *Math: Multiple-Choice/Algebra/Creating, Expressing, and Evaluating Algebraic Equations and Functions.* Let n equal the number of coffees sold to break even and create an equation setting the cost equal to the profit: $8,000 + 0.5n = cn \Rightarrow 8,000 = cn - 0.5n = n(c - 0.5) \Rightarrow n = \dfrac{8,000}{c - 0.5}$.

4. **(C) (p. 88)** *Math: Multiple-Choice/Algebra/Manipulating Algebraic Expressions/Evaluating Expressions.* Since x, y, and z are consecutive integers for which $x > y > z$, x is 1 more than y, y is 1 more than z, and x is 2 more than z. Therefore: $y = x - 1$ and $z = x - 2$. Plug these expression for y and z into the given equation and evaluate: $[x - (x-1)][x-(x-2)][(x-1)-(x-2)] = (x-x+1)(x-x+2)(x-1-x+2) = (1)(2)(1) = 2$.

5. **(B) (p. 88)** *Math: Multiple-Choice/Algebra/Creating, Expressing, and Evaluating Algebraic Equations and Functions.* Printer M prints $8d$ models in d days, so the total printed by M as a function of d is $120 + 8d$. Printer N prints $12d$ models in d days, so the total number of models printed by Printer N is $80 + 12d$. Set the two expressions equal and solve for d: $120 + 8d = 80 + 12d \Rightarrow 40 = 4d \Rightarrow d = 10$.

6. **(C) (p. 88)** *Math: Multiple-Choice/Geometry.* A cube has six faces, each with edge-length, e, so the surface area of the cube is: $6(e^2) = 54x^2 \Rightarrow e^2 = 9x^2 \Rightarrow e = \sqrt{9x^2} = 3x$. Thus, the volume of the cube is $(3x)^3 = 27x^3$.

7. **(A) (p. 88)** *Math: Multiple-Choice/Statistics/Measures of Center and Spread/Averages* and *Algebra/Solving Simultaneous Equations.* Use the technique for finding the missing elements of an average. Since the average of the five numbers is 26, the sum is $26(5) = 130$. The sum of 20, 23, and 24 is 67, and $130 - 67 = 63$. So, $x + y = 63$. Use the method for solving simultaneous equations: if $x + y = 63$ and $x = \dfrac{3}{4}y$, then $\dfrac{3}{4}y + y = 63 \Rightarrow 1.75y = 63 \Rightarrow y = 36$. And $x + 36 = 63 \Rightarrow x = 27$.

8. **(C) (p. 89)** *Math: Multiple-Choice/Algebra/Creating, Expressing, and Evaluating Algebraic Equations and Functions/Function Notation.* Perform the defined function on the values given: $[3] = 3 \cdot 3 = 9$ since 3 is odd, and $[4] = 2 \cdot 4 = 8$ since 4 is even. $9 \cdot 8 = 72$, so $[3] \cdot [4] = 72$. Now, reason that since 72 is an even number, it is the result of performing the defined function on a number equal to one-half of 72, or 36. Therefore, $[3] \cdot [4] = 72 = [36]$.

9. **(D) (p. 89)** *Math: Multiple-Choice/Algebra/Creating, Expressing, and Evaluating Algebraic Equations and Functions/Function Notation.* If x is a prime number greater than 2, then x must be odd and $x - 1$ is the next smaller number, which must be an even number. Since the quantity is even, the function tells you to multiply the quantity by 2: $2(x - 1) = 2x - 2$.

    Alternatively, test the test using $x = 3$: $[3 - 1] = [2]$, and 2 is even, so $[2] = 2(2) = 4$. Now test the answer choices:

    A) $3x = 3(2) = 6$, and $6 \neq 4$
    B) $2x = 2(3) = 6$, and $6 \neq 4$
    C) $3x - 3 = 3(3) - 3 = 6$, and $6 \neq 4$
    D) $2x - 2 = 2(3) - 2 = 4$, and $4 = 4$

10. **(A)** (p. 89) *Math: Multiple-Choice/Algebra/Creating, Expressing, and Evaluating Algebraic Equations and Functions.* For $t = 0$, the value of the car is $12,000; that is, the original purchase price of the car was $12,000.

11. **(A)** (p. 89) *Math: Multiple-Choice/Algebra/Creating, Expressing, and Evaluating Algebraic Equations and Functions.* Set up the formula by reasoning that Tom's age minus Y years is equal to 3 times Julie's age minus Y years: $T - Y = 3(20 - Y) \Rightarrow T - Y = 60 - 3Y \Rightarrow T = 60 - 2Y$.

12. **(B)** (p. 89) *Math: Multiple-Choice/Algebra/Manipulating Algebraic Expressions/Factoring Expressions.* Use prime factorization to solve this problem. As for (I), if x is a multiple of both 5 and 9, then the following are true: $x = 3 \cdot 3 \cdot 5 \cdot a$ (for some other integer, a) and $x \neq 45$ whenever a is any integer other than 1. So, (I) is not true. As for (II), x is a multiple of 15 because $x = (3 \cdot 5) \cdot 3 \cdot a$, so (II) must be true. As for (III) whenever a is even, x is even, so (III) is not true. The correct choice includes (II) only.

13. **(B)** (p. 89) *Math: Multiple-Choice/Coordinate Geometry/Graphs of Quadratic Equations and Relations and Algebra/Creating, Expressing, and Evaluating Algebraic Equations and Functions/Concepts of Domain and Range.* The domain of a function is the set of x-values and the range is the set of y-values, or $f(x)$. In this case, the function $f(x) = x^2 - 4$ is a quadratic in which the x is squared and has a positive coefficient (1), so the graph is a regular, up-right parabola. The minimum value of the parabola occurs for $x = 0$, so the minimum value for y is –4:

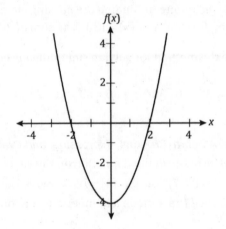

Therefore, the range of the function is all real numbers greater than or equal to –4.

14. (A) (p. 89) *Math: Multiple-Choice/Coordinate Geometry/The Coordinate System and Geometry/Triangles/ Properties of Triangles.* A sketch will help:

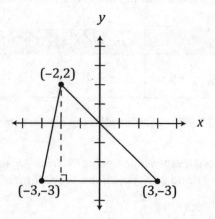

From the diagram, the length of the triangle's base is 6 and the height of the triangle is 5. So, the area is $\dfrac{bh}{2} = \dfrac{(6)(5)}{2} = 15.$

15. (D) (p. 90) *Math: Multiple-Choice/Trigonometry/Right Triangles/Trigonometric Ratios.* Since the points are both on the circle and the radius of the circle is 1, ΔMON is an isosceles triangle with two sides equal to 1:

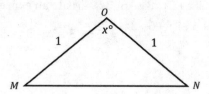

Draw a line segment from O to the center of $\overline{MN}$ to create two right triangles:

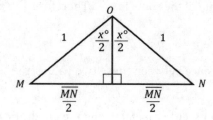

Now, use the trigonometric relationships to solve for $\overline{MN}$ in terms of $x°$. Since the side opposite $\dfrac{x°}{2}$ and the hypotenuse are both known values, relate these two: $\sin = \dfrac{\text{opposite}}{\text{hypotenuse}}$. Therefore,

$$\sin\frac{x}{2} = \frac{\overline{MN}/2}{1} = \frac{\overline{MN}}{2} \text{ and } \overline{MN} = 2\sin\frac{x}{2}.$$

16. **(15.5 or 31/2)** (p. 92) *Math: Student-Produced Responses/Algebra/Evaluating Sequences Involving Exponential Growth.* This item describes a situation demonstrating inverse exponential growth. The problem is simplified by writing the information in a table, decreasing the number of hours each day by half:

Monday	Tuesday	Wednesday	Thursday	Friday
8	$\frac{8}{2} = 4$	$\frac{4}{2} = 2$	$\frac{2}{2} = 1$	$\frac{1}{2} = 0.5$

Therefore: $8 + 4 + 2 + 1 + 0.5 = 15.5$. Note that the grid can also accommodate the fraction 31/2.

17. **(4)** (p. 92) *Math: Student-Produced Responses/Algebra/Solving Algebraic Equations or Inequalities with One Variable/Equations Involving Rational Expressions.* Solve for N:

$$\frac{1}{2N} + \frac{1}{2N} = \frac{1}{4} \Rightarrow \frac{2}{2N} = \frac{1}{4} \Rightarrow \frac{1}{N} = \frac{1}{4} \Rightarrow N = 4 \,.$$

18. **(29)** (p. 92) *Math: Student-Produced Responses/Statistics/Measures of Center and Spread/Mode and Averages and Algebra/Manipulating Algebraic Expressions/Evaluating Expressions.* A mode is the value with the greatest frequency in a set of numbers. There are three modes—x, y, and z—so each of these modes occur the same number of times and with a greater frequency than the other numbers, which include 4, $3(x+2)$, $3y-5$, and $3z$. This leaves six additional numbers, so the modes each occur twice. The complete set is $[4, x, x, y, y, z, z, 3(x+2), 3y-5, 3z]$. Create an expression for the average of the set of numbers: $\dfrac{4 + 2x + 2y + 2z + 3x + 6 + 3y - 5 + 3z}{10} = 15 \Rightarrow 5 + 5x + 5y + 5z = 150 \Rightarrow$

$5(x + y + z) = 145 \Rightarrow x + y + z = 29$.

19. **(1)** (p. 92) *Math: Student-Produced Responses/Algebra/Solving Quadratic Equations and Relations.* This problem is greatly simplified if you remember that the product of the roots of a quadratic equation $ax^2 + bx + c = 0$ is $\dfrac{c}{a}$ and the sum of the roots is $\dfrac{-b}{a}$. Therefore, the product of the roots of the quadratic equation $3x^2 - 2x - 1 = 0$, where $a = 3$, $b = -2$, and $c = -1$, is $-\dfrac{1}{3}$ and the sum of the roots is $\dfrac{-(-2)}{3} = \dfrac{2}{3}$. The absolute value of the difference between these two values, that is, the distance between the two values on a number line, is 1.

Alternatively, determine the roots, either by factoring the quadratic equation or by applying the quadratic formula. According to the quadratic formula, the roots are $\dfrac{-b \pm \sqrt{b^2 - 4ac}}{2a} = \dfrac{-(-2) \pm \sqrt{(-2)^2 - 4(3)(-1)}}{2(3)} =$

$\dfrac{2 \pm \sqrt{4 + 12}}{6} = \dfrac{2 \pm 4}{6} = -\dfrac{1}{3}$ and 1. The product of the roots is $-\dfrac{1}{3}$ and the sum is $\dfrac{2}{3}$, so the absolute value of the difference between these two values is 1.

20. (9) (p. 92) *Math: Student-Produced Responses/Geometry/Circles* and *Coordinate Geometry/Graphs of Quadratic Equations and Relations.* The item stem states that $\overset{\frown}{XY}$ is an arc of a circle with center O, and $\angle XOY = 90°$. Therefore, $\overset{\frown}{XY}$ is one-fourth of the circumference of the circle. Use this information and the length of $\overset{\frown}{XY}$ to find the radius of the circle: $\dfrac{3\pi}{2} = \dfrac{C}{4} = \dfrac{2\pi r}{4} \Rightarrow r = \dfrac{4(3\pi)}{2(2\pi)} = 3$. Thus, point X has coordinates $(3,0)$. Since point X is on both the circle and the parabola, substitute its coordinates into the given equation for the parabola and solve for a: $y = -x^2 + a \Rightarrow 0 = -(3)^2 + a \Rightarrow a = 9$.

Section 4: Math—Calculator

1. (B) (p. 94) *Math: Multiple-Choice/Algebra/Creating, Expressing, and Evaluating Algebraic Equations and Functions.* Each big slice equals $\dfrac{1}{6}$ of the whole. Each slice is then cut into thirds: $\dfrac{1}{6} \cdot \dfrac{1}{3} = \dfrac{1}{18}$, so each small slice is $\dfrac{1}{18}$ of the whole. Pete had 4 small slices, or $\dfrac{4}{18} = \dfrac{2}{9}$ of the whole pie: $\dfrac{2T}{9}$.

2. (A) (p. 94) *Math: Multiple-Choice/Problem Solving and Advanced Arithmetic/Common Advanced Arithmetic Items/Sets: Union, Intersection, and Elements.* Count the pairs that fit the requirement: $(2,1)$, $(3,1)$, $(3,2)$, $(4,1)$, $(4,2)$, and $(4,3)$, for a total of 6 pairs.

3. (C) (p. 94) *Math: Multiple-Choice/Probability/Arithmetic Probability.* Probability is the number of desirable outcomes divided by the total number of possible outcomes. In total, Estrella has $5 + 7 + 4 + 3 + 1 = 20$ coins. Of those coins, the nickels, dimes, quarters, and the half-dollar are not pennies—15 coins in total. Therefore, the probability of choosing a coin that is not a penny is $\dfrac{15}{20} = \dfrac{3}{4}$.

4. (A) (p. 94) *Math: Multiple-Choice/Problem Solving and Advanced Arithmetic/Common Problem Solving Items/Percentages.* First, determine the number of seniors going to college: 80 percent of the 150 graduating is $0.8(150) = 120$. Of those, 75 percent attend school in-state, so 25 percent attend school out-of-state: $0.25(120) = 30$.

5. (C) (p. 94) *Math: Multiple-Choice/Problem Solving and Advanced Arithmetic/Common Problem Solving Items/Proportions and Direct-Inverse Variation* and *Geometry/Complex Figures.* Since the shaded area, or $2\dfrac{1}{2}$ squares, is equal to 5 square miles, each full square is equal to 2 square miles. There are 9 squares in total, so the area of the entire piece of land is $9 \text{ squares} \cdot \dfrac{2 \text{ square miles}}{\text{square}} = 18$ square miles.

6. (D) (p. 94) *Math: Multiple-Choice/Algebra/Creating, Expressing, and Evaluating Algebraic Equations and Functions.* Create an equation, in which P represents the original price: $P - \left(\dfrac{1}{3}\right)P = B \Rightarrow \left(\dfrac{2}{3}\right)P = B \Rightarrow P = \dfrac{3B}{2}$.

7. **(B)** (p. 95) *Math: Multiple-Choice/Problem Solving and Advanced Arithmetic/Multi-Step Problem Solving Items.* Density is defined as mass divided by volume. The volume of the sample is $2.5 \text{ cm} \times 6 \text{ cm} \times 3 \text{ cm} = 45 \text{ cm}^3$. The density of the rock sample is $\dfrac{150 \text{ grams}}{45 \text{ cm}^3} \approx 3.33 \text{ g/cm}^3$, so it is most likely a chondrite meteorite.

8. **(D)** (p. 95) *Math: Multiple-Choice/Coordinate Geometry/Graphs of Linear Equations and Algebra/Solving Simultaneous Equations.* If two lines are parallel, but not identical, then they never intersect. In order for them to be parallel, they must have the same slope. Rewrite each equation in slope-intercept form: $\dfrac{x+y}{2} = 1 \Rightarrow y = -x + 2$ and $ax + 2y = 10 \Rightarrow y = -\dfrac{ax}{2} + 5$. Therefore, in order for the lines to have the same slope, $-\dfrac{a}{2} = -1 \Rightarrow a = 2$.

9. **(B)** (p. 95) *Math: Multiple-Choice/Geometry/Triangles/Properties of Triangles.* The triangle on the right is an equilateral triangle, so $2x = 8$, which means that $x = 4$. So, the length of side $\overline{AC}$ is $8 + 4 = 12$.

10. **(C)** (p. 95) *Math: Multiple-Choice/Problem Solving and Advanced Arithmetic/Common Problem Solving Items/Percentages.* In spite of the wordy item stem, simply compare $100 - (1 + 11) = 88\%$ of $25 with $100 - (2 + 14) = 84\%$ of $30. Avi's donation yields $0.88(25) = \$22$ and Brandon's donation yields $0.84(30) = \$25.20$. Therefore, Brandon's donation yields $\$25.20 - \$22 = \$3.20$ more than Avi's donation.

11. **(C)** (p. 96) *Math: Multiple-Choice/Statistics/Measures of Center and Spread/Averages.* Use the technique for finding a missing element in an average. Since the three scores average 75, the student earned a total score of $3 \cdot 75 = 225$. Since one score is 75, the remaining scores total $225 - 75 = 150$. The maximum that she could receive on any test is 100, and $150 - 100 = 50$. Thus, the lowest score that she could have received (and still maintain a 75 average) is 50.

12. **(B)** (p. 96) *Math: Multiple-Choice/Geometry/Complex Figures and Circles.* Let r be the radius of the original pool—its area is πr^2. Then, the radius of the larger pool is $2r$, so its area is $\pi(2r)^2 = 4\pi r^2$. The shaded part of the diagram is the larger circle minus the smaller one, so the area of the shaded part of the diagram is $4\pi r^2 - \pi r^2 = 3\pi r^2$. Therefore, the ratio of the shaded area to the unshaded area is $\dfrac{3\pi r^2}{\pi r^2} = \dfrac{3}{1}$.

13. **(A)** (p. 96) *Math: Multiple-Choice/Geometry/Circles and Problem Solving and Advanced Arithmetic/ Common Problem Solving Items/Percentages.* Let r be the radius of the original pool, so it has a surface area of πr^2. The radius of the new pool will be $1.2r$, so it has an area of $\pi(1.2r)^2 = 1.44\pi r^2$. Therefore, the area of the new pool is 144% of the area of the old pool.

Alternatively, choose some easy numbers to work with. Let the radius of the original pool equal 10. This means the radius of the new pool must be 12. Therefore, the area of the new pool is $\pi(12)^2 = 144\pi$ and the area of the original pool is $\pi(10)^2 = 100\pi$. And 144π is 144% of 100π.

14. **(A)** (p. 96) *Math: Multiple-Choice/Coordinate Geometry/Slope-Intercept Form of a Linear Equation.* Use the slope-intercept form for linear equations, $y = mx + b$, in which m, the slope, is equal to $\dfrac{y_2 - y_1}{x_2 - x_1}$. Thus, $m = \dfrac{5-1}{7-(-1)} = \dfrac{4}{8} = \dfrac{1}{2}$, so the equation is $y = \dfrac{x}{2} + b$. Substitute one of the given points into the equation to find the y-intercept, b: $1 = \dfrac{-1}{2} + b \Rightarrow b = \dfrac{3}{2}$. Therefore, $y = \dfrac{x}{2} + \dfrac{3}{2}$.

Alternatively, substitute the given points into the equations in the answer choices to determine which equation is true for both points.

15. **(C)** (p. 97) *Math: Multiple-Choice/Data Interpretation/Scatterplots and Statistics/Measures of Center and Spread/Median.* The median is the middle value of the data when the values are arranged in order. Since the x-axis shows the total grams of fat for the nine items arranged in order, simply pick the middle data point: the fish sandwich, which has 18 grams of fat.

16. **(C)** (p. 97) *Math: Multiple-Choice/Data Interpretation/Scatterplots and Algebra/Creating, Expressing, and Evaluating Algebraic Equations and Functions/Functions as Models and Coordinate Geometry/Slope-Intercept Form of a Linear Equation.* Written in slope-intercept form, the line of best fit has the form $y = mx + b$, where m is the slope of the line and b is the y-intercept (the y-value for $x = 0$). According to the graph, the y-intercept is 50. Next, pick two points on the line, say $(5,140)$ and $(8,200)$, to determine the slope of the line: $m = \dfrac{\text{rise}}{\text{run}} = \dfrac{\Delta y}{\Delta x} = \dfrac{200-140}{8-5} = \dfrac{60}{3} = 20$. Therefore, the relationship between the calories and total grams of fat is $y = 20x + 50$.

17. **(A)** (p. 97) *Math: Multiple-Choice/Data Interpretation/Scatterplots and Algebra/Creating, Expressing, and Evaluating Algebraic Equations and Functions/Functions as Models.* Based on the line of best fit, a 325-calorie fast food item will have approximately 15 grams of total fat, and (A) is closest, with 14 grams. Note that the equation determined in the previous item can also be used to determine the expected fat content of the 325-calorie item: $325 = 20(x) + 50 \Rightarrow x = \dfrac{325-50}{20} = 13.75$ grams. Therefore, (A) is the best approximation: 14 grams.

18. **(C)** (p. 98) *Math: Multiple-Choice/Geometry/Triangles/Properties of Triangles and Rectangles and Squares.* The rectangle has an area of $4 \cdot 9 = 36$. Since the triangle also has the same area as the rectangle, use this fact to solve for the height of the triangle: $\dfrac{1}{2} \cdot h \cdot 12 = 36 \Rightarrow 12h = 72 \Rightarrow h = 6$.

19. **(B)** (p. 98) *Math: Multiple-Choice/Problem Solving and Advanced Arithmetic/Common Problem Solving Items/Percentages and Ratios.* The acid concentration of each solution is the milliliters of acid per milliliters of solution. Create a table relating the given information and the unknown concentration of the final solution, x:

	$\dfrac{\text{mL acid}}{\text{mL solution}}$	mL solution	mL acid
35% acid solution	0.35	500	175
40% acid solution	0.40	250	100
Final solution	x	750	275

Therefore, the final solution has 275 mL acid in 750 mL solution, so its acid concentration is $\dfrac{275}{750} = 36\dfrac{2}{3}\%$.

20. **(D)** (p. 98) *Math: Multiple-Choice/Algebra/Solving Algebraic Equations or Inequalities with One Variable/Equations Involving Absolute Value.* Rewrite the equation by isolating the absolute value expression on one side: $\left|y^2 - 5\right| = 4$. This means that $y^2 - 5 = 4$ or $-\left(y^2 - 5\right) = 4$. Solve each equation for y: $y^2 = 9 \Rightarrow y = \pm 3$ or $y^2 = 1 \Rightarrow y = \pm 1$. Therefore, the complete solution set is $\{-3, -1, 1, 3\}$.

21. **(B)** (p. 99) *Math: Multiple-Choice/Data Interpretation/Bar, Cumulative, and Line Graphs and Problem Solving and Advanced Arithmetic/Common Problem Solving Items/Percentages.* According to the graph, 177×10^3 degrees were in social studies/history. Since the total number of degrees awarded was 1.716×10^6, the percentage of degrees that were in social studies/history was
$$\frac{177 \times 10^3}{1.716 \times 10^6} = \frac{177 \times 10^3}{1,716 \times 10^3} \approx \frac{1}{10} = 10\%.$$

22. **(D)** (p. 99) *Math: Multiple-Choice/Data Interpretation/Bar, Cumulative, and Line Graphs and Problem Solving and Advanced Arithmetic/Common Problem Solving Items/Ratios.* Determine the number of degrees awarded in the five most popular majors: $(365 + 177 + 143 + 104 + 101) \times 10^3 = 890 \times 10^3$. Notice that the item stem specifies that the comparison is with "all other undergraduate majors," which is $1.716 \times 10^6 - 890 \times 10^3 = (1,716 - 890) \times 10^3 = 826 \times 10^3$. Therefore, the ratio of the number of degrees in the five most popular majors to all other undergraduate majors was $\dfrac{890 \times 10^3}{826 \times 10^3} = \dfrac{890}{826} \approx \dfrac{1}{1} = 1:1$.

23. **(D)** (p. 100) *Math: Multiple-Choice/Statistics/Data Interpretation.* This item tests understanding of the terms "correlation" and "causation" in statistics. Correlation indicates the extent to which two or more variables fluctuate together. A positive correlation indicates the extent to which those variables increase or decrease in parallel; a negative correlation indicates the extent to which one variable increases as the other decreases. However, correlation doesn't explain how or why the relationship between two variables exists—only that it does exist. Causation goes a step further than correlation, stating that a change in the value of the x-variable will cause a change in the value of the y-variable. This item doesn't given enough information to assume that causation exists, but only that correlation exists.

24. **(D)** (p. 101) *Math: Multiple-Choice/Data Interpretation/Bar, Cumulative, and Line Graphs.* The fraction of uranium-235 remaining after 1.5 billion years is approximately 0.2. The fraction of uranium-235 remaining after 2.5 billion years is approximately 0.1. The uranium-235 remaining after 2.5 billion years is $\dfrac{0.1}{0.2} = \dfrac{1}{2} = 50\%$ of that remaining after 1.5 billion years, (D).

25. (A) (p. 101) *Math: Multiple-Choice/Algebra/Creating, Expressing, and Evaluating Algebraic Equations and Functions/Functions as Models.* After one half-life, the amount of uranium-235 remaining is $\dfrac{A_0}{2}$. After two

half-lives, the amount of remaining is $\dfrac{\frac{A_0}{2}}{2} = \dfrac{A_0}{4}$. After three half-lives, the amount remaining is $\dfrac{A_0}{8}$, and

after four half-lives, the amount remaining is $\dfrac{A_0}{16}$.

26. (C) (p. 101) *Math: Multiple-Choice/Coordinate Geometry/Graphs of Quadratic Equations and Relations.* This item tests your understanding of the general shape of a particular function. In this case, the data shows a negative relationship that slows with increasing time: a negative exponential, (C). Note that (A) would be a linear line with a negative slope; (B) would be a linear line with a positive slope; and (D) would be a positive relationship that increases with increasing time: a positive exponential.

27. (B) (p. 101) *Math: Multiple-Choice/Coordinate Geometry/Graphs of Linear Equations.* Both equations are linear (the power of x is 1 in both equations), so they intersect at most once, or if they are parallel, not at all.

They are parallel if they have the same slope, but the slope of the first equation is $-\dfrac{1}{2}$ and the slope of the

second is 4. Therefore, they are not parallel, so they must intersect at one point, so (B) or (C) must be correct. Only the first equation passes through the point (0,3), so (B) must be correct. Indeed, setting the two equations equal to one another shows that they intersect when

$$-\frac{x}{2}+3=4x+6 \Rightarrow -x+6=8x+12 \Rightarrow 9x=-6 \Rightarrow x=-\frac{2}{3}. \text{ For } x=-\frac{2}{3}, \; y=4\left(-\frac{2}{3}\right)+6=-\frac{8}{3}+\frac{18}{3}=\frac{10}{3}.$$

Therefore, the two lines intersect at $\left(-\dfrac{2}{3}, \dfrac{10}{3}\right)$.

28. (C) (p. 102) *Math: Multiple-Choice/Algebra/Solving Simultaneous Equations.* Since x and y are single digits, $x+2=6$ and $8+x=10+y$. Indeed, solving the system of equations shows that $x=4$ and $8+4=10+y \Rightarrow y=2$. The arithmetic problem is $84+42=126$.

29. (C) (p. 102) *Math: Multiple-Choice/Coordinate Geometry/Graphs of Linear Equations.* Two lines are perpendicular if the product of their slopes is –1, i.e., if the slopes of the two lines are negative reciprocals of

each other, then the two lines are perpendicular. The given line has a slope of $\dfrac{3}{2}$. The line in (C) has a slope

of $-\dfrac{2}{3}$.

30. (B) (p. 102) *Math: Multiple-Choice/Problem Solving and Advanced Arithmetic/Common Problem Solving Items/Proportions and Direct-Inverse Variation and Geometry/Circles.* Since the length of the needle is the radius of the circle swept by the needle, the distance the tip of the needle travels along the arc is

proportional to the angle swept by the needle: $\dfrac{30}{360} = \dfrac{1}{12}$. So, the pendulum moves through 1/12th of a circle

with radius 4, which is 1/12th of $C=2\pi r = 2\pi(4)=8\pi$ inches, or $\dfrac{8\pi}{12} = \dfrac{2\pi}{3}$ inches between each click. Since the setting is 30 beats per minute, the metronome clicks every 2 seconds—that is, the tip of the needle travels $\frac{2\pi}{3}$ inches every 2 seconds, or $\frac{2\pi/3}{2}=\frac{2\pi}{6}=\frac{\pi}{3}$ inches per second.

31. **(11) (p. 103)** *Math: Student-Produced Responses/Problem Solving and Advanced Arithmetic/Multi-Step Problem Solving Items.* Rate multiplied by time equals work; that is, the number of envelopes sealed is equal to the rate in envelopes per second multiplied by time in seconds. Work through the given scenario, a step at a time, setting up expressions so units cancel leaving the desired quantity. Rasheed's rate is 50 envelopes per 60 seconds and Tae-John's is 50 envelopes per 80 seconds. If Rasheed first seals 240 envelopes, this takes $\frac{60\ \text{seconds}}{50\ \text{envelopes}}\times 240\ \text{envelopes} = 288\ \text{seconds}$. Then, Tae-John working for 4 minutes seals $\frac{50\ \text{envelopes}}{80\ \text{seconds}}\times 4\ \text{minutes}\times\frac{60\ \text{seconds}}{1\ \text{minute}}=150\ \text{envelopes}$. This is a total of $240+150=390$ envelopes, leaving $500-390=110$ envelopes for Rasheed to seal:

$\frac{60\ \text{seconds}}{50\ \text{envelopes}}\times 110\ \text{envelopes} = 132\ \text{seconds}$. Therefore, the total time required to complete the job is

$288+(4\times 60)+132=660\ \text{seconds}\times\frac{1\ \text{minute}}{60\ \text{seconds}}= 11\ \text{minutes}.$

32. **(2) (p. 104)** *Math: Student-Produced Responses/Algebra/Solving Quadratic Equations and Relations.* The axis of symmetry for a quadratic equation gives the maximum or minimum of the equation, depending on whether the quadratic is upright or not. In this case, the coefficient of the x^2 term is negative, so it is an up-side down parabola—the vertex (on the axis of symmetry) is a maximum. For a quadratic equation in the form $y=ax^2+bx+c$, the x-value of the axis of symmetry (maximum or minimum y-value), is $\frac{-b}{2a}$. In the given equation, $b=4,000$ and $a=-1,000$, so $x=\frac{-4,000}{2(-1,000)}=2$—the number of sales staff that maximizes daily profits. Alternatively, test some numbers.

33. **(6000) (p. 104)** *Math: Student-Produced Responses/Algebra/Creating, Expressing, and Evaluating Algebraic Equations and Functions/Functions as Models.* This item builds on the previous one: the maximum daily profit is the value of the given quadratic equation for the x-value of the axis of symmetry. We've already determined that the number of sales staff that maximizes profit is 2. Therefore,
$y=-1,000x^2+4,000x+2,000= -1,000(2^2)+4,000(2)+2,000= -4,000+8,000+2,000= 6,000.$

34. **(4) (p. 104)** *Math: Student-Produced Responses/Algebra/Solving Quadratic Equations and Relations.* The roots of a quadratic equation correspond to the x-values that make the equation equal to zero—in this case, zero profit. Use the quadratic formula to find the roots of the equation $ax^2+bx+c=0$. To simplify, factor $-1,000$ out of the equation, so $-1,000(x^2-4x-2)=0\Rightarrow x^2-4x-2=0$: $\frac{-b\pm\sqrt{b^2-4ac}}{2a}=$

$\frac{-(-4)\pm\sqrt{(-4)^2-4(1)(-2)}}{2(1)}=\frac{4\pm\sqrt{16+8}}{2}=\frac{4\pm 2\sqrt{6}}{2}=2\pm\sqrt{6}$. Since $\sqrt{4}=2$ and $\sqrt{9}=3$, $2-\sqrt{6}$ is a negative value and not possible for the number of sales staff. The other root, $2+\sqrt{6}$ is between 4 and 5, so 5 employees would push the profit below zero (for x-values greater than the positive root, the corresponding y-value is negative; the same is true of x-values less than the negative root, but as already explained, a negative number of sales staff is not possible). Therefore, the maximum number of sales staff that can work on a given day and still yield positive profits must be the next lowest integer value (because sales staff must, by definition, be whole numbers of people): 4.

35. **(80)** (p. 104) *Math: Student-Produced Responses/Geometry.* After the pieces are cut out, the box will have the following dimensions: length $= 8$, width $= 10$, height $= 1$. $\text{Volume}_{\text{solid}} = \text{length} \cdot \text{width} \cdot \text{height} = 8 \cdot 10 \cdot 1 = 80$ cubic centimeters.

36. **(9)** (p. 105) *Math: Student-Produced Responses/Statistics/Measures of Center and Spread/Range.* Range is the difference between the smallest value and the greatest value. In the figure, the smallest value is 51 inches (Alli); the largest value is 60 inches (Azuany). Therefore, the range is 9 inches.

37. **(53)** (p. 105) *Math: Student-Produced Responses/Geometry/Lines and Angles and Circles.* When a line intersects a circle at only one point, that line is perpendicular to the radius at that point. Therefore, $\angle OPQ$ is $90°$.

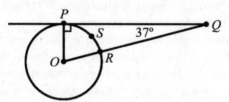

So, $90° + 37° + \angle POQ = 180° \Rightarrow \angle POQ = 53°$ $\angle POQ = \angle POR = 53°$. Since O is the center of the circle and an arc of a circle is equal to its central angle and $\angle POR = 53°$, $\overset{\frown}{PSR} = 53°$.

38. **(7/24)** (p. 105) *Math: Student-Produced Responses/Algebra/Solving Algebraic Equations or Inequalities with One Variable/Equations Involving Absolute Value.* Since $\left| \dfrac{1}{3} - \dfrac{1}{2} \right| = \dfrac{1}{6}$, create the derivative equations:

$k - \dfrac{1}{8} = \dfrac{1}{6}$ or $-k + \dfrac{1}{8} = \dfrac{1}{6}$. Solve for k: $k = \dfrac{14}{48} = \dfrac{7}{24}$ or $k = -\dfrac{1}{24}$. Since the item stem asks for a positive number, the answer must be $\dfrac{7}{24}$.

Section 5: Essay (p. 106)

Sample Essay Responses and Analyses

Above Average Response

Almost everyone can attest to the benefit of a good night's sleep. When we are well-rested, we feel energetic, our minds are sharp, and we feel ready to take on the day. If we get a poor night's sleep, we can feel the effects throughout the entire day. What most people may not know is that sleep deprivation is one of the major public health issues facing both adults and children. In her essay "Raising Awareness of Sleep as a Healthy Behavior," Geraldine S. Perry discusses the impact of sleep deprivation, and the effects are more seriously than simply feeling sleepy throughout the day. Perry uses clinical evidence to show how sleep deprivation affects adults and children and how clinicians are not as likely to provide patients with information on healthy sleep habits.

Perry begins her essay by discussing the percentages of adults and children who are sleep deprived in order to set up the context for her argument. The numbers are staggering: nearly 35% of adults and 70% of high school students are not getting the necessary amount of sleep. These numbers mean more than a lot of sleepy adults and teenagers: they mean an increased risk of dying of coronary heart disease (for adults) and higher instances of obesity (for children). Perry's claim that sleep is a public health issue becomes clear with the presentation of these effects of sleep deprivation. Both children and adults experience higher instances of mood disorders and see a decrease in overall performance. Sleep deprivation also leads to higher instances of workplace injuries, car accidents, and occupational/medical errors. This means that the sleep deprived person is not only hurting themselves, but their lack of sleep may very well be affecting the wellness and livelihood of those around them, making sleep deprivation the very definition of a public health issue. These statistics and facts are intended to make the information relevant to a broad audience and to shock and perhaps even scare that audience. They are successful persuasive devices because they affect, or have the potential to affect, everybody, and they address grave concerns of sleep deprivation. The reader's interest is won and the argument proceeds.

It is possible that the widespread sleep deprivation issue goes deeper than the demands of children's schoolwork and the busy schedules of adults. The public may not be receiving sufficient information from their health care professionals about healthy sleep habits. In fact, many people may not even be aware of the amount of sleep that they should be getting each night. Again, this lack of education puts sleep deprivation at the top of the list of public health concerns. It has been shown that health care providers do not generally assess sleep habits or provide counseling on healthy sleep behavior. In one survey, only about 10% of health care providers could say that they have a good knowledge of sleep and sleep disorders. This point about lack of information regarding sleep is included to show that the reader may be sleep deprived and not even realize it, increasing the gravity of the issue. This worries the audience and works because it exposes to us that not only we, but even our health care providers, may not even be aware that we are suffering the consequences of sleep deprivation.

Perry further builds the impact of her claim by addressing the public health burden of sleep deprivation. She argues, "there are substantial public health investments in all areas related to sleep, from obesity and other chronic conditions to motor vehicle accidents." This point is included in order to demonstrate the far reach of this issue of sleep deprivation. Everyone, she demonstrates, is affected, including the entirety of the audience of this text, whose tax dollars are paying for the consequences of sleep deprivation. This is meant to engage and concern the entire audience, and is effective because people generally do not like to see their tax dollars being used to pay for other people's bad decisions or for things that don't affect them. In this way, Perry gains the attention of those who may be getting enough sleep and who know that they are, but who do not like the idea of "substantial public health investments" for sleep-related issues.

Perry's essay includes some startling information about the general public's poor sleep habits and the lack of attention health care professionals give to sleep education. The combination, and perhaps interrelation, of these two topics show how sleep really is one of the most widespread public health issues facing both adults and children.

Analysis of Above Average Response

The writer is able to effectively take ideas discussed in the passage and connect them to make a case for the author's main argument. The sentence structure and vocabulary are appropriate and the tone remains consistent throughout the writer's response. The writer provides evidence from the passage to support the author's claims and is able to connect them appropriately.

Below Average Response

It's pretty obvious that people don't get enough sleep. That's why there are places like Starbucks and things like energy drinks, because people don't get enough sleep and have to find there energy somewhere else. For example, most car accidents happen because people are falling asleep at the wheel. I am going to explain to you what happens when people don't get enough sleep. They have health problems, they do not know how much sleep they should be getting, and there doctors don't know how to help them sleep more and better.

When you don't get enough sleep weird things start to happen. For example, people who don't get enough sleep are sick more often than people who get a good amount of sleep. The things that can happen are cardiovascular morbidity, metabolic disorders, obesity, diabetes, heart disease, and hypertension. People who don't get enough sleep tend to die sooner than people who do get enough sleep. So it's pretty much a major problem that can be solved really easily. All you need to do is sleep more. If people got more sleep, they could very easily avoid all these dangerous health issues.

Second of all people really don't know how much sleep they need. The author says that 35% of adults and 70% of children aren't getting enough sleep. Its possible that they think that they are getting enough sleep but they don't really know how much they should be getting so its not enough. What they need is some education that tells them exactly how much sleep they should be getting. This can be done by teaching students in school or telling adults when they visit their doctors.

Also, it seems like a lot of doctors don't really know a lot about how to help people get more sleep. They just don't provide the information like they should and so as a result people are uneducated on sleep. It would be good if doctors could have more information on sleep so they can give this information to their patients and let them know how much sleep they need and how they can sleep better.

In conclusion we would all be better off if we got more sleep and we were able to avoid all the problems that come with not sleeping enough. Its hard to do that when we don't know how much sleep we need to get and that our doctors can't really help us because they don't seem to know either. Not getting enough sleep leads to a lot of health problems, people don't know how much sleep to get, and doctors don't have the information to help people out. Maybe someday people will get more sleep, but right now it is just causing a lot of problems.

Analysis of Below Average Response

The writer does not follow the prompt: the response discusses aspects of the issue presented in the passage, but does not discuss how the author makes his/her argument. Some information from the passage is incorrectly interpreted. Grammatical errors make the response choppy and difficult to read at times. The information presented is somewhat repetitive, and the response is not well-developed.

PRACTICE TEST II

Answer Key

DIRECTIONS: For items answered <u>correctly</u>, circle the answer, then check any corresponding shaded box(es). Total the number of circled answers to determine the raw score for the test section. Total the number of checkmarks for each of the subscores and cross-test scores to determine each raw subscore and raw cross-test score.

Section 1: Reading (p. 111)

Item		Subscores		Cross-Test Scores	
		WC	CE	S	H/S
1.	A				
2.	C	■			
3.	B				
4.	B				
5.	C		■		
6.	D				
7.	A				
8.	A				
9.	A				
10.	C	■			
11.	C			■	
12.	B			■	
13.	B	■		■	
14.	B			■	
15.	B			■	
16.	A			■	
17.	A			■	
18.	B			■	

Item		Subscores		Cross-Test Scores	
		WC	CE	S	H/S
19.	D			■	
20.	B		■	■	
21.	B			■	
22.	B				■
23.	B		■		
24.	B				
25.	B		■		
26.	B	■			
27.	D				
28.	B	■			
29.	B	■			
30.	C				
31.	A				■
32.	D			■	
33.	C			■	■
34.	D			■	■
35.	B			■	■
36.	A			■	

Item		Subscores		Cross-Test Scores	
		WC	CE	S	H/S
37.	A	■		■	
38.	D		■	■	
39.	B				
40.	D		■		
41.	C	■			
42.	B				■
43.	C				■
44.	B				■
45.	B				■
46.	D		■		■
47.	C				■
48.	B	■			
49.	D				■
50.	C		■		
51.	A				
52.	D				

Raw Score: _____/52

Section 2: Writing and Language (p. 126)

#	Ans	Subscores WC	CE	Cross-Test S	H/S
1.	B				
2.	C				
3.	C		▓		
4.	A	▓			
5.	A				
6.	B				
7.	D				
8.	B				
9.	C				
10.	D	▓			
11.	A		▓		
12.	B	▓	▓		
13.	D	▓			
14.	C				
15.	D				

#	Ans	Subscores WC	CE	Cross-Test S	H/S
16.	C				
17.	A				
18.	C	▓			
19.	C				
20.	B				
21.	A				
22.	C				
23.	D				
24.	C				
25.	C				
26.	C				▓
27.	B				
28.	B				
29.	D		▓		▓
30.	B	▓	▓	▓	▓

#	Ans	Subscores WC	CE	Cross-Test S	H/S
31.	A				▓
32.	D	▓			▓
33.	D		▓		▓
34.	C	▓		▓	
35.	D				
36.	C				
37.	A		▓		
38.	A				
39.	A				
40.	B				
41.	B		▓	▓	
42.	B		▓	▓	
43.	B				
44.	D		▓	▓	

Raw Score: _____/44

Evidence-Based Reading and Writing Subscores

Words in Context (WC): _____/18   Command of Evidence (CE): _____/18

Section 3: Math—No Calculator (p. 140)

#	Ans	Cross-Test S	H/S
1.	A		
2.	B		
3.	D		
4.	A		
5.	C		
6.	B		▓
7.	D	▓	

#	Ans	Cross-Test S	H/S
8.	A		
9.	A		
10.	B		
11.	B		
12.	B		
13.	C	▓	
14.	C	▓	

#	Ans	Cross-Test S	H/S
15.	D		
16.	16		
17.	60		
18.	14		
19.	11		
20.	7/2, 3.5		

Section 4: Math—Calculator (p. 147)

#	Ans	S	H/S		#	Ans	S	H/S		#	Ans	S	H/S
1.	D				14.	B				27.	D		
2.	B				15.	C				28.	D		▓
3.	C				16.	B				29.	A		▓
4.	B				17.	D				30.	D		
5.	A		▓		18.	C				31.	125	▓	
6.	B				19.	A				32.	63		
7.	A				20.	C	▓			33.	240		▓
8.	C				21.	C				34.	18	▓	
9.	D				22.	D		▓		35.	20		
10.	C		▓		23.	B				36.	45		
11.	A				24.	B	▓			37.	250		▓
12.	A	▓			25.	A				38.	5		
13.	D				26.	B							

Math Raw Score (total of calculator and no-calculator sections): _____ /58

Cross-Test Scores (All four test sections)

Science (S): _____ /35   History/Social Studies (H/S): _____ /35

Explanations

Section 1: Reading

Passage 1

1. **(A)** (p. 112) *Reading/Literary Fiction/Implied Idea.* The two sisters are living in a cabin near a mansion that has fallen into disrepair. The text tells us "when the war began," the mansion was majestic. Although the author does not specifically say the mansion was destroyed during the war, that is a fair inference from the text. Certainly, the other choices are not supported by the text. As for (B), we know that the mansion was built by the father, not the sisters. And Petite's father is Léandre, brother of the sisters, and son of the man who designed the mansion. And as for (D), the text indicates that the mansion cost a lot of money to build and, in fact, stood on the Cote Joyeuse.

2. **(C)** (p. 112) *Reading/Literary Fiction/Vocabulary.* The meaning of "picayunes" is not obvious from the context, but careful attention to verbal clues coupled with the process of elimination gets you the correct answer. The most powerful verbal clue is the juxtaposition of "picayunes" and "dollars," strongly suggesting a contrast and pointing to "coins" as the best response. As for the other choices, while they have meanings associated with the theme of the paragraph, none of them describes something that the sisters would be accumulating over the years to rebuild their home.

3. **(B)** (p. 112) *Reading/Literary Fiction/Implied Idea.* The text strongly implies that the mansion was destroyed during the war and tells us specifically that the sisters live an impoverished life in a cabin nearby. In the picture painted by the author, the sisters are having afternoon coffee in a space that once had a roof but now is covered only by the sky.

4. **(B)** (p. 112) *Reading/Literary Fiction/Implied Idea.* This is an implied idea question and explores the relationship between Pelagie and Pauline. The text indicates that Pauline defers to her sister's judgment ("Yes, Sesoeur.") It is Pelagie who sets out the details of the plan to rebuild the house; Pauline simply agrees. Pelagie is the moving force.

5. **(C)** (p. 112) *Reading/Literary Fiction/Textual Evidence.* When we read about the plan to rebuild, every detail comes from Pelagie. The only thing we hear from Pauline is "Yes, Sesoeur" and "No, Sesoeur." Clearly, Pelagie is the driving force in the household and of the plan to rebuild. (A) is perhaps the second best answer because it helps to establish Pelagie's dominance in the situation, and Pelagie's dominance helps to explain the relationship between the sisters. But (A) does not really address the point of the plan to rebuild, while (C) does. (D) is weaker still, though it does put Léandre above Pauline in the pecking order. But Léandre is absent and not really involved in the big plan.

6. **(D)** *(p. 112) Reading/Literary Fiction/Implied Idea.* The final paragraph describes the arrival of La Petite. The author indicates that the sisters are not quite sure what to expect but hope that she could be accommodated. The "between" acknowledges that until this point these sisters have largely kept to themselves with no one else in their lives, a kind of unit bound each to the other. When La Petite arrives, they can no longer be absorbed in each other's company but must make room for the new arrival.

7. **(A)** (p. 113) *Reading/Literary Fiction/Implied Idea.* Paragraph 7 tells us that the younger sister always answers her older sister with a remark such as "as you please," implying that the younger sister agrees with whatever opinion the older sister expresses. "Condescendingly" might be a good description of the older sister's attitude toward her younger sibling but not vice versa.

8. **(A)** (p. 113) *Reading/Literary Fiction/Vocabulary.* Just before using the phrase "a true Valmet," Pelagie tells Pauline that La Petite is already familiar with the sisters' lifestyle and understands their frugality, the end of which is, of course, rebuilding the house. To the extent La Petite embraces the dream, Pelagie will consider her a "true" (or "real") Valmet.

9. **(A)** (p. 113) *Reading/Literary Fiction/Implied Idea.* Pauline expresses her disquiet in a series of questions put to her sister: What will we do with her? Where will she sleep? How will we amuse her? She is not comfortable with the idea and expresses misgivings about the arrangement.

10. **(C)** (p. 113) *Reading/Literary Fiction/Vocabulary.* The context in which the word "determination" is used makes it clear that Pelagie stood up with a clear plan in mind. She wanted to saddle the horse and look over the property. One might say that she has thought about her move and determined to go. A reasonable synonym for this attitude is "resolve," which suggests also that she considered her options, made a decision, and took action.

Passage 2

11. **(C)** (p. 115) *Reading/Natural Sciences/Main Idea.* This is a main idea that asks about the theme of Passage 1. Passage 1 begins by defining CCD, then the author explicitly cites the main conclusion of Lu's research followed by a description of the methodology used. The fourth paragraph provides the results of the experiment, and then in the last paragraph the author draws the conclusion explicitly that the neonicotinoids caused the CCD. (C) best describes this development. (A) goes beyond the scope of the passage. To be sure, the idea promoted by (A) is one that the author (or another writer) might go on to make using Passage 1, but it does not describe Passage 1 *as written.* The same is true for (D). The author may admire Dr. Lu for his work and think that the research deserves recognition, but the author does not take on that burden in the passage as written. Finally, (B) is a minor point mentioned in the passage, not the main theme.

12. **(B)** (p. 115) *Reading/Natural Sciences/Main Idea.* This is a main idea type question that asks about a specific part of the passage. As noted above, the five paragraphs of Passage 1 can be described as CCD

defined, preview of conclusions, description of the experiment, results of the experiment, and some implications of the results. Therefore, the correct answer is (B).

13. **(B)** (p. 115) *Reading/Natural Sciences/Vocabulary.* *Under the auspices of* means under the guidance or sponsorship of. The phrase does not imply that the sponsor has direct control of the project but only that the sponsor has authorized the project be undertaken and associated with its name. The sponsor may also provide funding for the project. Therefore, the only correct answer is (C).

14. **(B)** (p. 115) *Reading/Natural Sciences/Explicit Detail.* This an explicit detail question asking about the specific information contained in paragraph four of Passage 1. According to that part of Passage 1, a decline in the bee population with the onset of cold winter is expected. Normally, the population would then increase. Therefore, the correct answer is (B).

15. **(B)** (p. 116) *Reading/Natural Sciences/Application.* The definition of CCD provided in paragraph one includes: (1) few adult bees, (2) live queen, (3) honey, and (4) immature bees. The results of Dr. Lu's research, as reported by Passage 1, showed few adult bees (the bees either had died or fled). That is only the first element of the definition of CCD. In other words, Dr. Lu's research, even taken at face value, does show not CCD as the cause of the problems of the hives studied.

16. **(A)** (p. 116) *Reading/Natural Sciences/Vocabulary.* The context in which *sub-lethal* appears makes it clear that the word means "not deadly," which is answer (A). The passage, for example, specifically states that the dosage adversely affected various functions such as memory but did not kill the bees.

17. **(A)** (p. 116) *Reading/Natural Sciences/Voice.* This is a tone question that asks for a description of the author's attitude toward the publications mentioned. The author's voice, or position, is seen in the verbal clues given in the passage. For example, the author notes that the media coverage is not scholarly, that Dr. Lu is not himself an expert, and that the journal *Insectology* is not widely respected. Also, it is noted that the author made a "rush to judgment" and used sarcasm in the phrase "smoking gun." Therefore, (A) is the correct answer.

18. **(B)** (p. 116) *Reading/Natural Sciences/Main Idea.* This is a main idea question that asks about the final paragraph of the two passages. The opening sentence of the paragraph tells you the main point. The methodology was fatally flawed.

19. **(D)** (p. 116) *Reading/Natural Sciences/Main Idea.* Both authors state at the opening of their passages that honey bees are important to agriculture and that bee colonies have been hit by CCD. While passage 2 attacks the motivation of the reporters who prepared the article, passage 1 is silent on that article. The authors, however, have differing views about the validity of the research. Author 1 regards the research as conclusive and author 2 considers it weak.

20. **(B)** (p. 116) *Reading/Natural Sciences/Textual Evidence.* This is the second half of the evidence question; it asks for text excerpts that support the conclusion.

21. **(B)** (p. 116) *Reading/Natural Sciences/Data Presentations.* The graph shows that imidacloprid was introduced in 1994. From that year until 2003, the use of the chemical increased dramatically, but the number of managed honey bee colonies remained just about constant. This strongly suggests that there was no connection between the use of the chemical and the health of the bees.

Passage 3

22. **(B)** (p. 118) *Reading/Social Studies/Implied Idea.* The author states that the fabled mineral wealth of the region turned out to out to be just that, a fable. The Spanish Crown continued to maintain the colony primarily as a means of converting native peoples to the Catholic faith, so the correct answer is (A), and not agriculture, (B). Grazing lands and population are not mentioned in the text as reasons the Spanish government was originally interested in the Northern New Mexico and southern Colorado region, therefore (C) and (D) cannot be correct answers.

23. **(B)** (p. 118) *Reading/Social Studies/Textual Evidence.* As noted above, the mineral wealth of the area turned out to be a myth. In lines 5–7, the text uses the word "fable" to describe the wealth of the area.

24. **(B)** (p. 118) *Reading/Social Studies/Implied Idea.* The author makes it clear that members of the *Penitentes* were not ordained priests. The few priests who were sent to the region were assigned to the Pueblos or more populated areas.

25. **(B)** (p. 118) *Reading/Social Studies/Textual Evidence.* The distinction required by this question is between an ordained member of the formal priesthood and the status of members of the *Penitentes* as members of a lay organization. The excerpt cited makes this distinction clear.

26. **(B)** (p. 118) *Reading/Social Studies/Vocabulary.* You can determine the meaning of this vocabulary word by the context in which it appears. You can infer that *sodalities* has a meaning similar to *confraternities* and *religious volunteer associations*, the other two concepts that appear in the list.

27. **(D)** (p. 118) *Reading/Social Studies/Application.* The author uses the phrase "over-zealous" to describe the Franciscan friars, implying that they were abusive of the population.

28. **(B)** (p. 118) *Reading/Social Studies/Implied Idea.* The author mentions the confraternities of similar name to suggest that the Brotherhood originated in Spain and later spread to the New Mexico province.

29. **(B)** (p. 118) *Reading/Social Studies/Vocabulary.* In the paragraph in which the word appeared, the author describes how the settlers attended to their own needs because the central authority was relatively remote. Since the settlers relied on their own abilities and efforts, *resources* and *resourceful* are good synonyms.

30. **(C)** (p. 118) *Reading/Social Studies/Implied Idea.* In describing the political functions of the Brotherhood, the author mentions specifically that it was involved in decisions regarding the allocation of water. From this, you can infer that water allocation was a sensitive and important issue and draw the further conclusion that water must have been relatively scarce.

31. **(A)** (p. 119) *Reading/Social Studies/Application.* In the second paragraph, the author describes how the Hispanos provided for themselves in the absence of assistance from the centralized authority of the Spanish Crown.

Passage 4

32. **(D)** (p. 121) *Reading/Natural Sciences/Main Idea.* This is a main idea question. The author begins the passage by providing a simple definition of drought but then immediately says that definition is an oversimplification. The author spends the rest of the first paragraph clarifying in exactly what sense a drought is a lack of moisture. The second paragraph explains that "drought" can also be understood in ecological terms—as the effect of a relative lack of moisture on an area. The third paragraph talks about identifying dry period using meteorological tools. And the fourth explains that, in the final analysis, what we call a drought is largely dependent on human needs. Drought is the lack of sufficient water to meet human needs. (A) is an interesting response because the author does provide a correction. But the wording of (A) just doesn't describe very precisely what the author does, which is to make a <u>definition</u> more precise. As for

(B), while the author takes a position, the standard definition of "drought" is not treated as a discovery. And (C) is perhaps the weakest response as "correcting" is not "refuting."

33. **(C)** (p. 121) *Reading/Natural Sciences/Vocabulary.* The author begins with a very direct statement: drought is a lack of water. But then the author quickly states that this definition obscures various complexities. So the definition has been simplified: it is correct so far as it goes, but it is not the final word.

34. **(D)** (p. 121) *Reading/Natural Sciences/Development.* The author states that droughts are a function of time, not place. Any area on earth can experience drought condition so long as there is sufficient time without water. To dramatize the point, the author states that even a desert (which is pretty much dry all the time) can have a drought. (A) is wrong because a seasonal or usual dry spell is simply part of the baseline climate for the area and not an aberration that could be called a drought. (B) goes way beyond the text. Though the author would agree that dry conditions are not necessarily a drought, the author would probably not subscribe to the view that a drought could occur without a lack of water. (C) represents a misreading of the text. The point the author makes is that dry conditions do not necessarily constitute a drought, but the author would surely use "dry" as part of the definition of "desert."

35. **(B)** (p. 121) *Reading/Natural Sciences/Explicit Detail.* This is a detail question that asks the reader to show an understanding of the causal explanation provided in paragraph two. The passage explains that the extreme wet spell provides extra water for plants, so they grow. In particular, non-native plants that require more water than normally available take advantage of the wet spell. With native plants this is not true. Then when things return to normal, native plants are fine, but the invasive species dry up and pose a fire hazard.

36. **(A)** (p. 121) *Reading/Natural Sciences/Explicit Detail.* This is a detail question, and the answer is explicitly given in the first sentence of the third paragraph.

37. **(A)** (p. 122) *Reading/Natural Sciences/Vocabulary.* This is a vocabulary-in-context item. When the author says that weather is a "driver" in the calculation, the author means "cause" or "determinant."

38. **(D)** (p. 122) *Reading/Natural Sciences/Textual Evidence.* As the previous explanation lays out, the author defines drought in terms of human use, making (D) the strongest support for the answer to the previous question. Notice that (A) explains that various other types of drought such as hydrologic or agricultural drought highlight how meteorological drought impacts humans, pointing to the answer to the previous question. But it is not as directly supportive as (D).

39. **(B)** (p. 122) *Reading/Natural Sciences/Application.* This is an application question that asks for reading at the deepest level. In clarifying the definition of drought, the author eventually states that various terms that define "drought," such as hydrologic, agricultural, and socioeconomic, actually reflect determinations about human needs rather than objective measurements. And this is true of the underlying concept of meteorological drought. "Drought" is not whether the recorded precipitation is n milliliters less than c, the long-term average, but whether conditions are such that humans needs go unsatisfied, that is, there is not enough corn or the water level in the lake is too low to launch a boat.

40. **(D)** (p. 122) *Reading/Natural Sciences/Data Presentations.* This is a "pie chart," and pie charts typically show shares of a total. You can think of an actual pie: the larger the central angle of the slice, the bigger the portion. In this case, "Water Supply & Quality" accounts for 24.2% of the impacts reports, the largest of all the categories.

41. **(C)** (p. 122) *Reading/Natural Sciences/Data Presentations.* Remember that a pie chart provides information about the relative size of the slices. In order to know how much "pie" you have, you need to know how large the pie is. In this case, the note "Total Impacts: 218" tells you the size of the pie. So the number of "Society & Public Health" impacts is about 10% of 218 or 20.

Passage 5

42. (B) (p. 124) *Reading/Social Studies/Explicit Detail.* The author argues that the friendship coupled with prevailing attitudes about Dutch origins of New York institutions helps to explain the Dutch influences in "A Visit," thereby dating it to the time of "Dutch Revival" around 1822.

43. (C) (p. 124) *Reading/Social Studies/Main Idea.* The passage provides an overview of the debate concerning the authorship of "A Visit." The author of the passage presents evidence on both sides and offers analysis and even rebuttal to the evidence. The overall objective is to weigh the evidence and draw a conclusion as to which side of the debate is more persuasive.

44. (B) (p. 124) *Reading/Social Studies/Development.* This is a command of evidence item that asks about the function of the detail in the debate. One problem with attributing the poem to Moore is that Moore did not make such a claim himself at the time the poem was first published. Why didn't he? He wasn't aware the poem had been made public.

45. (B) (p. 124) *Reading/Social Studies/Voice.* After rehearsing the arguments for Livingston's authorship, the author of the passage presents a counterargument that the poem includes features pointing to Moore's authorship, and while Livingston seems likelier to have written in anapestic form, there is no evidence that Moore never wrote in that form. The best word to describe the evidence then is inconclusive.

46. (D) (p. 124) *Reading/Social Studies/Textual Evidence.* The author states at the end of the third paragraph that the likelihood of Livingston's using anapestic verse does not conclusively prove he is the author. This final sentence concisely summarizes the author's point in the third paragraph.

47. (C) (p. 124) *Reading/Social Studies/Implied Idea.* The author considers the significance of the names in paragraphs four and five. Scholars who support Livingston's authorship see the Dutch names used in the original publication as evidence that the author knew Dutch. The author of the passage rejects this theory, holding that Moore, who actually wrote the poem, used the German equivalents. This counter-theory is supported by the fact that in anticipation of a reprint Moore changed the originally printed version back to the German. Where did the original Dutch names come from? According to the passage, they were inserted by an editor at the newspaper.

48. (B) (p. 124) *Reading/Social Studies/Vocabulary.* The test clearly indicates that the "emendations" involved a change of the names, so *emendations* means *changes* or *corrections*.

49. (D) (p. 124) *Reading/Social Studies/Voice.* The author is generally skeptical of the Livingston claim, emerging as it does so many years after the poem's original publication and reprint in anthology form. Additionally, the main support for the claim is the recollections of Livingston's heirs, many years removed.

50. (C) (p. 124) *Reading/Social Studies/Textual Evidence.* This item asks for evidence to support the conclusion reached by the previous item. The author's attitude toward the heirs' claim to have once been in possession of an "original" of the poem is skepticism, and two words in the third sentence of paragraph two strongly point to this attitude: "claimed" and "allegedly."

51. (A) (p. 124) *Reading/Social Studies/Vocabulary.* The author is being generous to the Livingston family in trying to explain how it could, in good faith, have claimed authorship of the poem when so much evidence points to Moore. The author theorizes that Livingston's children may have made an honest mistake. The holiday poems written and read by their father would quite naturally have been similar to "A Visit," so it is forgivable that they would combine or confuse the two.

52. (D) (p. 125) *Reading/Social Studies/Main Idea.* This is a main idea question that asks about the final paragraph. The author's goal in that paragraph is to explain how the Livingston family could have make their claim when so much evidence points to Moore as the poet. The passage states that the similarity between the Moore poem and Livingston holiday tradition would have made it easy to think that "A Visit" was one of those holiday poems written by Livingston.

Section 2: Writing and Language

Passage 1

1. **(B)** (p. 127) *Writing and Language/Standard English Conventions/Grammar and Usage/Subject-Verb Agreement.* The problem with the original is the failure of the verb "is" to agree with the plural subject "jobs." This problem may be a little difficult to spot because of the inverted structure of the sentence, that is, the verb comes before the subject. The problem, once identified, is easily corrected by substituting the plural verb "are."

2. **(C)** (p. 127) *Writing and Language/Expression of Ideas/Style/Tone.* This item asks you to choose a phrase that is consistent with the overall tone of the passage. The author writes in a serious manner and avoids the use of slang. (C) is the phrase most consistent with the tone.

3. **(C)** (p. 127) *Writing and Language/Expression of Ideas/Strategy/Appropriate Supporting Material.* The value of the median salary is that it helps readers to understand how compensation is distributed in professional sports. Though the highest-paid athletes earn $190,000 a year, fully half earn less than $40,000 a year. Also, 40 percent earn between $40,000 and $190,000. So the median is an important number.

4. **(A)** (p. 127) *Writing and Language/Expression of Ideas/No Change.* The "even" provides a logical connection between the previous sentence and the following and dramatizes a point. The previous sentence says that a major injury can end an athlete's career. Then to dramatize the risk that athletes face, the author says that even a minor injury can end a career. The effect of the word "even" is to add special emphasis to the second sentence.

5. **(A)** (p. 128) *Writing and Language/Standard English Conventions/No Change.* The author means for the first sentence to identify the cause and the second to identify the effect in a cause-effect sequence: the intense competition causes the athletes to train constantly. A good way of joining the two sentences is to use "because" to express the connection. (B) and (D) create illogical connections. As for (B), the second idea is the effect of the first; the second is not contrary to the first. As for (D), the "when" reverses the connection. Finally, in (C), the "so" would require the first part of the sentence to be a clause, but the first part lacks a main verb.

6. **(B)** (p. 128) *Writing and Language/Standard English Conventions/Grammar and Usage/Verb Tense.* The problem with the underlined original is the verb tense. "Competed" is past tense, but all the other verbs in the paragraph are present tense. (B) solves the problem by changing the past tense to the present tense.

7. **(D)** (p. 128) *Writing and Language/Expression of Ideas/Style/Clarity of Meaning.* The problem with the original is the syntax of the sentence. The sentence, as written, defines group lessons as gymnastics or tennis and does not clearly say what the author means to say. The author intends to say that non-team sport athletes learn their skills by taking lessons. Examples of such sports are gymnastics and tennis.

8. **(B)** (p. 128) *Writing and Language/Standard English Conventions/Sentence Structure/Faulty Parallelism.* The problem with the original is a lack of parallel structure between "few" and "another." Both should have the same number. (B) solves the problem by substituting a plural form to parallel the plural "few."

9. **(C)** (p. 128) *Writing and Language/Standard English Conventions/Sentence Structure/Comma Splices.* The original contains a comma splice, that is, two independent clauses jammed together, separated only by a comma. (C) corrects the problem by adding the coordinate conjunction "and" and properly sets off the phrase "in turn" with commas.

10. **(D)** (p. 129) *Writing and Language/Expression of Ideas/Style/Conciseness.* The problem with the original is that it is needlessly wordy. A comparison of the various options will show how (D) eliminates the excess verbiage.

11. **(A)** (p. 129) *Writing and Language/Expression of Ideas/No Change.* The point of the final paragraph is that job prospects for the aspiring professional athlete are pretty grim. The author cites the example of men's basketball: only one in 12,000 candidates will make the grade. (A) summarizes this point.

Passage 2

12. **(B)** (p. 130) *Writing and Language/Expression of Ideas/Strategy/Effective Opening Sentence.* The first sentence establishes that the narrator was born in 1847, and the narrator says that he worked with circuses for sixty years. Allowing that the narrator was a young man when he first began, say 20 years old, his involvement with circuses would have covered the period 1867 to 1927, or thereabouts. So when the narrator contrasts the circus of "his time" with circuses of an earlier period, he is comparing those during that period with those that came earlier in the 1800s. This helps the reader appreciate references to "vaudeville," "horses," and "tallow dips." Without that first sentence, the reader knows only that the narrator's work spanned sixty years but does not know what era.

13. **(D)** (p. 130) *Writing and Language/Expression of Ideas/Style/Tone.* The problem with "was itchy" is that its use here amounts to slang. While the tone of the passage is not academic, it is a bit more formal than a dialect where "itchy" would be acceptable. Also, idiomatically it would be more appropriate to say "had an itch" or "was itching." For both reasons, (D) is the best answer.

14. **(C)** (p. 130) *Writing and Language/Standard English Conventions/Grammar and Usage/Pronoun Usage.* The underlined part of the sentence is followed twice by the pronoun "they," which must be intended to refer to "someone else." The problem is that "someone else" is singular while "they" is plural. The plural "others" solves the problem.

15. **(D)** (p. 130) *Writing and Language/Standard English Conventions/Sentence Structure/Faulty Parallelism.* The problem with the original is faulty parallelism. The first two elements in the series are –ing (gerund) forms while the third is a "to" (infinitive) form. All three elements need to have the same form. The problem with both (B) and (C) is that though the forms are parallel, the series uses a single object, "things," which means that one element asserts to be doing things or to do things. (D) avoids this problem. Additionally, (D) is better because the sequence of the elements parallels that of the preceding sentence.

16. **(C)** (p. 130) *Writing and Language/Standard English Conventions/Grammar and Usage/Faulty or Illogical Comparisons.* The original makes a false comparison. As written, the sentence seems to compare the modern "circus" with the "past," when, of course, it means to compare the circuses of the two different eras. (C) makes it clear that the comparison is between a modern circus and a past circus.

17. **(A)** (p. 130) *Writing and Language/Standard English Conventions/No Change..* The original is correct as written. The writer apparently means to distinguish between two types of promotion: the advance billing

(presumably posters and other ads that announce the coming of the circus) and the advertising done while the circus is in progress. Thus, there are two main categories with the second being a series of three elements. You do not want a comma following "billing" because there are only two elements in the overriding series: billing and the others.

18. (C) (p. 131) *Writing and Language/Expression of Ideas/Style/Precision.* Admittedly, the terms in this sentence are technical industry terms, but that does not mean that they are out of place. They seem to be the descriptive terms that people associated with a circus would use with great precision. A reader might wish that they had been defined, but one can understand from the context that these people were given the responsibility for stimulating interest in the circus.

19. (C) (p. 131) *Writing and Language/Expression of Ideas/Strategy/Main Idea.* The underlined part is a rhetorical question. The author does not intend to answer it; instead, the author believes that the answer is obvious: it's impossible to put anything that large indoors.

20. (B) (p. 131) *Writing and Language/Expression of Ideas/Strategy/Appropriate Supporting Material..* The aerial acrobat is obviously a highly skilled performer. One can imagine many workers being able to handle horses or raise the tent, but acrobatics requires special skills. So the "except" in the original is the author's way of saying to the reader that "jack-of-all-trades" does have limits. But the revision would make an exception to the exception by acknowledging that a handful of extremely talented people could even substitute as acrobats.

21. (A) (p. 132) *Writing and Language/Expression of Ideas/No Change.* The main point of the paragraph is that circuses were adaptable, taking advantage of new inventions and technology. The paragraph, as written, provides two examples: calcium flares and gaslights. (A) would provide a third example: railroads.

22. (C) (p. 132) *Writing and Language/Standard English Conventions/Grammar and Usage/Diction.* This item tests the proper choice of phrasing for making a comparison. The correct phrasing is "as . . . as," not "as . . . than."

Passage 3

23. (D) (p. 133) *Writing and Language/Standard English Conventions/Sentence Structure/Misplaced Modifiers.* The problem with the original is the placement of the introductory modifier. "One" will be attached by the reader to the first free-standing noun in the sentence, which in the original is "citizens." The other nouns such as "First Amendment" are objects of prepositions. But "citizens" is not "one of the group." (D) solves this problem by making it clear that it is the First Amendment that is one of the group of amendments called the Bill of Rights.

24. (C) (p. 133) *Writing and Language/Standard English Conventions/Punctuation/Dashes.* The material following "media" is an aside that provides further explanation or illustrates the concept. Since it is not an integral part of the logical structure of the sentence, it has to be punctuated so that the reader understands its secondary nature. A writer has two choices here. The material can be set aside using either commas or dashes, but not a mixture of both. And there must be one comma or dash to open the aside and another to close it.

25. **(C)** (p. 133) *Writing and Language/Standard English Conventions/Sentence Structure/Comma Splices.* The original contains a comma splice, that is, two independent clauses (each with its own subject and verb) jammed together and separated only by a comma. The commas splice can be eliminated by adding a conjunction, by substituting a semicolon for the comma, or by creating two sentences:

... speaker, and it ....

... speaker; it ....

... speaker. It ....

(C) uses the first approach. Note: Since the clauses are so short, a writer might choose to go with just a conjunction and omit the comma.

26. **(C)** (p. 133) *Writing and Language/Expression of Ideas/Style/Precision.* The syntax of the original is unnecessarily complex and makes the author's meaning unclear. The underlined portion needs to be rewritten so that it states the point directly, and (C) does this. (B) is wrong because "the government may do limited speech" is not idiomatic, and (D) is wrong because its passive voice obscures meaning.

27. **(B)** (p. 134) *Writing and Language/Standard English Conventions/Grammar and Usage/Pronoun Usage.* This item tests pronoun form. "It's" is the contraction for "it is," which is not what the author intends here. Instead, the author wants the possessive third person, singular pronoun: "its." "Its" signifies possession of "conclusion" and has as its antecedent "Court."

28. **(B)** (p. 134) *Writing and Language/Standard English Conventions/Sentence Structure/Fragments.* The problem with the original is that the word group lacks a main verb. (B) is the only choice that provides a main verb.

29. **(D)** (p. 134) *Writing and Language/Expression of Ideas/Strategy/Appropriate Supporting Material.* The case of *Schenck* dealt with speech that encouraged men to resist the draft during wartime. The Court ruled that such speech could be curbed because the interference with the government's ability to defend the nation constituted a clear and present danger.

30. **(B)** (p. 134) *Writing and Language/Expression of Ideas/Style/Conciseness.* The problem with the original is excess verbiage. "Popular" implies that the saying is used frequently and that the usage is widespread. (B) eliminates the redundancy and leaves a nice, succinct expression.

31. **(A)** (p. 135) *Writing and Language/Expression of Ideas/No Change.* This item asks you to choose the appropriate logical transition for the final sentence. Here the author intends to contrast the idea that the government may place some restrictions on speech with the idea that free speech is nonetheless an essential part of our system of government. "Despite" nicely signals that contrast.

32. **(D)** (p. 135) *Writing and Language/Expression of Ideas/Style/Conciseness.* The problem with the original is needless repetition. Anything that is critical is necessarily important, so the word "important" is unnecessary. Then, if something is "critical," it is of the utmost importance, so the "very" can be eliminated.

33. **(D)** (p. 135) *Writing and Language/Expression of Ideas/Organization/Sentence-Level Structure.* The new sentence provides an example of government regulation that does not ban speech but does restrict the way in which it can be presented. This is the topic of the final paragraph, and the sentence provides an example of the general idea set forth in the first sentence.

Passage 4

34. **(C)** (p. 136) *Writing and Language/Expression of Ideas/Style/Conciseness.* The original is needlessly wordy. "Subsequently" means later or following, so there is no reason to use both "subsequently" and "after that date."

35. **(D)** (p. 136) *Writing and Language/Standard English Conventions/Grammar and Usage/Adjectives versus Adverbs.* "Quickly" and "cheaply" modify the verb "built," so both must have the form of the adverb. You need to add –ly. Then, "relatively" modifies the two adverbs, so it must also be an adverb.

36. **(C)** (p. 136) *Writing and Language/Standard English Conventions/Grammar and Usage/Pronoun Usage.* The problem with the original is that the pronoun "it" refers to "gas plants," but "plants" is plural while "it" is singular. The error is easily corrected by changing "it" to "they" and conforming the verb.

37. **(A)** (p. 136) *Writing and Language/Expression of Ideas/No Change.* The first sentence of paragraph 2 is a topic sentence, and the author announces that gas plants are fast and cheap. The paragraph then develops the comparison between gas and coal plants on those two bases. First, the author provides some details about how long it takes to build the two different types of plant. Then the author talks about cost. (Smaller is cheaper.) The underlined sentence provides information about cost, so the best position is where it is in the original.

38. **(A)** (p. 137) *Writing and Language/Standard English Conventions/No Change.* The main problem with the original is the confusion between *less* and *few*. With count nouns, ones that can have a singular and plural, the correct choice is fewer, e.g., fewer pills and fewer cars. When the noun refers to a mass quantity, the correct choice is *less*, e.g., less water and less corn. But fewer quarts of water and fewer kernels of corn. In this case, "effects" refers to a mass quantity so the appropriate word is less, (A).

39. **(A)** (p. 137) *Writing and Language/Standard English Conventions/No Change.* The original is correct. The first part of the sentence is a dependent clause introduced by the subordinate conjunction "because." Its end should be signaled by a comma. (B) is incorrect because the comma is missing; the reader will have difficulty determining where the subordinate clause ends and the independent clause begins. (C) is wrong because this is a job for the comma, not the semicolon. And (D) is wrong because it creates a sentence fragment of the dependent clause.

40. **(B)** (p. 137) *Writing and Language/Standard English Conventions/Sentence Structure/Faulty Parallelism.* The author intends an elliptical construction here. The phrase "elliptical" derives from "ellipsis," which refers to the series of dots that signal that an element of the sentence has been intentionally omitted but is inferable or recoverable from the context. In this case, the author means: emits only about 40% as much as a typical coal plant does. For the construction to work, therefore, the word "does" is required.

41. **(B)** (p. 137) *Writing and Language/Expression of Ideas/Style/Idiomatic Expression.* The problem with the original is the use of the gerund "growing" with the definite article "the." While "growing" can be a noun form ("Growing corn requires extensive fertilization."), as used in this sentence the form is not idiomatic. The author does not mean that nuclear plants are "growing" in the same sense as a crop. Instead, the author is referring to the <u>increase</u> in capacity, and "growth *of*" is more precise for that purpose.

42. **(B)** (p. 138) *Writing and Language/Expression of Ideas/Strategy/Effective Concluding Sentence.* The main points of the passage are that technology has made gas a relatively cheap and benign energy source for generating electricity and that there is considerable underutilized capacity. In other words, gas-generated electricity is good and it's available. The conclusion naturally flows that it would be a wise idea to shift to gas—exactly what (B) concludes.

43. **(B)** (p. 138) *Writing and Language/Expression of Ideas/Strategy/Data Presentation.* The percentages given are:

Natural Gas	19%
Coal	42%
Nuclear	14%
All Other	15%

Therefore, (B), coal, is correct.

44. **(D)** (p. 139) *Writing and Language/Expression of Ideas/Strategy/Data Presentation.* The question stem suggests that the author might use the graph to make a claim about electricity *generated*, but the graph provides information about *capacity*. Indeed, in the final paragraph, the author is careful to draw this distinction: natural gas plants had greater *capacity*; coal plants produced more *electricity*.

Section 3: Math, No Calculator

1. **(A)** (p. 140) *Math: Multiple-Choice/Algebra/Creating, Expressing, and Evaluating Algebraic Equations and Functions.* This is a simple translation item: translate the English words into "algebrese." The product of 4 and x is written as $4x$, and 3 less than that is written as $4x - 3$.

2. **(B)** (p. 140) *Math: Multiple Choice/Algebra/Manipulating Algebraic Expressions/Manipulating Expressions Involving Exponents.* Given the item's place in the test (it is an easy item), look for an escape route rather than performing the indicated calculations. Cancel and factor:

$$\frac{10^3\left(10^5 + 10^5\right)}{10^4} = \frac{10^3\left[2\left(10^5\right)\right]}{10^4} = \frac{2\left(10^8\right)}{10^4} = 2\left(10^4\right).$$

3. **(D)** (p. 141) *Math: Multiple-Choice/Algebra/Solving Algebraic Equations or Inequalities with One Variable/Simple Inequalities.* This item can be solved by reasoning abstractly about the properties of the terms used. A negative number cubed is negative, but squared it is positive. Thus, x is not less than 0. A positive fraction grows smaller each time it is multiplied by itself. For example: $\left(\frac{1}{2}\right)^2 = \frac{1}{4} \Rightarrow \left(\frac{1}{4}\right)^2 = \frac{1}{16}$.

Thus, the fewer times it is multiplied by itself, the larger it is. Therefore, x cannot be a positive number less than 1. Finally, x cannot be 1, because $x^3 > x^2 \Rightarrow \left(1^3\right) > \left(1^2\right) \Rightarrow 1 > 1$, which is false. Therefore, (D) must be the correct choice.

A much more elegant approach to this item is to notice that x^2 is positive regardless of whether x is negative or positive. Furthermore, x cannot be zero or the original inequality would not hold true. Therefore, it is permissible to divide each side of the quantity by x^2: $x^3 > x^2 \Rightarrow \dfrac{x^3}{x^2} > \dfrac{x^2}{x^2} \Rightarrow x > 1$. Of the given choices, the only possible value for x is (D).

4. **(A)** (p. 141) *Math: Multiple-Choice/Algebra/Problem Solving and Advanced Arithmetic/Common Advanced Arithmetic Items/Properties of Numbers.* If n is the least of the three consecutive, even integers, then the other two can be represented as $n+2$ and $n+4$, so the sum of the three integers must be: $n + (n+2) + (n+4) = 156 \Rightarrow 3n + 6 = 156$.

5. **(C)** (p. 141) *Math: Multiple-Choice/Algebra/Manipulating Algebraic Expressions/Basic Algebraic Manipulations.* Perform the indicated operations: $(-3x^2 y - xy^2 + 2xy) - (-3xy + 2x^2 y - 5xy^2) =$ $-3x^2 y - 2x^2 y - xy^2 + 5xy^2 + 2xy + 3xy = -5x^2 y + 4xy^2 + 5xy = xy(-5x + 4y + 5)$.

6. **(B)** (p. 141) *Math: Multiple-Choice/Algebra/Creating, Expressing, and Evaluating Algebraic Equations and Functions.* This item asks you to interpret the given inequality. The inequality $|s - 28{,}600| \le 3{,}500$ means that the absolute value of the difference between a new bus driver's starting salary, s, and \$28,600 must be equal or less than \$3,500. In other words, $-3{,}500 \le s - 28{,}600 \le 3{,}500$, which is the same as $-3{,}500 + 28{,}600 \le s \le 3{,}500 + 28{,}600 \Rightarrow 25{,}100 \le s \le 32{,}100$. So, \$28,600 is the average possible starting salary, not the minimum, as stated in (B).

7. **(D)** (p. 141) *Math: Multiple-Choice/Coordinate Geometry/Graphs of Polynomial Functions and Algebra/Manipulating Algebraic Expressions/Factoring Expressions.* The zeros are those values of x for which the function equals to zero. Set each factor of the polynomial equal to zero and solve for x: $x = 0$, $2x + 3 = 0 \Rightarrow x = -\dfrac{3}{2}$, $x - 1 = 0 \Rightarrow x = 1$, and $x^2 - 1 = 0 \Rightarrow x = \pm 1$. The given polynomial has four distinct roots, or zeros: $-\dfrac{3}{2}$, -1, 0, and 1. Thus, the correct answer is (D).

8. **(A)** (p. 142) *Math: Multiple-Choice/Coordinate Geometry/The Coordinate System* and *Algebra/Creating, Expressing, and Evaluating Algebraic Equations and Functions/Creating Algebraic Expressions.* The coordinates establish that this figure is a rectangle. The width of the rectangle is a, and the length is $b - a$. So, the area is $a(b - a)$.

    Alternatively, assume values, such as $a = 2$ and $b = 4$. The rectangle has a width of 2, a length of $4 - 2 = 2$, and an area of $2 \cdot 2 = 4$. Substitute 2 for a and 4 for b into the formulas given in the answer choices and the correct formula will yield a value of 4.

9. **(A)** (p. 142) *Math: Multiple-Choice/Algebra/Solving Algebraic Equations or Inequalities with One Variable/Equations Involving Rational Expressions.* Solve the given equation for x: $\dfrac{6}{(x+3)(x-3)} = \dfrac{1}{x-3} + \dfrac{1}{x+3} \Rightarrow 6 = \dfrac{(x+3)(x-3)}{x-3} + \dfrac{(x+3)(x-3)}{x+3} \Rightarrow 6 = x+3 + x-3 \Rightarrow 2x = 6 \Rightarrow x = 3$. However, 3 cannot be the solution to the original equation because it would make the denominator of two of the fractions equal to zero, and division by zero is undefined. Therefore, 3 is an extraneous solution and the solution set is empty, $\{\ \}$.

10. **(B)** (p. 142) *Math: Multiple-Choice/Coordinate Geometry/Graphs of Linear Equations.* Create an equation in the form $y = mx + b$, in which m is the slope of the line and b is the y-intercept. Begin by calculating the slope: $m = \dfrac{(-2)-(4)}{(2)-(-1)} = \dfrac{-6}{3} = -2$. Therefore, $y = -2x + b$. (B) is the correct answer since it is the only equation with slope of –2. To further verify that (B) is correct, use one of the pairs of coordinates provided in the graph: $4 = -2(-1) + b \Rightarrow b = 2$. Therefore, the equation is indeed $y = -2x + 2$.

11. **(B)** (p. 142) *Math: Multiple-Choice/Algebra/Creating, Expressing, and Evaluating Algebraic Equations and Functions/Concepts of Domain and Range.* To be a function, a relation can have only one output for each input. In other words, for all ordered pairs (x, y), for any value x there can be only one y. Inspecting the relation defined by the given set, either $(0,3)$ or $(0,5)$ must be eliminated to make the relation a function. Only $(0,3)$ is given as a possible answer.

12. **(B)** (p. 143) *Math: Multiple-Choice/Coordinate Geometry/Graphs of Quadratic Equations and Relations.* First, determine what the graph of $y = x^2 - 3$ looks like. This equation is a parabola since the power of x is 2, and the parabola opens upward since the coefficient of x^2 is positive (+1). The axis of symmetry is $x = h$ and the vertex is k for $y = (x - h)^2 + k$. Therefore, the axis of symmetry is $x = 0$ and the vertex is $y = -3$. So, the graph of $y = x^2 - 3$ is as follows:

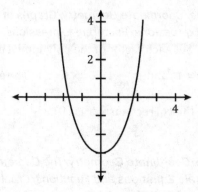

Now, the actual graphical representation in question is of an absolute value: $y = \left|x^2 - 3\right|$. Therefore, the graph of this equation is the same as that of $y = x^2 - 3$ but with any negative values transposed across the x-axis:

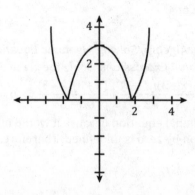

Alternatively, note that the graph of $y = |x^2 - 3|$ must always be positive since the absolute value is always positive. The only graph that does not depict negative y-values is (B).

13. (C) (p. 144) *Math: Multiple-Choice/Coordinate Geometry/Graphs of Quadratic Equations and Relations.* A graph relating kinetic energy as a function of velocity would have kinetic energy on the y-axis and velocity on the x-axis: $KE = \frac{1}{2}mv^2 \Rightarrow y \propto x^2$. Therefore, the correct graph will be a positive, upright (half) parabola representing a quadratic equation. Only (C) matches this requirement.

14. (C) (p. 144) *Math: Multiple-Choice/Algebra/Creating, Expressing, and Evaluating Algebraic Equations and Functions/Functions as Models.* KE is measures in joules, J, equivalent to $\frac{\text{kg} \cdot \text{m}^2}{\text{s}^2}$. For KE to equal $\frac{1}{2}mv^2$, m needs to have the unit kg and v needs to have the unit $\frac{\text{m}}{\text{s}}$. First, convert 2,000 grams to kilograms:

$$2,000 \text{ grams} \times \frac{1 \text{ kilogram}}{1,000 \text{ grams}} = 2 \text{ kg}.$$ Solve the given equation for velocity:

$$KE = \frac{1}{2}mv^2 \Rightarrow v = \sqrt{\frac{2KE}{m}} = \sqrt{\frac{2(120 \text{ kg} \cdot \text{m}^2 / \text{s}^2)}{2 \text{ kg}}} = 2\sqrt{30} \text{ m/s}.$$

15. (D) (p. 144) *Math: Multiple-Choice/Trigonometry/Right Triangles/Trigonometric Ratios.* The length of the side opposite the angle is 6 feet, so use the relation for the sine of an angle:

$$\sin\theta = \frac{\text{side opposite } \theta}{\text{hypotenuse}} \Rightarrow \sin 35° = \frac{6 \text{ feet}}{x} \Rightarrow x = \frac{6}{\sin 35°}$$ feet. Therefore, subtract the ramp's length from the purchased board: $12 - \frac{6}{\sin 35°}$.

16. (16) (p. 146) *Math: Student-Produced Responses/Algebra/Solving Algebraic Equations or Inequalities with One Variable.* If $\frac{3}{4}$ of x is 36, then $\frac{3}{4}(x) = 36 \Rightarrow x = 36\left(\frac{4}{3}\right) = 48$, and $\frac{1}{3}$ of 48 is 16.

17. (60) (p. 146) *Math: Student-Produced Responses/Geometry/Lines and Angles.* Label the other two angles in the triangle:

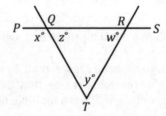

The angle measure of a straight line is 180°, so $x + z = 180 \Rightarrow 120 + z = 180 \Rightarrow z = 60$. Next, $z + w + y = 180$. And since $\overline{QT} = \overline{QR}$, $y = w$. Therefore, $60 + y + y = 180 \Rightarrow 2y = 120 \Rightarrow y = 60$.

18. (14) (p. 146) *Math: Student-Produced Responses/Algebra/Solving Algebraic Equations or Inequalities with One Variable/Equations Involving Absolute Value.* Solve using absolute value conventions. $|x-2|=6$, so either $x-2=6$ or $x-2=-6$; $x=8$ or $x=-4$ $|y+8|=10$, so either $y+8=10$ or $y+8=-10$. Thus, $y=2$ or $y=-18$. Since x and y are both negative, $x=-4$, $y=-18$, and $x-y=-4-(-18)=14$.

19. (11) (p. 146) *Math: Student-Produced Responses/Problem Solving and Advanced Arithmetic/Common Advanced Arithmetic Items/Complex Numbers.* Since $i=\sqrt{-1}$, $i^2=(\sqrt{-1})(\sqrt{-1})=-1$ and $i^4=(i^2)(i^2)=(-1)(-1)=1$. Simplify the expression: $3i^4+2i^2+10=3(1)+2(-1)+10=3-2+10=11$.

20. (7/2, 3.5) (p. 146) *Math: Student-Produced Responses/Algebra/Creating, Expressing, and Evaluating Algebraic Equations and Functions.* To determine for what value x the function k is undefined, set the denominator of the fraction equal to zero and solve for x: $(x+2)^2-\dfrac{x+2}{2}-3=0$. To make the algebra simpler, let $x'=x+2$, so $(x')^2-\dfrac{x'}{2}-3=0$. To determine the possible values of x', factor the left side of the equation: $x'^2-\dfrac{x'}{2}-3=(x'+\dfrac{3}{2})(x'-2)$. (Note: if the factor pattern is not immediately evident, the quadratic formula can be used to determine x'.) Thus, $x'=-\dfrac{3}{2}$ or $x'=2$, so $x+2=-\dfrac{3}{2}\Rightarrow x=-\dfrac{7}{2}$ or $x+2=2\Rightarrow x=0$.

Therefore, $m-n=0-\left(-\dfrac{7}{2}\right)=\dfrac{7}{2}$.

Alternatively, solve for x directly. Set the denominator of the fraction equal to zero and solve for x, as above. Now, multiply both sides by 2 and expand: $(x+2)^2-\dfrac{x+2}{2}-3=0\Rightarrow 2(x+2)^2-(x+2)-6=0$, so

$2x^2+8x+8-x-2-6=0\Rightarrow 2x^2+7x=0$. Factor to find the solutions:

$2x^2+7x=0\Rightarrow x(2x+7)=0\Rightarrow x=0$ and $x=-\dfrac{7}{2}$. Thus, $m-n=0-\left(-\dfrac{7}{2}\right)=\dfrac{7}{2}$.

Section 4: Math, Calculator

1. (D) (p. 148) *Math: Multiple-Choice/Problem Solving and Advanced Arithmetic/Common Advanced Arithmetic Items/Properties of Numbers* and *Algebra/Solving Simultaneous Equations.* Reason through each of the answer choices:

A) $2+n$ cannot be a multiple of 3. Since n is a multiple of 3, when $2+n$ is divided by 3, there will be a remainder of 2;

B) $2-n$ cannot be a multiple of 3 for the same reason that $2+n$ cannot be a multiple of 3;

C) $2n+1$ cannot be a multiple of 3 for the same reason that $2n-1$ cannot be a multiple of 3; and finally,

D) $2n+3$ is a multiple of 3. $2n$ is a multiple of 3; 3 is a multiple of 3; so, $2n+3$ is a multiple of 3.

Alternatively, use the "Plug-and-Chug" method. Select a value for n and test the answer choices. Let $n=9$.

A) $2+9=11$ ✗

B) $2-9=7$ ✗

C) $2(9)+1=19$ ✗
D) $2(9)+3=21$ ✓

2. **(B)** (p. 148) *Math: Multiple-Choice/Problem Solving and Advanced Arithmetic/Common Problem Solving Items/Percentages.* Use the "is-over-of" equation for percents. The "of," which is the denominator of the fraction, is the total quantity of the mixture. How much of the mixture is there? $2.5+12.5=15$ kilograms. The word "is," which is the numerator of the fraction, is the 2.5 kilograms of gravel. Thus:

$$\frac{is}{of}=\frac{gravel}{mixture}=\frac{2.5}{15}=\frac{1}{6}=0.1\overline{6}=16\frac{2}{3}\%.$$

3. **(C)** (p. 148) *Math: Multiple-Choice/Algebra/Solving Simultaneous Equations.* Set up a system of equations to solve this problem: $T+H=22$; $H+B=17$; and $B+T=15$. Using the first two equations:

$$\begin{array}{r} T+H=22 \\ -(H+B=17) \\ \hline T-B=5 \end{array}$$

Couple the result with the third equation:

$$\begin{array}{r} T-B=5 \\ +(B+T=15) \\ \hline 2T=20 \Rightarrow T=10 \end{array}$$

Since $T+H=22$ and Tom is 10, Herb must be 12.

4. **(B)** (p. 148) *Math: Multiple-Choice/Problem Solving and Advanced Arithmetic/Common Advanced Arithmetic Items/Properties of Numbers.* The trick to this item is that since both x and y are negative, xy, (B), is the only expression that generates a positive result. Therefore, (B) must be the greatest.

5. **(A)** (p. 148) *Math: Multiple-Choice/Algebra/Creating, Expressing, and Evaluating Algebraic Equations and Functions.* The formula will be x, the cost for the first ounce, plus some expression to represent the additional postage for each additional ounce over the first ounce. The postage for the additional weight is y cents per ounce, and the additional weight is w minus the first ounce, or $w-1$. Therefore, the additional postage is $y(w-1)$, and the total postage is $x+y(w-1)$.

Alternatively, assume some numbers. For ease of calculations, assume that the first ounce costs 1 cent and every additional ounce is 2 cents. If $x=1$ and $y=2$, then a letter, of say, 3 ounces ($w=3$) will cost $1+2(2)=5$ cents. Substitute these values for $x, y,$ and w into the answer choices, and the correct choice will return the value 5:

A) $x+y(w-1)=1+2(3-1)=1+2(2)=5$ ✓
B) $x(w-y)=1(3-2)=1(1)=1$ ✗
C) $x(w-1)+y(w-1)=1(3-1)+2(3-1)=1(2)+2(2)=6$ ✗
D) $x+wy=1+3(2)=7$ ✗

6. **(B)** (p. 148) *Math: Multiple-Choice/Geometry/Complex Figures* and *Coordinate Geometry/The Coordinate System.* This is a shaded area problem: $\text{area}_{\text{shaded portion}} = \text{area}_{\text{square}} - \dfrac{\text{area}_{\text{circle}}}{4}$. The area of the square is $s^2 = 2^2 = 4$, and the area of the circle is $\pi r^2 = \pi(2)^2 = 4\pi$. Therefore, the area of the shaded portion is $4 - \dfrac{4\pi}{4} = 4 - \pi$.

7. **(A)** (p. 148) *Math: Multiple-Choice/Algebra/Solving Algebraic Equations or Inequalities with One Variable.* Since $2^x = 16$, $x = 4$. Therefore, $4 = \dfrac{y}{2} \Rightarrow y = 8$.

   Alternatively, "test-the-test" with the answer choices. If $y = 8$, then $x = 4$, and since $2^4 = 16$, (A) must be the correct choice.

8. **(C)** (p. 149) *Math: Multiple-Choice/Algebra/Manipulating Algebraic Expressions/Basic Algebraic Manipulations.* Rewrite the equation so that it is in the form the question asks for, $x + y$: $12 + x = 36 - y \Rightarrow x + y = 36 - 12 = 24$.

9. **(D)** (p. 149) *Math: Multiple-Choice/Problem Solving and Advanced Arithmetic.* One way of analyzing this item is to reason that the larger square has four sides and each guard requires 10 minutes to walk the distance of a side (400 yards). In $3.5 \; \cancel{\text{hours}} \times \dfrac{60 \text{ minutes}}{1 \; \cancel{\text{hour}}} = 210$ $3.5 \; \cancel{\text{hours}} \times \dfrac{60 \text{ minutes}}{1 \; \cancel{\text{hour}}} = 210$ minutes, each guard will walk 210 minutes $\div 10$ minutes/side $= 21$ sides. So, each guard will make five complete trips around the lot plus one more side (21 sides $\div 4$ sides/trip $= 5$ trips, remainder 1 side), bringing each back to his or her original starting point, P, and then one side further. This puts both guards at the opposite side of the square: Jane at Q and Ed at S. Therefore, they are $400 + 400 = 800$ yards away from each other, as measured along the perimeter of the fence.

10. **(C)** (p. 149) *Math: Multiple-Choice/Statistics/Measures of Center and Spread/Averages* and *Median* and *Mode.* Adding the twelve temperatures and dividing by twelve gives an average slightly greater than 54°F, so (I) is true. Arrange the values in order: 30, 30, 35, 35, 35, 50, 55, 65, 65, 80, 80, and 90. The central values are 50 and 55, so the median (52.5°F) is greater than 50°F, so (II) is true. The mode is 35°F because it is the temperature that appears with the greatest frequency, so (III) is false.

11. **(A)** (p. 149) *Math: Multiple-Choice/Algebra/Manipulating Algebraic Expressions/Factoring Expressions.* Notice that $x^2 - y^2$ is the difference of two squares, so $x^2 - y^2 = (x + y)(x - y)$. Since $x - y = 3$, $(x + y)(3) = 3$, so $x + y = 1$.

12. **(A)** (p. 150) *Math: Multiple-Choice/Problem Solving and Advanced Arithmetic/Common Problem Solving Items/Proportions.* Panel A stores 40 kilowatts per hour and Panel B stores 50 kilowatts (kW) per hour in full sun. The panels are exposed to 12 hours of full sun. The energy credit in this problem is 2 cents per kW. Panel A's credit is $40\dfrac{\text{kW}}{\text{hr}} \cdot 12\text{hr} \cdot 0.02\dfrac{\text{dollars}}{\text{kW}} = \$9.60$. Panel B's credit is $50\dfrac{\text{kW}}{\text{hr}} \cdot 12\text{hr} \cdot 0.02\dfrac{\text{dollars}}{\text{kW}} = \$12.00$. The difference in solar credit between the two panels is $\$12.00 - \$9.60 = \$2.40$.

13. (D) (p. 150) *Math: Multiple-Choice/Algebra/Creating, Expressing, and Evaluating Algebraic Equations and Functions.* Eliminate (A) and (B) because whether they are odd or even depends on whether $3n$ is odd or even, which depends on whether n is odd or even. As for (C) and (D), n^2 could be odd or even. If n^2 is even, then the expression $n^2 + 1$ is equal to an odd number. And if n^2 is odd, the expression is equal to an even number. Therefore, (D) must be the correct choice: if n is odd, n^2 is odd, and an odd number plus an odd number is even; if n is even, n^2 is even, and an even number plus an even number is always even.

14. (B) (p. 150) *Math: Multiple-Choice/Problem Solving and Advanced Arithmetic/Multi-Step Problem Solving Items.* Create an expression to convert mils to centimeters, making sure that similar units cancel leaving the answer in units of mil: $0.2 \text{ mils} \times \dfrac{.0001 \text{ inch}}{1 \text{ mil}} \times \dfrac{2.54 \text{ centimeters}}{1 \text{ inch}} = .05 \text{ centimeters}$.

15. (C) (p. 150) *Math: Multiple-Choice/Problem Solving and Advanced Arithmetic/Multi-Step Problem Solving Items and Algebra/Creating, Expressing, and Evaluating Algebraic Equations and Functions.* This item can be solved using a Venn diagram:

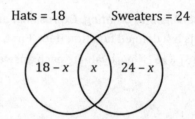

The twist here is that the diagram is not intended to represent all 36 people in the group. 6 of the 36 have neither hats nor sweaters on, so the total represented by the diagram is $36 - 6 = 30$. Therefore, $30 = (18 - x) + x + (24 - x) = -x + 42 \Rightarrow x = 12$.

16. (B) (p. 150) *Math: Multiple-Choice/Statistics/Measures of Center and Spread/Median.* Find the cost per meter for the four wires:

A) $\dfrac{\$6}{2 \text{ meters}} = \$3$ per meter

B) $\dfrac{\$10}{4 \text{ meters}} = 2\dfrac{1}{2} = \$2.50$ per meter

C) $\dfrac{\$7}{5 \text{ meters}} = 1\dfrac{2}{5} = \$1.40$ per meter

D) $\dfrac{\$10}{8 \text{ meters}} = 1\dfrac{1}{4} = \$1.25$ per meter

Since there are four values, the median value is the average of the two middle values when arranged in order. The two middles values are $1.40 and $2.50, so the median price per meter is $\dfrac{\$1.40 + \$2.50}{2} = \dfrac{\$3.90}{2} = \$1.95$.

17. **(D)** (p. 150) *Math: Multiple-Choice/Algebra/Solving Simultaneous Equations.* To find b in terms of x and y, set b equal to x and equal to y:

$$x = b + 4 \qquad y = b - 3$$
$$b = x - 4 \qquad \text{and} \qquad b = y + 3$$

Now, combine the two equations by adding:

$$b = x - 4$$
$$+ (b = y + 3)$$
$$\overline{2b = x + y - 1}$$
$$b = \frac{x + y - 1}{2}$$

Alternatively, substitute some numbers. Let $b = 1$, so $x = 1 + 4 = 5$ and $y = 1 - 3 = -2$. Substitute 5 for x and -2 for y into the choices; the correct choice will yield the value 1.

18. **(C)** (p. 150) *Math: Multiple-Choice/Algebra/Creating, Expressing, and Evaluating Algebraic Equations and Functions/Function Notation.* This is a defined function item. First, do "Δ" to 3 and "∇" to 5: $\Delta(3) = 3 + 1 = 4$ and $\nabla(5) = 5 - 1 = 4$. So, $\Delta(3) \cdot \nabla(5) = 16$. Now, evaluate each answer choice to find the one that equals 16:

A) $\Delta(12) = 12 + 1 = 13$ ✗
B) $\Delta(14) = 14 + 1 = 15$ ✗
C) $\nabla(17) = 17 - 1 = 16$ ✓
D) $\nabla(20) = 20 - 1 = 19$ ✗

19. **(A)** (p. 150) *Math: Multiple-Choice/Problem Solving and Advanced Arithmetic/Common Advanced Arithmetic Items/Absolute Value.* Since $|-3| = 3$, $|-3| \cdot |2| \cdot \left|\frac{1}{2}\right| + (-4) = 3 \cdot 2 \cdot \frac{1}{2} - 4 = 3 - 4 = -1$.

20. **(C)** (p. 151) *Math: Multiple-Choice/Statistics/Measures of Center and Spread/Averages and Data Interpretation/Bar, Cumulative, and Line Graphs.* Write an equation for the average well quality (sum of the quality scale points for all 22 wells/the total number of wells), in which x, y, and z represent the quality of the three new wells:

$$4 \leq \frac{2(1) + 0(2) + 6(3) + 4(4) + 8(5) + 2(6) + x + y + z}{25} \leq \frac{2 + 18 + 16 + 40 + 12 + x + y + z}{25} \leq \frac{88 + x + y + z}{25} \Rightarrow$$

$x + y + z \geq 4(25) - 88 = 12$. Therefore, the sum of the water quality for the three new wells must be at least 12. Since the item stem asks about the lowest quality that all three new wells can have that maintains an average well quality of at least 4, the three scores are the same: $x = y = z \Rightarrow 3x \geq 12 \Rightarrow x \geq 4$. Therefore, the lowest water quality that each of the new wells must have is 4.

21. **(C)** (p. 151) *Math: Multiple-Choice/Algebra/Manipulating Algebraic Expressions/Evaluating Expressions.* An expression is undefined when its denominator has a zero value. For $x = 1$, $x - 1 = 0$, so the entire expression is undefined. Similarly, for $x = -2$, $x + 2$ is 0, and the expression is undefined. For $x = -3$, $x + 3$ is equal to 0, so the value of the expression is 0 and that is perfectly allowable.

22. **(D)** (p. 151) *Math: Multiple-Choice/Coordinate Geometry/Graphs of First-Degree Inequalities.* First, determine the equations of the functions shown in the graph. The upright parabola corresponds to a quadratic equation, $y = x^2 + b$, where b is the y-intercept. In this case, $y = -2$ for $x = 0$, so the equation for the parabola is $y = x^2 - 2$. The other line is a constant value for y, $y = 4$. The shaded area represents the overlap for the y-values greater than the parabola $\left(y > x^2 - 2\right)$ and the y-values greater than the line $\left(y > 4\right)$.

23. **(B)** (p. 152) *Math: Multiple-Choice/Coordinate Geometry/The Coordinate System* and *Geometry/Triangles/ Properties of Triangles.* The base of the triangle is: $3k - k = 2k$. The height of the triangle is: $4k - k = 3k$. Therefore, $\text{area}_{\text{triangle}} = \dfrac{\text{base} \cdot \text{height}}{2} = \dfrac{3k \cdot 2k}{2} = 12 \Rightarrow 3k^2 = 12 \Rightarrow k^2 = 4 \Rightarrow k = 2$.

24. **(B)** (p. 152) *Math: Multiple-Choice/Coordinate Geometry/Graphs of Linear Equations.* According to the graph, the time it takes each ball to fall from the drop height to ground level increases as the drop heights increase in an almost constant manner. Only (B) shows a linearly increasing function (positive slope).

25. **(A)** (p. 153) *Math: Multiple-Choice/Probability/Arithmetic Probability.* For $xy = 0$, either x or y must be zero. If the first tile drawn is zero, it does not matter which tile is drawn next; the product of the two tiles will always be zero. The probability of drawing a zero in the first draw is $\dfrac{5}{9}$. Now, suppose that the first tile drawn is not a zero. The probability that the first tile is not a zero is $\dfrac{4}{9}$. With that tile gone, there are only eight tiles left to draw from. The probability that the second tile drawn is a zero is $\dfrac{5}{8}$. Thus, the probability that the first tile is not a zero and the second tile is a zero is $\dfrac{4}{9} \cdot \dfrac{5}{8} = \dfrac{5}{18}$. The question asks for the probability that one or the other of these events occur, so we add the probabilities: $\dfrac{5}{9} + \dfrac{5}{18} = \dfrac{15}{18} = \dfrac{5}{6}$.

Alternatively, count the number of times the product of x and y is zero in the table below. Then, divide that quantity by the total number of combinations of tiles: $\dfrac{\text{\# combinations with } xy = 0}{\text{total \# of combinations}} = \dfrac{60}{72} = \dfrac{5}{6}$.

First tile drawn	REMAINING TILES POSSIBLE FOR SECOND TILE								
	0	1	0	2	0	3	0	4	0
0		0	0	0	0	0	0	0	0
1	0		0	2	0	3	0	4	0
0	0	0		0	0	0	0	0	0
2	0	2	0		0	6	0	8	0
0	0	0	0	0		0	0	0	0
3	0	3	0	6	0		0	12	0
0	0	0	0	0	0	0		0	0
4	0	4	0	8	0	12	0		0
0	0	0	0	0	0	0	0	0	

26. (B) (p. 153) *Math: Multiple-Choice/Problem Solving and Advanced Arithmetic/Multi-Step Problem Solving Items.* The item stem states that the baker added 3 cups of flour instead of 2 cups, and then removes $\frac{1}{3}$ of

the mix of dry ingredients to correct her error. Assuming she removes $\frac{1}{3}$ of each ingredient, she removes

$\frac{1}{3}(3 \text{ cups}) = 1$ cup of flour, $\frac{1}{3}(3 \text{ teaspoons}) = 1$ teaspoon of sugar of sugar, and $\frac{1}{3}(2\frac{1}{4} \text{ teaspoons}) =$

$\frac{1}{3}\left(\frac{9}{4}\right) = \frac{3}{4}$ teaspoon of salt. Therefore, to correct her error, she must add back to the dry ingredient mix 1

teaspoon of sugar and $\frac{3}{4}$ teaspoon of salt.

27. (D) (p. 153) *Math: Multiple-Choice/Coordinate Geometry/Graphs of Linear Equations.* First, expand the equation: $3(x+2) = 3x + 6$. So, the correct graph is of the equation $y = 3x + 6$, which has a positive slope of 3 and a y-intercept of 6. Therefore, (D) is the correct graph: a line with positive slope of 3 that crosses the x-axis at $y = 6$. Alternatively, eliminate answer choices. We can eliminate (A) since it is nonlinear. We can also eliminate (B) and (C) since they have negative slopes. Thus, (D) must be the correct answer.

28. (D) (p. 154) *Math: Multiple-Choice/Problem Solving and Advanced Arithmetic/Common Problem Solving Items.* To determine the number of people in the group insurance plan that are expected to visit a doctor,

multiply together the two matrices: $\begin{bmatrix} 125 & 75 & 150 \end{bmatrix} \begin{bmatrix} 0.60 \\ 0.40 \\ 0.90 \end{bmatrix} = (125)(0.6) + (75)(0.4) + (150)(0.9) =$

$75 + 30 + 135 = 240$.

29. (A) (p. 154) *Math: Multiple-Choice/Algebra/Creating, Expressing, and Evaluating Algebraic Equations and Functions.* The family has one child in elementary school, one child in middle school, and one child in high school. The family buys breakfasts, lunches, and milks for each child. Each child eats twice as many lunches as breakfasts. Additionally, each child drinks milk with each meal. Now, create equations representing the total cost for each child. The cost for the child in elementary school is represented by $x + 4.20x + 1.5x = 6.70x$. The cost for the child in middle school is represented by $1.25x + 5.20x + 1.5x = 7.95x$. Finally, the cost for the child in high school is represented by $1.50x + 6.00x + 1.5x = 9.00x$. The total cost for all three children, in dollars: $6.70x + 7.95x + 9.00x = 23.65x$.

30. (D) (p. 154) *Math: Multiple-Choice/Probability/Arithmetic Probability and Geometry/Circles and Rectangles and Squares.* No figure is provided, so sketch one:

In the figure above, the unshaded area represents the favorable outcomes. The probability of the dart landing in the unshaded area is equal to the number of favorable outcomes divided by the number of total outcomes: $\dfrac{\text{area of circle} - \text{area of square}}{\text{area of circle}}$. Since the square has an area of 16, it has a side of 4 and a diagonal of $4\sqrt{2}$ (the diagonal forms the hypotenuse of a 45°-45°-90° triangle, so the diagonal is equal to the length of a side times $\sqrt{2}$). The diagonal of the square is also the diameter of the circle, so the circle has a radius of $2\sqrt{2}$ and an area of $\pi\left(2\sqrt{2}\right)^2 = \pi(8) = 8\pi$. Therefore, the probability is $\dfrac{8\pi - 16}{8\pi} = 1 - \dfrac{2}{\pi}$.

31. **(125)** (p. 156) *Math: Student-Produced Responses/Problem Solving and Advanced Arithmetic/Common Problem Solving Items/Proportions and Direct-Inverse Variation.* Let x denote the number of people to look at in order to find 50 with blue eyes. Recall that $\dfrac{2}{5}$ of the population has blue eyes. The number of people to look at, x, must contain 50 people with blue eyes, where the 50 people with blue eyes constitutes two-fifths of the population. To solve for x, set up a direct proportion and solve for the missing value:
$\dfrac{2}{5} = \dfrac{50}{x} \Rightarrow 2x = 250 \Rightarrow x = 125$.

32. **(63)** (p. 156) *Math: Student-Produced Responses/Statistics/Measures of Center and Spread/Averages.* Use the method for finding the missing element of an average. The smallest possible sum for six different positive integers is $1+2+3+4+5+6 = 21$. The sum of all seven integers is $7 \cdot 12 = 84$. So, with the average of the seven numbers still being 12, the largest the number could be is $84 - 21 = 63$.

33. **(240)** (p. 156) *Math: Student-Produced Responses/Problem Solving and Advanced Arithmetic/Common Problem Solving Items/Percentages.* This is a simple problem with multiple steps. You know that Company *A* has 800 employees, and Company *B* has half that, or 400 employees. Of those at Company *A*, 50 percent are women: $0.50(800) = 400$ women. At Company *B*, 40 percent are women: $0.40(400) = 160$ women. The difference is $400 - 160 = 240$.

34. **(18)** (p. 156) *Math: Student-Produced Responses/Probability/Arithmetic Probability.* The item asks for the minimum number of snakes that need to be removed from a tank in order to guarantee that two of each type of snake had been removed. The key word is *guarantee*. It is possible that the first ten snakes removed from the tank are unmarked and that the next six snakes removed are all striped. The next two snakes would both be spotted snakes, and, at that point, at least two of each type of snake would have been removed. Thus, the minimum number of snakes that need to be removed is $10 + 6 + 2 = 18$.

35. **(20)** (p. 157) *Math: Student-Produced Responses/Geometry/Triangles/Properties of Triangles.* Since $\overline{PQ} \parallel \overline{ST}$, $x = y$ because the alternate interior angles of parallel lines cut by transversal $\overline{QS}$ are equal. Furthermore, the sum of angles in $\triangle PRQ$ is 180°, so $75 + 65 + x + x = 180 \Rightarrow 2x + 140 = 180 \Rightarrow 2x = 40 \Rightarrow x = 20$ and $y = 20$.

36. **(45)** (p. 157) *Math: Student-Produced Responses/Data Interpretation/Tables* and *Problem Solving and Advanced Arithmetic/Multi-Step Problem Solving Items.* Multiply the rate given for each room by the number of rooms to determine the total time spent cleaning each type of room:

ESTIMATED TIME OF CLEANING			
Room	Number x	Time per Room =	Total Time
Bedroom	4	20 minutes	80 minutes
Bathroom	2	30 minutes	60 minutes
Kitchen	1	t minutes	t minutes
Living Area	4	25 minutes	100 minutes
Garage	1	75 minutes	75 minutes
TOTAL			$315 + t$ minutes

The entire house takes 6 hours to clean, or $6 \text{ hours} \times \dfrac{60 \text{ minutes}}{1 \text{ hour}} = 360$ minutes. Therefore,

$t = 360 - 315 = 45$ minutes.

37. (250) (p. 157) *Math: Student-Produced Responses/Algebra/Creating, Expressing, and Evaluating Algebraic Equations and Functions.* The payout for the first policy is $m = \dfrac{\$400,000}{(0.8)(\$500,000)}L - \$2,000 =$

$\dfrac{\$400,000}{\$400,000}(\$150,000) - \$2,000 = \$130,000$. The payout for the second policy is

$n = \dfrac{\$350,000}{(0.8)(\$500,000)}L - \$1,000 = \dfrac{\$350,000}{\$400,000}(\$150,000) - \$1,000 = \$131,250 - \$1,000 = \$130,250$. The

difference is $\$130,250 - \$130,000 = \$250$. The final answer, in dollars, is 250.

38. (5) (p. 157) *Math: Student-Produced Responses/Coordinate Geometry/Slope-Intercept Form of a Linear Equation* and *Slope of a Line* and *The Coordinate System.* To determine the *x*-intercept—the point at which the line crosses the *x*-axis ($y = 0$)—determine the equation for the line, $y = mx + b$, where *m* is the slope and *b* is the *y*-intercept, –10. Since the *y*-intercept is the point where the line crosses the *y*-axis, that is, the value of *y* for *x* = 0, the item stem actually gives two points: $(0, -10)$ and $(3, -4)$. Using these two points,

calculate the slope of the line: $m = \dfrac{\text{rise}}{\text{run}} = \dfrac{\Delta y}{\Delta x} = \dfrac{-4 - (-10)}{3 - 0} = \dfrac{6}{3} = 2$, so $y = 2x - 10$. Finally, to determine the

x-intercept, substitute $y = 0$ and solve for *x*: $0 = 2x - 10 \Rightarrow x = 5$.

Section 5: Essay

Sample Essay Responses and Analyses

Above Average Response

Due to Teddy Roosevelt's pioneering of conservation, the US has known a hundred years of environmental awareness. At the turn of the century, he called Americans to patriotism and responsible management of US natural resources in his speech, "Conservation as a National Duty," given in 1908 to the Conference of Governors. In response to increasing depletion of natural resources, President Roosevelt effectively argues that resources must be both protected and wisely used. Through his use of statistics, appeals to logos and pathos, and vivid imagery, which appeal both to his countrymen's minds and to their hearts, he persuades Americans to prioritize the conservation of natural resources.

Roosevelt reasons that the dramatically higher use of resources in the last century in comparison to the previous six millennia reveals the need for conservation. In order to increase the impact of this sharp contrast, he has his audience imagine the early life on the Nile and Euphrates, which was slow in progress, in juxtaposition to the hum of discovery and innovation in the 1800s. He notes that coal, water, and wood were used primitively until our discovery of their power, which resulted in a "hundred-fold" increase. Roosevelt includes this quantity, and several others ("more space...covered...than during the preceding six thousand years," "the mere increase...during 1907 over 1906 exceeded the total consumption in 1876," etc.) to awe the audience and compel them to agree that the large increase is tangible and to earn their support for an urgent response to it. This method is effective because the numbers offer solid factual evidence for Roosevelt's argument and combat counter-arguments that suggest that he is exaggerating about the gravity of the issue. He drives home the point with an ominous observation: "rapid development" of resources will result in "rapid destruction."

Roosevelt appeals to both pathos (emotion) and logos (logic) to further increase the impact of his message. He connects the value of the natural resources to the continuation of the human population, saying that foresight will result in the "assurance of well-being for himself and his children." This is meant to invest the audience in the cause personally; it is effective because he picks up on a broad human desire and even instinct (protection of future generations) in order to earn the support of a huge portion of the audience for contributing to the cause at least for the sake of their children. Roosevelt also appeals to logos by referring to one of our Constitution's original purposes, which was to help unite the people to wisely use our national resources. Roosevelt observes that we are now seeing "enormous consumption" of resources which would result in the "threat of imminent exhaustion" of them due to "reckless and wasteful use," and he urges us to pursue the kind of wise conservation promoted in the document at the foundation of our nation once again. In citing the Constitution, he ties the need for conservation to our nation's very identity, making the audience realize that it is indeed against our very principles as a people to ignore the issue. This point is effective because it presents abuse of resources as irrational and unpatriotic to those in the audience invested in their national identity.

Through the use of vivid imagery, Roosevelt makes a strong case for conservation using an emphatic description of a world minus its resources. He has us imagine sobering sensory details such as depleted soils that are "washed into the streams," eliminated forests, and polluted rivers, details meant to make us prematurely nostalgic for a lush environment that we are urgently at risk for losing. These details are effective because they make us picture and appreciate those things that we already have and compel us to imagine losing them, fostering a sense of attachment to and gratitude for these precious natural resources. Roosevelt also creates an allegorical character whom he calls the "prudent man." His man, a metaphor of wisdom, learns to exercise "foresight in conserving and wisely using" the earthly resources. This imagery of the man conveys the importance and tangibility of conservation by showing that we as individuals each have the incentive (protecting ourselves and our children) and potential (through exercising foresight) to contribute to the cause.

Having used dramatic statistics, appeals to pathos and logos, and vivid imagery, Roosevelt clinches the deal at the conclusion of his speech when he specifically asks the people to prioritize the conservation of natural resources. Because he has shown the imminence of the approaching exhaustion of non-renewable resources such as coal, oil, gas, and metals, and because he has induced aversion to this exhaustion, Roosevelt can appeal to the nation to "guard its own future in the essential matter of natural resources."

Analysis of Above Average Response

This writer's use of textual evidence in both paraphrasing and direct quotation demonstrates a high level of comprehension and understanding of the central themes. The writer provides three relevant aspects and supports claims with logical and persuasive elements. The writer's development of several rhetorical devices, such as statistics, pathos, logos, and imagery, reveals an intuitive grasp of the author's intention and impact. The response is well-organized, logically developed, and free of distracting errors. The writer has mastered proper grammatical structure and usage, including spelling, punctuation, and word choices that strengthen the thesis.

Below Average Response

Roosevelt gives a very persuasive speech on the topic of conservation in America. He uses several points to make his argument about conservation. Roosevelt uses American history, facts, and patriotism to make his argument more persuasive.

One of the things that Roosevelt uses in his speech is logic. He talks about American history and how natural resources help America become great. I think that that his points about how far Americans have come since the early days shows how essentel natural resources are. America's growth is dependent on its natural resources.

Roosevelt also discusses facts in his speech. He talks about how conservation is important because Americans need to make sure that there are natural resources for the next generations. I believe that helped his speech be more persuasive because it appeals to people's emotions because everyone wants the best for their kids. Roosevelt talks about a man who uses foresight to take care of his children and their future, I think that he means that by conserving natural resources, America will be like that man.

Another point Roosevelt uses to make his argument about conservation is American patriotism. I think that this is Roosevelt's strongest point in his speech. He uses American history to remind people about how important natural resources were to the Founding Fathers. Roosevelt also says that it is the duty of every American citizen to strive to be better and to conserve natural resources for America's future.

I think that Roosevelt's speech is very convincing and well done. He uses logical reasoning, facts, and American history to make his point about the importance of conservation to America's present and future success. This makes his speech more persuasive and likeable.

Analysis of Below Average Response

This writer demonstrates some understanding of the source text. This response illustrates that the writer understands Roosevelt's argument for the importance of conserving America's natural resources. The writer conveys understanding of the text and the details that contribute to the persuasiveness of Roosevelt's argument. However, the writer misspells words and misuses them, which distracts from the response itself. The writer starts to explain Roosevelt's argument but is not cohesive in his/her explanation. The writer also does not support his/her argument with evidence from the text source.

PRACTICE TEST III

Answer Key

DIRECTIONS: For items answered <u>correctly</u>, circle the answer, then check any corresponding shaded box(es). Total the number of circled answers to determine the raw score for the test section. Total the number of checkmarks for each of the subscores and cross-test scores to determine each raw subscore and raw cross-test score.

Section 1: Reading (p. 163)

Item	Subscores WC	CE	Cross-Test Scores S	H/S
1. B				
2. D		■		
3. B	■			
4. A	■	■		
5. A				
6. B				
7. B				
8. C				
9. B				
10. B				
11. A	■		■	
12. B			■	
13. A			■	
14. C			■	
15. C	■		■	
16. B			■	■
17. A			■	■
18. D			■	■

Item	Subscores WC	CE	Cross-Test Scores S	H/S
19. D			■	
20. A		■	■	
21. C		■	■	
22. B				■
23. C				■
24. A				■
25. C				■
26. D	■			■
27. B				■
28. C		■	■	
29. B		■		
30. A	■			
31. B		■		
32. D		■		
33. A			■	
34. A			■	
35. D			■	
36. B			■	

Item	Subscores WC	CE	Cross-Test Scores S	H/S
37. C		■	■	
38. C			■	
39. A			■	
40. B		■	■	
41. A			■	
42. A			■	
43. A			■	
44. B		■	■	
45. A			■	
46. D			■	
47. A			■	
48. A			■	
49. D	■		■	
50. B			■	
51. B			■	■
52. A		■		■

Raw Score: _____ /52

Section 2: Writing and Language (p. 179)

#	Answer	Subscores WC	CE	Cross-Test Scores S	H/S
1.	C				
2.	B	■			
3.	B				
4.	D				
5.	B				
6.	D				
7.	A				
8.	D	■			
9.	B		■		
10.	C				
11.	B		■		
12.	B				
13.	D	■			
14.	A				
15.	D				

#	Answer	Subscores WC	CE	Cross-Test Scores S	H/S
16.	A				
17.	B		■		
18.	B				
19.	D				
20.	D	■			
21.	A				
22.	D		■		
23.	A				
24.	D		■	■	
25.	C				
26.	C				
27.	C	■		■	
28.	B		■	■	
29.	A			■	
30.	A			■	

#	Answer	Subscores WC	CE	Cross-Test Scores S	H/S
31.	D	■		■	
32.	D				
33.	A				■
34.	D	■			■
35.	D				
36.	C	■			■
37.	B				
38.	C				
39.	A				
40.	A				
41.	C				■
42.	A				
43.	A		■		■
44.	D	■	■		■

Raw Score: _____/44

Evidence-Based Reading and Writing Subscores

Words in Context (WC): _____/18   Command of Evidence (CE): _____/18

Section 3: Math—No Calculator (p. 193)

#	Answer	Cross-Test Scores S	H/S
1.	C		
2.	C		
3.	B		
4.	D		
5.	A		
6.	A		
7.	B	■	

#	Answer	Cross-Test Scores S	H/S
8.	A		
9.	D	■	
10.	C	■	
11.	B	■	
12.	C		
13.	D		
14.	D		

#	Answer	Cross-Test Scores S	H/S
15.	D		
16.	0		
17.	9/10, 0.9		
18.	90		
19.	10		
20.	26		

Section 4: Math—Calculator (p. 199)

		Cross-Test Scores				Cross-Test Scores				Cross-Test Scores	
		S	H/S			S	H/S			S	H/S
1.	B			14.	B			27.	B		
2.	A			15.	B		■	28.	A	■	
3.	C		■	16.	C			29.	B		■
4.	D			17.	B	■		30.	A		
5.	A			18.	A	■		31.	35		
6.	C			19.	C			32.	1		
7.	C			20.	A		■	33.	4		■
8.	C			21.	C		■	34.	9		
9.	B			22.	A			35.	9		
10.	D	■		23.	C			36.	1		
11.	C			24.	B			37.	7		
12.	A			25.	B			38.	10		
13.	D			26.	A						

Math Raw Score (total of calculator and no-calculator sections): _____ /58

Cross-Test Scores (All four test sections)

Science (S): _____ /35   History/Social Studies (H/S): _____ /35

Explanations

Section 1: Reading

1. **(B)** (p. 164) *Reading/Literary Fiction/Implied Idea.* You are asked to form a conclusion about Master Horner's demeanor based on the information given. In the first part of the first paragraph, the author describes the physical appearance of Master Horner; in the second part (signaled by "his address corresponded very well with his appearance . . ."), the author describes his demeanor: prim and never smiling. So, (B) is the correct answer choice.

2. **(D)** (p. 164) *Reading/Literary Fiction/Textual Evidence.* How do you know that Master Horner was severe and stern? He has a prim mouth and never smiles. So, (D) is the correct answer choice.

3. **(B)** (p. 164) *Reading/Literary Fiction/Vocabulary.* "Address" can mean any of the first three choices (though not the fourth), so context is critical in this case; do not confuse "address" with "dress" (style of clothing), which sounds like the term in question and is related to the idea of physical appearance. The author is sketching a picture of Master Horner who presents a physical appearance that is stern and dour. Since his "address" is consistent with this physical appearance, the use of the word cannot point to either (A) or (C); it must, therefore, refer to Master Horner's manner of speaking, (B).

4. **(A)** (p. 164) *Reading/Literary Fiction/Implied Idea.* This question asks about rhetorical technique. The sad faces of the students and their angry gestures directed toward Master Horner are in no sense positive benefits; instead, they represent negative feelings. So, the author chooses the word "rewards" for a specific reason: to express irony, (A).

5. (A) (p. 164) *Reading/Literary Fiction/Development.* This is a Command of Evidence question that asks about the structure of the author's reasoning. In the third paragraph, the author states that Horner was not inherently cruel; the author acknowledges, though, that there are other teachers who might indeed be cruel and goes on to describe how certain college preparatory teachers use corporal punishment. The author theorizes about such teachers in order to set up a contrast between their particularly cruel demeanor and that of Master Horner. So, (A) is the correct answer choice.

6. (B) (p. 164) *Reading/Literary Fiction/Implied Idea.* The phrase "infant giant" is an oxymoron, or a phrase whose terms possess a contradictory relationship. Of the four answer choices, only (B) expresses such a relationship: Joshua is a physically intimidating person, but he is intellectually and emotionally underdeveloped.

7. (B) (p. 165) *Reading/Literary Fiction/Implied Idea.* The author explains that Master Horner returned the following autumn "all the broader-chested and stouter-armed after having spent the summer performing "labors in [his father's] harvest-field." Physical strength, according to the author, was for a teacher equally if not more important a characteristic than was intelligence. Since Master Horner lacked such strength during the first term, Joshua was able to intimidate him. In the second term, however, Joshua no longer enjoyed this physical advantage. So, (B) is the correct choice.

8. (C) (p. 165) *Reading/Literary Fiction/Voice.* This question asks about the author's attitude toward Master Horner's faults. We've already noted that the author believes that Horner was not an evil person despite his tendency to be overly-authoritarian. The author suggests that Horner was "determined to make his empire good" (line 59) and that one must "make all due allowance" (line 70) for Horner's not recognizing in his first term the need for physical strength. So, (C), "understanding," is the best answer choice.

9. (B) (p. 165) *Reading/Literary Fiction/Explicit Detail.* According to the author, a teacher must first show physical strength, as mental agility will be taken for granted. And in lines 63–64, the author states specifically that the uneducated are impressed by physical strength.

10. (B) (p. 165) *Reading/Literary Fiction/Application.* This is an Application question that asks you to apply what you know about the overall development of the passage in order to predict how it might be further developed. Throughout the passage, the author describes Master Horner's shortcomings and subsequent development as a teacher. In the first term, Horner is physically intimidated by Joshua. At the start of the second term, Horner returns to school physically stronger after spending the summer working on his father's farm, and Joshua no longer poses a threat. So, the author has set the stage for a discussion of Horner's continued development, both as an individual and as a teacher. Therefore, (B) is the correct answer choice.

11. (A) (p. 168) *Reading/Natural Sciences/Implied Idea.* One of the clues you need is provided in the same sentence: "again breed," (line 71). Notice also the root word "pause" in "diapause." So, you can infer that "reproductive diapause" refers to a suspension of breeding (reproductive activity), (A).

12. (B) (p. 168) *Reading/Natural Sciences/Explicit Detail.* This question asks you to synthesize details from both passages. Both passages state that milkweeds are the only food that caterpillars eat. So, (B) is the correct answer choice. (A) is wrong because the overwintering forests in California are at low altitudes. (C) is wrong because both authors specifically mention that the monarchs are reproductively inactive in the winter. And (D) is a point made by Passage 1 only in reference to the eastern monarchs.

13. (A) (p. 168) *Reading/Natural Sciences/Development.* Both passages discuss monarch butterflies, but Passage 1 discusses the eastern monarch while Passage 2 discusses the western monarch. So, (A) is the correct answer choice. (B) is an interesting choice because the eastern monarch is apparently in greater danger than the western monarch, but the idea of endangerment is not the fundamental organizing principle of either passage. The authors begin with a discussion of what makes the eastern monarchs "eastern" (they live, migrate, and overwinter east of the Rockies) and the western monarch "western" (they live, migrate, and overwinter west of the Rockies). Threats to population are treated as consequences of where the insects live. (C) is wrong because the western subspecies is also migrational, even if the migrations are less spectacular than those of the eastern subspecies. And (D) is wrong because both the eastern and the western monarchs are subspecies of the monarch species.

14. **(C)** (p. 168) *Reading/Natural Sciences/Explicit Detail.* Just as with item #12, this question asks you to synthesize details from both passages. In this case, both passages make the point that the adult monarchs forage for nectar, (C). As for (A), both authors note that caterpillars, not adult monarchs, feed on milkweeds. As for (B), while nectar is converted into lipids that the monarchs metabolize ("[eastern] monarchs live off of their lipid reserves and do not feed again until February" and "[western] [m]onarchs metabolize these lipid reserves as an energy source for winter survival"), the monarchs do not *feed on* the lipids. As for (D), though both subspecies overwinter in forests and the author of Passage 1 mentions that "[e]ggs are laid on milkweed leaves," neither author states that tree leaves are a food source.

15. **(C)** (p. 168) *Reading/Natural Sciences/Implied Idea.* This is a Word-in-Context item. As you may already know, "complete" means "total" and "metamorphosis" means "change." In lines 22–24, the author of Passage 1 refers to the monarch butterflies' complete metamorphosis and then refers to how the "[e]ggs are laid on milkweed leaves." So, you can infer that "complete metamorphosis" refers to the process of change from an egg to an adult (butterfly), (C).

16. **(B)** (p. 168) *Reading/Natural Sciences/Explicit Detail.* In the last paragraph, the author of Passage 2 says that "drought conditions associated with ongoing climate change are the most likely cause of decreases in monarch population size" and that these conditions "reduced the diversity of milkweed and monarch nectar sources." So, (B) is the correct answer choice.

17. **(A)** (p. 168) *Reading/Natural Sciences/Voice.* The author of Passage 1 states that the decline of the eastern monarch population is due to loss of milkweed as a result of things like herbicides, pesticides, mowing, and deforestation, which are all practices that can be regulated and controlled. Thus, the first author seems to think that there is hope for the eastern monarchs (lines 53–55). The author of Passage 2, on the other hand, states that the decline of the western monarch population is due to long-term climate change and "that the population decline is likely to continue." So, (A) is the correct answer choice.

18. **(D)** (p. 169) *Reading/Natural Sciences/Explicit Detail.* The author says that many of the overwintering sites are at low elevations near the Pacific Ocean or San Francisco Bay "(where these bodies of water moderate temperatures)," (D).

19. **(D)** (p. 169) *Reading/Natural Sciences/Explicit Detail.* The author of Passage 1 identifies the most important cause of the decline of the eastern monarch population as agricultural practices that have resulted in the loss of milkweed, a crucial food in the monarch life-cycle. So the most important first step to correcting this problem would be to reverse the trend so that more milkweed would be available.

20. **(A)** (p. 169) *Reading/Natural Sciences/Data Presentations.* Figure 1 provides data about the total forest area (in hectacres) used by the eastern population of monarchs during overwinter. In order for the figure to support the magnitude of the decline in the eastern population of monarchs, though, you can infer that the number of butterflies per hectacre would be a necessary assumption. (A) is the only answer choice that provides this information: about 50 million butterflies per hectacre (lines 10–11).

21. **(C)** (p. 169) *Reading/Natural Sciences/Data Presentations.* The data provided in Figure 2 support each of the quantified claims made in the fourth paragraph. Of the four answer choices, only (B) and (C) refer to lines in the fourth paragraph. (C), however, is the only answer choice that refers to one of the aforementioned quantified claims.

22. **(B)** (p. 171) *Reading/Social Studies/Main Idea.* In the first paragraph, the author explains what originalism is and how this legal theory informed the decision-making practices of Justice Scalia, (B). As for (A), while the first paragraph mentions that Justice Scalia had differences with some of the Supreme Court's constitutional rulings, that is not the author's primary concern. And as for (C) and (D), while these things are touched on in the first paragraph, neither is the author's primary concern.

23. **(C)** (p. 171) *Reading/Social Studies/Application.* This item describes a constitutional provision from 1868 that is not specifically mentioned in the passage and asks you to apply this idea in the current context, based on what is explicitly said about Scalia, in order to draw a conclusion. The first paragraph describes how Scalia was influenced by originalism, that is, the practice of deciding the meaning of legal language based on its text as it was understood when it was adopted. So, Scalia would have interpreted the provision according to its meaning when it took effect in 1868, (C).

24. **(A)** (p. 171) *Reading/Social Studies/Textual Evidence.* This question asks you to determine the statement that supports the correct answer to the preceding question. That Scalia would have interpreted the provision according to its meaning when it took effect in 1868 is representative of the fact that he advocated originalism, a term that is defined at the very beginning of the passage in lines 2–5. So, (A) is the correct answer choice.

25. **(C)** (p. 171) *Reading/Social Studies/Development.* This question asks about the logical role played by the author's use in the first paragraph of the 2008 Supreme Court decision on handguns. In that paragraph, the author defines the practice of originalism and explains why Scalia was attracted to the doctrine. Then the author writes that "Scalia's originalism was perhaps most famously displayed in the Court's 2008 decision striking down the . . . ban on handguns," which indicates that the decision was a good example of Scalia's use of originalism, (C).

26. **(D)** (p. 171) *Reading/Social Studies/Implied Idea.* This is an unusual vocabulary question in that it tests a purely contextual understanding of the word "friends," which in this case does not have its usual meaning or any related connotation. Instead, Justice Scalia draws an analogy between "judges [who] could select the materials that support their preferred policy positions" and "a person 'walking into a . . . party and looking over the heads of the guests to pick out [his] friends'." So, (D) is the correct answer choice.

27. **(B)** (p. 172) *Reading/Social Studies/Implied Idea.* The author makes it fairly clear that Justice Scalia's thinking was "influential," (B), saying that "Scalia shaped the manner in which his colleagues . . . approach the interpretation of a legal text" (lines 87–89). Notice also that each of the other answer choices contradicts the idea that Scalia's thinking was influential, and this is a good indication that "influential" is the correct answer.

28. **(C)** (p. 172) *Reading/Social Studies/Textual Evidence.* To support the contention that "Scalia shaped the manner in which his colleagues . . . approach the interpretation of a legal text," a connection must be seen between two factors cited by the author. Scalia's influence on approach to interpretation deals with a "focus on the ordinary meaning of words and his general skepticism about the value of historical context" (89–91). Knowing this, you can infer that "the greater use of dictionaries and lesser reliance on legislative history" (69–70) provides strong support for Scalia's influence. So, (C) is the correct answer choice.

29. **(B)** (p. 172) *Reading/Social Studies/Explicit Detail.* In the fourth paragraph, the author explains that Justice Scalia was "[u]nlike some other supporters of textualism . . . even object[ing] to the use of legislative history materials to confirm text-based interpretations of statutes," (B).

30. **(A)** (p. 172) *Reading/Social Studies/Vocabulary.* The word "jurisprudence" appears in the first sentence of the last paragraph. The sentence is not really a summary of the whole passage, but it does refer, at least indirectly, to the entire development up to that point. So we can infer that "jurisprudence" refers to the totality of Justice Scalia's thinking on the issues discussed, or his philosophy of the law, (A).

31. **(B)** (p. 172) *Reading/Social Studies/Voice.* The author does make a small criticism of Justice Scalia in the last paragraph, mentioning that he may not have lived up to his claim about judicial restraint as did his

colleagues. Overall, however, the author is very "respectful," (B), treating all of Justice Scalia's theories and practices as worthy of discussion and neutrally drawing distinctions between them and those of other justices.

32. **(D) (p. 172)** ***Reading/Social Studies/Data Presentations.*** The graph shows how Justice Scalia's decisions measure up as a Republican (100%, so very committed), as a conservative (82%, which is considerably more than the Court as a whole), and as a judicial activist (75%, which is equal to the Court as a whole). The third measure immediately catches our attention because Justice Scalia supposedly advocates judicial restraint and opposes judicial activism. One would expect this measure, therefore, to be much less than 75% and certainly much less than that of the rest of the Court. These equal measurements show that Justice Scalia was just as much a judicial activist as was anyone else on the Court. So, the third bar of the graph supports the statement that "[q]uestions have been raised about the extent to which Justice Scalia" followed through on his position when compared to his colleagues, (D).

33. **(A) (p. 174)** ***Reading/Natural Sciences/Vocabulary.*** In the first half of the passage, the author lays out the claims made by the proponents of raw milk; in the second half of the passage, the author debunks those claims. So, when referring to "the supposed nutritional and health benefits of raw milk," the author uses the word "supposed" to mean "assumed but not proved." So, (A), "speculative," is the correct answer choice.

34. **(A) (p. 174)** ***Reading/Natural Sciences/Voice.*** This is a Voice question. Notice that the answer choices reflect a continuum of attitudes, with (D) describing the most favorable view and (A) describing the least favorable view. It's hard to imagine a more negative attitude than that expressed by the author. In the first paragraph, the author calls the proponents of raw milk "naive" and "uncritical" and goes on to say that they have "misconceptions about [its] benefits." In the fourth paragraph, the author simply dismisses the claims, saying that they do not "withstand scientific scrutiny." So, (A) must be the correct answer choice.

35. **(D) (p. 174)** ***Reading/Natural Sciences/Explicit Detail.*** In the second paragraph, the author talks about pasteurization, saying that the process is performed "to kill harmful bacteria" and that proponents of raw milk claim that it is performed "simply to prolong shelf life." So, (D) is the correct answer choice.

36. **(B) (p. 174)** ***Reading/Natural Sciences/Main Idea.*** As already discussed in the explanation for item #33, the second half of the passage is where the author debunks the claims made by proponents of raw milk. Since the author debunks the claims and also makes the important point that pasteurization prevents food-borne illnesses, a summary of the second half of the passage would best be characterized as critical of raw milk's proponents and supportive of pasteurization. Of the four answer choices provided, only (B) satisfies these conditions: it "is not nutritionally superior to pasteurized milk and poses health risks that can be avoided by pasteurization." (A) is a restatement of the first part of the passage from the point of view of the "back to nature" advocates. (C) provides only half of the correct answer, promoting the use of pasteurization but failing to criticize the raw milk proponents. Finally, (D) is much too broad as the passage focuses on raw milk, not on the "back to nature" movement.

37. **(C) (p. 174)** ***Reading/Natural Sciences/Development.*** One of the challenges to understanding the passage is matching the claims of the proponents of raw milk that are mentioned in the first half of the passage to the points made by the author in the second half of the passage. In the second paragraph, the author says that those who drink raw milk claim that the altered fat content that comes with pasteurization makes it difficult to absorb the vitamins and minerals in milk. In the fifth paragraph (lines 45–53), however, the author provides evidence that "[p]asteurized milk has essentially the same fat composition" as does raw milk, thereby refuting the proponents' claim. So, (C) is the correct answer choice.

38. **(C) (p. 174)** ***Reading/Natural Sciences/Vocabulary.*** The image that the author hopes to create is one where dairy cows reside in a clean and natural setting that is free from such sources of bacteria as manure and contaminated equipment. So, "pristine" means "pure," (C).

39. **(A) (p. 174)** ***Reading/Natural Sciences/Implied Idea.*** The author mentions the allergenicity of milk in the sixth paragraph. The key word used is "therefore." The author says that "the protein quality of pasteurized milk is not different from that of raw milk" and that "therefore" it is no surprise that "pasteurization does not change the allergenicity of milk." From this, we can infer that allergic reactions are caused by milk proteins, (A).

40. (B) (p. 174) *Reading/Natural Sciences/Development.* The author mentions the low concentration of immunoglobulins in cow's milk to make the point that these concentration levels cannot possibly affect the human immune system as expressed in lines 61–64, (B).

41. (A) (p. 175) *Reading/Natural Sciences/Explicit Detail.* Microorganisms in raw milk have a bovine origin. In lines 66–68, the author specifically states that the microorganisms in raw milk are not helpful to humans because in order for them to be probiotic, they must have a human origin, (A).

42. (A) (p. 175) *Reading/Natural Sciences/Main Idea.* The author uses the final paragraph to argue that the idea of cows residing in a pristine, bacteria-free environment is one of a manipulative advertising campaign— one that hides the fact that the cows' environment is outdoors in the dirt and involves animal waste, germs, and other unsanitary conditions that make raw milk potentially dangerous. So, (A) is the correct answer choice.

43. (A) (p. 177) *Reading/Social Studies/Implied Idea.* In the third paragraph, the author notes that the original membership was chosen by the commander and included only officers junior in rank and status to the captain of the *Maine*. The author implies that this was done for the very reason that it would have been nearly impossible for those officers to accuse their superior of negligence. So, (A) is the correct answer choice.

44. (B) (p. 177) *Reading/Social Studies/Textual Evidence.* As already mentioned in the previous explanation, the discussion of who was chosen to be on the board is in the third paragraph. In lines 34–39, the author notes that the original board consisted of junior officers, a membership that would have made it impossible for the board to function effectively, (B).

45. (A) (p. 177) *Reading/Social Studies/Implied Idea.* In the second paragraph, the author notes that the conclusions of the Spanish board were not reported by the American press. The first and last paragraphs make it clear that the American press advocated the theory that the sinking was caused by an enemy mine. It is reasonable to infer, then, that the press was not the least bit interested in evidence that contradicted its preferred theory. So, (A) is the correct answer choice.

46. (D) (p. 177) *Reading/Social Studies/Main Idea.* The sixth paragraph discusses the theory of the Navy's Chief Engineer, presumably someone of considerable experience with the needed expertise to make an informed judgment. The Chief Engineer's theory was "that the cause of the disaster was a magazine explosion" brought on by the spontaneous combustion of coal in the coal bunker. So, the Chief Engineer offered an alternative to enemy mine theory, (D).

47. (A) (p. 177) *Reading/Social Studies/Development.* As already discussed in the previous explanation, the Chief Engineer's theory was "that the cause of the disaster was a magazine explosion" brought on by the spontaneous combustion of coal in the coal bunker. The fact that bituminous coal, which was the type burned by the *Maine*, was particularly likely to spontaneously combust makes this theory even more probable. So, (A) is the correct answer choice.

48. (A) (p. 177) *Reading/Social Studies/Voice.* In the sixth paragraph, the author makes clear his or her support for the Chief Engineer's theory: "fires from coal bunkers were frequent occurrences" and "the *Maine* took on bituminous coal, which was particularly subject to spontaneous combustion." And since the American rallying cry during the Spanish-American War was "Remember the *Maine*! To Hell with Spain!", it is safe to say that the author believes that war to have been ill-advised and therefore unwarranted, (A).

49. **(D)** (p. 177) *Reading/Social Studies/Vocabulary.* The passage states that "magazines" were where ammunition was stored, so it is a fairly easy step to the conclusion that magazines are storage areas, (D).

50. **(B)** (p. 177) *Reading/Social Studies/Vocabulary.* The word "yellow" in line 78 is immediately followed by terms that describe its meaning in this context: "exaggerating," "distorting," and "fabricating." (B), "sensational," best captures this meaning.

51. **(B)** (p. 177) *Reading/Social Studies/Implied Idea.* The author does not explicitly say why the Spanish government called for a joint inquiry, but the first sentence of the second paragraph does say that "the Spanish government feared [the] possibility [of a war with the United States] and immediately proposed a joint US-Spanish investigation." So, we can infer that the joint inquiry came as a result of the Spanish government's fear of going to war with the United States, (B).

52. **(A)** (p. 178) *Reading/Social Studies/Textual Evidence.* Again, as already discussed in the previous explanation, the first sentence of the second paragraph explains that the Spanish government proposed the joint inquiry because it feared that the incident on the *Maine* would lead to war with the United States. This sentence consists of lines 12–14, so (A) is the correct answer choice.

Section 2: Writing and Language

1. **(C)** (p. 180) *Writing and Language/Standard English Conventions/Grammar and Usage/Pronoun Usage.* This item asks about correct pronoun usage. Several factors are in play here. First, when referring to people, as opposed to animals or objects, the proper pronouns to use are "who" and "whom." Second, the choice between those two depends on the role the pronoun takes in the sentences. "Whom" is an objective case pronoun and so should be used for functions such as direct and indirect objects and objects of prepositions. "Who" is the nominative case of the pronoun to be used for subjects. In this case, the "whom" takes the role of direct object: he calls *whom*.

2. **(B)** (p. 180) *Writing and Language/Expression of Ideas/Style/Conciseness.* This question asks about word choice. The original is needlessly wordy. A "new" acquaintance is necessarily someone "just met," so there is no need for both of those elements.

3. **(B)** (p. 180) *Writing and Language/Standard English Conventions/Punctuation/Commas.* This item is a straightforward test of the rules for using commas. Here you have a series: story, watercolors, and insights. While the comma following the penultimate element of a series is considered optional, all other elements must be marked with commas. So there is no room here for debate; a comma must follow "story" since it is the first element in a series.

4. **(D)** (p. 180) *Writing and Language/Expression of Ideas/Strategy/Appropriate Supporting Material.* This is a Command of Evidence question. The author provides the reader with several elements of the plot from *The Little Prince*. Which of them most strongly suggests that the story is fiction? The notion that a small boy could have a home on an asteroid and travel to Earth clearly marks the story as fantasy.

5. **(B)** (p. 180) *Writing and Language/Expression of Ideas/Strategy/Appropriate Supporting Material.* This is an Expression of Ideas question that asks you to provide an introduction to the second paragraph. Paragraph 2 provides biographical details about multiple career choices Saint-Exupéry tried and failed in until he joined the army. (B) is the best summary of this paragraph. The other choices are by comparison weak, as Saint-Exupéry really did not seem to have any life-long plans or definite ambitions.

6. **(D)** (p. 180) *Writing and Language/Standard English Conventions/Sentence Structure/Faulty Parallelism.* The original sentence suffers from a lack of parallelism. The three elements, "transferred, trained, and he was assigned," should all be in the past tense: transferred, trained, and assigned.

7. **(A)** (p. 181) *Writing and Language/Standard English Conventions/No Change.* How can these two sentences be combined? (B) and (D) involve the comma splice—jamming together two independent clauses separated only by a comma. And (C) creates a run-on sentence. So the best course is to leave the original unchanged.

8. **(D)** (p. 181) *Writing and Language/Expression of Ideas/Style/Conciseness.* The original version of the underlined part is needlessly repetitive. "Dehydration" is by definition a condition that results from a lack of water. So you do not need both of those elements.

9. **(B)** (p. 181) *Writing and Language/Expression of Ideas/Strategy/Appropriate Supporting Material.* If the sentence is deleted, what will be lost? An explanation of how Saint-Exupéry was rescued from the desert.

10. **(C)** (p. 182) *Writing and Language/Standard English Conventions/Grammar and Usage/Misplaced Modifiers.* The original sentence is afflicted with the infamous dangling modifier. The underlined part of the sentence is an adjective phrase anchored by "rejected," the past participle of "to reject." And an adjective phrase needs a noun to modify. So a reader will naturally look for the first important noun to follow, and that is "Eisenhower." The sentence seems to say that Eisenhower was rejected for combat duty. What the sentence means to say, however, is that Saint-Exupéry was rejected, and (C) makes this clear by replacing the adjectival phrase with a complete sentence that is properly joined to the second independent clause, which begins with "General Eisenhower."

11. **(B)** (p. 182) *Writing and Language/Expression of Ideas/Strategy/Main Idea.* This is a Command of Evidence question. The author tells of several clues that support the conclusion that the debris discovered came from the plane flown by Saint-Exupéry: P-38, unarmed ID bracelet. The author is careful, however, to use phrases like "might" and not to say, for example, that the bracelet must have belonged to Saint-Exupéry. So the strongest conclusion supported by this information is that the debris was likely from Saint-Exupéry's plane, but the connection is by no means certain.

12. **(B)** (p. 183) *Writing and Language/Standard English Conventions/Punctuation/Commas.* This item asks about comma usage. The tendency is for students to use commas where they are not needed and actually disrupt the structure of the sentence. That is the case here. You have a gratuitous comma that separates the direct object ("portion") from the verb ("retains"). There is no reason for the comma, and its presence seems to orphan the rest of the sentence. And as a general rule, if you can't think of an affirmative reason to insert a comma, don't use one. In other words, "When in doubt, leave it out."

13. **(D)** (p. 183) *Writing and Language/Expression of Ideas/Style/Conciseness.* This is a Words in Context question. The original is unnecessarily wordy. "Anticipate" and "expect" have pretty much the same meaning, so you should use one or the other but not both.

14. **(A)** (p. 183) *Writing and Language/Standard English Conventions/No Change.* This item focuses on the use of the apostrophe. Here, the sentence requires the third person singular possessive pronoun "its," so the original is correct. As for the other choices, "its'" is not an English spelling, and "it's" and "they're" are the contraction of "it is" and "they are," respectively, neither of which make sense in the sentence.

15. **(D)** (p. 183) *Writing and Language/Standard English Conventions/Sentence Structure/Faulty Parallelism.* The original suffers from a lack of parallelism. There is a sequence of three elements to the process: locates, dispatches, and confirms. But as written, the original uses a subject and verb for the third element rather than just a verb. (D) corrects the error.

16. **(A)** (p. 183) *Writing and Language/Expression of Ideas/Organization/Paragraph-Level Structure.* This item asks about the logical organization of paragraph 2. The paragraph is pretty much organized in a chronological fashion: The company is in business; the client downloads the app; the client requests a ride; the company dispatches the car; the company notifies the client; the client rides; the ride is billed to the client. And the driver gets paid.

17. **(B)** (p. 183) *Writing and Language/Expression of Ideas/Strategy/Main Idea.* This is a Command of Evidence question. The author spends a paragraph discussing the operation of Uber. Why? In order to give the reader a concrete example of the workings of a gig economy company. The author wants to make the abstract discussion in paragraph 1 more understandable by using a specific case.

18. **(B)** (p. 184) *Writing and Language/Standard English Conventions/Sentence Structure/Fragments.* The second underlined element is not a complete sentence because it lacks a main verb. "Is being made" is a participle form, not a conjugated verb. There are several ways to eliminate the problem. You might turn the participle into a main verb and let the sentence stand on its own:

... employees. This arrangement is usually made ....

But that option is not available. You might also turn the fragment into an independent clause and join it to the preceding sentence. (C) tries this but fails. The result is a comma splice (no conjunction). (D) uses an acceptable procedure for joining two independent clauses, but the second part is not an independent clause. You still have the "being" form of the verb.

19. **(D)** (p. 184) *Writing and Language/Standard English Conventions/Grammar and Usage/Pronoun Usage.* Here you have a Conventions of Usage problem that focuses on agreement. The problem with the original is that "its" refers to "companies," but "its" is singular while "companies" is plural. The "its" should be "their." Then, since each of the companies has a brand, you need the plural "brands."

20. **(D)** (p. 184) *Writing and Language/Expression of Ideas/Style/Tone.* This is a Words in Context item that tests tone and precision of the words used. The problem with the original is that "back in the day" is informal usage. The phrase is supposed to mean "old" or "traditional," so "traditional" is a good alternative. The other two choices don't have the same precision.

21. **(A)** (p. 184) *Writing and Language/Expression of Ideas/No Change.* The author develops the final paragraph by pointing out first some disadvantages to gig work and then noting that gig work offers the big advantage of flexibility. There is a contrast here, and the original "on the other hand" is the best choice available to signal that contrast.

22. **(D)** (p. 184) *Writing and Language/Expression of Ideas/Organization/Paragraph-Level Structure.* The sentence that the author wishes to add discusses a disadvantage to being a gig worker; namely, that gig workers don't usually receive benefits. The third sentence of the final paragraph is the first place the author mentions disadvantages to being a gig worker—not under the protection of employment laws and not receiving benefits. The key word "also" in the added sentence is a verbal clue that this sentence is a continuation of a previous discussion, and that is the discussion mentioned in sentence 3. So the best place for the added sentence would be after sentence 3.

23. **(A)** (p. 185) *Writing and Language/Standard English Conventions/No Change.* This is a straightforward question testing subject-verb agreement. The subject of the noun clause is "that" which refers to "those," a plural pronoun. So the verb in the original is correct.

24. **(D)** (p. 185) *Writing and Language/Expression of Ideas/Strategy/Data Presentation.* This is a Command of Evidence question that asks about the connection between the graph and the text. The lines in the graph shows the percentage of acreage planted in each of the GM varieties shown, and the acreage is clearly increasing, making (D) correct. (A) is probably the weakest answer, since there is no connection at all to "thousands of years." (B) is superficially attractive because the graph covers a 15-year span, but the graph does not show the progress of an individual cross-breeding. And (C) is wrong because the graph does not compare the crops mentioned with other crops, and without some sort of cross-comparison, there is nothing in the graph to support the conclusion that those crops are more important than others (even though the text itself says this).

25. **(C)** (p. 186) *Writing and Language/Standard English Conventions/Grammar and Usage/Pronoun Usage.* The problem with the original is that the pronoun "they" is intended to refer to "insect," but "they" is plural and "insect" is singular. "They" is also ambiguous, so "the insect" should be used. (B) introduces a new error: "stopped" is inconsistent with the present tense used in the rest of the paragraph. And (D) destroys entirely the internal logic of the sentence.

26. **(C)** (p. 186) *Writing and Language/Standard English Conventions/Punctuation/Commas.* Here you have a fairly long introductory phrase, so you should mark the end with a comma. The other options turn the first part of the sentence into a fragment.

27. **(C)** (p. 186) *Writing and Language/Expression of Ideas/Style/Precision.* This is a Words in Context item. The problem with the original is that "traditionally" doesn't really fit the sense of the sentence. A tradition is a practice settled upon over time; it is human behavior. So what is needed here is a word that describes conditions that develop without regard to human choice. "Usually" provides the best alternative.

28. **(B)** (p. 186) *Writing and Language/Expression of Ideas/Strategy/Appropriate Supporting Material.* This question asks about the significance of the underlined part of the sentence in the context of the paragraph. In the paragraph, the author explains that HT genes protect GM plants from glufosinate so that glufosinate can be used as an herbicide to eliminate weeds without killing the desirable plants.

29. **(A)** (p. 187) *Writing and Language/Expression of Ideas/Organization/Effective Transitional Sentences.* The first part of the passage provides background on the workings of genetic modifiers, then the rest of the passage provides information to show that GM crops are safe. So (A) provides an excellent introduction to the second part of the passage.

30. **(A)** (p. 187) *Writing and Language/Expression of Ideas/Strategy/Appropriate Supporting Material.* This is a Command of Evidence question that asks about a clever twist of reasoning used by the author. The author cites the lack of litigation involving GM foods as evidence for the conclusion that these foods do not cause serious harm to humans. This is further clarified by adding the idea presented in (A): if there were harm, people would be filing lawsuits.

31. **(D)** (p. 187) *Writing and Language/Expression of Ideas/Style/Conciseness.* This is a Words in Context item that asks you to eliminate unnecessary wordiness in the underlined portion. As a comparison of the available choices will make clear, (D) is the shortest and clearest option.

32. **(D)** (p. 187) *Writing and Language/Standard English Conventions/Grammar and Usage/Verb Tense.* The problem with the original is that the verb tense of the underlined element is inconsistent with the tense of rest of the sentence. "Contain" is the present tense and in this case implies an ongoing action. "Have consumed" is a past tense verb. (Imperfect tense be precise.) Both verbs, however, should be expressed in the same time frame. (D) corrects this error by matching the present tense "contain" with the present tense "consume."

33. **(A)** (p. 188) *Writing and Language/Standard English Conventions/No Change.* This is a straightforward item that tests punctuation. In a series of three or more elements, all of the elements except the penultimate must be followed by a comma. (The comma following the next-to-last element is optional.)

34. **(D)** (p. 189) *Writing and Language/Expression of Ideas/Style/Tone.* This is a Words in Context item. The original sentence uses an informal phrasing that is inconsistent with the formal tone of the passage. (D) is much better suited to the author's style.

35. **(D)** (p. 189) *Writing and Language/Standard English Conventions/Sentence Structure/Misplaced Modifiers.* The main weakness of the original sentence is the position of the introductory modifier in relation to the noun "theorists." Since the introductory modifier will be associated with the first major noun that appears in the main clause that follows the comma, it now seems to modify "theorists." But the "theorists" were not "established in 1787"; the system was. (D) eliminates the problem by moving the intended modifier "electoral college" to the beginning of the clause, where it functions as the subject.

36. **(C) (p. 189)** *Writing and Language/Expression of Ideas/Style/Conciseness.* This is a fairly direct Words-in-Context item. The underlined portion of the sentence is needlessly wordy. "For the time being" and "into the foreseeable future" say essentially the same thing, so one can be eliminated.

37. **(B) (p. 190)** *Writing and Language/Expression of Ideas/Strategy/Main Idea.* This is a Command of Evidence item that asks that you show an understanding of the main point of paragraph 2. The problem with the 2000 election, according to the author, is that the electoral college chose Bush even though Gore received more votes.

38. **(C) (p. 190)** *Writing and Language/Standard English Conventions/Grammar and Usage/Verb Tense.* This question asks about appropriate verb form. The author here is suggesting what <u>might</u> happen in the event of a malfunction of the electoral system. The best available choice for describing an outcome that is not definite is "could arguably lead," (C).

39. **(A) (p. 191)** *Writing and Language/Standard English Conventions/No Change.* The original is correct. The problem with (B) and (C) is that they create comma splices: the dependent clause introduced by "although" becomes an independent clause attached to the existing independent clause by only a comma. (D) introduces an error of pronoun agreement.

40. **(A) (p. 191)** *Writing and Language/Standard English Conventions/No Change.* This is a fairly subtle question. The original is correct. Ordinarily, you should be reluctant to sprinkle commas throughout a sentence too liberally. Over-punctuating is an error students are more likely to make than under-punctuation. In this case, however, the comma is needed to separate "indirect" and "deliberative" because they are coordinate adjectives. That is, "indirect" is intended to modify "process," not "deliberative." A good test is to insert the word "and" between them. If the result makes sense, then the comma is probably needed: they intended it to be an indirect and deliberative process.

41. **(C) (p. 191)** *Writing and Language/Expression of Ideas/Strategy/Effective Transitional Sentence.* In the third paragraph, the author contrasts the intended working of the electoral system with its actual functioning. It was supposed to be insulated from politics, but now it actually incorporates party politics. The best available transitional phrase to signal the reader that a contrast is intended is "instead."

42. **(A) (p. 191)** *Writing and Language/Standard English Conventions/No Change.* This question tests a fairly simple rule of punctuation. With a series of elements, each element, save for the last, should be followed by a comma. So the original is correct. (A comma following the second-to-last element is considered optional, and, fortunately, the test would not force students to make a choice on an optional comma.)

43. **(A) (p. 191)** *Writing and Language/Expression of Ideas/Strategy/Appropriate Supporting Material.* This item asks about the main theme of the passage. The author's primary point is that the electoral college system, for all its faults and the occasional unintended result, still works pretty well.

44. **(D) (p. 192)** *Writing and Language/Expression of Ideas/Strategy/Data Presentation.* This is a Command of Evidence question. When dealing with a graph, it is important to read the descriptive information that accompanies the picture—the title, the units, the names, and any clarifying notes. In this case, the graph provides information about presidential elections from 1920 to 2004. It neither supports nor weakens a conclusion about an election outside of that time frame. So both (B) and (C) are incorrect. (A) is wrong because the graph provides data about votes cast; it doesn't support any qualitative conclusion such as "durable" or "adaptable."

Section 3: Math, No Calculator

1. **(C)** (p. 194) *Math: Multiple-Choice/Algebra/Creating, Expressing, and Evaluating Algebraic Equations and Functions.* This is a translation item: translate the English words to "algebrese." The product of x and 5 is $5x$, and the sum of $3x$ and 3 is $3x + 3$. Since the first expression is equal to $\dfrac{1}{2}$ of the second expression, the

    entire statement can be written as $5x = \dfrac{3x + 3}{2}$.

2. **(C)** (p. 194) *Math: Multiple-Choice/Algebra/Solving Simultaneous Equations.* Use the technique for solving simultaneous equations. Solve the first equation for x: $x + 2 = 7 \Rightarrow x = 5$. Substitute this value for x in the second equation and solve for y: $5 + y = 11 \Rightarrow y = 6$.

3. **(B)** (p. 194) *Math: Multiple-Choice/Algebra/Creating, Expressing, and Evaluating Algebraic Equations and Functions and Probability/Arithmetic Probability and Statistics/Measures of Center and Spread/Averages.*

    The average is the sum of all the numbers divided by the total number of numbers: $\dfrac{4x + 3x}{7} = \dfrac{7x}{7} = x$.

    Alternatively, substitute numbers. Assume $x = 10$: the average of 7 numbers would be

    $\dfrac{4(10) + 3(10)}{7} = \dfrac{70}{7} = 10$. Substitute 10 for x in the given expressions—only (B) returns a value of 10.

4. **(D)** (p. 194) *Math: Multiple-Choice/Algebra/Creating, Expressing, and Evaluating Algebraic Equations and Functions/Function Notation.* Substitute 3 for x in the function and evaluate it:

    $-2x^2 + 2 = -2(3)^2 + 2 = -18 + 2 = -16$.

5. **(A)** (p. 194) *Math: Multiple-Choice/Algebra/Manipulating Algebraic Expressions/Basic Algebraic Manipulations.* Apply the distributive property to the given expression: $w(x + y + z) = wx + wy + wz$. (B), (C), and (D) are also equal to $wx + wy + wz$. (A) is incorrect because $w(xy) + w(yz) = wxy + wyz$.

    Alternatively, assume some values. Let w, x, y, and z each be equal to 1. On that assumption: $w(x + y + z) = 1(1 + 1 + 1) = 1(3) = 3$. Then, substitute 1 for w, x, y, and z into the answer choices. Every choice yields the value 3 except for (A).

6. **(A)** (p. 194) *Math: Multiple-Choice/Algebra/Manipulating Algebraic Expressions/Manipulating Expressions Involving Exponents.* Simply use the laws of exponents: $(-3x)^3 \left(\dfrac{-3x^{-3}}{27} \right) = -27x^3 \left(\dfrac{-3}{27x^3} \right) = 3$.

7. **(B)** (p. 194) *Math: Multiple-Choice/Algebra/Manipulating Algebraic Expressions/Manipulating Expressions Involving Exponents.* In spite of the elaborate setup, this is simply a "rearrange the equation" item. Solve the

    given equation for the desired quantity, the height, h: $v = \sqrt{2gh} \Rightarrow v^2 = (\sqrt{2gh})^2 = 2gh \Rightarrow h = \dfrac{v^2}{2g}$.

8. **(A)** (p. 194) *Math: Multiple-Choice/Geometry/Complex Figures* and *Triangles/45°-45°-90°Triangles* and *Pythagorean Theorem.* Draw a diagram of the provided and needed information:

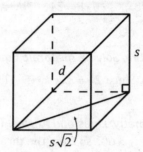

Notice that the diagonal of the face, the edge of the cube, and the diagonal of the cube form a right triangle, the hypotenuse of which is the diagonal of the cube. Since the edge has a length of s, the diagonal of the face has a length of $s\sqrt{2}$ (45-45-90 triangle). Now, use the Pythagorean theorem: $d^2 = s^2 + (s\sqrt{2})^2 =$
$s^2 + 2s^2 = 3s^2 \Rightarrow d = \sqrt{3s^2} = s\sqrt{3}$. This is the length of the diagonal. The distance from any vertex to the center of the cube is one half of that, or $\dfrac{s\sqrt{3}}{2}$.

9. **(D)** (p. 195) *Math: Multiple-Choice/Coordinate Geometry/Slope of a Line* and *Graphs of Linear Equations.* The slope of a line is defined as the rise divided by the run; that is, the difference between y-values divided by the difference in the corresponding x-values. In this case, the y-values represent the total pressure and the x-values represent the depth below the surface of the water. Note that the slope is increasing—the increase in total pressure due to the corresponding increase in depth.

10. **(D)** (p. 195) *Math: Multiple-Choice/Coordinate Geometry/Graphs of Linear Equations.* Locate the point on the line corresponding to a total pressure of 40, which is recorded on the y-axis. This point corresponds to a depth of 56 feet.

11. **(B)** (p. 195) *Math: Multiple-Choice/Coordinate Geometry/Slope-Intercept Form of a Linear Equation* and *Graphs of Linear Equations.* The slope-intercept line of an equation is $y = mx + b$, where m is the slope and b is the y-intercept. In this case, the x-variable is d (depth) and y-variable is p (total pressure): the graph shows how p changes with d. As covered in #9 above, the slope is the change in total pressure per change in depth. Points crossing directly on the intersections of the grid on the graph are convenient to use in the equation for slope. Thus, we use (0,15) and (100,60): $m = \dfrac{\Delta y}{\Delta x} = \dfrac{60-15}{100-0} = \dfrac{45}{100} = \dfrac{9}{20}$. The y-intercept is at (0,15), so $b = 15$. Therefore, the equation of the line is $p = \dfrac{9d}{20} + 15$.

12. **(C)** (p. 196) *Math: Multiple Choice/Geometry/Triangles/Properties of Triangles.* Complete the sketch:

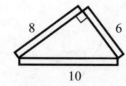

The triangle has sides of 6, 8, and 10, which you should recognize as multiples of 3, 4, and 5. So, the triangle is a right triangle. The sides of 6 and 8 form the right angle, so they can be used as altitude and base for finding the area: $\text{area} = \dfrac{1}{2} \cdot \text{altitude} \cdot \text{base} = \dfrac{1}{2} \cdot 6 \cdot 8 = 24$.

13. **(D)** (p. 196) *Math: Multiple-Choice/Algebra/Solving Algebraic Equations or Inequalities with One Variable/Equations Involving Exponents.* Since $2^x = 32$, $x = 5$. Therefore, $y^2 = \sqrt{5(5)} + 4 = 9 \Rightarrow y = \pm 3$.

14. **(D)** (p. 196) *Math: Multiple-Choice/Geometry/Lines and Angles.* From the three angles in the large triangle, $x + 30 + 90 = 180 \Rightarrow x = 60$. Since $x < y$, $y > 60$, so from the three angles in the smaller triangle, $y + 30 + z = 180 \Rightarrow z = 150 - y$. Since $y > 60$, $z < 90$.

15. **(D)** (p. 196) *Math: Multiple-Choice/Algebra/Solving Quadratic Equations and Relations/The Quadratic Formula.* Rewrite the given equation in the standard form for a quadratic ($ax^2 + bx + c = 0$):

$$mg(H+s) = \frac{k}{2L}s^2 \Rightarrow \frac{k}{2L}s^2 - mg(H+s) = 0 \Rightarrow \left(\frac{k}{2L}\right)s^2 - (mg)s - mgH = 0.$$ Therefore, $a = k/2L$, $b = -mg$, and

$c = -mgH$. Use the quadratic formula to solve for s: $s = \dfrac{-b \pm \sqrt{b^2 - 4ac}}{2a} =$

$\dfrac{-(-mg) \pm \sqrt{(-mg)^2 - 4(k/2L)(-mgH)}}{2(k/2L)} = \dfrac{mg \pm \sqrt{(mg)^2 + 2kmg(H/L)}}{k/L}$. Since the quantity under the square root sign is bigger than mg, the use of the minus sign from the $\pm$ symbol would lead to a negative value for s, which is an extraneous root because distance must be positive. Therefore, the correct expression for s includes only the positive sign, (D).

16. **(0)** (p. 198) *Math: Student-Produced Responses/Algebra/Manipulating Algebraic Expressions/Evaluating Expressions.* Substitute 2 for x in the expression and evaluate it: $x^2 - 2x = (2)^2 - 2(2) = 4 - 4 = 0$.

17. **(9/10, 0.9)** (p. 198) *Math: Student-Produced Responses/Algebra/Manipulating Algebraic Expressions/Evaluating Expressions.* The least possible value for the expression $\dfrac{x+y}{z}$ occurs when x and y are the least and z is the greatest: $\dfrac{6+3}{10} = \dfrac{9}{10}$.

18. **(90)** (p. 198) *Math: Student-Produced Responses/Geometry/Lines and Angles.* Vertical angles created by intersecting lines are congruent, so label the missing angles:

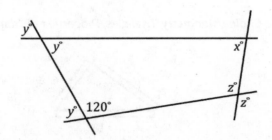

Since a straight line has 180°, $y + 120 = 180 \Rightarrow y = 60$. Furthermore, the sum of the interior angles of a quadrilateral (four-sided polygon with four angles) is 360° and the stem states $x = z$, so $x + y + z + 120 = 360 \Rightarrow x + 60 + x + 120 = 360 \Rightarrow 2x = 360 - 180 = 180 \Rightarrow x = 90$.

19. **(10)** (p. 198) *Math: Student-Produced Responses/Algebra/Manipulating Algebraic Expressions/ Manipulating Expressions Involving Exponents.* Use prime factorization to solve:

$200 = (2)(100) = (2)(2)(50) = (2)(2)(2)(25) = (2)(2)(2)(5)(5) = (2^3)(5^2)$. Therefore, $x = 2$, $y = 5$, and $xy = (2)(5) = 10$.

20. **(26)** (p. 198) *Math: Student-Produced Responses/Algebra/Solving Simultaneous Equations.* First, rewrite both equations in slope-intercept form: $x = 6y - 2 \Rightarrow 6y = x + 2 \Rightarrow y = \dfrac{x+2}{6} \Rightarrow y = \dfrac{1}{6}x + \dfrac{1}{3}$ and

$a(y + 3) = x - b \Rightarrow ay + 3a = x - b \Rightarrow ay = x - b - 3a \Rightarrow y = \dfrac{x - b - 3a}{a} \Rightarrow y = \dfrac{1}{a}x - \dfrac{b}{a} - 3$. If the system has an infinite number of solutions, the two lines are actually the same: one is the other multiplied by some constant. Set the two equations equal to each other: $\dfrac{1}{6}x + \dfrac{1}{3} = \dfrac{1}{a}x - \dfrac{b}{a} - 3$. Since a and b are constants, set the x-terms equal to one another and the constant terms equal to each other and use this new system of equations to determine a and b: $\dfrac{x}{6} = \dfrac{x}{a} \Rightarrow a = 6$ and $\dfrac{1}{3} = -\dfrac{b}{a} - 3 \Rightarrow -\dfrac{b}{a} = \dfrac{10}{3} \Rightarrow b = -\dfrac{10}{3}(6) = -20$. Therefore, $|a - b| = |6 - (-20)| = |6 + 20| = 26$.

Section 4: Math, Calculator

1. **(B)** (p. 200) *Math: Multiple-Choice/Probability/Arithmetic Probability* and *Statistics/Measures of Center and Spread/Averages.* Use the concept of an average to create an equation to solve this problem: average $= x =$

$\dfrac{5 + 5 + 10 + 12 + x}{5} \Rightarrow x = \dfrac{32 + x}{5} \Rightarrow 5x = 32 + x \Rightarrow 4x = 32 \Rightarrow x = 8$.

Alternatively, test each answer choice, starting with (A). Let $x = 6$. On that assumption, the total of the five elements is 38, and the average is $\dfrac{38}{5}$, which is not equal to 6, so (A) is wrong. Next, try (B). If $x = 8$, then

the total of the five elements is 40, and the average is $\dfrac{40}{5} = 8$. Since $8 = 8$, (B) is the correct choice.

2. **(A)** (p, 200) *Math: Multiple-Choice/Algebra/Solving Quadratic Equations and Relations/Factoring Expressions.* To find the possible values of x, factor the given equation: $x^2 + 2x + 1 = (x + 1)(x + 1) = 0$. The expression is equal to zero for $x + 1 = 0 \Rightarrow x = -1$.

3. **(C)** (p. 200) *Math: Multiple-Choice/Geometry/Triangles/Pythagorean Theorem.* Observe that the direct path between Fuller Acres and Farmers' Market is the hypotenuse of a triangle that can be completed as follows:

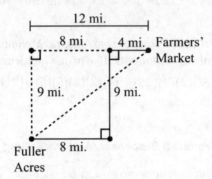

The easiest way to solve the problem is to see that the two known sides of this triangle form a ratio of $\frac{9}{12} = \frac{3}{4}$, suggestive of a $3:4:5$ right triangle. The hypotenuse is determined by the following proportion: if all of the sides are proportional to $3:4:5$, then $\frac{9}{3} = \frac{12}{4} = \frac{x}{5}$, where $x = 15$. (Note that the distance of the direct path can be determined using the Pythagorean theorem: $a^2 + b^2 = c^2 \Rightarrow 9^2 + 12^2 = x^2 \Rightarrow x = \sqrt{81 + 144} = 15$. Since the indirect path measures $8 + 9 + 4 = 21$ miles and the direct path measures 15 miles, the difference in miles between the two paths is $21 - 15 = 6$.

4. **(D)** (p. 200) *Math: Multiple-Choice/Problem Solving and Advanced Arithmetic/Multi-Step Problem Solving Items.* If the original prize is x, each student would receive $\frac{x}{11}$. When another student is added, each student would receive $\frac{x}{12}$. Thus, each student would then receive $\frac{x}{12} \div \frac{x}{11} = \frac{11}{12}$ of what he or she would have originally received.

Alternatively, assume some values. For example, assuming that the prize is worth \$132 (a convenient assumption since $11 \cdot 12 = 132$), each student originally receives \$12. After the addition of another student, the prize is worth only \$11. Thus, the second prize must be worth only $\frac{11}{12}$ of the first prize.

5. **(A)** (p. 200) *Math: Multiple-Choice/Algebra/Creating, Expressing, and Evaluating Algebraic Equations and Functions* and *Problem Solving and Advanced Arithmetic/Common Problem Solving Items/Proportions and Direct-Inverse Variation.* To create the expression, set up a direct proportion between the ratios of the number of items bought at sale price and the number bought at regular price: ($\frac{\text{sale price}}{\text{regular price}}$):

$\frac{3}{2} = \frac{x}{y} \Rightarrow y = \frac{2x}{3}$.

6. **(C)** (p. 200) *Math: Multiple-Choice/Problem Solving and Advanced Arithmetic/Common Problem Solving Items/Ratios.* Since 6 items out of 30 are inspected, the number of non-inspected items is: $30 - 6 = 24$. Thus, the ratio of inspected items to non-inspected items is: $6:24 = 1:4$.

7. **(C)** (p. 201) *Math: Multiple-Choice/Algebra/Manipulating Algebraic Expressions/Evaluating Expressions.*

Since 13 is not divisible by 7, t must be divisible by 7 in order for the expression $\dfrac{13t}{7}$ to produce an integer. 3 is the only answer choice that is not divisible by 7.

Alternatively, "test-the-test." Each of the numbers given in the choices will produce an integer except for (C): $\dfrac{13(3)}{7} = \dfrac{39}{7}$, which is not an integer.

8. **(C)** (p. 201) *Math: Multiple-Choice/Algebra/Solving Simultaneous Equations.* Assume $x \neq 0$ and $y \neq 0$.

Rewrite the equations: $\dfrac{(x+y)}{x} = 4 \Rightarrow x + y = 4x \Rightarrow y = 3x$; $\dfrac{(y+z)}{z} = 5 \Rightarrow y + z = 5z \Rightarrow y = 4z$. Therefore:

$3x = 4z \Rightarrow \dfrac{x}{z} = \dfrac{4}{3}$.

9. **(B)** (p. 201) *Math: Multiple-Choice/Algebra/Creating, Expressing, and Evaluating Algebraic Equations and Functions.* Create an equation. Let x equal the original amount:

$\dfrac{x}{2} - \$60 = \dfrac{x}{5} \Rightarrow \dfrac{x}{2} - \dfrac{x}{5} = \$60 \Rightarrow \dfrac{3x}{10} = 60 \Rightarrow x = 200$.

Alternatively, "test-the-test" with the answer choices.

10. **(C)** (p. 201) *Math: Multiple-Choice/Problem Solving and Advanced Arithmetic/Common Problem Solving Items/Ratios and Data Interpretation/Tables.* The number of people having X is: $10 + 30 = 40$; the number of people having Y is: $10 + 40 = 50$. Thus, the ratio of people having X to people having Y is: $40 : 50 = 4 : 5$.

11. **(C)** (p. 201) *Math: Multiple-Choice/Coordinate Geometry/The Coordinate System and Geometry/Triangles/Properties of Triangles.* The length of the base of the triangle is $4x - x = 3x$, and the length of the altitude is $3x - 0 = 3x$ (the difference in the y-coordinate). Use the formula for finding the area of a triangle to determine x: $\dfrac{1}{2}(3x)(3x) = 54 \Rightarrow 9x^2 = 108 \Rightarrow x^2 = 12 \Rightarrow x = \sqrt{12} = 2\sqrt{3}$ (distance must be positive).

12. **(A)** (p. 201) *Math: Multiple-Choice/Problem Solving and Advanced Arithmetic/Common Problem Solving Items/Proportions and Direct-Inverse Variation.* This is a direct variation problem, so create a proportion grouping like terms on the same side of the equality: $\dfrac{20 \text{ minutes}}{35 \text{ minutes}} = \dfrac{40\%}{x} \Rightarrow x = 40\left(\dfrac{35}{20}\right) = 70\%$.

Alternatively, note that the bushel fills 10 percent every 5 minutes, so it fills another 30 percent in 15 minutes. Therefore, $40\% + 30\% = 70\%$.

13. **(D)** (p. 202) *Math: Multiple-Choice/Problem Solving and Advanced Arithmetic/Common Problem Solving Items/Percentages.* Begin by finding 40 percent of 5: $\dfrac{40}{100} \cdot 5 = \dfrac{200}{100} = 2$. Now, find 50 percent of 2:

$\frac{50}{100} \cdot 2 = 1$. If 1 person had a score averaging 250 or better, and there are 5 people in all, 4 people had a score averaging below 250.

14. (B) (p. 202) *Math: Multiple-Choice/Algebra/Creating, Expressing, and Evaluating Algebraic Equations and Functions and Problem Solving and Advanced Arithmetic/Common Problem Solving Items/Proportions and Direct-Inverse Variation.* Since $n > m$, the net drain from the tank per minute is: $n - m$. Therefore, the time required to empty the tank is: $\frac{g}{(n-m)}$.

Alternatively, substitute numbers and "test-the-test."

15. (B) (p. 202) *Math: Multiple-Choice/Algebra/Creating, Expressing, and Evaluating Algebraic Equations and Functions.* For each of the x morning sessions, there are y lunch roundtables, or $x \times y$ combinations. And for each of the $x \times y$ morning/lunch combinations, there are z afternoon sessions, or $x \times y \times z = xyz$.

Alternatively, assume some numbers for x, y, and z, and determine the total number of combinations—compare this value with the value returned by the expressions in each answer choice.

16. (C) (p. 202) *Math: Multiple-Choice/Algebra/Solving Algebraic Equations with Two Variables.* For one equation with two variables, you cannot solve for x and y individually. Instead, look for a way to rewrite the first equation in terms of $x + y$: $\frac{x}{y} = -1 \Rightarrow x = -y \Rightarrow x + y = 0$.

17. (B) (p. 203) *Math: Multiple-Choice/Data Interpretation/Bar, Cumulative, and Line Graphs.* This is a simple "read the graph" item. According to the graph, the density of water at its maximum (4°C) is 1.0 g/cm³ and the density of ice at -2°C is 0.9170 g/cm³. The difference is $1.0 - 0.9170 = 0.083$ g/cm³.

18. (A) (p. 203) *Math: Multiple-Choice/Data Interpretation/Bar, Cumulative, and Line Graphs.* The graph shows that as water approaches its freezing point and cools below 4°C, its density begins to decrease until it freezes at 0°C (32°F). This is why ice floats. In a freezing freshwater lake, the top of the lake is frozen water, and the bottom of the lake is the densest: unfrozen water at 4°C. Therefore, the correct figure is (A).

19. (C) (p. 204) *Math: Multiple-Choice/Data Interpretation/Bar, Cumulative, and Line Graphs and Coordinate Geometry/Slope of a Line.* Change in the y-axis per change in the x-axis is the definition of slope: $\frac{\Delta y}{\Delta x}$. The greatest slope in the graph relates to the greatest increase in the weight of strawberries, which directly corresponds to the greatest rainfall (starting 24 hours previously). The greatest slope in the graph corresponds to June 28 through June 30, when the weight of strawberries increased from 1.7 pounds per quart to 2.3 pounds per quart. Therefore, it is likely that there was significant rainfall in the 24 hours preceding that period: June 27, (C). Note that while the slope in the period following June 21, (A), does increase, it does not increase as much as the period following June 27. Similarly, the weight on June 27 is the same as on June 26, so while there was probably rain on June 26, (B) (the decline in weight stops), it is not as much as on June 27, when the period following shows significant increase in slope. Finally, nothing can be said about June 30, (D), because the graph does not extend to July 1.

20. (A) (p. 204) *Math: Multiple-Choice/Data Interpretation/Bar, Cumulative, and Line Graphs and Statistics/Measures of Center and Spread/Range and Problem Solving and Advanced Arithmetic/Common*

Problem Solving Items/Percentages. The range is the difference between the greatest value and the lowest value. According to the graph, the greatest weight was 2.3 pounds per quart (June 12th and 16th) and the lowest weight was 1.5 pounds per quart (June 26th and June 27th) . So, the range is $2.3 - 1.5 = 0.8$ pounds. The maximum weight is 2.3 pounds per quart, so the range of the weight of strawberries is $\frac{0.8}{2.3} \approx 0.35 = 35\%$ of the maximum weight of strawberries.

21. **(C)** (p. 204) ***Math: Multiple-Choice/Data Interpretation/Bar, Cumulative, and Line Graphs*** and ***Problem Solving and Advanced Arithmetic/Common Problem Solving Items/Proportions and Direct-Inverse Variation.***

Work through the item a step at a time. Twelve pints of jam is $12 \text{ pints} \times \frac{2 \text{ cups}}{\text{pint}} \times \frac{8 \text{ ounces}}{\text{cup}} = 192$ ounces.

The recipe produces eight half-pint jars of jam—a pint is 2 cups, so the recipe produces 8 cups or 64 ounces of jam. Set up a direct proportion to determine the amount of crushed strawberries needed:

$\frac{5 \text{ cups}}{x \text{ cups}} = \frac{64 \text{ ounces}}{192 \text{ ounces}} \Rightarrow x = \frac{5 \times 192}{64} = 15$ cups of crushed strawberries, or 15 pounds of fresh strawberries.

Note that u-pick strawberries are sold per pound, so this is enough to determine the cost of 15 pounds of u-pick strawberries sold on June 27: $15 \text{ pounds} \times \frac{\$1.65}{\text{pound}} = \$24.75$. The cost of the pre-picked strawberries

on June 27 is directly related to the weight per quart on June 26, as given in the graph:

$15 \text{ pounds} \times \frac{1 \text{ quart}}{1.5 \text{ pounds}} = 10$ quarts of pre-picked strawberries. Thus, the cost of the pre-picked

strawberries is $10 \text{ quarts} \times \frac{\$4.25}{\text{quart}} = \$42.50$ The difference in price is $\$42.50 - \$24.75 = \$17.75$.

22. **(A)** (p. 205) ***Math: Multiple-Choice/Algebra/Creating, Expressing, and Evaluating Algebraic Equations and Functions*** and ***Probability/Arithmetic Probability and Statistics/Measures of Center and Spread/Averages and Median.*** There is an even number of numbers, so the median is halfway between the two middle

numbers: $\text{median} = \frac{(b+c)}{2}$. The average is twice the median, so

$\frac{a+b+c+d}{4} = 2 \cdot \frac{b+c}{2} \Rightarrow \frac{-2c+0+c+nc}{4} = 0+c \Rightarrow -c+nc = 4c \Rightarrow nc = 5c \Rightarrow n = 5.$

23. **(C)** (p. 205) ***Math: Multiple-Choice/Coordinate Geometry/Graphs of Quadratic Equations and Relations.*** The center-radius form of a circle is given by $(x-h)^2 + (y-k)^2 = r^2$, where the point (h,k) represents the center of the circle and the radius is r. Rewrite the equation in center-radius form: $(x-2)^2 + (y-(-1))^2 = 9$. The circle is of radius 3 centered at point $(2,-1)$. Therefore, only (C) is true: a line drawn through the center of the circle parallel to the x-axis intersects the y-axis at -1 :

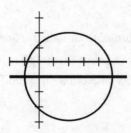

24. **(B) (p. 205)** *Math: Multiple-Choice/Coordinate Geometry/Graphs of Quadratic Equations and Relations* and *Transformations and Their Effects on Graphs of Functions.* To determine how the graph of the original is transformed, compare the original with the new equation to determine what is different: the coefficient of the x-squared term is positive when it was originally negative and 2 is added to the term. Take each of these in turn. A number added to or subtracted from the x term shifts the graph left or right, respectively. In this case, the graph is shifted one unit horizontally to the right. Next, the negative sign leading the squared x term turns the graph upside down—every x value is converted from positive to negative (and vice versa). Finally, the number added after the squared x term shifts the graph upward (if positive) or downward (if negative). In this case, the graph is shifted 2 units upward. Therefore, the correct transformation of the graph is (B).

25. **(B) (p. 206)** *Math: Multiple-Choice/Data Interpretation/Scatterplots* and *Coordinate Geometry/Graphs of Linear Equations.* The graph shows $y(x)$ where T^2 (the square of the period) is the y variable and l (the pendulum arm length) is the x variable. Draw a line of best fit through the data, extrapolating beyond the given data points:

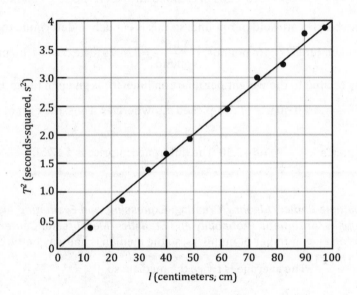

Based on the extrapolation, for a pendulum arm length of 100 cm, T^2 would be approximately 4 seconds-squared. So, the expected period, T, is $\sqrt{4} = 2$ seconds.

26. **(A) (p. 207)** *Math: Multiple-Choice/Coordinate Geometry/Graphs of Linear Equations* and *Algebra/Creating, Expressing, and Evaluating Algebraic Equations and Functions.* The line of best fit should be close to as many points as possible. The proposed lines of best fit in (B) and (D) show the correct trend of the points but do not correctly fit the points. Graph (C) shows a proposed line of best fit in the incorrect direction. Thus, (A) must be the correct answer. Indeed, the proposed line of best fit in (A) intersects several of the data points.

27. **(B) (p. 207)** *Math: Multiple-Choice/Coordinate Geometry/Graphs of Linear Equations* and *Slope of a Line.* The period of the pendulum is $\sqrt{2}$ seconds but the graph is in terms of period-squared, T^2. If the period is $\sqrt{2}$ seconds, then the period-squared is 2 seconds-squared. This corresponds to arm length of approximately 48 centimeters.

28. **(A)** (p. 207) *Math: Multiple-Choice/Algebra/Creating, Expressing, and Evaluating Algebraic Equations and Functions.* The graph shows an exponential increasing relationship. Specifically, the metabolic rate doubles every 10°C. The equation that represents this relationship is known at the doubling equation: $N = N_0 2^{T/d}$, where d is the quantity of T required to double and N_0 is the quantity of N when $T = 0$. In this case, $d = 10$, so R doubles every 10°C. This relationship can be inferred from the information: at $T = 0$, $R = x$; at $T = 10$, $R = 2x = x(2)^1$; at $T = 20$, $R = 4x = x(2)^2$; at $T = 30$, $R = 8x = x(2)^3$; etc. Setting the exponent to 1, 2, 3, etc. shows that the exponent must be $T/10$: 10/10 = 1, 20/10 = 2, 30/10 = 3, etc. Therefore, $R = x(2)^{T/10}$.

Alternatively, test the answer choices with values for T in each equation—only the correct choice, (A), returns values for R that match those in the graph.

29. **(B)** (p. 208) *Math: Multiple-Choice/Algebra/Creating, Expressing, and Evaluating Algebraic Equations and Functions.* Each sponsor pledges Cooper at least $5, so that's at least $5s$ dollars. Plus, $\frac{s}{3}$ pledged five cents, for a subtotal of $\frac{s}{3}\left(\frac{5}{100}\right) = \frac{s}{60}$ dollars per word; and $\frac{s}{4}$ pledged ten cents, for a subtotal of $\frac{s}{4}\left(\frac{10}{100}\right) = \frac{s}{40}$ dollars per word; and the remainder, $s - \frac{s}{3} - \frac{s}{4} = s\left(1 - \frac{1}{3} - \frac{1}{4}\right) = \frac{5s}{12}$, pledged twenty-five cents, for a subtotal of $\frac{5s}{12}\left(\frac{25}{100}\right) = \frac{5s}{48}$ per word. Therefore, the total pledges per word spelled correctly is $\frac{s}{60} + \frac{s}{40} + \frac{5s}{48} = s\left(\frac{4}{240} + \frac{6}{240} + \frac{5(5)}{240}\right) = s\left(\frac{35}{240}\right) = \frac{7s}{48}$ dollars per word. Since Cooper spelled c words correctly, the total amount raised by Cooper in the fundraiser is $5s + \frac{7sc}{48} = s\left(5 + \frac{7c}{48}\right)$.

30. **(A)** (p. 208) *Math: Multiple-Choice/Algebra/Creating, Expressing, and Evaluating Algebraic Equations and Functions.* This item builds on the previous one, giving the values for s and c for Cooper's fundraising equation, and requires comparison of the total raised with another student, Maya. Write a similar equation for Maya's fundraising: $5 per sponsor, s, plus ten cents per sponsor per word spelled correctly, $sc(0.10)$. The total raised by Maya is $.5s + 0.1sc = s(5 + 0.1c)$ .. Plug the given values for s and c into each student's fundraising equation:

Cooper ($s = 25$, $c = 72$): $s\left(5 + \frac{7c}{48}\right) = 25\left(5 + \frac{7(72)}{48}\right) = \$387.50$

Maya ($s = 50$, $c = 55$): $s(5 + 0.1c) = 50(5 + 0.1(55)) = \$525$

Therefore, the difference in the amounts raised is $525 - 387.50 = \$137.50$.

31. **(35)** (p. 209) *Math: Student-Produced Responses/Problem Solving and Advanced Arithmetic/Common Problem Solving Items/Proportions and Direct-Inverse Variation.* Set up a direct proportion, grouping like terms on the same side of the equality and solve for the missing value:
$$\frac{2 \text{ pounds}}{10 \text{ pounds}} = \frac{7 \text{ pots}}{x \text{ pots}} \Rightarrow x = \frac{7 \cdot 10}{2} = 35.$$

32. (1) (p. 209) *Math: Student-Produced Responses/Algebra/Solving Algebraic Equations with Two Variables.*
Perform the indicated operations: $(x+y)^2 = (x-y)^2 + 4 \Rightarrow x^2 + 2xy + y^2 = x^2 - 2xy + y^2 + 4 \Rightarrow$
$2xy = -2xy + 4 \Rightarrow xy = 1$.

33. (4) (p. 210) *Math: Student-Produced Responses/Data Interpretation/Tables* and *Probability/Arithmetic Probability* and *Statistics/Measures of Center and Spread/Median.* Determine the "Difference" values:

AGE DIFFERENCE FOR CHILDREN IN FIVE FAMILIES					
Family	Oldest	Age	Youngest	Age	Difference
LaTours	Joan	15	Ed	12	$15 - 12 = 3$
Pickett	Harold	17	Claire	8	$17 - 8 = 9$
Thibault	Rene	16	Henri	3	$16 - 3 = 13$
Barber	Fred	9	Gloria	7	$9 - 7 = 2$
Newcomb	Danny	12	Syd	8	$12 - 8 = 4$

Arrange the "Difference" values in order: 2, 3, 4, 9, and 13. Therefore, the median age difference is 4.

34. (9) (p. 210) *Math: Student-Produced Responses/Problem Solving and Advanced Arithmetic/Common Advanced Arithmetic Items/Properties of Numbers* and *Algebra/Creating, Expressing, and Evaluating Algebraic Equations and Functions.* Let n be the smallest integer: $n + (n+1) + (n+2) + (n+3) + (n+4) = 55 \Rightarrow$
$5n + 10 = 55 \Rightarrow 5n = 45 \Rightarrow n = 9$.

Alternatively, for an odd number of consecutive integers, the middle integer is the sum of the integers
divided by the number of integers. So, the middle number is $\dfrac{55}{5} = 11$ and the 5 integers are:
$\{9, 10, 11, 12, 13\}$. Therefore, 9 is the smallest integer.

35. (9) (p. 210) *Math: Student-Produced Responses/Problem Solving and Advanced Arithmetic/Multi-Step Problem Solving Items* and *Algebra/Creating, Expressing, and Evaluating Algebraic Equations and Functions.* Create an equation relating the original height of the sapling, h, to the heights after trimming and
growth. From the information given in the item stem, $h = \dfrac{9}{10}(h) + \dfrac{9}{10}$. Now, solve for h:

$10h = \dfrac{9}{10}(h)(10) + \dfrac{9}{10}(10) \Rightarrow 10h = 9h + 9 \Rightarrow h = 9$ feet.

36. (1) (p. 210) *Math: Student-Produced Responses/Trigonometry/Right Triangles/Trigonometric Ratios* and *Geometry/Lines and Angles* and *Triangles/Pythagorean Theorem/45°-45°-90° Triangles.* Draw a picture of
the triangle described:

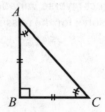

Clearly, the 90° angle must be $\angle ABC$ because the two legs of the right triangle are congruent and must both be shorter than the hypotenuse. Thus, the two congruent angles, $\angle BAC$ and $\angle ACB$, must each equal 45°. Therefore, the item stem is asking for the value of $\dfrac{\sin 45°}{\cos 45°} = \tan 45°$. Recall (or use your calculator) that $\tan 45° = 1$ (or that $\sin 45° = 1$ and $\cos 45° = 1$).

Alternatively, use the relations between the sides of a 45°-45°-90° triangle and the definitions of the trigonometry functions to determine the value of $\dfrac{\sin 45°}{\cos 45°} = \tan 45°$.

37. (7) (p. 210) *Math: Student-Produced Responses/Algebra/Creating, Expressing, and Evaluating Algebraic Equations and Functions/Function Notation.* To find the value of x for which $f(x-1) = g(x+2)$, set the functions equal to one another, substituting $x-1$ for x in $f(x)$ and substituting $x+2$ for x in $g(x)$. Then solve for x: $2(x-1)-5 = (x+2)-2 \Rightarrow 2x-2-5 = x \Rightarrow x = 7$.

38. (10) (p. 210) *Math: Student-Produced Responses/Geometry/Circles.* First, determine the circumference of the bed. Since the bed has a diameter of 12 feet, it has a radius of 6 feet and a circumference of $2\pi r = 12\pi \approx 37.7$ feet. Therefore, the landscaper needs $\dfrac{37.7}{4} = 9.425$ edging lengths. This must be rounded to the nearest whole length, or 10 lengths.

Section 5: Writing (p. 211)

Sample Essay Responses and Analyses

Above Average Response

Rebecca Lindsey uses rhetorical elements, evidence, and reasoning to make the case that tropical deforestation must be combatted. Tropical deforestation puts countless species in jeopardy, threatens biodiversity, and contributes to climate change. After demonstrating how problematic tropical deforestation is and illustrating its harmful effects with evidence, Lindsey uses reasoning to discuss a number of possible solutions.

Firstly, Lindsey demonstrates how deforestation is affecting genetic diversity; deforestation is especially harmful in the tropics where about half of all species on earth find a home. Genetic diversity, potential resources, and keys to improving everyday life are all lost with deforestation. By emphasizing the importance of what is lost when deforestation happens, Lindsey highlights how damaging the lasting effects of deforestation can be. This is an emotional appeal to the people who read Lindsey's article and is meant to make them realize how serious the problem is. Lindsey notes that deforestation can contribute to global warming, also highlighting how serious deforestation can be. Lindsey's use of emotional appeals makes her argument more persuasive.

Secondly, Lindsey argues that the deforestation stems from global, national, and local demands. She points out that vast expanses of rainforest are being cleared to meet the needs of industrial producers as well as to meet agricultural demands. In one decade, Brazil lost around 163,436 square miles of forest—leading the world in terms of total deforested area. Lindsey develops her argument through examples of tropic countries that deal with deforestation. These examples help to situate her argument and to connect her claims with evidence. Since Lindsey has already illustrated the seriousness of deforestation, she reiterates the importance of combating deforestation by using statistics about Brazil to demonstrate how much land is lost.

Lastly, Lindsey proposes a multitude of solutions that work to address the problem on several levels. Lindsey proposes the "sustainable harvesting of native plants, shade farming, nature preserves, and management by indigenous peoples." Lindsey's argument is that incentivizing countries, businesses, and individuals to adopt forest-

friendly practices will make preserving the rainforest more realistic. By suggesting possible solutions, Lindsey develops her argument further; having claimed that deforestation is a problem and supported her claim with evidence, she uses reasoning to address the problem of deforestation on local, national, and global levels. Lindsey's use of possible solutions makes for a compelling conclusion to her article.

Lindsey illustrates that fighting deforestation is crucial because tropical deforestation threatens biodiversity, makes entire species vulnerable to extinction, and contributes to climate change. Lindsey uses rhetorical elements, reasoning, and evidence to support her argument. This leads to a well-founded and persuasive argument that makes the case for global strategies that are crucial in preserving tropical rainforests.

Analysis of Above Average Response

The writer followed proper structure: introduction, body, and conclusion; and each paragraph contains one main idea followed by examples from the text, which are appropriately paraphrased and quoted. The writer's comprehension of many of the important themes introduced by Lindsey and the attempt to describe three of her central ideas was successful. However, the writer could strengthen this response by expanding the discussion of the impact of Lindsey's rhetoric. The tone of the response is professional and objective, analyzing the author's development of argument. The writer analyzed how Lindsey's argument was logically and persuasively constructed, building strong, cohesive paragraphs. Word choice is specific, objective, and descriptive.

Below Average Response

In her fabulous article titled "Tropical Deforestation," Rebecca Lindsay uses great evidence to support her claims and prove that yes indeed deforestation destroys the earth and puts every single plant, animal and person at risk. She claims that deforestation has significant ramifications for the planet, such as climate change and species extinction and that the answer is to discover and implement various strategies in which we preserve our tropical forests and find sustainable options for the land and peoples involved.

First, it seems really important to understand what is happening when deforestation occurs. Lindsay explains that "entire species are vanishing." It's not just the species that goes extinct that is a big deal; everything around the extinct species is effected and harmed. These dangers may bring climate change and other really scary things to our earth, such as when Brazil lost over 160,000 square miles of forest.

Second, the evils of industrialization, are really described by Lindsay. It's the fault of devuloping countries who need so many more wood products, roads, and farming space. The Amazon is one place that bears the scars of consumerism at its worst. No thought is given to the people of that area or to the future of the country.

Last, Lindsay advocates for a plan that would help us perserve instead of destroy the forests. Her plans includes "sustainable harvesting of native plants, shade farming, nature preserves, and management by indigenous peoples." In the past years: many people have started businesses with these goals in mind, such as fair trade chocolate, the idea is catching on everywhere.

There are so many more good ideas that Lindsay has proposed in her article, but there is not time here to discuss them all. One way people can get envolved is to make direct payments to tropical countries, and it would be a great way for wealthier countries to make a difference.

Analysis of Below Average Response

The writer followed proper structure: introduction, body, and conclusion; and each paragraph contains one main idea followed by appropriately quoted textual examples. The writer's comprehension of many of the important themes introduced by Lindsey and the attempt to describe her central ideas was adequate. Several times the writer lapsed into personal opinion instead of keeping an objective position. The writer did not analyze how Lindsey's argument is persuasively constructed, nor does the essay include coherent paragraphs. Word choice in this essay can be improved so that descriptions are specific. Words like "fabulous and "really" must be replaced by objective words that fit the context. Several mechanical, spelling, and punctuation errors should be revised in the final read-through. The author's name (Lindsey) is also misspelled. In the conclusion, the writer apologizes for not being able to discuss every element in the article, but the purpose is rather to focus on the most relevant aspects of the author's argument. Also, new material should not be introduced in concluding comments.

ITEM INDEX

In the following index, all of the numeric references are designed as follows: **Page #/Item #**. The parenthetical information beside each item category refers to the subject-area in which that item category appears.

45°-45°-90° Triangles (Math: Multiple-Choice and Student-Produced Responses)

Practice Test III, Section 3 (MC): **194**/8
Practice Test III, Section 4 (SPR): **210**/36

Absolute Value (Math: Multiple-Choice and Student-Produced Responses)

Practice Test II, Section 4 (MC): **150**/19

Adjectives versus Adverbs (Writing and Language)

Quiz II: **26**/7
Practice Test II: **136**/35

Algebra (Math: Multiple-Choice and Student-Produced Responses)

Quiz I—No Calculator (MC): **30**/2–4
Quiz I—Calculator (MC): **31**/1–2; **32**/5; **33**/9–10
Quiz II—No Calculator (MC): **34**/1–2; **35**/3–5
Quiz II—Calculator (MC): **37**/1; **38**/7; **39**/9
Quiz I—No Calculator (SPR): **42**/1–2
Quiz I—Calculator (SPR): **44**/1
Quiz II—No Calculator (SPR): **47**/1
Quiz II—Calculator (SPR): **50**/2
Practice Test I, Section 3 (MC): **88**/2–5, 7; **89**/8–13
Practice Test I, Section 3 (SPR): **92**/16–19
Practice Test I, Section 4 (MC): **94**/1, 6; **95**/8; **97**/16–17; **98**/20; **101**/25; **102**/28
Practice Test I, Section 4 (SPR): **104**/32–34; **105**/38
Practice Test II, Section 3 (MC): **140**/1–2; **141**/3, 5–7; **142**/8–9, 11; **144**/14
Practice Test II, Section 3 (SPR): **146**/16, 18, 20
Practice Test II, Section 4 (MC): **148**/1, 3–5, 7; **149**/8, 11; **150**/13, 15, 17–18; **151**/20–21; **153**/27; **154**/29
Practice Test II, Section 4 (SPR): **157**/37
Practice Test III, Section 3 (MC): **194**/1–7; **196**/13
Practice Test III, Section 3 (SPR): **196**/15; **198**/16–17, 19–20
Practice Test III, Section 4 (MC): **200**/2, 5; **201**/7–9; **202**/14–16; **205**/22; **207**/26, 28; **208**/29–30
Practice Test III, Section 4 (SPR): **209**/32; **210**/34–35, 37

Apostrophes (Writing and Language)

Practice Test I: **80**/20

Application (Reading)

Quiz I: **4**/3; **5**/8; **7**/10, 15, 17–18
Quiz II: **15**/28
Practice Test II: **116**/15; **118**/27; **119**/31; **122**/40
Practice Test III: **165**/10; **171**/23

Appropriate Supporting Material (Writing and Language)

Quiz I: **21**/18; **24**/34
Practice Test I: **81**/24
Practice Test II: **127**/3; **131**/20; **134**/29
Practice Test III: **180**/4–5; **181**/9; **186**/28; **187**/30; **191**/43

Arithmetic Probability (Math: Multiple-Choice and Student-Produced Responses)

Quiz I—Calculator (MC): **32**/7
Practice Test I, Section 4 (MC): **94**/3
Practice Test II, Section 4 (MC): **153**/25
Practice Test II, Section 4 (SPR): **156**/34
Practice Test III, Section 3 (MC): **194**/3
Practice Test III, Section 4 (MC): **200**/1; **205**/22
Practice Test III, Section 4 (SPR): **210**/33

Audience (Writing and Language)

Quiz I: **24**/33

Averages (Math: Multiple-Choice and Student-Produced Responses)

Quiz I—Calculator (MC): **32**/4
Quiz II—Calculator (MC): **38**/6
Practice Test I, Section 3 (MC): **88**/7
Practice Test I, Section 3 (SPR): **92**/18
Practice Test I, Section 4 (MC): **96**/11
Practice Test II, Section 4 (MC): **149**/10; **151**/20
Practice Test II, Section 4 (SPR): **156**/32
Practice Test III, Section 3 (MC): **194**/3
Practice Test III, Section 4 (MC): **200**/1; **205**/22

Bar, Cumulative, and Line Graphs (Math: Multiple-Choice and Student-Produced Responses)
Quiz I—Calculator (MC): 32/4
Practice Test I, Section 4 (MC): 99/21-22; 101/24
Practice Test II, Section 4 (MC): 149/10; 151/20
Practice Test III, Section 4 (MC): 203/17-18; 204/19-21

Basic Algebraic Manipulations (Math: Multiple-Choice and Student-Produced Responses)
Practice Test II, Section 3 (MC): 141/5
Practice Test II, Section 4 (MC): 149/8
Practice Test III, Section 3 (MC): 194/5

Circles (Math: Multiple-Choice and Student-Produced Responses)
Quiz I—No Calculator (MC): 30/5
Practice Test I, Section 3 (SPR): 92/20
Practice Test I, Section 4 (MC): 96/12-13; 102/30
Practice Test I, Section 4 (SPR): 105/37
Practice Test II, Section 4 (MC): 148/6; 154/30
Practice Test III, Section 4 (SPR): 210/38

Clarity of Meaning (Writing and Language)
Quiz II: 26/8; 28/17, 19-20
Practice Test II: 128/7

Colons (Writing and Language)
Practice Test I: 76/4

Comma Splices (Writing and Language)
Practice Test I: 80/22
Practice Test II: 128/9; 133/25

Commas (Writing and Language)
Quiz I: 18/7-8
Practice Test I: 85/42
Practice Test III: 180/3; 183/12; 186/26

Common Advanced Arithmetic Items (Math: Multiple-Choice and Student-Produced Responses)
Practice Test I, Section 4 (MC): 94/2
Practice Test II, Section 3 (MC): 141/4
Practice Test II, Section 3 (SPR): 146/19
Practice Test II, Section 4 (MC): 148/1, 4; 150/13
Practice Test III, Section 4 (SPR): 210/34

Common Data Representations (Math: Multiple-Choice and Student Produced Responses)
Quiz II—Calculator (MC): 39/10

Common Problem Solving Items (Math: Multiple-Choice and Student-Produced Responses)
Quiz I—Calculator (MC): 32/6-7
Quiz II—Calculator (MC): 37/1
Practice Test I, Section 4 (MC): 94/4-5; 95/10; 96/13; 98/19; 99/21-22; 102/30
Practice Test II, Section 4 (MC): 148/2; 150/12; 154/28
Practice Test II, Section 4 (SPR): 156/31, 33
Practice Test III, Section 4 (MC): 200/5, 6; 201/10, 12; 202/13-14; 204/20-21
Practice Test III, Section 4 (SPR): 209/31

Complex Figures (Math: Multiple-Choice and Student-Produced Responses)
Practice Test I, Section 4 (MC): 94/5; 96/12
Practice Test II, Section 4 (MC): 148/6
Practice Test III, Section 3 (MC): 194/8

Complex Numbers (Math: Multiple-Choice and Student-Produced Responses)
Practice Test II, Section 3 (SPR): 146/19

Concepts of Domain and Range (Math: Multiple-Choice and Student-Produced Responses)
Practice Test I, Section 3 (MC): 89/13
Practice Test II, Section 3 (MC): 142/11

Conciseness (Writing and Language)
Quiz I: 22/19
Quiz II: 26/9
Practice Test I: 81/28; 84/37; 85/41
Practice Test II: 129/10; 134/30; 135/32; 136/34
Practice Test III: 180/2; 181/8; 183/13; 187/31; 189/36

Coordinate Geometry (Math: Multiple-Choice and Student-Produced Responses)
Quiz I—No Calculator (MC): 30/1
Quiz I—Calculator (MC): 33/8
Quiz II—Calculator (MC): 37/2-3; 38/4-5
Quiz II—No Calculator (SPR): 48/2
Quiz II—Calculator (SPR): 50/1; 51/3

Practice Test I, Section 3 (MC): **89**/13–14
Practice Test I, Section 3 (SPR): **92**/20
Practice Test I, Section 4 (MC): **95**/8; **96**/14; **97**/16; **101**/26–27; **102**/29
Practice Test II, Section 3 (MC): **141**/7; **142**/8, 10; **143**/12; **144**/13
Practice Test II, Section 4 (MC): **148**/6; **151**/22; **152**/23; **153**/27
Practice Test II, Section 4 (SPR): **157**/38
Practice Test III, Section 3 (MC): **195**/9–11
Practice Test III, Section 4 (MC): **201**/11; **204**/19; **205–207**/23–27

Creating Algebraic Expressions (Math: Multiple-Choice and Student-Produced Responses)

Practice Test II, Section 3 (MC): **142**/8

Creating, Expressing, and Evaluating Algebraic Equations and Functions (Math: Multiple-Choice and Student-Produced Responses)

Quiz I—No Calculator (MC): **30**/2
Quiz I—Calculator (MC): **32**/5
Quiz II—No Calculator (MC): **34**/1
Quiz I—No Calculator (SPR): **42**/1–2
Quiz I—Calculator (SPR): **44**/1
Practice Test I, Section 3 (MC): **88**/3, 5; **89**/8; **89**/9–13
Practice Test I, Section 4 (MC): **94**/1, 6; **97**/16–17; **101**/25
Practice Test I, Section 4 (SPR): **104**/33
Practice Test II, Section 3 (MC): **140**/1, 6; **142**/8, 11; **144**/14
Practice Test II, Section 3 (SPR): **146**/20
Practice Test II, Section 4 (MC): **148**/5; **150**/13, 15, 18; **151**/20; **154**/29
Practice Test II, Section 4 (SPR): **157**/37
Practice Test III, Section 3 (MC): **194**/1, 3–4
Practice Test III, Section 4 (MC): **200**/5; **201**/9; **202**/14–15; **205**/22; **207**/26, 28; **208**/29–30
Practice Test III, Section 4 (SPR): **210**/34–35, 37

Dashes (Writing and Language)

Practice Test II: **133**/24

Data Interpretation (Math: Multiple-Choice and Student-Produced Responses)

Quiz I—Calculator (MC): **32**/4
Quiz II—Calculator (MC): **39**/10
Practice Test I, Section 4 (MC): **97**/15–17; **99**/21–22; **101**/24
Practice Test II, Section 4 (MC): **149**/10; **151**/20; **152**/24; **154**/28
Practice Test II, Section 4 (SPR): **157**/36
Practice Test III, Section 4 (MC): **201**/10; **203**/17–18; **204**/19–21; **206**/25
Practice Test III, Section 4 (SPR): **210**/33

Data Interpretation (Statistics) (Math: Multiple-Choice and Student-Produced Responses)

Practice Test I, Section 4 (MC): **100**/23

Data Presentations (Writing and Language)

Quiz I: **19**/13; **20**/14–15
Practice Test I: **82**/32
Practice Test II: **138**/43; **139**/44
Practice Test III: **185**/24; **192**/44

Data Presentations (Reading)

Quiz II: **10**/11; **15**/31
Practice Test I: **71**/41; **74**/51
Practice Test II: **116**/21; **122**/41–42
Practice Test III: **169**/20–21; **172**/32

Determining Values on the Unit Circle (Math: Multiple-Choice and Student-Produced Responses)

Quiz II—Calculator (MC): **39**/8

Development (Reading)

Quiz II: **15**/26
Practice Test I: **61**/7; **64**/18; **66**/27; **70**/34; **70**/36; **70**/37; **70**/38
Practice Test II: **121**/34; **124**/44
Practice Test III: **164**/5; **168**/13; **171**/25; **174**/37; **177**/47

Diction (Writing and Language)

Quiz I: **17**/2; **23**/25; **23**/29

Drawing Inferences (Math: Multiple-Choice and Student-Produced Responses)

Quiz II—Calculator (MC): **39**/10

Effective Concluding Sentence (Writing and Language)

Practice Test II: **138**/42

Effective Opening Sentence (Writing and Language)

Practice Test II: **130**/12

Effective Transitional Sentence (Writing and Language)

Quiz I: **17**/3
Practice Test I: **80**/17
Practice Test III: **187**/29; **191**/41

Equations Involving Absolute Value (Math: Multiple-Choice and Student-Produced Responses)

Practice Test I, Section 4 (MC): **98**/20
Practice Test I, Section 4 (SPR): **105**/38
Practice Test II, Section 3 (SPR): **146**/18

Equations Involving Exponents (Math: Multiple-Choice and Student-Produced Responses)

Quiz I—No Calculator (MC): **30**/3
Quiz II—No Calculator (SPR): **47**/1
Practice Test II, Section 4 (MC): **148**/7
Practice Test III, Section 3 (MC): **196**/13

Equations Involving Radical Expressions (Math: Multiple-Choice and Student-Produced Responses)

Quiz I—Calculator (MC): **33**/9
Quiz II—No Calculator (MC): **35**/5
Quiz II—Calculator (SPR): **50**/2

Equations Involving Rational Expressions (Math: Multiple-Choice and Student-Produced Responses)

Quiz I—Calculator (MC): **31**/1
Quiz II—Calculator (MC): **39**/9
Practice Test I, Section 3 (SPR): **92**/17
Practice Test II, Section 3 (MC): **142**/9

Evaluating Expressions (Math: Multiple-Choice and Student-Produced Responses)

Practice Test I, Section 3 (MC): **88**/4
Practice Test I, Section 3 (SPR): **92**/18
Practice Test II, Section 4 (MC): **148**/4; **151**/21
Practice Test III, Section 3 (SPR): **198**/16; **198**/17
Practice Test III, Section 4 (MC): **201**/7

Evaluating Sequences Involving Exponential Growth (Math: Multiple-Choice and Student-Produced Responses)

Practice Test I, Section 3 (SPR): **92**/16

Explicit Detail (Reading)

Quiz I: **4**/4: **5**/6–9; **7**/11–14, 16
Quiz II: **9**/3; **11**/13; **12**/16; **14**/23; **15**/24–25
Practice Test I: **61**/9; **64**/19; **66**/21, 23; **73**/45, 47; **74**/48, 52
Practice Test II: **115**/14; **121**/35–36
Practice Test III: **165**/9; **168**/12, 14, 16;**169**/18–19; **172**/29; **174**/35; **175**/41

Expression of Ideas (Writing and Language)

Quiz I: **17**/3–4; **18**/9; **19**/13; **20**/14–15; **21**/16–18; **22**/19, 23; **23**/26; **24**/32–34
Quiz II: **26**/8–10; **27**/16; **28**/17, 19–20
Practice Test I: **76**/2–3; **77**/6–8; **78**/11; **79**/12–13, 16; **80**/17–18, 21; **81**/24–26, 28; **82**/32–33; **84**/37; **85**/39–41; **86**/43–44
Practice Test II: **127**/2–4; **128**/7; **129**/10–11; **130**/12–13; **131**/18–20; **132**/21–22; **133**/26; **134**/29–30; **135**/31–33; **136**/34, 37; **137**/41; **138**/42–43; **139**/44
Practice Test III: **180**/2, 4–5; **181**/8–9; **182**/11; **183**/13, 16–17; **184**/20–22; **185**/24; **186**/27–28; **187**/29–31; **189**/34, 36; **190**/37; **191**/41, 43; **192**/44

Factoring Expressions (Math: Multiple-Choice and Student-Produced Responses)

Practice Test I, Section 3 (MC): **89**/12
Practice Test II, Section 3 (MC): **141**/7
Practice Test II, Section 4 (MC): **149**/11; **153**/27
Practice Test III, Section 4 (MC): **200**/2

Faulty or Illogical Comparisons (Writing and Language)

Quiz II: **27**/14
Practice Test I: **82**/29
Practice Test II: **130**/16

Faulty Parallelism (Writing and Language)

Quiz I: **18**/10; **23**/31
Quiz II: **25**/1; **26**/5
Practice Test I: **76**/1, 5
Practice Test II: **128**/8; **130**/15; **137**/40
Practice Test III: **180**/6; **183**/15

Fragments (Writing and Language)

Quiz I: **17**/5; **22**/21
Practice Test I: **84**/34
Practice Test II: **134**/28
Practice Test III: **184**/18

Function Notation (Math: Multiple-Choice and Student-Produced Responses)

Quiz I—No Calculator (SPR): **42**/2
Practice Test I, Section 3 (MC): **89**/8–9
Practice Test II, Section 4 (MC): **150**/18
Practice Test III, Section 3 (MC): **194**/4
Practice Test III, Section 4 (SPR): **210**/37

Functions as Models (Math: Multiple-Choice and Student-Produced Responses)

Quiz II—No Calculator (MC): **34**/1
Practice Test I, Section 4 (MC): **97**/16–17; **101**/25
Practice Test I, Section 4 (SPR): **104**/33
Practice Test II, Section 3 (MC): **144**/14

Geometric Probability (Math: Multiple-Choice and Student-Produced Responses)

Practice Test II, Section 4 (MC): **154**/30

Geometry (Math: Multiple-Choice and Student-Produced Responses)

Quiz I—No Calculator (MC): **30**/5
Quiz II—Calculator (MC): **37**/2
Quiz I—Calculator (SPR): **44**/2; **45**/3
Practice Test I, Section 3 (MC): **88**/6; **89**/14
Practice Test I, Section 3 (SPR): **92**/20
Practice Test I, Section 4 (MC): **94**/5; **95**/9; **96**/12–13; **98**/18; **102**/30
Practice Test I, Section 4 (SPR): **104**/35; **105**/37
Practice Test II, Section 3 (SPR): **146**/17
Practice Test II, Section 4 (MC): **148**/6; **152**/23; **154**/30
Practice Test II, Section 4 (SPR): **157**/35
Practice Test III, Section 3 (MC): **194**/8; **196**/12, 14
Practice Test III, Section 3 (SPR): **198**/18
Practice Test III, Section 4 (MC): **200**/3; **201**/11
Practice Test III, Section 4 (SPR): **210**/36, 38

Grammar and Usage (Writing and Language)

Quiz I: **17**/1–2; **18**/11–12; **22**/20, 22; **23**/25, 27, 29
Quiz II: **25**/4; **26**/6–7, 10; **27**/14
Practice Test I: **77**/9; **78**/10; **79**/15; **80**/19; **82**/29–30; **85**/38

Practice Test II: **127**/1; **128**/6; **130**/14, 16; **134**/27; **136**/35–36
Practice Test III: **180**/1; **182**/10; **184**/19; **186**/25; **187**/32; **190**/38

Graphs of First-Degree Inequalities (Math: Multiple-Choice and Student-Produced Responses)

Practice Test II, Section 4 (MC): **151**/22

Graphs of Linear Equations (Math: Multiple-Choice and Student-Produced Responses)

Quiz II—Calculator (MC): **37**/3
Practice Test I, Section 4 (MC): **95**/8; **101**/27; **102**/29
Practice Test II, Section 3 (MC): **142**/10
Practice Test II, Section 4 (MC): **153**/27
Practice Test III, Section 3 (MC): **195**/9–11
Practice Test III, Section 4 (MC): **206**/25; **207**/26–27

Graphs of Polynomial Functions (Math: Multiple-Choice and Student-Produced Responses)

Quiz I—Calculator (MC): **33**/8
Quiz II—Calculator (SPR): **51**/3
Practice Test III, Section 3 (MC): **141**/7

Graphs of Quadratic Equations and Relations (Math: Multiple-Choice and Student-Produced Responses)

Quiz II—Calculator (MC): **38**/5
Quiz II—No Calculator (SPR): **48**/2
Practice Test I, Section 3 (MC): **89**/13
Practice Test I, Section 3 (SPR): **92**/20
Practice Test I, Section 4 (MC): **101**/26
Practice Test II, Section 3 (MC): **143**/12; **144**/13
Practice Test II, Section 4 (MC): **151**/22; **205**/23–24

Histograms (Math: Multiple-Choice and Student-Produced Responses)

Quiz II—Calculator (MC): **39**/10

Idiomatic Expression (Writing and Language)

Quiz I: **18**/9
Quiz II: **26**/10; **28**/19–20
Practice Test I: **85**/40
Practice Test II: **137**/41

Implied Idea (Reading)

Quiz II: **9**/4, 6, 8; **12**/15, 19
Practice Test I: **60**/3, 5; **61**/8, 10; **63**/11, 13, 15; **66**/24; **67**/29; **73**/43
Practice Test II: **112**/1, 3–4, 6; **113**/7, 9; **118**/22, 24, 28; **118**/30; **122**/38; **124**/47
Practice Test III: **164**/1; **165**/7; **172**/27; **174**/39; **177**/43, 45, 51

Incomplete Split Constructions (Writing and Language)

Quiz II: **25**/2

Lines and Angles (Math: Multiple-Choice and Student-Produced Responses)

Quiz I—Calculator (SPR): **45**/3
Practice Test I, Section 4 (SPR): **105**/37
Practice Test II, Section 3 (SPR): **146**/17
Practice Test III, Section 3 (MC): **196**/14
Practice Test III, Section 3 (SPR): **198**/18
Practice Test III, Section 4 (SPR): **210**/36

Literary Fiction (Reading)

Practice Test I: **60**/1–6; **61**/7–10
Practice Test II: **112**/1–6; **113**/7–10
Practice Test III: **164**/1–6; **165**/7–10

Main Idea (Reading)

Quiz I: **5**/6
Quiz II: **9**/1; **12**/17; **14**/22
Practice Test I: **64**/20; **66**/22; **71**/40; **74**/50
Practice Test II: **115**/11–12; **116**/18–19; **121**/32; **124**/43; **125**/52
Practice Test III: **171**/22; **174**/36; **175**/42; **177**/46

Main Idea (Writing and Language)

Quiz I: **21**/16
Practice Test I: **78**/11; **80**/18; **82**/33
Practice Test II: **131**/19
Practice Test III: **182**/11; **183**/17; **190**/37

Manipulating Algebraic Expressions (Math: Multiple-Choice and Student-Produced Responses)

Quiz II—Calculator (MC): **38**/7
Practice Test I, Section 3 (MC): **88**/4; **89**/12
Practice Test I, Section 3 (SPR): **92**/18
Practice Test II, Section 3 (MC): **140**/2; **141**/5, 7
Practice Test II, Section 4 (MC): **148**/4; **149**/8, 11; **151**/21; **153**/27

Practice Test III, Section 3 (MC): **194**/5–7
Practice Test III, Section 3 (SPR): **198**/16–17, 19
Practice Test III, Section 4 (MC): **201**/7

Manipulating Expressions Involving Exponents (Math: Multiple-Choice and Student-Produced Responses)

Quiz II—Calculator (MC): **38**/7
Practice Test II, Section 3 (MC): **140**/2
Practice Test III, Section 3 (MC): **194**/6, 7
Practice Test III, Section 3 (SPR): **198**/19

Measures of Center and Spread (Math: Multiple-Choice and Student-Produced Responses)

Quiz I—Calculator (MC): **32**/4
Quiz II—Calculator (MC): **38**/6; **39**/10
Practice Test I, Section 3 (MC): **88**/7
Practice Test I, Section 3 (SPR): **92**/18
Practice Test I, Section 4 (MC): **96**/11; **97**/15
Practice Test I, Section 4 (SPR): **105**/36
Practice Test II, Section 4 (MC): **149**/10; **150**/16; **151**/20
Practice Test II, Section 4 (SPR): **156**/32
Practice Test III, Section 3 (MC): **194**/3
Practice Test III, Section 4 (MC): **200**/1; **204**/20; **205**/22
Practice Test III, Section 4 (SPR): **210**/33

Median (Math: Multiple-Choice and Student-Produced Responses)

Quiz II—Calculator (MC): **38**/6
Practice Test I, Section 4 (MC): **97**/15
Practice Test II, Section 4 (MC): **149**/10; **150**/16
Practice Test III, Section 4 (MC): **205**/22
Practice Test III, Section 4 (SPR): **210**/33

Misplaced Modifiers (Writing and Language)

Quiz II: **25**/3; **27**/11; **28**/18
Practice Test I: **81**/23
Practice Test II: **133**/23
Practice Test III: **182**/10; **189**/35

Mode (Math: Multiple-Choice and Student-Produced Responses)

Practice Test I, Section 3 (SPR): **92**/18
Practice Test II, Section 4 (MC): **149**/10

Multi-Step Problem Solving Items (Math: Multiple-Choice and Student-Produced Responses)

Quiz I—Calculator (MC): **32**/3
Practice Test I, Section 3 (MC): **88**/1
Practice Test I, Section 4 (MC): **95**/7
Practice Test I, Section 4 (SPR): **103**/31
Practice Test II, Section 4 (MC): **149**/9; **150**/14; **150**/15; **153**/26
Practice Test II, Section 4 (SPR): **157**/36
Practice Test III, Section 4 (MC): **200**/4
Practice Test III, Section 4 (SPR): **210**/35

Natural Sciences (Reading)

Quiz I: **7**/9–18
Quiz II: **14**/22–23; **15**/24–31
Practice Test I: **66**/21–28; **67**/29–30; **73**/42–47; **74**/48–52
Practice Test II: **115**/11–14; **116**/15–21; **121**/32–36; **122**/37–42
Practice Test III: **168**/11–17; **169**/18–21; **174**/33–40; **175**/41–42

Organization (Writing and Language)

Quiz I: **21**/17; **24**/32
Practice Test I: **79**/13; **86**/44
Practice Test II: **132**/22; **135**/33
Practice Test III: **183**/16; **184**/22; **187**/29

Paragraph-Level Structure (Writing and Language)

Practice Test III: **183**/16; **184**/22

Passage-Level Structure (Writing and Language)

Quiz I: **21**/17; **24**/32
Practice Test I: **86**/44

Percentages (Math: Multiple-Choice and Student-Produced Responses)

Quiz I—Calculator (MC): **32**/6
Quiz II—Calculator (MC): **37**/1
Practice Test I, Section 4 (MC): **94**/4; **95**/10; **96**/13; **98**/19; **99**/21
Practice Test II, Section 4 (MC): **148**/2; **154**/28
Practice Test II, Section 4 (SPR): **156**/33
Practice Test III, Section 4 (MC): **202**/13; **204**/20

Precision (Writing and Language)

Practice Test I: **79**/12; **81**/25

Practice Test II: **131**/18; **133**/26
Practice Test III: **186**/27

Probability (Math: Multiple-Choice and Student-Produced Responses)

Quiz I—Calculator (MC): **32**/7
Practice Test I, Section 4 (MC): **94**/3
Practice Test II, Section 4 (MC): **153**/25; **154**/30
Practice Test II, Section 4 (SPR): **156**/34
Practice Test III, Section 3 (MC): **194**/3
Practice Test III, Section 4 (MC): **200**/1; **205**/22
Practice Test III, Section 4 (SPR): **210**/33

Problem Solving and Advanced Arithmetic (Math: Multiple-Choice and Student-Produced Responses)

Quiz I—Calculator (MC): **32**/3, 6, 7
Quiz II—Calculator (MC): **37**/1
Practice Test I, Section 3 (MC): **88**/1
Practice Test I, Section 4 (MC): **94**/2, 4–5; **95**/7, 10; **96**/13; **98**/19; **99**/21–22; **102**/30
Practice Test I, Section 4 (SPR): **103**/31
Practice Test II, Section 3 (MC): **141**/4
Practice Test II, Section 3 (SPR): **146**/19
Practice Test II, Section 4 (MC): **148**/1–2, 4; **149**/9; **150**/12–15, 19; **153**/26; **154**/28
Practice Test II, Section 4 (SPR): **156**/31, 33; **157**/36
Practice Test III, Section 4 (MC): **200**/4–6; **201**/10, 12; **202**/13–14; **204**/20–21
Practice Test III, Section 4 (SPR): **209**/31; **210**/34–35

Problems of Coordination and Subordination (Writing and Language)

Quiz II: **27**/13, 15
Practice Test I: **84**/35

Pronoun Usage (Writing and Language)

Quiz I: **17**/1; **18**/12; **22**/22
Practice Test I: **78**/10; **79**/15; **80**/19
Practice Test II: **130**/14; **134**/27; **136**/36
Practice Test III: **180**/1; **184**/19; **186**/25

Properties of Numbers (Math: Multiple-Choice and Student-Produced Responses)

Practice Test II, Section 3 (MC): **141**/4
Practice Test II, Section 4 (MC): **148**/1, 4; **150**/13
Practice Test III, Section 4 (SPR): **210**/34

Properties of Triangles (Math: Multiple-Choice and Student-Produced Responses)
Practice Test I, Section 3 (MC): **89**/14
Practice Test I, Section 3 (MC): **95**/9; **98**/18
Practice Test I, Section 4 (MC): **152**/23
Practice Test II, Section 4 (SPR): **157**/35
Practice Test III, Section 3 (MC): **196**/12
Practice Test III, Section 4 (MC): **201**/11

Proportions and Direct-Inverse Variation (Math: Multiple-Choice and Student-Produced Responses)
Practice Test I, Section 4 (MC): **94**/5; **102**/30
Practice Test I, Section 4 (MC): **150**/12
Practice Test II, Section 4 (SPR): **156**/31
Practice Test II, Section 4 (MC): **200**/5; **201**/12;
202/14; **204**/21
Practice Test III, Section 4 (SPR): **209**/31

Punctuation (Writing and Language)
Quiz I: **18**/7-8
Practice Test I: **76**/4; **80**/20; **85**/42
Practice Test II: **133**/24
Practice Test III: **180**/3; **183**/12; **186**/26

Pythagorean Theorem (Math: Multiple-Choice and Student-Produced Responses)
Quiz II—Calculator (MC): **37**/2
Quiz I—Calculator (SPR): **44**/2
Practice Test II, Section 3 (MC): **194**/8
Practice Test III, Section 4 (MC): **200**/3
Practice Test III, Section 4 (SPR): **210**/36

Range (Math: Multiple-Choice and Student-Produced Responses)
Practice Test I, Section 4 (SPR): **105**/36
Practice Test III, Section 4 (MC): **204**/20

Ratios (Math: Multiple-Choice and Student-Produced Responses)
Quiz I—Calculator (MC): **32**/7
Practice Test I, Section 4 (MC): **98**/19; **99**/22
Practice Test III, Section 4 (MC): **200**/6; **201**/10

Rectangles and Squares (Math: Multiple-Choice and Student-Produced Responses)
Practice Test I, Section 4 (MC): **98**/18
Practice Test II, Section 4 (MC): **148**/6; **154**/30

Right Triangles (Math: Multiple-Choice and Student-Produced Responses)
Practice Test I, Section 3 (MC): **90**/15
Practice Test II, Section 3 (MC): **144**/15
Practice Test III, Section 4 (SPR): **210**/36

Run-On Sentences (Writing and Language)
Quiz I: **23**/30

Scatterplots (Math: Multiple-Choice and Student-Produced Responses)
Practice Test I, Section 4 (MC): **97**/15, 16; **97**/17
Practice Test III, Section 4 (MC): **206**/25

Sentence Structure (Writing and Language)
Quiz I: **17**/5; **18**/10; **22**/21; **23**/30-31
Quiz II: **25**/1-3; **26**/5, 7; **27**/11, 13, 15; **28**/18
Practice Test I: **76**/1, 5; **79**/14; **80**/22; **81**/23;
84/34-35
Practice Test II: **128**/8-9; **130**/15; **133**/23, 25;
134/28; **137**/40
Practice Test III: **180**/6; **183**/15; **184**/18; **189**/35

Sentence-Level Structure (Writing and Language)
Practice Test I: **79**/13
Practice Test II: **132**/22; **135**/33

Sequence and Verb Tense (Writing and Language)
Quiz I: **18**/11; **22**/20

Sets: Union, Intersection, and Elements (Math: Multiple-Choice and Student-Produced Responses)
Practice Test I, Section 4 (MC): **94**/2

Simple Equations (Math: Multiple-Choice and Student-Produced Responses)
Practice Test I, Section 3 (MC): **88**/2

Simple Inequalities (Math: Multiple-Choice and Student-Produced Responses)
Practice Test II, Section 3 (MC): **141**/3

Slope of a Line (Math: Multiple-Choice and Student-Produced Responses)
Quiz I—No Calculator (MC): **30**/1

Practice Test II, Section 4 (SPR): 157/38
Practice Test III, Section 4 (MC): 204/19; 207/27
Practice Test III, Section 3 (MC): 195/9

Slope-Intercept Form of a Linear Equation (Math: Multiple-Choice and Student-Produced Responses)
Quiz II—Calculator (MC): 37/3
Practice Test I, Section 4 (MC): 96/14; 97/16
Practice Test II, Section 4 (SPR): 157/38
Practice Test III, Section 3 (MC): 195/11

Social Studies (Reading)
Quiz I: 4/1-4; 5/5-8
Quiz II: 9-12/1-21
Practice Test I: 63/11-17; 64/18-20; 69-71/31-41
Practice Test II: 118/22-30; 119/31; 124/43-51; 125/52
Practice Test III: 171/22-26; 172/27-32; 177/43-51: 178/52

Solving Algebraic Equations or Inequalities with One Variable (Math: Multiple-Choice and Student-Produced Responses)
Quiz I—No Calculator (MC): 30/3
Quiz I—Calculator (MC): 31/1; 33/9
Quiz II—No Calculator (MC): 35/5
Quiz II—Calculator (MC): 39/9
Quiz II—No Calculator (SPR): 47/1
Quiz II—Calculator (SPR): 50/2
Practice Test I, Section 3 (MC): 88/2
Practice Test I, Section 3 (SPR): 92/17
Practice Test I, Section 4 (MC): 98/20
Practice Test I, Section 4 (SPR): 105/38
Practice Test II, Section 3 (MC): 141/3; 142/9
Practice Test II, Section 3 (SPR): 146/16, 18
Practice Test II, Section 4 (MC): 148/7
Practice Test III, Section 3 (MC): 196/13

Solving Algebraic Equations with Two Variables (Math: Multiple-Choice and Student-Produced Responses)
Practice Test III, Section 4 (MC): 202/16
Practice Test III, Section 4 (SPR): 209/32

Solving Quadratic Equations and Relations (Math: Multiple-Choice and Student-Produced Responses)
Quiz I—No Calculator (MC): 30/4
Quiz I—Calculator (MC): 33/10
Quiz II—No Calculator (MC): 35/4

Practice Test I, Section 3 (SPR): 92/19
Practice Test I, Section 4 (SPR): 104/32, 34
Practice Test III, Section 3 (SPR): 196/15
Practice Test III, Section 4 (MC): 200/2

Solving Simultaneous Equations (Math: Multiple-Choice and Student-Produced Responses)
Quiz I—Calculator (MC): 32/5
Quiz II—No Calculator (MC): 34/2; 35/3
Quiz II—Calculator (MC): 37/1
Quiz I—Calculator (SPR): 44/1
Practice Test I, Section 3 (MC): 88/7
Practice Test I, Section 4 (MC): 95/8; 102/28
Practice Test II, Section 4 (MC): 148/1, 3; 150/17
Practice Test III, Section 3 (MC): 194/2
Practice Test III, Section 3 (SPR): 198/20
Practice Test III, Section 4 (MC): 201/8

Standard English Conventions (Writing and Language)
Quiz I: 17/1-2, 5, 18/6-8, 10-12; 22/20-22, 24; 23/25, 27-31
Quiz II: 25/1-4, 26/5-7, 10, 27/11-15; 28/18
Practice Test I: 76/1, 4-5, 77/9, 78/10, 79/14-15; 80/19-20, 22; 81/23, 27, 82/29-31; 84/34-36; 85/38, 42
Practice Test II: 127/1, 128/5-6, 8-9, 130/14-17; 133/23-25, 134/27-28, 136/35-36, 137/38-40
Practice Test III: 180/1, 3, 6, 181/7, 182/10, 183/12, 184/14-15, 185/18-19, 186/25-26, 187/32, 188/33, 189/35, 190/38, 191/39-40, 42

Statistics (Math: Multiple-Choice and Student-Produced Responses)
Quiz I—Calculator (MC): 32/4
Quiz II—Calculator (MC): 38/6; 39/10
Practice Test I, Section 3 (MC): 88/7
Practice Test I, Section 3 (SPR): 92/18
Practice Test I, Section 4 (MC): 96/11; 97/15; 100/23
Practice Test I, Section 4 (SPR): 105/36
Practice Test II, Section 4 (MC): 149/10; 150/16; 151/20
Practice Test II, Section 4 (SPR): 156/32
Practice Test III, Section 3 (MC): 194/3
Practice Test III, Section 4 (MC): 200/1; 204/20; 205/22
Practice Test III, Section 4 (SPR): 210/33

Strategy (Writing and Language)

Quiz I: **17**/3; **19**/13; **20**/14–15; **21**/16, 18; **24**/33–34
Practice Test I: **78**/11; **80**/17–18; **81**/24; **82**/32–33
Practice Test II: **127**/3; **130**/12; **131**/19–20; **134**/29; **138**/42–43; **139**/44
Practice Test III: **180**/4–5; **181**/9; **182**/11; **183**/17; **185**/24; **186**/28; **187**/30; **190**/37; **191**/41, 43; **192**/44

Style (Writing and Language)

Quiz I: **18**/9; **22**/19
Quiz II: **26**/8–10; **28**/17, 19–20
Practice Test I: **76**/3; **79**/12, 16; **81**/25, 28; **84**/37; **85**/40–41
Practice Test II: **127**/2; **128**/7; **129**/10; **130**/13; **131**/18; **133**/26; **134**/30; **135**/32; **136**/34; **137**/41
Practice Test III: **180**/2; **181**/8; **183**/13; **184**/20; **186**/27; **187**/31; **189**/34, 36

Subject-Verb Agreement (Writing and Language)

Quiz I: **22**/20
Quiz II: **26**/10
Practice Test I: **77**/9; **82**/30
Practice Test II: **127**/1

Tables (Math: Multiple-Choice and Student-Produced Responses)

Practice Test II, Section 4 (MC): **152**/24; **154**/28
Practice Test II, Section 4 (SPR): **157**/36
Practice Test III, Section 4 (MC): **201**/10
Practice Test III, Section 4 (SPR): **210**/33

Textual Evidence (Reading)

Quiz II: **9**/5, 7; **12**/14, 20; **15**/29
Practice Test I: **60**/4, 6; **63**/14, 16; **66**/25; **67**/30; **69**/32; **70**/39; **73**/44, 46
Practice Test II: **112**/5; **116**/20; **118**/23, 25; **122**/39; **124**/46, 50
Practice Test III: **164**/2; **171**/24; **172**/28; **174**/40; **177**/44; **178**/52

The Coordinate System (Math: Multiple-Choice and Student-Produced Responses)

Quiz II—Calculator (MC): **37**/2–3
Practice Test I, Section 3 (MC): **89**/14
Practice Test II, Section 3 (MC): **142**/8
Practice Test II, Section 4 (MC): **148**/6; **152**/23
Practice Test II, Section 4 (SPR): **157**/38

Practice Test III, Section 4 (MC): **201**/11

The Quadratic Formula (Math: Multiple-Choice and Student-Produced Responses)

Practice Test III, Section 3 (SPR): **196**/15

Tone (Writing and Language)

Practice Test I: **76**/3; **79**/16
Practice Test II: **127**/2; **130**/13
Practice Test III: **184**/20; **189**/34

Transformations and Their Effects on Graphs of Functions (Math: Multiple-Choice and Student-Produced Responses)

Quiz II—Calculator (MC): **38**/4
Quiz II—Calculator (SPR): **50**/1
Practice Test III, Section 4 (MC): **205**/24

Triangles (Math: Multiple-Choice and Student-Produced Responses)

Quiz II—Calculator (MC): **37**/2
Quiz I—Calculator (SPR): **44**/2
Practice Test I, Section 3 (MC): **89**/14
Practice Test I, Section 4 (MC): **95**/9; **98**/18
Practice Test II, Section 4 (MC): **152**/23
Practice Test II, Section 4 (SPR): **157**/35
Practice Test III, Section 3 (MC): **194**/8; **196**/12
Practice Test III, Section 4 (MC): **200**/3; **201**/11
Practice Test III, Section 4 (SPR): **210**/36

Trigonometry (Math: Multiple-Choice and Student-Produced Responses)

Quiz II—Calculator (MC): **39**/8
Practice Test I, Section 3 (MC): **90**/15
Practice Test II, Section 3 (MC): **144**/15
Practice Test III, Section 4 (SPR): **210**/36

Trigonometric Ratios (Math: Multiple-Choice and Student-Produced Responses)

Practice Test I, Section 3 (MC): **90**/15
Practice Test II, Section 3 (MC): **144**/15
Practice Test III, Section 4 (SPR): **210**/36

Unintended Meanings (Writing and Language)

Quiz II: **26**/7; **27**/13
Practice Test I: **79**/14

Verb Tense (Writing and Language)

Quiz I: **23**/27

Quiz II: **25**/4; **26**/6
Practice Test I: **85**/38
Practice Test II: **128**/6
Practice Test III: **187**/32; **190**/38

Vocabulary (Reading)

Quiz I: **4**/1; **4**/2
Quiz II: **9**/2; **10**/10; **12**/18; **12**/21; **15**/27; **15**/30
Practice Test I: **60**/1; **60**/2; **63**/12; **63**/17; **66**/26; **66**/28; **69**/33; **70**/35; **73**/42; **74**/49
Practice Test II: **112**/2; **113**/8; **113**/10; **115**/13; **116**/16; **118**/26; **118**/29; **121**/33; **122**/37; **124**/48; **124**/51
Practice Test III: **164**/3; **164**/4; **164**/6; **168**/11; **168**/15; **171**/26; **172**/30; **174**/33; **174**/38; **177**/49; **177**/50

Voice (Reading)

Quiz I: **4**/4
Quiz II: **10**/9; **11**/12
Practice Test I: **69**/31; **116**/17; **124**/45; **124**/49
Practice Test III: **165**/8; **168**/17; **172**/31; **174**/34; **177**/48

Cambridge *The Practice Book, 13th Edition*
Error Correction and Suggestion Form

Name/Location: _____   Day Phone: _____   E-mail Address: _____

Part of Materials: ☐ Student Text, Specify Subject: _____   Page: _____ Item: _____
☐ Teacher's Guide, Specify Subject: _____   Page: _____ Item: _____
☐ Test Explanations, Specify Code: _____   Page: _____ Item: _____

Error/Suggestion: _____

Part of Materials: ☐ Student Text, Specify Subject: _____   Page: _____ Item: _____
☐ Teacher's Guide, Specify Subject: _____   Page: _____ Item: _____
☐ Test Explanations, Specify Code: _____   Page: _____ Item: _____

Error/Suggestion: _____

Part of Materials: ☐ Student Text, Specify Subject: _____   Page: _____ Item: _____
☐ Teacher's Guide, Specify Subject: _____   Page: _____ Item: _____
☐ Test Explanations, Specify Code: _____   Page: _____ Item: _____

Error/Suggestion: _____

Part of Materials: ☐ Student Text, Specify Subject: _____   Page: _____ Item: _____
☐ Teacher's Guide, Specify Subject: _____   Page: _____ Item: _____
☐ Test Explanations, Specify Code: _____   Page: _____ Item: _____

Error/Suggestion: _____

Part of Materials: ☐ Student Text, Specify Subject: _____   Page: _____ Item: _____
☐ Teacher's Guide, Specify Subject: _____   Page: _____ Item: _____
☐ Test Explanations, Specify Code: _____   Page: _____ Item: _____

Error/Suggestion: _____

Mail form to Cambridge Educational Services, Inc. or fax form to 1-847-299-2933. For teacher's assistance, call 1-800-444-4373 or e-mail solutions@CambridgeEd.com. Visit our website at www.CambridgeEd.com.